DATE			

UTOPIAN COMMUNISM
IN FRANCE

Cabet and the Icarians, 1839–1851

UTOPIAN COMMUNISM IN FRANCE

Cabet and the Icarians, 1839–1851

Christopher H. Johnson

Cornell University Press | ITHACA AND LONDON

First published 1974 by Cornell University Press.
Published in the United Kingdom by Cornell University Press Ltd., 2-4 Brook Street, London W1Y 1AA.

International Standard Book Number 0-8014-0895-4
Library of Congress Catalog Card Number 74-10409

Printed in the United States of America by York Composition Co., Inc.

For My Father

Is it so astonishing that an intelligent but poor worker such as Rolland should sympathize with M. Cabet's newspaper? Is it not easy to understand and explain why a part of the working class lends its support to the only periodical that it can afford to buy and almost the only one where the intolerable suffering of the people has found a true and profound compassion? Well! Read, then, hard critics of the proletarians, read the established works of MM. de Villeneuve, de Morogues, and Villermé, of Eugène Buret and of Duchâtelet! Look below you and see whether you are able to face the spectacle of the unbelievable distress and the dreadful torment of the poor and the workers without feelings of anguish and of fear.

—M. Detours, lawyer for the Icarian stonecutter, Rolland, at the Toulouse conspiracy trial, 1843

Community! The true promised land where the human family will be able to rest after its hard work. There tears will no longer flow, the vultures will no longer drink our blood. Young men, you will know the joys of family life, you will love your wives, your mothers, your sisters, because misery will no longer come to destroy your noble sentiments. Young virgins will no longer put their virtue up for auction, for egotism and pauperism will no longer open houses of prostitution. Children, you will learn early in life to live as brothers; old men, we will respect you for your wisdom; women, we will render you all the respect you merit. Let us be the apostles of this new faith that will make this earth into a valley of pleasure, hope, and love. For such a noble cause, let us pledge today to give all our efforts to advance its reign; if we are faithful to this pledge, our names will shine in posterity, as will those thousands of globes that we illuminate.

—Discourse by an Icarian silkworker of Lyons, sequestered by the police, 1843

Acknowledgments

The obligations I have incurred in preparing this book are numerous. Special thanks are due the Social Science Research Council, whose Graduate Research Fellowship enabled me to carry out the basic research for the study in 1964–1965. Later research and writing time was made available through financial assistance from the University of Wisconsin, Wayne State University, the Leverhulme Foundation (London), and the American Philosophical Association. The kindness of the library and archival staffs whose holdings I have consulted can never be adequately repaid. B. van Tijn, former head of the French Section at the International Instituut voor Sociale Geschiedenis in Amsterdam, set me on the proper course, and without the guidance and special knowledge of staff members at the Archives Nationales de France and the Bibliothèque Historique de la Ville de Paris, several important aspects of this book would never have come to light.

Sections of this book have been drawn from my previously published articles, "Etienne Cabet and the Problem of Class Antagonism," *International Review of Social History,* XI (1966), 403–43, and "Communism and the Working Class before Marx: The Icarian Experience," *American Historical Review,* LXXIV (1971), 642–89. Thanks are due both journals for permission to republish these sections. The editorial staff of Cornell University Press has been of immense assistance at every stage of the publication process.

Many friends and colleagues have offered encouragement and criticism. I particularly wish to thank Harvey Goldberg, Rondo Cameron, John F. C. Harrison, David Sabean, Roger Price, Austin F. Johnson, Lynn Parsons, Melvin Small, Peter Coleman, and Sándor and Carol Agócs. It is hoped that the historical wisdom and humanistic temperament of Henry Bertram Hill, now retired from the University of Wisconsin, are in some way reflected in this book. Samuel F. Scott has been a constant source of inspiration, from our seminars in graduate school to our daily contacts as colleagues at Wayne. Both have my deepest appreciation.

Finally, I want to thank my wife, Lois. She has lived every moment of the Icarian story, both in history and in its recreation. She has also typed every word of every draft through which the book has gone.

Responsibility for the interpretation offered here, of course, rests with me alone.

CHRISTOPHER H. JOHNSON

Detroit, Michigan

Contents

Tables

UTOPIAN COMMUNISM IN FRANCE

Cabet and the Icarians, 1839–1851

Introduction

The roots, dynamics, and composition of pre-Marxian socialist movements are only vaguely understood. Curiously, this is particularly the case in the classic context of utopian socialism, France during the July Monarchy. There is no shortage of studies on the founders and major disciples of various socialist schools, but the bulk of this research has been biographical. Even Sébastien Charléty's outstanding work on the Saint-Simonians is primarily an intellectual history, and we still await systematic analysis of Saint-Simon's influence not only upon working-class opinion but upon the French business community as well. Fourierism has suffered much the same fate, although historians have pierced beneath the level of the doctrinal journal and the propaganda brochure into the active world of at least one area of Fourier's influence, the worker cooperative movement. Babouvist writers, "romantic" socialists, the wide variety of Jacobin socialists, and the more idiosyncratic leaders and thinkers of the era, such as François-Vincent Raspail, Louis-Auguste Blanqui, and Pierre-Joseph Proudhon, have all found their historians.[1] There is certainly no reason to regret this work, for it has created an extraordinarily full picture of the intellectual universe of the French left in the first half of the nineteenth century. Nor is there any reason to doubt the conclusion of E.-C. Labrousse that this was an age marked essentially by the "ideological force of socialism and the weakness of the working-class movement."[2]

[1] Sébastien Charléty, *Histoire de Saint-Simonisme (1825–1864)* (Paris, 1965), and Jean Gaumont, *Histoire générale de la coopération en France* (Paris, 1924). The range of works on the socialist thinkers of this era is indicated by the citations in the Bibliographical Note.

[2] Such are his terms in introducing the problem. *Le Mouvement ouvrier et les théories sociales en France de 1815 à 1848* (Paris, 1948), 9.

But socialism was something more than an idea, especially in the 1840s. For a minority of working people, it was also becoming a source of political identity; men and women were beginning to make conscious decisions to link themselves with socialist organizations or at least to describe themselves as socialists or communists of this or that persuasion. The dimensions of this affiliation, the kinds of people who made this commitment, their rationale for doing so, and the deeper social and economic forces that motivated them all remain obscure.[3]

To explore this larger problem, I undertook a study of the Icarian communist movement and the work of its leader, Etienne Cabet. The result is the first full history of a pre-Marxian socialist movement in France and the popular influence wielded by a prominent utopian socialist.

Frank Manuel has remarked that "the utopia may well be a sensitive indicator of where the sharpest anguish of an age lies."[4] The level of response and the types who responded to certain utopian doctrines give further specificity to the needs and yearnings found within a society at a particular point in its development. Cabet's utopia was born in a society confronting the initial impact of industrial capitalism. At this point mechanization as such was perhaps less important as a source of change than more efficient forms of capitalist production and exchange in which the division of labor and the exploitation of resources were moving toward new levels of sophistication. The 1840s appear to have been the crucial decade during which this general process began to have a broad and telling effect on French society.[5] Simultaneously, the central tension arising from the French Revolution—between, on the one hand, possessory individualism and the implicit right of the "responsible," substantial property owner to rule, and, on the other, popular sovereignty interlaced with concepts of the social regulation of

---

[3] This is not to say that such analysis has not been undertaken at all. But it is largely limited to detailed local studies, such as Fernand Rude, "L'Arrondissement de Vienne en 1848," in Rude, ed., *La Révolution de 1848 dans la département de l'Isère* (Grenoble, 1949), 209–423, and Maurice Agulhon, *Une Ville ouvrière au temps du socialisme utopique: Toulon, 1815–1851* (Paris, 1970).

[4] "Toward a Psychological History of Utopia," *Daedalus*, XCIV (1965), 294.

[5] See below, Chapter 4.

property relationships—agitated French political life with a force unparalleled since Year II of the Revolution itself. But such manifestations of societal modernization should not be allowed to mask the fact that many aspects of French life, to a greater or lesser extent depending on the region or the particular locality involved, remained essentially preindustrial. The sickle and the flail, long-fallow rotation systems, and subsistence agriculture marked the lives of millions of peasants. Occupational diversity and the maintenance of the family economy were facets of the work patterns of many wage-earners. While guilds were officially dead, guild patterns of promotion and control still played a vital role in artisanal production. Retailing remained overwhelmingly in the hands of petty operators. Even big business continued to be predominantly a family affair. Social and political power, while on the national level increasingly falling into the hands of a *grande bourgeoisie* (very wealthy bourgeois) of commerce and finance, locally was still largely rooted in more traditional sources of prestige—above all land ownership and family name.[6] Lower-class deference, though it had been profoundly shaken by the French Revolution, was a continuing fact of life in the mid-nineteenth century.

Simply put, France during the July Monarchy was a society in transition; the forces of modernity, powerful and ineffaceable as they might be, were not yet triumphant. But they were locked in a struggle unleashed a generation earlier against the weight of another, preindustrial world. The anguish of this transition—perhaps the most profound social transformation since the neolithic revolution—pushed those caught up in it toward new dreams of different, less troubled worlds. To be effective, such visions somehow had to be in touch with both the moral and social universe that was being lost and the one coming into being. If any one element of Cabet's utopia might be singled out as fundamental to its appeal, it is that it served this function. For while it promised a plenitude founded upon advanced technology, it also presented images of community and economic morality, both nostalgic of an idealized artisan past. And, most fundamentally, Cabet invoked the dictum that Icarian communism was "Christianity in its primitive purity," thus linking it to the central moral impulse of traditional Western culture. This

---

[6] This is clear especially in the great work of Jean-André Tudesq, *Les Grands Notables en France, 1840–1849* (Paris, 1964).

Janus-faced utopia also possessed the allure of granitic stability, of an unchanging garden of pleasures that, unlike many of the "open-ended" utopias of the nineteenth century, appeared as a haven above and beyond the chaos of the bewildering present. Cabet's was among the last "utopias of calm felicity"—to borrow again from Manuel—but perhaps was better suited to the troubled minds of workingmen than the sophisticated theory of progress of a Saint-Simon or psychological calculus of a Fourier for that very reason.

Yet the staticity and simplicity of Cabet's plan and the numerous archaic elements bound into his appeal (including his own excessive paternalism) also played a large part in the collapse of the Icarian movement in 1847–1848. I shall attempt to show that Icarian communism, while certainly a child of its era, did not have within it, either as an ideology or as an organized movement, the components necessary for moving with the rapid social and economic changes of its decade. Its rise and fall, chronicled in the following pages, thus also can be viewed as an important sequence in the broader history—and sociology—of movements of social protest. It takes a place beside a wide variety of *transitional* social movements that arise in the earlier and more traumatic stages of industrialization but are inherently incapable of becoming viable mass movements in the modern industrial context.

The nature of the Icarian movement thus occupies center stage in this book. Of greatest interest to me has been a series of questions relating to the composition of the movement and the stimuli that brought individuals from particular socioeconomic groups in various localities throughout France into it. The most important finding is that Icarianism drew its following overwhelmingly from the urban working classes, above all from among distressed artisans whose livelihood was threatened less by the direct impact of machinery than by concentration of ownership, increasing division of labor, and generally more efficient modes of organization in their still largely handicraft occupations. Their crafts, such as tailoring and shoemaking, required only medium skill and generally provided lower than average wages but were certainly respectable trades with important traditions of craftsmanship and a penchant for organization. In this light, we are viewing one of the reactions to the deterioration of the economic position of the traditional artisan classes. Another striking feature of the movement was its geographical extent. In many smaller industrial towns Cabet's doctrine was the first to achieve any significant following in the artisan population. The response to Icarian communism, which sought total social transformation, among artisan elements contrasts sharply with the largely defensive reaction to "industrial freedom" in Germany in the same period.[7] Moreover, the strength of the French movement demonstrates that state communism was not inimical to large numbers of traditional artisans, despite the documented significance of producer cooperation among artisan elements in the 1848 era.[8]

In should be understood from the outset, however, that Cabet's ideology was not merely taken by those under his influence as received doctrine. Among the most fascinating elements in Icarianism are the internal conflicts in the movement and what working people did with Cabet's ideas. Quite often, much to the leader's dismay, the more sophisticated of his people—especially in Lyons—challenged major precepts of his gospel. Such independence, along with his own growing awareness of the changing social structure in France, began to expose important inadequacies in his system. Chief among these were its ahistorical foundations and the tactical position favoring class collaboration. The failure to appreciate trends in capitalist development and the historical reality of class antagonism became a basic feature of internal Icarian discord and, increasingly, was recognized as a serious problem by Cabet himself. Cabet's struggle with the issue allows one to peer directly into the heart of what might be called the utopian dilemma and to test, quite specifically, the validity of Marx's and Engels' theses regarding the shortcomings of utopian socialism in theory *and* practice. In a related issue the movement's turn toward sectarianism and its final abandonment of the battle in Europe can be followed. This development, while in part caused by Cabet's failure to bring his

[7] See P. H. Noyes, *Organization and Revolution: Working-class Associations in the German Revolutions of 1848–1849* (Princeton, 1966).

[8] On the significance of cooperation at this time, see, for instance, Gaumont, *Histoire générale,* and Rémi Gossez, *Les Ouvriers de Paris* (Paris, 1967). An American historian, Bernard Moss of the University of Southern California, is currently studying the implications of the cooperative movement for later French socialism.

thought into conformity with emergent social realities, also grew out of a large body of sentiment in the movement itself, particularly the religious enthusiasm of many of its members.

These remarks indicate the central problem to be dealt with. The examination of the work of Etienne Cabet and the dynamics of the movement he founded provide a window through which to view aspects of working-class consciousness in France's most trying era of economic modernization. The conclusions that can be drawn —given the inevitable shortage of precise information on the mentalities of common people—are no more than suggestive. But I hope that the crying need to advance the "history of the inarticulate" will nevertheless be served.

This book is neither a biography of Cabet nor an analysis of his thought. The former has been largely accomplished in the work of Jules Prudhommeaux,[9] and the latter, alas, hardly seems worth doing. While Cabet's communism may lay claim to a unique position in the history of nineteenth-century thought, and while it combined a variety of ingredients appealing to numerous working people in its day, it introduced no new themes into the currents of radical social theory. It was hardly a system and certainly not a philosophy. While exiled in London after being convicted for anti-Monarchist press offenses in 1834, Cabet wrote a novel called *Voyage en Icarie* (borrowing the format from Thomas More and the plot from the *Nouvelle Héloise*), which described the structure of an ideal communist society; he completed it, "like a good lawyer" as Marx once remarked, with a series of statements by famous people allegedly supporting the communist principle. The inclusion in this list of Napoleon Bonaparte and John Locke serves as a preliminary warning, perhaps, that we are not in the presence of a great mind. But Cabet remains in the pantheon of early socialists. The reason is not his originality but his influence, and this, unfortunately, is the only aspect of Cabet's life and work that Prudhommeaux failed to examine in any detail. Amédée Dunois, the able syndicalist writer, put it succinctly in a review: "I am persuaded that if Cabet had only written his *Voyage* and founded his colony, he would not at all merit being dragged out of historical oblivion. The Cabet who counts for history is . . . the Cabet of the years

[9] *Icarie et son fondateur, Etienne Cabet* (Paris, 1907).

before 1848, the founder and leader of one of the first proletarian groupings, of a veritable worker's party."[10]

This is the Cabet we seek to discover. To do so, however, a few pertinent biographical details concerning his long life before his conversion to communism will be necessary, as will a rapid sketch of his utopia. It should become quickly apparent that one persistent myth about Cabet has little foundation. Far from being a lofty dreamer, the quintessential utopian, Cabet possessed remarkable political acumen and immense powers as a propagandist. To be sure, once convinced of the truth of communism, he exhibited some of the traits that caused Jakov Talmon to place him in the mainstream of nineteenth-century "political messianism."[11] But there was a notable consistency in Cabet's political tactics and his overall strategy throughout his career. He became an *homme politique* in the early 1820s and remained so for the rest of his life. The success his communism enjoyed owed as much to his abilities as a political organizer and tactician as to the concept itself.[12] And we shall see that the one truly utopian flaw in his history—the decision of May 1847 to create an experimental community in the United States— arose less from previous conviction than from his earlier misconception of the nature of social change and the growing recognition that his strategy of left-wing cross-class unity was untenable.

[10] *L'Action directe*, May 20, 1908. My thanks to Harvey Goldberg for bringing this review to my attention. For Prudhommeaux's justification of this lacuna, see his *Cabet*, 194.

[11] J. L. Talmon, *Political Messianism, The Romantic Phase* (New York, 1960), 163–76. See also his *Utopianism and Politics* (London, 1957).

[12] Cabet is usually regarded as the most utopian of utopians. This is largely because of the general ignorance of his activity in July Monarchy politics. See G. D. H. Cole, *A History of Socialist Thought*, I, *The Forerunners* (London, 1959), 6, and M. L. Berneri, *Journey through Utopia* (London, 1957), 222. The "other Cabet" is treated to an extent in Pierre Angrand, *Etienne Cabet and the Revolution of 1848* (Paris, 1948); Fernand Rude, "Introduction," in Rude, ed., *Voyage en Icarie: Deux Ouvriers viennois aux Etats-unis en 1855* (Paris, 1955); Georges Duveau, *1848* (Paris, 1965), 229–32. For an extremely cynical view of Cabet and his motivations, see Janice Fotion, "Cabet and Icarian Communism," Ph.D. dissertation (State University of Iowa, 1966). The practical side of Cabet, his political realism above all, does not conform to the image of the utopian mind presented in Raymond Ruyer, *L'Utopie et les utopies* (Paris, 1957), 25–40. As is the case with Talmon, Ruyer would have benefited from a more thorough study of real life as opposed to the history of ideas.

1 | The Long Apprenticeship, 1788–1839

An engraving widely circulated in 1848 pictures Etienne Cabet and several other notable socialists hawking their ideas in sideshow fashion before the wondering eyes of the plain folk crowded below.[1] This withering image, for all its ill will, captures the contemporary view of Cabet with some accuracy. Daniel Stern has left this appreciation: "A man of much less scientific worth than Raspail, but infinitely better suited for the governance of the common people [was] M. Cabet. . . . [He] possessed a talent for organization to a high degree and hid, under the exterior of a communicative bonhomie, the instinct and even the qualifications for power." Karl Marx felt that Cabet should "be respected for his practical attitude toward the proletariat," by which he meant that Cabet knew how to operate in the political arena and had no romantic illusions about those with whom he wished to communicate.[2] That Cabet was a remarkable salesman and an indefatigable organizer will become obvious as we examine the Icarian movement. But by the forties he possessed several decades of experience in such matters. The development of these skills, the roots of his political strategy of compromise, conciliation, and coalition, and the paths that led him to communism will be the main emphasis of this chapter.

The Formation of a Republican Leader

Cabet's origins are a matter of some controversy. Although he became a lawyer and adopted a bourgeois life style, he never tired of reminding his followers that he sprang from the working class.

[1] Collection of Lithographs relating to the Revolution of 1848, Cabinet d'Estampes, Bibliothèque Nationale de France.

[2] Daniel Stern, *Histoire de la Révolution de 1848* (Paris, 1850) II, 165. Marx to J. B. Schweitzer, Jan. 24, 1865, quoted in the Appendix to Marx, *The Poverty of Philosophy* (New York, 1963), 199–200.

This was true perhaps in the general sense of the early nineteenth-century conception of the term, which tended to include all persons whose income derived from work with their hands. But the child born on New Year's Day 1788 in Dijon was the son of Claude Cabet, a master cooper, and the former Françoise Bertier. His godfather was a master joiner and his godmother the wife of an innkeeper.[3] While it was not unusual to call upon people of slightly higher social status to act in such functions, we cannot forget that Dijon was the scene of considerable journeyman-master conflict among joiners in the years before the Revolution.[4] In such an atmosphere the common corporate status of Etienne's father and godfather perhaps has a greater significance. Moreover, coopering, especially in a town at the center of the Burgundy wine trade, was among the more remunerative crafts of the day, and to be a skilled craftsman at all, no matter what one's status, placed one considerably above the common mass of working people. Claude Cabet wished Etienne to take up his craft, but when the boy's eyesight proved too weak for the exacting work of a barrelmaker he had little trouble in financing his son's preliminary academic training for a professional career. Cabet never spoke of having suffered any particular hardships as a child and no doubt would have done so if they had existed in order to impress his worker-followers in the forties. Furthermore, a brother became a relatively successful businessman in Dijon, probably assisted by capital or an inheritance from his father. Still, in the twenties Cabet went to a former teacher rather than his family for loans.[5] The evidence is skimpy, but it would appear that the status of Cabet's family was a cut above that of the common worker.

Very little is known about the political atmosphere in the Cabet home or about Etienne's early ideological development. Prudhommeaux has left us with a picture of Cabet as a Jacobin Republican from his early childhood, citing the strength of Jacobinism in Dijon, Claude Cabet's social status, the elder Cabet's joy upon hearing of

[3] Details from Cabet's birth certificate in the Archives Nationales de France (hereafter A.N.), C 1194 (Côte d'Or).

[4] Henri Hauser, *Les Compagnonnages d'arts et métiers à Dijon au XVII*[e] *et XVIII*[e] *siècles* (Paris, 1907), 67.

[5] Proudhon *fils* to Cabet, May 17, 1826, Correspondance, Archief Cabet, Internationaal Instituut voor Sociale Geschiedenis, Amsterdam (hereafter IISG).

the execution of Girondist leaders, and Etienne's alleged relations with Prieur de la Côte d'Or.[6] If so, then Cabet must have actually drifted to the right as he reached maturity, for in his first political statement of any significance, written in 1828, he reveals himself to be a liberal Orleanist.[7] It is clear, however, that Cabet's major intellectual influences, his lycée mentor, Joseph Jacotot, and Victor Proudhon, dean of the Dijon school of law, must be ranged somewhere on the left. Both, having supported Napoleon's liberal promises of the Hundred Days, lost their jobs thereafter, and Jacotot ended up in permanent exile in Belgium, where he developed an important reputation in pedagogical theory.[8] Moreover, Cabet, after a prayerful search for the God of Christianity, gave in to rationalist skepticism at an early age and, by way of contrast, apparently was more impressed with Fénelon's *Télémaque* than any other book of his youth. Prudhommeaux considered the latter his "first lesson in communism."[9]

But it would seem that Cabet's main preoccupation as a young man was professional success. Having achieved a brilliant record at the lycée, he first tried medical school but then shifted to law, aiming for a chair in jurisprudence at Dijon. When he received his law degree in May 1812, however, no position was available and so he became a practicing lawyer. He must have been successful, for he was chosen to defend several high-ranking Bonapartist administrators during the "legal white terror" that followed the Hundred Days; among them were General Antoine Vaux, military commander of Burgundy, for whom he won an acquittal, and Piogy, former mayor of Dijon. Such activity raised Cabet to prominence in local liberal circles and no doubt helps explain his popu-

---

[6] Prudhommeaux, *Cabet,* 31. On Jacobinism in Dijon see A. Kleinclauz, *Histoire de Bourgogne* (Paris, 1909), 372–86.

[7] "Exposé d'une révolution nécessaire dans le gouvernement de France," Archief Cabet, Manuscrits, IISG.

[8] E. Méssine, "Un Pedagogue bourguignon: Joseph Jacotot (1770–1844)," *Annales de Bourgogne,* XXVI (1964), 5–43, and Colette Sadowsky, "La Crise et le relèvement des collèges en Côte d'Or sous la Restauration," *Annales de Bourgogne,* XXXII (1960), 37. Proudhon was allowed to return as a professor in 1816, however, and became dean again in 1818.

[9] *Cabet,* 3. See also H. Carle and J. P. Beluze, *Biographie de Etienne Cabet, fondateur de l'école icarienne* (Paris, 1861–62), 18. On Cabet's early religious experience see his *Voyage en Icarie,* 3d ed. (Paris, 1845), 281–82.

larity in 1831, when he was elected deputy from Dijon.[10] He also discovered that the promotion of one's career and political involvement, even in opposition, could go hand in hand.

The Piogy trial dragged on until February 1820 and resulted in a turn of events that proved decisive for Cabet's future. While his client was cleared after a third appeal, Cabet found himself faced with a trumped-up malpractice charge—a result more of the repressive atmosphere produced by the assassination of the Bourbon heir, the Duc de Berry, than of his own improprieties—and was suspended from the bar for a whole year. Moreover, he suffered from temporary blindness toward the end of the trial, a condition he attributed to overwork.[11] These circumstances motivated him to seek a new life in Paris. He had apparently established contacts there during a visit in 1816 through the Comtesse de Chastenay, a Parisian patroness of prominent Burgundians; upon his arrival he became the personal secretary of Félix Nicod, a wealthy lawyer. This connection threw Cabet into the midst of the active liberal-Bonapartist opposition to the Bourbon regime. He frequented the salons of Lafayette and came to know Jacques Laffitte, Jacques Charles Dupont de l'Eure, and Jacques Antoine Manuel, whom he admired above all the others.[12] Inevitably, he became associated with the Charbonnerie, the only major conspiracy against the Bourbons during the Restoration.

In retrospect, the Charbonnerie may be viewed as the training ground for the radical activism that burst forth in 1830 and after. Cabet, however, was not connected with such youthful republican militants as Bazard, Buchez, and Raspail. Rather, because of his links with the liberal establishment, he figured among the more mature—and generally more conservative—cadres. Ostensibly, the *vente suprême*, the highest "cell" in the organization, which in-

[10] See Cabet, *Lettre de M. Cabet, ex-Procureur-général en Corse, aux électeurs du deuxième arrondissement de Dijon (Côte-d'Or)* (Dijon, June 16, 1831), 24; Bissey, *Note* (Dijon: Frantin, 1820); *Le Moniteur universel,* Aug. 24, 1816; Cabet, *Le "National" traduit devant le tribunal de l'opinion publique et M. Cabet accusé par le "National"* (Paris, May 5, 1841), 40; G. Bertier de Sauvigny, *La Restauration* (Paris, 1955), 181–82; and Piogy to Cabet, May 5, 1839, Archief Cabet, IISG.

[11] Prudhommeaux, *Cabet,* 12.

[12] Carle and Beluze, *Biographie,* 58–59.

cluded such luminaries as Manuel, Dupont de l'Eure, and Lafayette, directed the Charbonnerie; but the Parisian *vente centrale,* controlled by Buchez and Bazard, carried out most of the practical operations. Cabet became a member of the former late in 1821.[13] Even within this directorate, there was considerable division. Lafayette thought the determination of the precise form of government should await the nation's will as expressed through a constituent assembly, though he personally leaned toward a republic. Manuel, on the other hand, "believed that after the revolution the nation could not be left in suspense as to its destiny and that one should, if not impose, at least indicate a solution." A postrevolutionary provisional government should frankly declare for a monarchy.[14] By and large the younger militants favored Lafayette's position while "those more eminent by virtue of age and position" followed Manuel.[15] Cabet functioned with considerable success as director of communications for the Manuel faction: "with regard to the arrangement of meeting places, precautions to foil the police, guards to establish, the means of flight or defense in case of attack, he excelled, and everyone rendered homage to his services, even those who did not like him."[16] He also undertook several dangerous liaison missions before the revolt, including one to Joigny that resulted in his arrest.[17] There is no evidence, as Théodore Dézamy later charged, that Cabet exhibited any cowardice in this role.[18]

Besides fulfilling his technical role, Cabet was a major voice on the vente suprême in promoting reconciliation between the wings of the Charbonnerie. He even counseled a wait-and-see attitude with regard to the removal of the Bourbons. Pierre Leroux insisted on

[13] *Ibid.,* 61.

[14] Duvergier de Hauranne, *Histoire du gouvernement parlementaire en France* (Paris, 1864), VI, 398. On the Charbonnerie see Joseph Calmette, "Les Carbonari en France sous la Restauration," *La Révolution de 1848,* IX (1913–14), 401–17, X (1913–14), 52–73, 117–37, 214–30, and the recent work by Alan Spitzer, *Old Hatreds and Young Hopes: The French Carbonari against the Bourbon Restoration* (Cambridge, Mass., 1971).

[15] See Paul-François Dubois, "Étienne Cabet," *Revue bleue* (March 14, 1908), 322. My thanks to Alan Spitzer for informing me of this valuable source.

[16] *Ibid.*

[17] Carle and Beluze, *Biographie,* 64.

[18] *Calomnies et politique de M. Cabet: Réfutation par des faits et par sa biographie* (Paris, 1842), 7.

the importance of Cabet within the Charbonnerie and seriously compared his influence to that of the Fayettiste leader, Bazard. Finally, Cabet helped to launch the revolutionary tradition surrounding the martyrdom of the four sergeants of La Rochelle, who voluntarily gave their lives to save those of many of their fellow conspirators, by authorizing a famous account of their heroism.[19]

Cabet's role in the Charbonnerie firmly established him among the parliamentary liberal opposition. Perhaps because of this connection, more fruitful for a man with developing political ambitions, he divorced himself from the two vital manifestations that seduced so many young radicals during the last years of the Restoration, Saint-Simonism and neo-Jacobinism.

Paul-François Dubois, a founder of the Saint-Simonian *Globe* and later a high official under the July Monarchy, has left a valuable portrait of Cabet during these years. Through their close association in the Charbonnerie, Dubois formed a generally unfavorable opinion of Cabet's potentialities: "If, when I knew Cabet in 1822, someone had said to me that he would become anything more than a lawyer—politically inclined, restless, impassioned, narrow-minded, with no education beyond that of his profession, and, even so, limited and superficial—he would have greatly surprised me." Cabet's capacities seemed limited to those of an efficient and constricted bureaucrat. At a planning session, Cabet, "speaking with a slow and methodical precision, astonished me by a narrative in which all the words appeared prepared in advance and engraved in his memory with such imperturbable fidelity that one would have said that he was reading a written document." The only thing he could discuss intelligently was the Revolution. "His life, however, was honorable and pure. Evidently very poor, with bread and a bowl of milk in the morning and in the evening [to be found] in some little out-of-the-way restaurant like a simple worker, a veritable political ascetic, he was always working, running to the four corners of Paris, to the suburbs, and even farther . . . in a word, inde-

---

[19] Dubois, "Cabet," 321; Pierre Leroux, *La Grève de Samarez* (Paris, 1863–64), I, 364. Cabet's piece was entitled "Mort héroique de Bories, Goubin, Raoulx et Pommer: Récit fait, raconté et distribué le lendemain de l'exécution," *Almanach populaire de la France* (Paris: Pagnerre, 1848). According to the editor, "This handwritten essay bore no signature, but within the Charbonnerie it was known to be the work of Cabet."

fatigable."[20] This austerity and single-minded devotion to a cause remained important facets of Cabet's character. But one cannot ignore his emphasis on unity and factional reconciliation as a member of the vente suprême. It is also evident that he had discovered his true profession: the life of political opposition.

Cabet was readmitted to the bar, and he may have even pleaded some cases in 1823 and 1824. For the next three years he became a partner in a bank linking English and French commercial interests that was financed by liberal bankers and lawyers. The venture had to be liquidated in 1827 because of the commercial crisis.[21] In 1828 he gained employment with the legal publishing house of Dalloz, another illustrious liberal leader. Cabet directed the gathering of materials and the planning of a *Recueil de jurisprudence générale,* the purpose of which was to expose the need for legal reform. A M. Grün replaced him the following year, and one suspects, in light of the silence of Carle and Beluze about the circumstances, that Cabet may have performed less than satisfactorily.[22] Broadly viewed, Cabet's activity during the twenties secured his position as one of the lesser lights of the group surrounding the far left in the Chamber of Deputies and established associations that would be professionally rewarding in the future.

In 1827, in a tract entitled "Une Exposé d'une révolution nécessaire dans le gouvernement de France,"[23] Cabet made his first serious attempt to set down his political opinions. His central theme was that while a republic might be the "most perfect" form of government, France was not yet sufficiently mature to sustain one. Did he therefore opt for the liberal Empire that he defended in 1815 and 1816 and still flirted with as late as 1822?[24] Not at all. Napolean destroyed the gains for liberty made by the Revolution, and the constitutionalism of the *Acte additionel* was a ruse. Cabet argued that no single individual, emperor or king, could legitimately take it upon himself to govern a state; rather it was "exclusively up to the nation" to form its own laws and constitute its

[20] All quotations in this paragraph are from Dubois, "Cabet," 321 and 323.
[21] Cabet, *Lettre aux électeurs* (June 16, 1831), 34; Carle and Beluze, *Biographie,* 66.
[22] Carle and Beluze, *Biographie,* 66.
[23] See above, n. 7.
[24] Dubois (p. 321) refers to Cabet as "semi-Bonapartist, semi-Orleanist."

own government. This was the grand principle of the "just and glorious" Revolution of 1789. Even the Convention and the Terror were justified, for the former saved France from invasion and the latter eliminated the threat from the aristocrats, who merited death "one hundred times over." The Restoration had destroyed the sacred Revolutionary principle of national sovereignty, and thus a "new revolution" was necessary to revive it. "That which essentially constitutes a republic is this principle: that sovereignty belongs to the nation, that all power emanates from it and ought to be exercised in its interest alone." At the time, however, France was not ready for a purely elective government. Ambitions and rivalries might "overwhelm the state." Instead, a "representative and constitutional monarchy" alone could produce a stable polity. And his candidate? Naturally, the hero of Jemappes, a true son of the Revolution, the Duc d'Orléans. Louis-Philippe would be the best of republics.[25]

This was only his opinion, for the choice must be left to the "will of the nation." Did he mean that universal (manhood) suffrage should be adopted? Nowhere did he specifically say so, and it is rather doubtful that this was his intention. In discussing the issue of how the revolution should be fomented, Cabet made clear his low opinion of the political capacity of the uneducated masses.[26] The "middle class" (*classe moyenne*) would make the revolution and presumably ought to constitute the principal force of the national will. Cabet disavowed not only real republicanism but formal democracy as well. Given his associates at the time, this should not come as a great surprise.

Extending Manuel's argument for a firm hand after the upheaval, Cabet proposed the creation of a brief postrevolutionary dictatorship under Louis-Philippe. The function of such an emergency government would be to call elections for a constituent assembly and to organize the defense of the revolution against aristocratic plots and foreign intervention. The other duties of the dictator, according to Cabet's formula, should be to establish complete

---

[25] "Exposé," 4, 77, and 87.
[26] *Ibid.*, 42–43. The "poor class," he indicated, is too absorbed in its work, when work is available, to take an informed interest in politics and, when times are bad, reacts blindly to hunger without recourse to political ideals.

freedom of the press and to choose from among the "young, en-lightened, active, and courageous patriots" new functionaries to replace the aristocrats.[27]

Cabet diverged (at least in emphasis) from his mentors' outlook when he discussed "the principal object of administration," which ought to be "the improvement of the conditions of the popular classes," the element "most useful" to society and in the greatest need of "social protection." All men should be guaranteed enough work to allow them to be well fed, clothed, and housed. Only through their amelioration could a country achieve "solid grandeur" and "veritable glory."[28] Perhaps this opinion reflects the impact of Saint-Simon's thought, but it may have simply derived from the fact that Cabet, unlike most of his friends, was a son of the people.

With this exception, Cabet rested firmly in the mainstream of the political thought that was to characterize the revolution of 1830; his revolution was essentially the one that occurred. In 1830 he was not to be found, even in spirit, among the disgruntled republicans who opposed the accession of Louis-Philippe.[29] Politically to the right of even Lafayette, he would concur with those of his associates who convinced the old general that a "monarchy with republican institutions" was necessary.

Like most of his associates, Cabet remained far from the barricades during the revolution but joined them in the consolidation of victory, acting as a member of a local revolutionary committee. Shortly after Louis-Philippe was declared lieutenant-general of the kingdom, Cabet sent him a long letter that argued for a national plebiscite sanctioning his elevation to the throne. But on August 7, the rump Chamber, led by Dupont and Laffitte, overwhelmingly voted the Duc d'Orléans the crown. Cabet changed his tune quickly, publishing a brochure endorsing the move, particularly in light of the international situation. He did, however, reiterate the need for a widened suffrage in all elections.[30] Such opportunism should be

[27] "Exposé," 71. On the subject of postrevolutionary dictatorship, pp. 64–72 are relevant.

[28] *Ibid.*, Chap. 10, Sec. 11.

[29] See Louis Blanc, *Histoire de dix ans,* 13th ed. (Paris, 1883), I, 358–61. Cabet even said that he might have had some influence on the recalcitrant republicans by urging them not to declare for a republic before the nation had been called upon; see his *Révolution de 1830,* 2d ed. (Paris, 1833), 237.

[30] C——, avocat, *Au duc d'Orléans* (Paris, Aug. 7, 1830), 1 and 8. This

no surprise: Cabet was among the thousands of place-seekers spawned by the revolution. In the blunt terms of Charles de Rémusat, "Dupont made a procureur-général of him";[31] Cabet received a patronage appointment as the chief judicial official of Corsica from the man for whom he had been serving as personal secretary. In a letter to Nicod's wife, Elisa, Cabet indicated that he was satisfied with the independence and power the new post offered, despite its distance from the center of things, and considered it to be the logical steppingstone toward his "one serious ambition," to become a deputy.[32]

Such an opportunity would soon arise. No sooner had he been installed and begun to institute the jury system in Corsica than Dupont resigned as Minister of Justice. It soon became apparent to Cabet—as it had to Dupont, Laffitte, and the more liberal elements of the revolutionary leadership—that, politically, the new regime was less bent on innovation than they had assumed. He received virtually no support from Mérilhou and Barthe, who succeeded Dupont. The government's dismissal of Lafayette as commander of the National Guard, its failure to render even moral support to the Polish revolutionaries, its unwillingness to call new elections, and the determination of the increasingly powerful Casimir Périer faction to repress popular societies and to develop a conservative suffrage law convinced him that he could not honestly serve the new regime, especially after Périer came to power on March 13, 1831.[33] But more exciting opportunities were in the offing. Cabet

---

brochure is located among the printed matter in the Archief Cabet, IISG. See also Cabet, *Lettre aux électeurs* (June 16, 1831), 36–37; Cabet, *Poursuites du Gouvernement contre M. Cabet* (Paris, 1834), 11–12; and Cabet, *Correspondance depuis le 1er août 1830 avec S. M. Louis-Philippe 1er*, *Dupont de l'Eure, Barthe, etc.* (Paris, 1833), 4.

[31] *Mémoires de ma vie*, ed. Charles Pouthas (Paris, 1959), II, 119.

[32] Cabet to Mme Nicod, Nov. 20, 1830, Archief Cabet, Manuscrits, IISG. This is not to contest the fact that Cabet felt isolated in Bastia. But Prud-hommeaux (*Cabet*, 38ff), not familiar with the Nicod letter, argues that Cabet did not really want the post at all.

[33] See Cour Royale de Bastia, *Procès-verbal de l'installation de M. Cabet en qualité de Procureur-général de S. M.* (Bastia, n.d. [Nov. 1830]), 15 (A.N., BB6 188 dos Cabet); Cabet, *Correspondance avec Louis-Philippe*, 23, 35, 38–41; A. Fortier, "Dupont (de l'Eure) et la Révolution de Juillet 1830," *La Révolution de 1848*, XIII (1916–17), 151–52; Carle and Beluze, *Biographie*, 178; and Cabet to the Garde des Sceaux, Nov. 3, 1830, and May 22, 1831, A.N., BB6 188 dos Cabet.

had been asked by Dupont to run for the Chamber of Deputies from Dijon. He could count on the suport of Aide-toi, le ciel t'aidera, a liberal electoral organization now led by Garnier-Pagès the elder, which had become the haven for Fayettist monarchists. It officially supported the constitutional outcome of the revolution but wished to hold the king to the promise of a "monarchy with republican institutions."[34] Cabet's candidacy was announced on April 7 in Dijon, and on May 3 the Council of Ministers voted to revoke his appointment in Corsica. On May 9 *Le Moniteur* carried the news of his dismissal, and this is where Cabet read about it; no one ever bothered to inform him officially.[35]

But no matter. Aged forty-three, Etienne Cabet, the son of a barrelmaker, was on his way back to mount a campaign for national office in his native city. Arrangements were quickly made. Because Cabet paid only 46 francs in taxes on some land near Dijon that he had acquired "several years" before, one Mme Legéas, a friend of his Parisian patroness, made legal transfer to his name of property she owned worth 509 francs in taxes, and he became eligible for office.[36] (This arrangement provides an interesting example of how a poor politician with the right connections might break the stranglehold of the *régime censitaire*.) Cabet's main opponent, a Périer candidate, was a former deputy and a marquis named Chauvelin. Success came with remarkable ease. Although the arrondissement claimed only 439 eligible voters, a majority of these men of sub-

[34] See H. Duval, "Documents pour servir à l'histoire des sociétés populaires sous la Monarchie de Juillet: La Société Aide-toi, le ciel t'aidera," *La Révolution de 1848*, XIII (1916–17), 373–96.

[35] See unofficial letter of Cabet to Mérilhou (Cabet's copy), March 9, 1831, Archief Cabet, Correspondance, IISG; Cabet, "Aux électeurs de l'arrondissement de Dijon," *Journal politique et littéraire de la Côte d'Or*, April 24, 1831 (copy in Archief Cabet, IISG); and Carle and Beluze, *Biographie*, 164–65. My interpretation here contradicts that of Prudhommeaux (*Cabet*, 47), who asserts that Cabet's dismissal came as a "stunning disgrace." But the fact that Cabet decided to run for a deputyship as an opposition candidate well before the government's move against him began indicates that he was ready to resign. Moreover, as he remarked in his brochure formally opening his campaign (not utilized by Prudhommeaux): "I thus voluntarily exposed myself to revocation the moment I resolved to write my letter to the electors [on April 7]"; Cabet, *Lettre aux électeurs* (June 16, 1831), 39.

[36] Cabet, *Lettre aux électeurs*, (June 16, 1831), 4; A.N., C 1194 (Côte d'Or); and Cabet, *Correspondance*, 46.

stance professed to be liberal; on July 5, responding to the electoral propaganda of Aide-toi, Cabet's past record of opposition to the Bourbons, and his assurances that he was not a republican, they accorded him an overwhelming victory in a turnout well above the national average.[37]

Cabet took his seat in the Chamber in a crisis atmosphere. Périer's "party of resistance" had gained in the July elections and appeared firmly established in power. And Louis-Philippe had already begun to demonstrate that he was not willing to play a passive role in the regime. The monarchy with republican institutions was not to become a reality. Moreover, the new regime did nothing to mitigate the working-class and artisan distress that had resulted from a further disintegration of economic stability following the revolutionary events. Indeed, the Périer ministry made every effort to harass those middle-class elements who had moved to develop programs and organizations to agitate for social justice, above all the avowedly republican Société des Amis du Peuple, led by François-Vincent Raspail. This conservative policy served to drive such moderates as Dupont, Garnier-Pagès, and the editor of the influential *Le National,* Armand Carrel, toward overt republicanism. Cabet, who, in a brochure published after his election,[38] had already vowed to fight against property qualifications and for the payment of elected officials, willingly followed their lead. By early 1832 he was a republican and rapidly becoming one of the most acerbic critics of the "betrayal of July." Unfortunately, the Chamber of Deputies did not prove the arena best suited to his abilities. He appeared constricted, overwhelmed, even frightened when he took the floor. He was totally inept as an orator and generally uncreative as a legislator.[39] One can only guess at his reaction to this failure, but given his high expectations he must have been heartbroken.

But the evolution of Cabet's political opinions was making for-

[37] Cabet, *Lettre aux électeurs* (June 16, 1831), 6 and 10–11; A.N., C 1194 (Côte d'Or); and Sherman Kent, *Electoral Procedure under Louis-Philippe* (New Haven, 1937), 26.

[38] *Lettre aux électeurs* (July 8, 1831), 4 and 6–7.

[39] See Janice Fotion, "Cabet and Icarian Communism." Although correct with regard to Cabet's undistinguished career as a legislator, Fotion's attempts to prove Cabet's general incompetence are unconvincing, especially in light of his leadership role in extraparliamentary politics, analyzed in the following paragraphs.

mal politics increasingly irrelevant for him. The republicans claimed only a handful of deputies and possessed virtually no support from the narrow electorate. The evident channel for Cabet's energies was extraparliamentary, in the realm of organizational activity and propaganda among the disenfranchised. Most historians agree that the revolution of 1830 "had brought the people, particularly the people of Paris, back into politics in a way they had not been involved since the 1790s."[40] The patent failure of the new regime to satisfy even the least desires of the popular classes who made the revolution possible tended to radicalize large numbers of these common folk. A sense of the growing frustration, and the degree of political consciousness, among them may be found in this remarkable epigram written by a Parisian coachman, Millon. Before July

there existed that class of imposters and weaklings . . . called the noble and religious aristocracy; another class, the people, the active and laboring part [of the population], from whom derives all industrial wealth, found itself tributary to and exploited . . . by the first. But Nature, irritated by such a state of things, awakened from its long slumber . . . and crushed the head of the aristocracy with a single blow. And it is to that, citizens, that we must react; to pursue the debris of that same aristocracy that has formed anew under the dominion of the bourgeoisie and eradicate it to its very foundations, creating on its debris the government most conformable to our social needs. In my opinion, this government is the Republic.[41]

While such an attitude may have been more advanced than that of most Parisian working people at the time, it captures the idea of both the fruitlessness of the revolution and the expected social transformation that should accompany the establishment of a republic, sentiments doubtless shared by all workers who considered such questions at all. The winter and spring of 1831–1832 must be regarded as a crucial period in the growth of popular republicanism. The brief triumph and brutal suppression of the great silk-weavers' uprising in Lyons in November, the traumatic late-winter

[40] David H. Pinkney, *The French Revolution of 1830* (Princeton, 1972), 367.

[41] From among the papers of Millon seized by the police in preparation for the trial of Droits de l'Homme members in April 1833, in Gisquet, *Mémoires d'un Préfet de Police* (Paris, 1840), III, 77–78. On the Société des Droits de l'Homme, see Georges Weill, *Histoire du parti républicain en France 1814–1871* (Paris, 1928), 75ff.

experience of the cholera epidemic and its socially unequal death toll, the furious conflict between the government and republican political societies seeking working-class support, and, finally, the insurrection of June 5–6, 1832, which brought thousands of workers and students together into armed conflict with the bourgeois National Guard of Paris, all contributed to a massive broadening of the republican political base.[42]

This was the context in which Etienne Cabet became a true political leader. Although supported by a sinecure subscribed by his supporters in Dijon, he increasingly neglected parliamentary life and built instead a formidable reputation as a propagandist and organizer. His general political strategy was one of republican unity. The range of republican opinion in 1832–1833 was wide, stretching from the Babouvist communism of Filipo Buonarroti on the left to simple belief in expanded suffrage and a republican constitution shared by the former Orleanists, such as Dupont and Garnier-Pagès. The central issue dividing the various factions was the relationship between the constitutional and socio-economic structures of their projected republics. On the practical level, the dividing line came between those who incorporated the Jacobin heritage into their vision (although Blanqui was an exception here) and those who did not. Cabet's influence in large measure resulted from the fact that he could function as a liaison between these elements, both because of personal contacts and because of his middle-ground ideological stance.

He revealed the latter in his first major written work, *La Révolution de 1830,* which he finished on October 11, 1832. This book enjoyed considerable success and was described by Armand Marrast of *La Tribune* as the "patriots' manual." It chonicled the perfidies of the king and the Périer ministry, focusing especially on

---

[42] See Weill, *Histoire,* 72ff; Irene Collins, *The Government and the Newspaper Press in France* (Oxford, 1959), 61ff; Jean Lhomme, *La Grande Bourgeoisie au pouvoir (1830–1880),* (Paris, 1960), 71ff; Louis Chevalier, *Classes laborieuses et classes dangereuses* (Paris, 1958), xvii–xxii; and Christopher H. Johnson, "The Regeneration of French Social Republicanism, 1830–1832," master's thesis (University of Wisconsin, 1962), *passim.* On the significance of June 5–6 for Cabet's own radicalism (he was in fact arrested because he was one of the leaders of General Lamarque's funeral cortege), see Cabet, *Correspondance,* 48–49; Blanc, *Dix Ans,* III, 268–77; A.N., F⁷ 5886 and C 753 dos 5.

how they had ignored the needs of the working classes. Despite the often bitter tone that underpinned his critique, Cabet steered clear of open support for Jacobinism, then fully embraced by the famous Société des Droits de l'Homme. His discussion of the Revolution of 1789 established his position. He endorsed all the articles of the Declaration of the Rights of Man and Citizen and the constitution of 1791 except for the latter's property qualifications on voting rights, substituting instead the electoral law that produced the Convention. But he had reservations about the untried constitution of 1793, which, "by giving the people direct participation in the government, was perhaps too democratic for the epoch. That of the Year III, . . . less democratic than the preceding one, as liberal and popular as that of 1791, appeared to reconcile better the rights and interests of all the classes of society." At the same time, he condemned other aspects of the Thermidorian reaction, particularly the persecution of Jacobins, who, said Cabet, were the "patriots" of the period. His admiration for them had a simple source: they saved France in her most desperate hour. Whereas the Girondins dangerously compromised the war effort and dealt timidly with counterrevolution at home, the Mountain consisted of "men of action, convinced that force alone could defeat so many external and internal enemies." He went on to justify, though very briefly, the dictatorship of the Committee of Public Safety and the Terror. " '93 was not the republic but war; and throughout the duration of this stormy epoch, it was a question not of liberty or of institutions but of combat, of defense, of life or death for the nation." This, however, was as far as Cabet was willing to go in defense of Robespierre and the Jacobins.[43] His social theory showed the same restraint. Despite his repeated assertion that the sole end of good government was to promote the welfare of the people, he still held fast to a belief in the inviolable right of private property. While such devoted Jacobins as Godefroy Cavaignac wished to redefine property as a mere "natural sentiment," and founded their arguments on Robespierre's Declaration of April 24, 1793, Cabet, even in mid-1833, included property among the "natural rights of

---

[43] Quotations are from Cabet, *La Révolution de 1830*, I, 59, 52, 47, 54, and 53. See also Cabet, *Procès devant la cour d'assises contre M. Cabet* (Paris, 1833), 39–40, and A.N., BB[18] 1214 dos 8792 and C 753 dos 5.

man." Existence, which along with liberty was the first of these rights for Robespierre, did not figure among them.[44]

The publication of *La Révolution de 1830* gave Cabet considerable stature in the republican camp, and his prosecution and acquittal for five "press offenses" allegedly committed in the book added further prestige.[45] Of equal importance in this long-delayed rise to fame was Cabet's prominent role in the Association Libre pour l'Education du Peuple. Shortly after the revolution of 1830, several students from the Ecole Polytechnique had formed a group to offer courses in various fields to the workers of Paris. The following year the program was expanded when several politically active professors of the lycées and colleges joined. The society was named the Association pour l'Instruction gratuite du Peuple and took on a markedly republican flavor. The days of June 1832 caused the suppression of the organization, but it was not long before it revived as the Association Libre.[46] Governmental authorization was contingent upon its pledge to avoid all political questions. The association offered a large variety of courses, mostly ranging from beginning reading and arithmetic to zoology and history.

Victor Lechevalier guided the association throughout 1832, but toward the end of the year an internal crisis began to develop. While Lechavalier was content to adhere to the nonpolitical requirements imposed by the government, several of the teachers, the history professors particularly, mixed republican politics with pedagogy. In December, Lechevalier apologized to the Minister of Public Instruction, François Guizot (who knew a thing or two about the political uses of history himself), and asked for reauthorization, guaranteeing future obedience. He had also meekly complied with an unspecified "order of the Minister of War." The

[44] Cabet, *La République du "Populaire"* (Paris, 1833), 11. For the Jacobin position see, for instance, the point-by-point analysis of the social implications of Robespierre's Declaration made by Dupont de Bussac in *Procès des vingt-sept* (Paris, 1834), 63–96 and G. Cavaignac, "Defense de Cavaignac," *Procès du droit de l'association* (Paris, 1833), 32.

[45] Cabet, *5ᵉ publication du "Populaire"* (Paris, 1833), 4; Digeon *et al.* to Pagnerre, April 28, 1833, Papiers Pagnerre, A.N., 67 AP dos 3; A.N., F⁷ 3886.

[46] Weill, *Histoire*, 58–59.

members of the society felt that he had "sold out to the ministry,"[47] and Lechevalier decided to resign.

These events had created a rift within the society between the "fanatics" and the "moderates," but Lechevalier's resignation soothed the passions of the former, and a "treaty of peace" was effected on February 2. Precisely who comprised each faction is not clear, but it is likely that Camille Berrier-Fontaine and Marc-René Voyer d'Argenson, also members of the Droits de l'Homme, led the advanced wing, while Odilon Barrot and Dupont de l'Eure were among the moderates. Cabet, who participated in the central committee of the association in 1832, was asked to take Lechevalier's place and seems to have been a compromise candidate suitable to both factions. *Le Fondateur,* the society's newspaper, reported that he was "unanimously proposed by the twelve commissions of the arrondissements."[48]

On February 9, 1833, Cabet became the association's secretary-general, a function automatically making him president of the central committee and editor-in-chief of *Le Fondateur.* Under his direction, the association expanded its membership and scope of activity. Previously restricted to Paris, the society found contributing members in the departments. After two months under Cabet, the number of professors, organizers, and contributors had risen to 2,000, while 2,500 persons were paying 25 centimes weekly to take one or more of the 42 courses offered. "Each day [the association] makes new gains: workers, manufacturers, merchants, savants, deputies hasten to involve themselves, some to receive knowledge, others to give it." By November it would have 3,000 contributing members and be offering 50 courses. In line with Cabet's vow of action to promote the material well-being of the people, a commission of doctors and lawyers was created in each arrondissement to assist members and nonmembers alike free of charge. They would also attempt to find work and provide short-term relief for the unemployed.[49] As editor of *Le Fondateur,* Cabet successfully

[47] Report on Lechevalier of Jan. 19, 1833, A.N., F17 6674 dos Association Libre pour l'Education du Peuple.

[48] *Le Fondateur,* Feb. 1833. (A copy is located among the Cabet papers at the IISG.) On the internal conflict and Cabet's election see an informant's report of Feb. 2, 1833, Gisquet to Guizot, Feb. 5, 1833, and the "Rapport spécial" of Feb. 10, 1833, A.N., F17 6674.

[49] Informant's report of Feb. 9, 1833, A.N., F17 6674; Association Libre

learned the difficult trade of the journalist and in June brought out a new paper, *Le Populaire,* a weekly that became the most widely circulated republican sheet of the era.

Its prospectus, which appeared on June 24, 1833, revealed that the paper was not simply another opposition journal but undertook the specific mission of defending the rights and interests of the people. And it would be designed so that the common man could understand it. *Le Populaire* asserted that the "people" produced all by its work and defended the nation by its courage. Therefore it "ought to participate in all social rights, in all benefits of civilization." Yet for centuries society had meant nothing more than its "organized oppression." The Revolution had announced its liberation and fulfillment, but this emancipation was short-lived. Once again oppression reigned. Why? Very simply, because the "laws are made by the minority. . . . Let the people be admitted to the election of its representatives and to the making of the laws; the evil will soon cease." The goals of the paper would be to propagandize for material improvement without harm to the rich (for the wonders of machine production under the aegis of "liberty of industry" held the key to the betterment of the poor), to agitate for universal suffrage, and "to develop in the people a sense of its dignity." To accomplish the last, it would publish "popular biographies" of men of the people who had succeeded.[50] This self-help doctrine did no harm to the paper's circulation. *Le Populaire* was destined to sell 12,000 copies in Paris alone by its seventh number and still more later on.[51]

Cabet's ideology, which ran through the pages of *Le Populaire* and its separate brochures, remained a rather pedestrian, non-Jacobin republicanism adorned with a humanitarian desire to better

---

pour l'Education du Peuple, *Discours d'installation de M. Cabet* (Paris, Feb. 9, 1833), 2; A.N., 67 AP dos 3; Association Libre pour l'Education du Peuple, *But de la société: Sa Composition* (Paris, April 1833); and a brochure of the same title published in November 1833.

[50] Quotations are from the Prospectus to *Le Populaire,* June 24, 1833 (Bibliothèque Nationale).

[51] Cabet, *Nécessité de populariser les journaux républicains* (Paris, n.d.). Prudhommeaux gives a circulation figure of 27,000 for the eighth number; this is an exaggeration which he drew from Favard, *et al., Biographie de M. Cabet* (Paris, 1846).

the conditions of the working classes. Still, ideas conformable to the Jacobin tradition had begun to appear. In a brochure issued in October 1833, Cabet outlined *La République du "Populaire."* A new tone entered his writing. For example, he promoted a devotion to the principle of popular sovereignty almost bordering on a civic religion. "Citizen" became sanctified. All the arts should glorify this perfect polity. The political life had taken on the omnipresence that would be one of the fundamental characteristics of Icaria. Furthermore, Cabet affirmed the "necessity of a revolution by legislation or by force." Though he naturally favored the former, he did not hesitate to justify the use of violence. "If the people were united, if it existed as a people for a single day, a single hour, its powerful hand or its voice alone would at once resuscitate its rights, and force would then be acting only to assure the triumph of justice."[52] But, foreshadowing his position in the 1840s, he cautioned against partial action such as conspiracies or uprisings because the forces at the disposal of the government were far too strong.

Thus, despite his maintenance of property as a natural right, Cabet seemed to be veering toward the camp of the neo-Jacobin society of the Droits de l'Homme. And with good reason, even from a purely practical point of view: his association was increasingly subject to the influence of members of this society. Indeed, a coup had taken place within the central committee of the Association Libre that at least momentarily affected Cabet's power. According to police intelligence, a marked shift to the left had occurred by July 1833 as purges ousted moderates from the central committee and Lafayette was attacked. Moreover, "things have come to the point where even M. Cabet finds himself outflanked, on several occasions, he has been accused of tepidity and of aristocracy."[53] The coup was completed by July 12. Although Cabet maintained his functions as editor and secretary-general, Voyer d'Argenson, deputy, friend of Buonarroti, and a leader in the Droits de l'Homme, replaced him as president of the central committee.[54] On the same day a circular, signed by Cabet, noted that Camille Berrier-Fontaine, future secretary of the central com-

[52] Cabet, *La République du "Populaire,"* 6 and 11.
[53] Minister of Interior d'Argout to Guizot, June 25, 1833, A.N., F17 6674 dos Association Libre pour l'Education du Peuple.
[54] Informant's report of July 14, 1833, A.N., BB18 1338 dos 9306.

mittee of the Droits de l'Homme in Paris, had been elected the association's Inspector-general of Courses by the central committee.[55] On July 15, Gisquet, Prefect of Police, apprised the Minister of the Interior: "I have had the honor of calling to the attention of Your Excellency the dangers that [this association] presents to the public tranquility"; the danger was now patent, having "taken in the majority of the members of the Société des Droits de l'Homme. The central committee and especially the committees of the arrondissements are so many clubs of political propaganda."[56] The Association Libre had become, for all intents and purposes, a front organization for the unauthorized Société des Droits de l'Homme.

Cabet apparently did not fight this development in any way. While he never become a member of Droits de l'Homme, he was reported to have sympathized with the society. A delegate of the Droits de l'Homme was present at a Dijon banquet in Cabet's honor. "He had the honor of conversing with Deputy Cabet, who praised the plan and the goal of our association, which is destined to form citizens . . . cognizant of their rights and duties, as well as the political and moral ideas that ought to distinguish a free man."[57] Such approbation was also necessitated by the new relationship between Droits de l'Homme and the Association Libre. Both practical and ideological considerations thus figured in Cabet's slow conversion to Jacobinism.

But Cabet still resisted socialism. While *Le Populaire* might publish bitter outbursts of working-class resentment,[58] the struggle was to be carried on within the current social system. In an excellent brochure, *Moyens d'améliorer l'état déplorable des ouvriers,* Cabet stressed the need for craft unionism. "If the associations ar-

---

[55] In a dossier concerning the Association Libre in the Archief Cabet, IISG. Berrier-Fontaine became one of Cabet's closest friends. A report on various instructors of the association (Jan. 19, 1833) stated that he "is very closely linked with les Srs Laponneraye and Caunes," important members of Droits de l'Homme. A.N., F17 6674 dos Association Libre.

[56] A.N., BB18 1338 dos 9306.

[57] From an "order of the day" of Dec. 8, 1833 prepared by the central committee of the society at Châlons-sur-Saône and printed in Cour des Pairs, *Affaire du mois d'avril 1834: Rapport fait à la Cour par M. Girod (de l'Ain)* (Paris, 1834), I, 93.

[58] See, for instance, the poem by H. Demolière directed against bourgeois "monopolizers," in the 11th publication of *Le Populaire, La Justice du peuple* (Paris, n.d.).

range a common plan of action and give one another mutual support you will have enough power to have the justice of your claims
recognized." He endorsed the expansion of the functions of mutual
benefit societies and the creation of worker cooperatives. He also
showed a deep understanding of the misery of the workers, their
falling wages, the irregularity of employment, their inadequate
housing. But, despite his support for specific institutions, the thrust
of his arguments remained in the realm of self-help and moral up-
lift: "Instruct yourselves, sense your dignity as men, make yourselves respected, do not endure injury, humiliation, and aggres-
sion."[59]

Despite Cabet's efforts to maintain a moderate tone, the government's attitude toward the Association Libre hardened. On December 22, 1833, the Ministry of Education informed the central
committee that the association's authorization had been withdrawn
because it was actually organized for political purposes. A circular
of the association announced its dissolution shortly thereafter.[60]
This was but one of the repressive measures in the armory of the
government. It had already begun its unrelenting struggle against
the republican press and its prosecution of workers' "societies of
resistance." In January 1834, completing its campaign against the
Association Libre, it indicted *Le Populaire* on two counts. Late
that month discussion began on a measure to require authorization
for all associations of more than twenty members, no matter how
subdivided. Its sights were set on the Société des Droits de
l'Homme. On February 2, 1834, Dupont de l'Eure made the most
dramatic move of his long career. To protest this avalanche of reaction, he resigned from the Chamber of Deputies. The present
monarchy, he said, was operating "in the tradition of the Restoration."[61]

The move against *Le Populaire* was to end Cabet's career as a
republican leader. On January 20 the prefect of the Seine requested
formal authorization from the Chamber of Deputies permitting the
indictment of Cabet for articles written on January 12 and January
19. The first, "La République est dans le Chambre," asserted that

[59] Cabet, *Moyens* (Paris, Nov. 1833), 6 and 4.
[60] Undated circular (probably early Jan. 1834), A.N., 67 AP dos 3.
[61] Dupont to the president of the Chamber of Deputies, Feb. 2, 1834,
A.N., C 760 dos 7.

the reaction, led by the king himself, only made the coming of the republic more probable because the Chamber would shift to the left. More serious, however, was the second, "Crimes des rois contre l'humanité." The recent refusal to grant political asylum to dozens of Poles exiled from Prussia led Cabet to compare Louis-Philippe to the most reactionary monarchs of the day. The illegal utterance followed: Louis-Philippe is "resolved, if necessary, to have Frenchmen shot, gunned down in the streets."[62] On February 8 a parliamentary debate, bordering on a free-for-all, ensued over the requested authorization. Almost helplessly, Cabet lashed out at the Ministry of the Interior for its alleged vendetta against him; this had been backed in the press by *Le Figaro,* a paper "paid by the government." The Minister of the Interior, Argout, amid an immense hubbub, shouted his denial and challenged Cabet to a duel for attacking his integrity. The question was almost immediately settled by hastily chosen seconds.[63] A voice vote sufficed to send Cabet before the tribunal.

As he awaited his fate, republicanism in France approached the final showdown of its "heroic" period. Within two months, Lyons, then Paris, would flame into revolt while the Chamber passed the Draconian law on associations. Cabet came to trial on February 28, 1834. His condemnation was swift and severe despite the efforts of his friends, who even intimidated the jury. Not only did he receive the maximum penalty allowed by law, two years in prison and a 4,400-franc fine, but the judge also condemned him to four years of civil death, a sentence never before rendered in a press offense. "That will deliver us of him," exclaimed the conservative Baron Dupin.[64]

Instead of going to prison in France and, especially, in light of the four-year suspension of all his civil rights, Cabet chose an alternative legally open to him: a five-year exile. A number of his associates contributed to a subscription of 4,000 francs annually for his support while he was out of the country.[65] Cabet first chose

[62] The indictment request and the relevant issues of *Le Populaire* are to be found in A.N., C 760 dos 5.

[63] Cabet, *Poursuites du Gouvernement contre M. Cabet,* 22; *Le Moniteur universel,* Feb. 10, 1834.

[64] André Dupin, *Mémoires* (Paris, 1860), III, 160. On the trial, see A.N., F7 6783 and F7 3887; Cabet, *Poursuites, passim.*

[65] Prudhommeaux, *Cabet,* 96–97. There is some controversy over why

the traditional haven of French exiles, Brussels, where he was "welcomed at the residence" of the prominent liberal deputy, A. Gendebien. His sojourn was brief, however, for the Belgian government expelled him after the anti-Orangist troubles known as the *haras de Tervueren* on April 5 and 6.[66] He then departed for England.

Cabet's activities prior to his conversion to communism reveal a number of facts that need to be borne in mind in assessing his later role as leader of the Icarian movement. First, despite his lower-middle-class origins, his associations were largely with liberal bourgeois. His closest friend was an established Parisian lawyer, and his protector, Dupont de l'Eure, was the recognized leader of the constitutional monarchist, then moderate republican professional middle-class opposition. Cabet's relationships with these notables was to have a lasting impact on his political outlook, for they influenced his belief that any sincere democrat could rationally come to communism as well as his position favoring class collaboration. Second, the development of Cabet's political philosophy was strongly rooted in these associations. Simply put, he

Cabet decided to leave France. Fotion ("Cabet and Icarian Communism," 57) suggests that he may have done so in order to avoid responsibilities with regard to Delphine Lesage, who was supposedly pregnant in March 1834. This would make Cabet's condemnation a most fortuitous occurence! More generously, Fotion also suggests that Cabet might have chosen exile to avoid undue embarrassment for himself and his mistress. Fotion's hypotheses are drawn from p. 98 n. 3 of Prudhommeaux, *Cabet.* The latter, no doubt in deference to Beluze (Cabet's closest associate after 1848), who married the Cabets' only daughter in 1860, makes only passing reference to the situation: "Delphine Lesage had already given birth to a daughter, Céline, when she came to London to join Etienne Cabet who, a little later, regularized the situation of the mother and child by marriage." The crux of the matter is the approximate birthdate of Céline, which would seem to be, according to this statement, the summer of 1834. This is most unlikely, for Céline married one of Cabet's most loyal Icarians, Firman Favard, sometime before the latter's tragic death in March 1847. At that time Céline could have been twelve years old at the very most if we accept the summer of 1834 as her date of birth. This is highly improbable. There is no doubt, however, that she was born out of wedlock (probably in the late 1820s).

[66] Julien Kuypers, *Les Egalitaires en Belgique: Buonarroti et ses sociétés secrètes d'après des documents inédits (1824–1836)* (Brussels, 1960), 38. The royal order effecting this expulsion may be found among the Cabet papers at the IISG. On Gendebien (1789–1869), see Kuypers, 4, 6, and 43; E. van Turenhoudt, *Louis de Potter* (Brussels, 1946), 133–35; and T. Juste, "Alexandre-Joseph-Celestin Gendebien," *Biographie nationale* (Brussels, 1880–83), vol. VII.

swam with the tide. The only element of his thought distinguishing him from many of his associates was an abiding concern for the condition of the workers. This was essential, of course, to the final evolution of his thought, but even in 1834 he showed no signs of endorsing socialism. Third, Cabet's abilities, while by no means modest, were of a particular kind. He showed himself to be a remarkable organizer and propagandist. He could also speak to the working man at his own level while simultaneously relating to "respectable" society. These traits, along with his political common sense, played a fundamental part in the formulation of Icarian tactics and the successful development of the movement in the 1840s. Finally, there can be no question of Etienne Cabet's stature as a leader of the republican opposition. If he failed to become an important deputy, he left an indelible imprint on the extraparliamentary politics of the day. *La Révolution de 1830,* the secretary-generalship of the Association Libre, and the editorship of *Le Populaire,* the largest-selling republican newspaper of the day, all stand as contributions of lasting significance. His fame and abilities would be remembered by workingmen in the forties. To cite two of the most famous of them, Martin Nadaud first attached himself to Cabet in the thirties and preached from *Le Populaire* in the cabarets of Paris, while Agricole Perdiguier, the great reformer of the ancient journeymen's association known as the *compagnonnage,* "especially admired Cabet, 'true patriot, courageous republican, zealous defender of the rights of the people [who was] prosecuted by the king, the ministers, and the potbellied deputies, for a press offense.' "[67]

Exile

The lack of information about Cabet's years in London makes it difficult to establish the reasons for his move from bourgeois republicanism to communism. Fortunately, the question is not of great importance for the purposes of this study and can be treated summarily. Cabet's private view of history and the needs of French society probably always ran several steps ahead of his public utterances. His noninvolvement in political activity after

[67] Quoted in Jean Briquet, *Agricole Perdiguier, compagnon du Tour de France* (Paris, 1955), 126–27; Nadaud, *Mémoires de Léonard, ancien garçon maçon* (Bourganeuf, 1895), 99.

1834 allowed him the intellectual freedom that circumstances had previously prevented. A variety of influences came to bear upon him in 1834, 1835, and 1836 all of which must have played a role in his conversion to communism, but it is impossible to determine the order of their impact or their relative significance.

His personal life was substantially transformed. Cabet had married his long-time mistress, Delphine Lesage, thus legitimizing his daughter, Céline, shortly after his arrival in London. Although we know little about Delphine beyond the facts that she was a Dijonnaise of lower-class origins and a headstrong woman with some political sophistication, she may have had something to do with her husband's rejection of those moderate views that had been molded in part out of consideration for his past bourgeois associates. Cabet may have felt betrayed by those associates, since the sinecure they were to have provided him during his exile was not maintained. He knew real poverty during most of his stay in London.[68] The evidence indicates, too, that he became increasingly distraught in late 1835 and early 1836, the period that appears to have been crucial in his transition to communism. Unfortunately the precise source of his depression cannot be identified.[69]

Intellectually, three direct influences can be documented. The first came from the community of exiled members of the Société des Droits de l'Homme who had escaped from St. Pélagie prison on July 12, 1835. Armand Marrast and Godefroy Cavaignac were among them, but Cabet became tied to the more radical and socialist elements, above all to Dr. Berrier-Fontaine, with whom he and his family shared a house for the bulk of their exile. Berrier had been one of the "fanatics" in the Association Libre and was a recognized Jacobin socialist. One of his closest friends was Albert Laponneraye, whose quasi-Babouvist history of the French Revolution is well known. Berrier regarded himself as a disciple of

[68] Dézamy, *Calomnies,* 32; Cabet to Nicod, Feb. 10, 1836, Archief Cabet, IISG.

[69] Three surviving draft letters help clarify Cabet's emotions during his first two years of exile. The first, to his mother and dated Sept. 4, 1834, indicates that while he missed France he was not unhappy and was willing to brave the inconveniences of exile. But in a letter to Nicod of Jan. 16, 1836, he stated bluntly: *"J'ai trop de noir dans l'âme* to speak to you of anything else." The same attitude appears in another letter to Nicod the following month (Feb. 10, 1836). All three located in the Archief Cabet, IISG.

Bounarroti and Voyer d'Argenson; while Cabet knew them both, nothing in his writings before he left France would imply that he shared their views. Probably his daily contact with Berrier—who remained one of his most trusted counselors in the forties—contributed in a major way to his changing outlook.[70] Cabet also met and discussed social theory with Robert Owen while in London. The similarity of many of their opinions, especially the extreme environmental determinism that appears in the thought of both, indicates Owen's influence on Cabet.[71] Finally, there was the power of Thomas More's vision. Cabet himself declared that *Utopia,* which he apparently read during that troubled winter of 1835–1836, was the crucial influence upon his thought.[72]

However these various elements may have influenced the evolution of Cabet's outlook, we cannot discount his personal evaluation of French historical development since 1789 and the way it had affected his life and career. Now, with time to reflect and the well-stocked library of the British Museum at hand, he was in a position to consider recent history seriously. The French Revolution, as whole, was for him—as for Jules Michelet—a moral good. His parents had lived it and apparently gained from it. He must have felt some personal ambivalence about the Empire, for he was clearly one of those who could not deny the reality of "careers open to talent." Moreover, for a while, defense of the "liberal" Napoleon was both intellectually and professionally rewarding. Opposition to the Restoration was a foregone conclusion. Not only did it violate his every principle, but—as for so many of his class and his generation—it also afforded no possible avenue for career advancement.[73] The July Revolution, in his mind, took France

---

[70] On Berrier see A.N., F[17] 6674 dos Association Libre pour l'Education du Peuple; A. Chenu, *Les Conspirateurs* (Paris, 1850), II, 20–21; Cour des Pairs, *Affaire du mois d'avril 1834,* III, 15–16; and Jean Maitron, ed., *Dictionnaire biographique du mouvement ouvrier français, 1789–1864* (Paris, 1966), III, 492 (hereafter *Dict. Biog.*).

[71] Cabet to Owen, Paris, Aug. 15, 1847, letter no. 1,503, University of Wisconsin microfilm 1,090 (copies of the Owen Papers, Cooperative Library, Manchester, England). Thanks due to Judi Bullerwell for guiding me to this source. See also Stern, *Histoire,* II, 166; Leroux, *La Grève de Samarez,* II, 360.

[72] Cabet, *Toute La Vérité au peuple* (Paris, 1842), 93.

[73] Bertier de Sauvigny, *The Bourbon Restoration* (Philadelphia, 1966), 239–40.

back to 1789. A liberal monarchy under the son of Philippe Egalité rather than the traitorous Louis XVI: why not? A son of the people, sophisticated by a knowledge of political realities and associated with the best liberal minds of the day could certainly support that. This was why he regarded the course of the first four years of the July Monarchy with such utter dismay. He actually held Louis-Philippe responsible for a kind of personal betrayal. In a brochure published in late 1835 he attacked the king with a singularity and violence that approached monomania.[74] The repressive measures embodied in the September press laws were the last straw. Moreover the Jacobins had been correct: the root of Louis-Philippe's policy was the defense of a new bourgeois aristocracy. Thus Cabet's crowning test of any government—what kind of framework it provided for the amelioration of the conditions of the masses—could not be met as long as private property remained an inviolable right. It would appear that once Cabet grasped this principle (and one can imagine his conversations with Berrier during the dreary winter of 1835–1836), the floodgates were let open. In a way, private property replaced Louis-Philippe as the source of all evil, and Cabet moved, possibly overnight, through the entire range of republican opinion that had been represented in the Association Libre, though the entire spectrum of social theories founded upon varying degrees of property rights limitation—and became a communist.

He set feverishly to work on two books, a history of the French Revolution and the *Voyage en Icarie*. Both were completed by early 1838.[75] In the first he reveals his new direction: Maximilien Robespierre was actually a communist. This thesis had already been developed by Buonarroti in his famous book on the Babeuf conspiracy, which clearly influenced Cabet's analysis. But there are too many aspects of Cabet's thought (his patent antimaterialism and his opposition to conspiratorial means, above all) that diverge from Babeuf for his thought to be seen as largely of "Babouvist inspiration."[76]

[74] Cabet, *Lettre à Louis-Philippe* (London, 1835), especially 35–36.
[75] See Chenu, *Les Conspirateurs*, II, 57; Voyer d'Argenson to Cabet, May 15, 1838, Archief Cabet, IISG.
[76] Prudhommeaux, *Cabet*, 144. The Buonarroti volume in question is *La Conspiration pour l'égalité dite de Babeuf* (Brussels, 1828).

Cabet's four-volume *Histoire populaire de la Révolution française* (Paris, 1839–40) was a sustained encomium of the grandeur and wisdom of Robespierre.[77] The following summary illustrates the place he held in Cabet's interpretation of the Revolution.

Up to this point, we have seen the Committee [of Public Safety] and the Convention proclaim, in principle, Equality, Unity in Society and Government, that the right of disposing of persons and things belongs to the Nation, complete freedom of religion, the necessity of free and republican education; we have seen them make Justice and probity the order of the day. We are going to see them proclaim the reign of *morality,* the abolition of misery, ease and happiness for all, and develop their new system the end of which is to realize all the hopes of Philosophy in radically regenerating France and Humanity.

But the guiding spirit of the Committee of Public Safety and "the principal cause of everything that the Convention did well" was a single man, Robespierre. "Thus it is Robespierre who is able to give France peace in founding the Republic of equality, justice, virtue, the happiness of the People, and fraternity of the human race." Cabet justified the Terror and waxed ecstatic over the cult of the Supreme Being. He denied that Robespierre sought to create a dictatorship, recalling the need for unity under the dire circumstances of the Year II. If Robespierre made any mistake it was that he attempted to move on to "communism" too quickly. The conservatives marshaled their forces and organized the tragedy of 9 Thermidor. "Far from being fortunate, the catastrophe of 9 Thermidor is perhaps the most unfortunate thing that could have occurred for France and for the world." In a final eulogy Cabet says: "The

---

[77] This work presented the popular view of the Revolution more simply and clearly than any other of its day. Published at the same time as Albert Laponneraye's superior *Histoire de la Révolution française depuis 1789 à 1814* (Paris, 1838–39), it was Cabet's study that again won the reputation as the "patriot's manual" of the 1840s (Stern, *Histoire de la Révolution de 1848,* II, 166). New editions were published in 1846 and 1851. Ange Guépin, the erudite Jacobin and socialist physician of Nantes, assessed it quite positively: "Cabet is the author of a history of the French Revolution in which the facts are always perfectly appreciated. Others have narrated the events of this period in a more brilliant style, but none has better judged them" (Guépin, *Philosophie du socialisme* [Paris, 1850], 599). And it was Cabet's history from which T.W. Thornton, an Owenite writer, chose to translate parts as the "communist view" of the French Revolution in *The Reasoner* (Dec. 13 and 20, 1848, 453–55, 474–76).

day of justice will not fail to arrive . . . for the martyr of 9 Thermidor; and, we are profoundly convinced, his disinterestedness, his love of the People, and his devotion to Humanity, finally recognized, will give to him a lofty place in the gratitude and the esteem of Peoples."[78] Thus, with the exceptions perhaps of Laponneraye and Albert Mathiez, Cabet presented the most positive assessment of Robespierre in the range of historical writing on the French Revolution. In his view, among the great harbingers of communism, only Jesus Christ and Sir Thomas More rank on the same level. There seems little reason, therefore, to disagree with Karl Grün that Cabet was "the last consequence of '93."[79] Jacobinism, not Babouvism, lay at the heart of his new orientation.

Thus, Cabet's path to communism combined the influences of More, Owen, and Buonarroti and was catalyzed by a mood of frustration and depression and his personal relationship with the neo-Jacobin activist Berrier-Fontaine. The final product was the ideological basis for a new socialist "school" that may be conveniently described as utopian Jacobin communism.

Journey to Icaria

The French workingman who read the *Voyage en Icarie* found himself in the midst of a serene world where not the least whisper of unhappiness, not the slightest ripple of discontent troubled the lives of the inhabitants. This new world stood in stark contrast to the tragic realities of his daily life. He visualized himself residing with his family in a single home; he was well clothed and fed; his wife did not have to face the daily struggle with the local shopkeepers and their faulty weights; his children went to school rather than to the shop; his own workday was short, easy, and pleasant; he could venture into the beautiful countryside without paying a fare and picnic in spacious parks open to anyone; and no police agents hounded him. All this could be effected by the simplest of measures: eliminate private property.

Numerous studies of Cabet's utopia have been published, [80] and no more is needed here than a brief summary of the life Cabet char-

---

[78] *Histoire populaire*, IV, 5–6, 119, 40, 29–30, 136, 137.

[79] Karl Grün, *Die Soziale Bewegung in Frankreich und Belgien* (Darmstadt, 1845), 325–32.

[80] See below, 000–000.

acterized thus: "Community (la communauté) is a mutual and universal guarantee, of all for all. In return for moderate labor, the Community . . . guarantees education, the possiiblity of marriage, food, housing; in a word, everything."[81]

Icaria is a centrally planned but democratically directed and absolutely egalitarian nation-state in which neither property nor money, regular courts of law nor police exist. Cabet held that "it is necessary to opt for all or nothing"; either total communism or a world of misery.[82] Anything short of this logical (but not necessary) consequence of all human history is commensurate with accepting defeat, the status quo. Cabet offered two proofs in deducing the fundamental rationality of complete social and economic equality. First, it is natural, in the sense made so familiar by seventeenth- and eighteenth-century philosophy: it was the original condition of man.[83] Second, all men and women are born equal in physical and mental capabilities.[84] Even for the time, both arguments were extremely tenuous, but Cabet glibly lays them down in the briefest manner. Given this natural equality, the only way that men may become truly human is to construct a social organism conformable to it.

Thus, social equality must be the rule. In housing, food, clothing, and furnishings, every Icarian has as much as every other. But while Cabet is often accused of complete regimentation with regard to the daily needs of life, a careful reading shows that all houses

[81] *Voyage en Icarie,* 3 ed., 568. *La Communauté* was employed by Cabet to designate his communist society. The English word "Community" is used here, but the reader should be aware of the specific connotation it involves.

[82] *Ibid.,* 531.

[83] *Ibid.,* 407.

[84] Physique is obviously a matter of environment and "if there exist some intellects that are naturally superior, they are rare exceptions." The basic problem is that people are unequally educated. *Ibid.,* 385. This is precisely the argument of Babeuf in his *Cadastre perpetuel* (M. Dommanget, *Pages choisies de Babeuf* [Paris, 1935], 81–87). Cabet altered his position on this question in 1847. In an article in *Le Populaire* he admits natural inequality of intelligence, capacity, strength, beauty, and so on, but stands on this argument: do these gifts from nature mean that those more liberally endowed should *by right* receive greater material benefits than the others? That one man is more talented than another is an accident of nature; it is not the fault of the man of lesser talent that he was born that way. Should a man be penalized materially for something that is beyond his control? (*Le Populaire,* April 18, 1847).

are not exactly the same, and on the question of clothing, some individual taste is allowed, though the variety of production is not large. The guiding principle in this matter is "to reconcile all the pleasures of *variety* with all the advantages of *uniformity*."[85]

The fundamental social unit in Icaria is the family, not the nuclear family of the industrial age but a veritable kinship group; the average size appears to be twenty living under the same roof. There is a nostalgia for the supposedly idyllic situation of the family in the preindustrial countryside. Cabet deplored the condition of the family under capitalism and felt, like Marx, that it had been reduced to an economic unit.[86] Cabet thought that the close and harmonious relationship existing in the family not overwhelmed by capitalism could and should exist on the societal level. The essence of his vision of human relations in the Icarian utopia is the concept of community, of an integrated, loving oneness among all individuals. And the only obstacle standing between love and antagonism is private property.

The units of production and the means of distribution in the Icarian economy are owned by the state or, more strictly speaking, by the community of Icarians. They are established and synchronized by central committees, chosen from among the members of a popularly elected national assembly. The members of the committees of industry, agriculture, and commerce are generally experts in these fields (the size of the assembly—2,000 members—would allow this), and thus the technocracy that exists, for instance, in the Saint-Simonian construct is apparently overcome.

The basic units of production are large family farms and immense factories. In agriculture, Cabet, more prescient than certain other communist thinkers, appreciated the probable effects of collectivization on efficiency and seems to have recognized the peasant desire for relative autonomy. Besides individual holdings, he also allowed for a greater degree of differentiation in the physical appearance of the buildings and in the layout of the farm than is the case in Icarian cities. As in all other spheres of production, agriculture is highly scientific, and prospective farmers, like everyone else, are given rigorous specialized instruction as the last phase of

[85] *Voyage en Icarie,* 71.

[86] He explains himself more fully in Cabet, *Douze Lettres d'un communiste à un réformiste sur la Communauté* (Paris, 1841–42), 7.

their education. New knowledge is constantly being circulated through the *Journal d'agriculture* and many other publications. Cabet did not indicate whether each farm was to be devoted to raising one specific crop or type of livestock, although he did recommend heavy regional specialization.[87] Industrial production is pursued entirely on the basis of the factory system in which a highly coordinated process puts out a single product in each factory unit. Icaria is without artisans. Even such processes as printing are carried out in huge mechanized public workshops. Management of each factory and of the system as a whole is democratic: "In each factory, the rules are deliberated and the functionaries elected by the workers themselves, while the laws common to all the factories are made by those elected by the entire People."[88]

The system of distribution is equally simple and uniform. Although Cabet did not go into all the intricate details of the exchange mechanisms, several points are worth noting. Unlike many utopias, Icaria is by no means autarchic. Impressed by free-trade arguments of the day, Cabet noted that "the Republic takes great care not to cultivate or manufacture anything that it can obtain easily from another country, if its agriculture and its industry can be employed more usefully in other products." Internal commerce is coordinated by agencies of the national assembly. Demographic data are carefully scrutinized, and production remains in accord with them. Great central and regional warehouses maintain a surplus of necessary goods. The economy responds to consumer demand, but the ballot rather than money is the instrument that registers consumer preferences. The use of new products is thus previously assured. On the local level huge warehouses store direct consumption items other than food, and apparently the Icarian simply goes in and takes what he needs. Money has been eliminated in Icaria, although Cabet gives no indication as to the concrete means of acquisition. Certainly there are no "labor notes," for this is communism; one's contribution to the economy has nothing to do with his reward. Is there a rationing system based on family size, special needs, and so forth? Cabet does not say. Apparently Icarian education has been so effective as to eliminate greed entirely; no one would ever take more than he needs. Food is de-

---

[87] *Voyage en Icarie,* 147, 152, 163.
[88] *Ibid.,* 105.

livered directly to the door. Each household has two containers on file with every food distribution warehouse in the locality. A special niche is built in the exterior of each dwelling; the Icarian places his empty container there, and it is soon replaced by the other one, full of new food supplies.[89] It is unnecessary to comment on the myriad problems that could arise under this arrangement.

Cabet recognized the enormous promise of the railroad. Icaria has "twelve great lines that traverse the country in all directions and a multitude of small ones connecting them." Then, allowing himself a bit of true fantasy, our guide says that "they have just discovered an agent more powerful than steam, produced by *sorub,* a material more abundant than coal, that is going to produce a revolution in industry and that will permit, in particular, the still greater multiplication of railroads."[90] Canals and well-channeled rivers complete the transportation system.

In general, the economy of Icaria is believable except for its system of exchange. Cabet demonstrates a fantastic naïveté in submitting to the popular whim against money as such. An economy—especially one as advanced as he wished to see created—without some medium of exchange and without a certain possibility for immediate consumer choice simply could not exist.

Working conditions, of course, are wonderful. The factories are clean, brightly painted, well lighted. For the most part, all that workers are required to do is tend machines. The uniform workday, which has been constantly decreasing since the beginning of Icarian history, stands at seven hours in the summer, six in the winter, and ends at one in the afternoon. This indicates Cabet's attitude toward work. Unlike Marx, who was deeply concerned with the problem of alienation, the psychosocial condition resulting from the commoditization of labor and the radical separation of work from its product, Cabet pictures work as an evil necessity to be made as pleasant and as short as possible. He was not entirely unaware of the problem of alienation (though he never used the term), for the system of worker control obviously means that each worker must identify with the total process of production, the process of collective creativity. He recommends considerable on-

[89] *Ibid.,* 164, 55.
[90] *Ibid.,* 15.

the-job communications and even mass singing to keep spirits high. The latter measures are of course aimed at relieving the anxiety of industrial alienation, not at eliminating it.

In his essentially negative attitude toward work, Cabet betrayed his outlook on creativity in general. If work is not intended to be particularly creative, then leisure activities should fill the void. But what does an Icarian do with his leisure? After all, he has the whole afternoon and evening. He promenades, chats with his neighbor, is "sociable." He participates in politics—in primary assemblies and in the great festivals organized to honor national historical figures and dates. He tends his garden, to the social end of making Icaria more beautiful and "pleasurable" to live in. The question of incentive was for Cabet a simple one. One works hard because he realizes that the total aims of the society, this joyous existence, depend on it. "Each considers his work as a public function, in the same way that each functionary considers his function only as a job."[91]

To acquire this consciousness, however, requires a lifetime of education and constant propaganda. As Cabet conceives of it, education is not simply instruction but should permeate every level of life. In Icaria it is the "foundation of our entire social and political system."[92] Thus Cabet has the committee on education outline a grand program covering all the essentials of life and work in Icaria. It includes, first of all, physical education and detailed instructions on prenatal care and child-rearing practices. Parents are required to allow their children to mingle with others, under strict supervision, so as to develop their natural sociability from an early age. All children should know how to read and write before they go to school. Cabet discussed no measures to enforce these private aspects of education so we must assume that he thought their basic rationality would be sufficient motivation. Formal education begins at the age of six, and the first dozen years are devoted to a broad development of the intellect and the creation of a disposition that readily accepts discipline and duty. The latter is already begun at home, where "the first sentiments that the mother takes care to develop in her child are filial love, an unreserved confidence [in the parent], and a blind obedience"—to which Cabet ambiguously

[91] *Ibid.*, 107.
[92] *Ibid.*, 74, and *Douze Lettres,* 82.

adds, "of which the mother herself knows how to prevent an excess."[93]

Such a conception is then transferred into formal educational channels, where further regimentation is achieved through uniforms, collective recitation, group singing, and mass gymnastic exhibitions. Girls and boys, in conformity with Cabet's purported ideal of perfect sex equality, are given exactly the same education, though coeducation is limited at the lower levels. At age eighteen for boys, seventeen for girls, specialized education begins, when the adolescents choose their professions. Their education has been such that all occupations carry equal prestige and honor. They therefore select the kind of work best suited to their "natural inclinations." If there are more applications for jobs than openings, examinations are held and judged by the competitors themselves. (This difficult problem of job placement is by no means adequately handled by Cabet.)[94] Professional education is accompanied by a preliminary introduction to the mechanisms of Icarian politics. After three years, responsible citizens and skilled workers emerge from this system. As for those professions requiring longer training, such as medicine, research science, and education, Cabet felt that the number pursuing them would be properly limited because of their greater difficulty.

The educational system naturally lays heavy emphasis upon the concept of civic duty. This is absolutely necessary since the maintenance of law and order in Icaria is the responsibility of all members of the community. As Cabet puts it, "Nowhere is the police so numerous; for all our public functionaries and even all our citizens are obliged to see to the execution of the laws and to proceed against or denounce offenses that they witness." Naturally these are rare, for, in line with Cabet's single-cause analysis of evil, "There is no crime nor instance of human misery which is not provoked and sustained by inequality of wealth, by property and money." Nevertheless, minor offenses do occur. Any citizen may lodge an accusation against any other and judgment is rendered by ad hoc people's courts. The locale of the offense normally determines the nature of the court—factory, restaurant, street, even

[93] *Voyage en Icarie,* 87.
[94] *Ibid.,* 105–7.

a single home suddenly becomes a court when an offense is committed. The exact nature of these offenses is not spelled out, but there are indications that they are usually simple cases of avarice, uttering unkind comments about another person, and such unfraternal acts. More serious offenses (undefined) are handled by popular assemblies, which include all the citizens of each locality (approximately 2,000 persons). Order in Icaria is thus based, as in More's *Utopia,* on a vast system of public censure. For Cabet, this represents the highest form of democracy, but can one doubt that the reality would consist of little more than a great network of mutual suspicion? This was certainly to become manifest in the Icarian experiment in America.[95]

Obviously a sharp differentiation between the political and the social, the economic, or even the moral in Icarian life is quite difficult to make. The total integration, the lack of separate spheres of existence, the complete absence of a sense of relativism, the regimentation, and the public nature of all actions remind one of modern totalitarianism. It could be argued that Cabet was one of the first totalitarian theorists.[96] Yet the principal characteristic of totalitarian society is not to be found in Cabet's construct: this *Gleichschaltung* is entirely voluntary, and decisions in Icaria are made not by an elite party or a single dictator who supposedly manifests the general will but through the agency of universal suffrage. All major political issues are discussed and all representatives are elected by the popular assemblies of Icaria, each of which contains all the citizens of a commune. Cabet's ideal, therefore, is direct democracy. The members of the national assembly, a 2,000-member body renewed by a third every year, are direct mandatories for their constituencies; all decisions made here are previously discussed in the primary assemblies. The national assembly subdivided into fifteen specialized decision-making committees, consists of two representatives from every commune. There is no party organization, since this would create an allegiance separate from that to the people. The executive, directed by a president and elected by the national assembly, has the sole function of carrying

[95] On law and order in Icaria see *ibid.,* 128–35, 310–22, and 577.

[96] Such is the view of Talmon in his section on Cabet in *Political Messianism,* 157–66. Fernand Rude also stresses this theme in the introduction to his *Voyage en Icarie.*

out its decisions. What kind of decisions are made? Construction of new roads and railroads, introduction of new products and of new courses in the schools, organization of patriotic celebrations, creation of new journals and newspapers. The state, therefore, does not "govern men" but attends to "the administration of things."

The principal question, a very practical one, concerns majority rule in the face of theoretical organic unity. Here Cabet follows Rousseau to the letter, though he sidesteps the issue that gives the *Contrat social* latent totalitarian implications. For Rousseau the original social compact requires unanimous consent. Those who oppose it "become so many foreigners among the citizens."[97] This foreign element is, therefore, at the mercy of the popular sovereignty. Rousseau does not discuss how small it must be for the contract still to be unanimous. This confusion strips the general will of any quantifiable elements and implies that the small number not adhering to its presuppositions are expendable. Cabet avoids these potentialities simply by declaring that all Icarians adhered to the original contract. Thus the transitional constitution was "accepted unanimously by the People in the midst of celebrations and transports of joy."[98] Beyond the original contract, for Cabet as for Rousseau, "the voice of the greater number always binds the rest." Cabet, however, again tells his readers that most decisions gain nearly unanimous approval.

Icarian political life, unreal as it may appear, is not totalitarian. Cabet simply *makes* it democratic. It may involve total regulation, but no coercion is present because the individual regulates himself, through the medium of society and for his own good. Cabet's system is obviously riven with authoritarian implications, but with a series of outrageous oversimplifications, he just blots them out.

Let us turn to Cabet's goals, or, rather, his goal. Simply put, it was "the ideal of the nineteenth century," as Marius Leblond called it, human happiness. Cabet apparently conceived of happiness in two ways. The first, the only one generally attributed to him by his commentators, is the simple joy derived from Icaria's material abundance. "Everything is filled with delight and voluptuous

[97] J.-J. Rousseau. *The Social Contract,* trans. Wilbert Kendall (Chicago: Gateway, 1954), 122.

[98] *Voyage en Icarie,* 361.

emulation in the naïve pleasure of the community of goods."[99] It is the land of milk and honey, the millennium. Cabet's conception of art supports this thesis. In the past the fine arts were only for the rich anyway; their diminution is therefore no great loss.[100] The function of painting and sculpture is simply to render Icaria more beautiful. Literature should provide the same kind of titillation but also plays a role in moral guidance. Music seems to be the freest and most pervasive art form in Icaria. It usually requires cooperation among performers—thus contributing to the fraternal bond—and, in its integral harmony, aesthetically reflects Icaria's social ideal. Nowhere do we find the art of longing and criticism, and, if we follow the argument of Herbert Marcuse in his penetrating critique of art in the Soviet Union,[101] real art, therefore, does not exist. There is no stimulation to think. Cabet showed no concern over the probable moribund state of intellectual and artistic endeavor in Icaria. Indeed, he proposed a censorship heavier than that of Metternich himself. All books and works of art must be approved by the republic before they can be published. Shortly after the communist revolution in Icaria all "harmful" books were burned. Icarians are, therefore, well insulated against "wrong ideas." The brief justification for censorship runs as follows: "But it seems to me that the Republic should permit only certain persons to publish a work just as it only permits pharmacists to prepare drugs. . . . liberty is not the right to do anything indiscriminately; it consists only in doing that which does not harm other citizens, and certain songs can be moral poisons as fatal to society as physical poisons."[102]

There appears, however, to be another side to Cabet's idea of happiness that is closely linked to the principle of equality of goods. With absolute equality all men are essentially naked; they are, in the fullest sense of the word, individuals, with no outward accoutrements to shield them. Their self-expression and self-fulfillment evolve only through the development of their intellects and personalities and on the basis of their relationships with others.

[99] M.-A. Leblond, *L'Idéal de XIXᵉ siècle* (Paris, 1909), 266.
[100] *Voyage en Icarie*, 394.
[101] *Soviet Marxism* (New York: Vintage, 1961), 116ff.
[102] *Voyage en Icarie*, 124.

This is one of the strongest arguments in favor of material equality, for it provides a reasonable rebuttal to the usual charge that the human personality would be submerged under communism. In fact, the personality that derives its identity mainly from the possession of titles and goods is a mere façade and disintegrates entirely when these meaningless things are taken away. Bruno Bettelheim points out that the first to crack in the Nazi camps were those who defined themselves in this fashion, while those whose identities were founded upon deep intellectual or emotional commitments, such as the Jehovah's Witnesses and the Communists, maintained their psychic integration.[103] Cabet also said later that the ultimate extension of machines into all aspects of production would be morally beneficial: "The end of community is, moreover, to create machines infinitely, to do all work with machines, and to reserve for man the noble role of a spiritual being, creator and commander of machines." Because of the leisure given by machine production, "spiritual or intellectual and moral happiness will be given greater than material happiness. . . . Thus, no more ignorance, demoralization, or brutalization; but men, true men sensing their dignity and always consulting their reason to direct themselves."[104] The sad part of all this in the case of Cabet's utopia, however, is that the available sources of commitment are limited. Indeed, there is but one commitment possible: to the community. This would perhaps suffice if the building of this society were as yet incomplete, or better still if it would never be complete. But, as pointed out earlier, there was nothing open-ended about Cabet's utopia. All problems have been overcome. No great goals remain. The perfect can only be manipulated, never improved upon. Icaria is a world where real action or creative endeavor is impossible. And without this possibility the dehumanization of man is assured. This, then, is the grave danger in any final-state-of-mankind theory. One of the great utopians of the twentieth century, Martin Buber, insists that the very essence of his community be the continual "unfolding of the possibilities" of a "right order," an order that must only be an unrealizable ideal.[105] Indeed, Cabet himself even hints that life in

---

[103] *The Informed Heart: Autonomy in a Mass Age* (Glencoe, Illinois, 1960), Chap. 4.

[104] *Le Populaire,* June 5, 1844.

[105] *Paths in Utopia* (Boston: Beacon Press, 1958), 8.

Icaria might ultimately be devoid of meaning when he has the historian, Dinaros, say, in discussing the transitional period before the perfection of communism: "Our fathers, more unhappy than we in their youth, found, in their successes and victories of all types, more intellectual, moral, and material pleasures than community gives us today!"[106]

In the decade following the creation of his ideal city, Cabet toiled tirelessly to implement Icaria in France. How would an Icarian world be brought into existence? Cabet rejected the tactics universally associated with communism on the Continent—the promotion of violent revolution by means of conspiratorial secret societies. He desired to bring communism out into the open. Through propaganda, the overwhelming majority of Frenchmen were to be convinced of the efficacy of his society. Once convinced, they would exert pressure for the reform of the suffrage; then, armed with the vote, they would democratically decide to initiate the transition to communism. This transition would be facilitated, at its inception, by a dictatorship that would coordinate the first steps toward the new society and, if necessary, provide leadership in the defense of the pacific revolution against foreign intervention. Thus, in its original form, Cabet's tactical program consisted of three steps: (1) the development of a great cross-class movement through propaganda and organization; (2) the legal conquest of political power by the communist majority; and (3) the election (or, rather, acclamation) of a dictator who would initiate the transition to communism. Ideally, the new order was to be ordained by the "general will" of the useful citizens of the entire nation.

Cabet realized that the immediate establishment of communism would be out of the question and therefore proposed a fifty-year transitional regime. Property would not simply be wrenched from the hands of its possessors. Instead, inheritance would be abolished; as each property owner died (or decided voluntarily to give up ownership), title to his capital would go to the state. At the same time, all property would be heavily taxed, and a progressive income tax would be instituted. Much of this revenue would be used to

[106] *Voyage en Icarie,* 371.

support ever-increasing public services. Education, both practical and communitarian, public works and employment bureaus, and public housing would be the most important of these during the transitional period. But the revenue raised would also be used to create state-run factories, mines, and farms to compete with the private sectors of the economy. By the end of this half century, private ownership of property would thus be nearly eradicated and the foundation for communism would have been laid. In Cabet's mind, this gradualism would considerably mitigate the apprehensions of the rich, for, while inequalities of wealth would be reduced and in the end eliminated altogether, the contemporary generation would not simply find itself pillaged of its possessions.[107] The entire program was dependent upon a particular conception of the social structure and of class relations. Cabet's original opinions on these questions were typically utopian. He "habitually appeal[ed] to society at large, without distinction of class; nay, by preference, to the ruling class."[108] Though he revised his position with regard to class relations in the mid-forties, and was therefore forced into a serious tactical dilemma, in 1838 he viewed class collaboration as entirely feasible. Antagonism existed to be sure, but it ranged the very rich against the rest of society, and aristocracy against the people. He thus analyzed the social structure in the terminology of the French Revolution. At this point, "bourgeoisie" does not figure prominently in Cabet's vocabulary but seems to be used, whenever the term crops up, to describe an element situated between the aristocracy and the people. He thought of the bourgeoisie as a natural ally of the people.

Persuasion, the presentation of rational arguments for the adoption of communism, was the sole means by which Cabet wished to implement his ideal. Despite the fact that Icaria itself was established by a revolution—Cabet could not resist the temptation to model Icarian history after that of France—he was theoretically opposed to violence. Hence the famous phrase, summarizing a lengthy argument against revolutionary violence near the end of

---

[107] On the transitional regime, see *ibid.*, 338–70.

[108] Karl Marx and Friedrich Engels, *Manifesto of the Communist Party*, in L. Feuer, *Marx and Engels: Basic Writings on Politics and Philosophy* (Garden City, N.Y.: Anchor Books, 1959), 38.

Voyage en Icarie, "If I held a revolution in my hand, I would keep it closed even though I should die in exile."[109]

The essential points supporting his argument were rooted in recent experience. The "aristocracy," by which he means the tiny elite of notables of both gentle birth and wealth governing France, monopolizes the instruments of power so completely that violent opposition would be fruitless. "You cannot stop a cannonball with your hand." Moreover, every violent outburst works to the advantage of the governing elite because it gives further excuse for repression. The agent provocateur has no other reason for existence. Finally, violent revolution, even if successful, could lead only to a new form of oppression—that of the rich by the poor. The goal of brotherhood would be indelibly tarnished from the beginning. Instead, the aim of communists must be to demonstrate how modern society constrains and demoralizes the rich and well-born as much as the poor. Cabet took special pains to show that "merchants and manufacturers" are burdened with anxieties arising from the uncertainty of the market, eaten up in the daily competitive struggle, and haunted by the fear that their property might be destroyed by the desperate poor. Indeed, "is it not especially the rich that one must convert?" They have more influence in society and will greatly ease the task of converting the poor. Hence, no conspiracies and no "partial communities." "Only proselytism and always proselytism, until the mass of men adopts the principle of Community."[110]

Such was Cabet's tactical program on the eve of his return from exile. He was to make monumental efforts to fulfill his dream of a pacific revolution in French society and to mold a party of considerable numerical significance. But rare were his bourgeois adherents and rarer still the aristocrats. His self-image as the fatherly *bonhomme* who grandly linked all classes had to fade before the realization that he was in fact a working-class leader. As the forties progressed Cabet came to understand that as an opponent of property, he, the apostle of panhuman fraternity, had no friends among the possessing classes.

[109] *Voyage en Icarie,* 564.
[110] *Ibid.,* 560–64.

2 | The Roots of the Icarian Movement

Cabet's term in exile expired on March 28, 1839. Although he was lonely and impoverished in London, this phase of his activity was the turning point of his life. At an age when most men of his class would be seeking to secure their retirement with a few wise investments, Cabet had only begun his career. He arrived in Paris without fanfare less than a month before the abortive insurrection of Auguste Blanqui's Society of the Seasons.

Among his old associates, Cabet's new opinions were already suspect. In 1838 he had sent a copy of *Voyage en Icarie* to Nicod, and his old friend responded with a thoroughly negative critique. Equality should never take precedence over liberty; without property, "individual initiative would die."[1] Nicod progressively cut off relations with Cabet. While still in London, Cabet had also written to his co-worker on *Le Populaire,* L. A. Pagnerre, in the hope of publishing his communist novel, but the latter refused, apparently on the advice of a friend of Nicod.[2] Thus the republican-turned-communist seems to have soft-pedaled his true position, even to the point of publishing the first edition of the *Voyage* under another name.[3] His friends had no objection to the *Histoire populaire,* however, and Pagnerre published its first two volumes toward the end of 1839. Cabet's communism nevertheless continued to isolate

---

[1] Nicod to Cabet, dated only 1838, Archief Cabet, IISG.

[2] Cabet, *Toute La Vérité,* 94.

[3] Both a private printing of 1839 and this first edition (January 1840) carried the title *Voyage et adventures de lord William Carisdall en Icarie, traduit de l'anglais de Francis Adams par Théodore Dufruit.* Dufruit was a real person, a professional translator. See his letter to Cabet, Sept. 12, 1839, Papiers Cabet, Bibliothèque Historique de la Ville de Paris (hereafter BHVP).

him from his old coterie. On August 22, 1839, he completed a manuscript, "Note à X," in which he said that it was necessary for what he called the patriot party to create a shadow government prepared to take dictatorial power if a revolution should occur. He sent it to Dupont de l'Eure[4] and intended that it be circulated among the reformist elements. Cabet thought that both the legitimists and the Bonapartists were ready to move and that the leftists were obliged to organize as well, although they should not act as the spearhead of revolution. As for the program outlined, Cabet avoided socialist goals even though he proposed a broad range of social reforms.[5] His sense of coalition politics had not been overwhelmed by doctrinal rigidity. He saw no reason why the entire left should not unite. But apparently his old associates did, for he was ignored. "Judging finally that his efforts were useless in face of the apathy of the most influential men, he gave himself over exclusively to the publication of his writings."[6]

While Cabet did not give up on unity politics, he must have had an inkling that a new situation was at hand. Times had changed since such communists as Voyer d'Argenson and Charles Teste could stand shoulder to shoulder with Jacques Laffitte and Dupont. Communism had ceased to be an academic issue. It had posed itself as the radical challenge to the whole framework of what Lorenz von Stein called industrial society, that is, liberal-bourgeois society. By 1840 "communism" had become more than a variation on social republican theory. It was rapidly becoming "the great protest

[4] This manuscript is located among the Cabet papers at the IISG. It is dated only Wednesday, August 22. Despite the fact that August 22 fell on a Thursday in 1839, the repeated mention of May 12 (Blanqui's insurrection) indicates that the document dates from this year. The only Wednesdays, August 22, during the July Monarchy were in 1832 and 1838. Cabet probably erred in dating his manuscript. The "Note" was sent to a deputy and at one point Cabet crossed out a capital D, replacing it with X: Dupont, his old patron, is therefore the likely recipient.

[5] *Ibid.*, 1–3.

[6] Cabet, *Ma Ligne droite* (Paris, 1841), 44. This was not quite the case, however. Perhaps already sensing that he was destined to carry on without a close connection with the moderate reformists, Cabet applied, alone, for authorization to present a public course on "universal history, considered especially in its relation to legislation and Philosophy." It was turned down by the Royal Council. A.N., F[17] 6687 dos Cabet.

of labor against the domination of capital."[7] Stein's analysis is useful in understanding the meaning of this:

Even at present, communism, growing in strength and scope, has no specific doctrine; all the individual communist trends and systems have little or no power at all over communism as a whole; communism has sometimes accepted, sometimes refuted them, has temporarily embraced them but again forgotten them without changing its character or its direction. This is precisely why communism is so much more important and more powerful than socialism. It cannot be denied that socialism is much superior as a system than anything communism has offered; socialism has had a deep influence on the various communistic systems, more than communists ever like to acknowledge. *Socialism is the scientific expression of the interpretation of the social movement by an individual, while communism is the response of a whole class, the expression of a whole social situation.* Its specific doctrines, its pamphlets and the other material it offers give but a superficial picture of communism. Its inner meaning cannot be understood like that of socialism—through one definite principle; communism can be understood only as part of the elements of industrial society and the inherent contradictions of this society.

Therefore it is useless to attempt a doctrinaire definition of communism. Communism is a phenomenon and a trend in the contemporary world, which has first drawn attention to the contradictions within industrial society and which has made both major classes [bourgeoisie and proletariat] aware of this contradiction. It has not developed logically but grown historically; it is not a teaching, rather it is a condition [*Zustand*].[8]

Communism was thus a kind of ur-theorie of the working class nurtured by the conditions of its existence. Doctrinal sophistication was not the foundation of its success. "It was a crude, rough-hewn, purely instinctual sort of communism; still it touched the cardinal point and was powerful enough among the working class to pro-

[7] Armand Cuvillier, "Action ouvrière et communisme en France vers 1840 et aujourd'hui," *La Grande Revue,* Dec. 1921, 25–35, quoting Auguste Ott in the *Revue nationale,* Feb. 1848.

[8] Lorenz von Stein, *Geschichte der Sozialen Bewegung in Frankreich von 1789 bis auf unsere Tage* (Leipzig, 1850), II, 334–35. Translation by Kaethe Mengelberg in her welcome (though abridged) English edition, *The History of the Social Movement in France, 1789–1850* (Totowa, N.J.: Bedminster Press, 1964), 282–83, save for the final clause; my italics.

duce the Utopian communism, in France, of Cabet, and in Germany, of Weitling."[9]

Although Cabet saw himself as something more than a historical by-product, Stein and Engels touched upon an essential chord in the history of early industrial societies. In the present state of historical research it is impossible to determine, even roughly, the actual number of committed communists in the French working class in 1840. But the unconscious urge to transform their oppressive environment must have animated large numbers of working people. They lived in a society undergoing bewildering economic change, one in which immiseration was a poignant reality, which was under the political control of men whose national power—won for them by the workers—rested less upon the traditional prestige of rank and title or any demonstrable capacity for statesmanship than upon the possession of property. Should it not be expected that the vision of a world without property and its attendant rights would occupy a corner of the minds of those who possessed none? Considered in this framework, the various doctrines of communism appear to be expressions of a fundamental instinct of the working class. We are at the beginning of what Adam Ulam, echoing Stein, terms the Marxist phase of social development in France.[10] But this instinct had to be articulated; only then would working people begin to think through their situation. And this would open the way to a profound change:

In '92 and since, the proletarians have shown that they could fight as well as the aristocrats . . . ; it remains for them to prove that they can reason as well and better: and this is what they are doing. It is the announcement of a new era: it is impossible that the order of things founded upon the stupefaction of the people can continue when the people thinks. The people will thus conquer—which is not new; but what is new is that it will not conquer for others.[11]

The question, however, remained *how* this stupefaction would be transcended. Cabet occupied but one place in a panoply of social thought unfolding in the first years after his return from exile. The ultimate success of his doctrine was rooted in the general so-

[9] Freidrich Engels, "Preface to the English Edition [of the *Communist Manifesto*] of 1888," in Feuer, *Marx and Engels: Basic Writings,* 4.

[10] *The Unfinished Revolution* (Garden City, 1959), *passim.*

[11] *Journal du peuple,* Sept. 27, 1840.

cial, economic, and political conditions of these years and the means by which he exploited them. These circumstances and the theoretical response to them, especially that of communist writers, must be briefly examined to illuminate the emergence of Icarian communism.

The Crisis of 1840 and the Communist Response

We all agree, citizens, that political reform is indispensible, but it is also necessary to consider that without social reform the large class of proletarians will continue to vegetate in Helotism and servitude. . . . The democratic element should understand this logic: in restoring the political rights of the proletarian, it will have to restore his social rights as well. . . .

To the triumph of social equality, that is to say, to distributive justice, to the complete liberation of the masses and to the reorganization of work on just and equitable bases![12]

The year is 1840, the year of Louis Blanc's *Organisation du travail,* of Proudhon's *Qu-est-ce que la propriété?,* of Cabet's *Voyage en Icarie.* Villermé's monumental study of the condition of the textile workers in France circulates; the *Livre du compagnonnage* cries for reform of that archaic institution. Communist writings of all varieties are to be found in the bookshops: Alphonse Esquiros has published *L'Evangile du peuple,* Abbé Constant, *La Bible de la liberté,* J.-J. Phillot, the bitter *Ni Chateaux, ni chaumières.* Beyond the efflorescence of ideas, 1840 witnessed an unprecedented strike movement; by September the walkout had reached the proportions of a general strike in Paris. Simultaneously, the bourgeois movement for suffrage reform made its way into the working classes. The "first communist banquet" took place at Belleville on July 1. Nor was working-class violence a stranger to the events of 1840. The strikes produced a certain amount of conflict, and in October a communist worker, Darmès, attempted to assassinate the king.

Suddenly and dramatically, the social question exploded, showering the nation with a torrent of ideas and events the historical impact of which went far beyond her boundaries.

Several factors combine to explain the new atmosphere. The law

[12] Toast at a "communist" banquet in Rouen, July 29, 1840, by Hésine, son of a Babouvist militant of Blois; quoted in the *Journal du peuple,* Aug. 9, 1840.

on associations, the subsequent repression of the republican societies, and the September 1835 press laws, which forbade any
allusion to the republic, all tended to throttle open development of
working-class republicanism. The later thirties, therefore, witnessed
the spread of illegal revolutionary secret societies on the one hand
and the publication of socialist and communist thought divorced
from any specific republican connotations on the other. By pushing
the doctrines of protest beyond the framework of republicanism in
which universal suffrage all too often appeared to be the great
panacea, these restrictions gave communism and socialism currency
as independent theories. The repression of 1834–1835, by making
the political avenues of protest more difficult, also stimulated economic action, whether in the form of mutual benefit societies, trade
unions, or cooperatives.

The government's policy of resistance, however, does not explain
the timing of the outburst. Throughout 1839 and 1840 France was
troubled by a prolonged ministerial crisis. She also found herself
isolated in her support of Mohammad Ali's claims in Syria, and a
general European war loomed. Preoccupation with foreign affairs
reduced the government's ability to control internal agitation. In
the midst of the double crisis, the great suffrage reform movement
of 1839–1841 expanded its activities. But many workers, ignored
in the great banquets spearheading the campaign, soon became disillusioned with the middle-class rhetoric of mere political reform
and withdrew their support, a move that ultimately vitiated the entire reform movement.[13]

Although the economic crisis of 1837–1839 was probably the
least severe of the first half of the nineteenth century, certain areas
(such as Lyons, because of its large exports to deeply depressed
England and America) were hard hit, money became tight, and
industrial production in general was considerably curtailed. In the
spring of 1840 affairs picked up, and the cost of living diminished
somewhat due to the very good harvest of 1839.[14] Octave Festy
clearly described its results:

[13] A. Gourvitch, "Le Mouvement pour la Réforme, 1839–1841," *La
Révolution de 1848*, XII (1915–16), 106ff and 262.
[14] On this crisis, see Bertrand Gille, *La Banque et le crédit en France,
1815–1848* (Paris, 1959), 337–46.

A long period of misery [during the crisis], accompanied by troubles and, in the departments, several worker associations; social, or rather at once social and political, propaganda which, under diverse forms and indirect rather than direct, came to have an effect on working-class opinion; and indifferent, if not hostile Government; a Chamber wherein the "poorest and most numerous class" hardly had a handful of defenders—such were the essential elements of the social situation in May of 1840, at the moment when a light upswing in business was manifested and when the strikes began in Paris.[15]

Cabet thus began to circulate his ideas in an atmosphere well prepared for their acceptance. It was a time of general crisis. Indeed, 1840 introduced a prolonged crisis that, despite the oft-cited stability of the long Guizot ministry, agitated France for the next eight years. While the Eastern Question, ministerial difficulties, and the economic troubles passed, the broad social movement to which each had given stimulation continued. The social question could no longer be repressed or ignored. Its manifestations could be, and were of course, resisted: and here one confronts the fundamental cause of the revolution of 1848.

Communism burst fully into public view in 1840. Neo-Babouvism dominated French communism in 1840, although Owenism and the spiritual egalitarianism of Pierre Leroux had some impact as well.[16] The heritage of Babeuf and Bounarroti had diversified

---

[15] Festy, "Le Mouvement ouvrier à Paris en 1840," *Revue des sciences politiques*, XXX (1913), 68. On the general development of the strikes, see J.-P. Aguet, *Les Grèves sous la Monarchie de Juillet* (Geneva, 1954), 194–225.

[16] On communist doctrine in the early forties see Pierre Angrand, "Notes critiques sur la formation des idées communiste en France," *La Pensée*, nos. 19 and 20 (1948), 38–46 and 57–67; Samuel Bernstein, "Le Néo-babouvisme d'après la presse (1837–1848)," in A. Soboul, ed., *Babeuf et les problèmes du Babouvisme* (Paris, 1963), 247–76; Georges Sencier, *Le Babouvisme après Babeuf* (Paris, 1911) (very unreliable); Roger Garaudy, *Les Sources Françaises du socialisme scientifique* (Paris, 1949); and V. P. Volguine, "Jean-Jacques Pillot, communist utopique," *La Pensée*, no. 84 (1959), 37–53. On Babouvism itself see especially Claude Mazauric, *Babeuf et la conspiration pour l'égalité* (Paris: Editions sociales, 1962); Soboul, ed., *Babeuf et les problèmes de Babouvisme;* and *Annales historiques de la Révolution française* (1961). Leroux published his main works, *De L'Egalité* and *De L'Humanité* in 1838 and 1840. His principal influence was upon Richard Lahautière. On Owenism see the Owen Papers (University of Wisconsin microfilm 1090), nos. 891, 907, 916, 936, and 1,655.

by this time, but it retained one essential element: a belief that social change would come through conspiratorial secret societies and
violent revolution. A brief review of the main voices of communism
in 1840 will place Cabet's doctrine in the proper perspective. The
pivotal figure in the communist camp was Jean-Jacques Pillot.[17]
Born in 1808, Pillot took the vows of the priesthood but during the
1830s made a rapid conversion, first to the Socialistic "Église catholique française" founded by Abbé Chatel in 1835, and then to
materialist communism.[18] In 1938–1839 he brought out several
numbers of *La Tribune du peuple*—an illegal newspaper—and won
a prison term for his efforts. His most famous work, a bulky pamphlet entitled *Ni Chateaux, ni chaumières,* appeared in 1840. Although he considered himself a "progressive Babouvist" there was
little evidence that he had gone beyond his revolutionary forebear.
The brochure's title itself indicated his economic pessimism. His
progressivism rested with his historical outlook, which pictured
human development as the story of the continual blossoming of
equality since ancient times. By 1840, "la communauté n'est pas
une utopie"—the pear was ripe.[19] According to Pillot, the unfolding of equality depended upon the decreasing influence of the
"slave morality" implanted by religion. The full-scale attack against
l'infâme in the eighteenth century had opened the way for the
triumph of modern socialism. The "revolution of '93" then destroyed all religious mystification. Thus the conclusion: "Before
1793, the people had masters; since 1793, the people have had
exploiters."[20] Pillot was an unabashed apostle of violent revolution
but eschewed conspiratorial methods. Instead he recommended in-
cessant propaganda to prepare the masses for revolt. The actual
overthrow of "the rich" would be led, however, by a highly organized communist clique.

A more trenchant thinker was Théodore Dézamy. In May and
June of 1840, Dézamy published two issues of a newspaper, *L'Egalitaire.* He felt that the key to the worker's emancipation was a

[17] See Cour des Pairs, *Attentat de 15 octobre: Rapport de Girod de l'Ain*
(Paris, 1841), 33.
[18] Volguine, "Jean-Jacques Pillot," 37–38.
[19] See Jean-Jacques Pillot, *La Communauté n'est pas une utopie! Conséquences du procès des communistes* (Paris, 1841).
[20] Quoted in Garaudy, *Les Sources,* 187.

comprehension of his situation and of the nature of things from a philosophical point of view. Unlike Cabet, he was thoroughly suspicious of liberalism in any form: "interest, gain, advantage, profit: such is the essence of its cult; laissez-faire, laissez-passer, each to himself, each to his right: such is its favorite motto." In fact, however, "these Machiavellian doctrines" added up to nothing more than a brutal rationalization for the oppression of the poor by the rich. Dézamy presented a broad tableau of current misery: while wheat prices skyrocket, wages are cut; under the aegis of free competition, industrialists struggle against one another to the inevitable annihilation of many of them, a process throwing men out of work; the grain dealers—also in the name of free competition—monopolize paltry harvests to drive prices even higher; and all of this is sanctioned by the present political regime. The people, as is its habit, suffers this misery, this anarchy, with "a magnanimity of which it alone is capable." But how long will it continue to do so? "Not by ridiculous lamentation, by stupid submission will the unfortunate better his lot, break his chains! . . . No, no! the oppressors will not give in to vain words. Liberty smiles on whoever desires to march boldly to its conquest." Hence his call to "the proletarians": "The moment has come for you to wake up and to realize that you are men." Only through the "fraternal union" of workingmen, a thoughtful consideration of their condition, and the concentration of their energies on "political matters" may the road to equality be opened.[21]

Together, Pillot and Dézamy, despite their differences, represent the core of the Babouvist position in 1840. Both spoke for working-class solidarity and militant political opposition to the possessing classes, their "oppressors." Theirs was the doctrine of the "materialists," the "violents," and "immediates" against whom Cabet would struggle so doggedly in the following years.

Another current of communist thought in 1840 was decidedly spiritualist. While it may be true that Alphonse Esquiros and Abbé Constant owed something to the Babouvist legacy,[22] their ideas, presented in *L'Evangile du peuple* and *La Bible de la liberté* (both

---

[21] *L'Egalitaire,* no. 1 (May 1840), 9 and 13; and no. 2 (June 1840), 36, 39 and 40.

[22] Sencier labels their position "babouvist spiritualism" (*Le Babouvisme après Babeuf,* 213).

published by Rouanet in 1840), seem to derive more fundamentally from the Judeo-Christian tradition of millennialism. Both fortified their points of view with allusions to the Book of Daniel and the Revelations of St. John, foreseeing the sudden destruction of the world of sin, of the world controlled by the rich, and its replacement by an egalitarian New Jerusalem. As Constant preached at his trial on charges of inciting "hatred of the rich" in 1841: "Angels of war and death fly on the red wings of fire and announce to the Earth the fall of Babylon! . . . Then Christ, become the People, will put the world between the hands of his father and will sit at the right hand of God. . . . And his reign will be endless. Amen."[23] Esquiros demonstrated the same kind of lyrical frenzy: "[Humanity] must die in the old world in order to be reborn in the new society. The old worm-eaten edifice . . . must be demolished from top to bottom and thrown to the earth." Thereafter "a just and liberal father will distribute to each according to his needs and, like the sun, will make equality shine on all men."[24] Jesus Christ, "the first sans-culotte," had shown the way toward equality. In view of Esquiros' excellent and highly rational *Histoire des Montagnards,* one should not place him in the same category with Constant, who was either a charlatan or mentally unbalanced. While in prison for the publication of his *Bible,* Constant recanted his communist and democratic views and outlined a royalist position. At the same time he took up a new crusade, female equality. His *Assomption de la femme* preached his new doctrine and simultaneously allowed him to discourse on the nature of love—an exercise throwing him into a new variety of ecstasy bordering on obscenity.[25] The *Bible de la liberté* achieved a fairly wide circulation, however (it was often among the works found in the libraries of workers investigated by the Ministry of Justice), and Cabet felt that its author's influence was strong enough to warrant a brochure against him.[26]

These were the principal communist ideas, besides those of

[23] Quoted *ibid.,* 224–25.
[24] *L'Evangile du peuple,* 144 and 155.
[25] Sencier, *Le Babouvisme,* 227–28.
[26] Cabet, *Réfutation ou examen de tous les écrits ou journaux contre ou sur la communauté: Réfutation des trois ouvrages de l'abbé Constant* (Paris, Sept. 1841).

Cabet, circulating in 1840. But the great works of Blanc and Proudhon—both often called communist—were available in the bookshops as well. And a year before, Auguste Blanqui had presented the reality of "communist" insurrection. In the public mind, there was no question that a red specter had arisen. There seems to have been little comprehension within the government or the public at large of the varieties of communist opinion. They were indiscriminately lumped together and labeled "dangerous to property and security."

But the number of workingmen calling themselves communists grew. In 1840 the movement was in the main a Parisian one, although Charles Nioret led a group of communists in Rouen, and in Lyons the Buonarrotian Charbonnerie Réformée made some progress among the workers. It appears that the insurrection of May 12 and the subsequent trial of the conspirators had the effect of spreading the popularity of Babouvist communism.[27] The reformist banquets then served to bring communism into open public debate. Many workers and their defenders among the intelligentsia participated in the banquet campaign. But simultaneously the split between communism and reformism became manifest:[28] "It appeared that the [communists] sincerely wished to unite with the others and demanded only the liberty to make toasts and speeches like the reformists. But the reformists . . . proscribed all communist manifestations, claiming that they would impede the cause of reform. The passion on both sides became extreme; attacks, injuries, calumnies flew back and forth; in short, the two factions declared war on each other.[29] Two banquets held in June brought the conflict to a head. Communists, among them Dézamy and Pillot, forced themselves upon their audiences and explained their doctrines. They were violently rebuked by the bourgeois reformists.

Such was the background for the banquet of communists held in Belleville on July 1, 1840. Pillot and Dézamy were instrumental in its organization. Cabet, who by this time had fully acknowledged his communist principles, was invited but refused to attend. His

[27] Cabet, *Ma Ligne droite*, 42.

[28] Gourvitch, "Le Mouvement pour la réforme," 262.

[29] Cabet, *Ma Ligne droit*, 43. Dézamy presents the same picture in *L'Egalitaire*, no. 2, p. 62.

reasons are obscure. He claimed that the whole reformist drive was premature and that the great issue of the day was the Eastern Question.[30] A more plausible explanation is that he already recognized that his reputation was going to be based on his legalism. Moreover, he still sought a wider unity on the left, and this banquet appeared to be motivated by "the spirit of contradiction, of rivalry, of hostility between certain communists and the reformists and not [by] the reflective and prudent concern for Community."[31]

At six o'clock on this balmy summer evening some 1,200 workers and sympathizing publicists were called to order by the provisional presidents of the banquet, Pillot and Homberg. With the gathering of this assembly, wrote Dézamy, "the glorious flag of social community" had been planted. "From the aristocrats of *La Quotidienne* to the radicals of the *Journal du peuple,* all the conservatives are in a flutter: a new era has just begun for the world." To demonstrate their fervor for equality, the assembly refused to elect a permanent chairman; the idea of a leader was repulsive. This air of naïve enthusiasm lasted for the duration of the banquet. In the toasts and orations that ensued many of the ideals and values, resentments and frustrations that made up the working-class mentality of the 1840s were in evidence. Pillot himself opened the speeches by stressing "the first two qualities that ought not to cease to shine among us . . . : the *dignity* that characterizes the man capable of enjoying his rights and the gentle candidness inspired by the sentiments of a sincere fraternity."[32] Although many of the toasts were merely vague slogans, several expressed a somewhat more sophisticated understanding of society and the goals of communism. Perhaps the most interesting of all was that of the barber Duval, "to the abolition of free competition." "It is this dreadful evil that excites such cruel discord among the workers, and that . . . sullies, wastes, and empoisons all the products of industry and science. Let this monster, enemy to the peace of all, which even tyrannizes its beneficiaries themselves, expire under the sword of equality." The bootmaker Villy added, "If the sun were an exploitable material, the proletarian would never see it." To combat

[30] Cabet, *Ma Ligne droite,* 45.

[31] *Toute La Vérité,* 38.

[32] Théodore Dézamy, *et al., Premier Banquet communiste, le 1ᵉʳ juillet 1840* (Paris, July 1840), 1–3.

their exploiters, "our enemies," the painter William-Louis counseled: "Let us strive to know them well, and if we cannot lead them to a better path let us abandon them to the fate of their incurable egotism." Several others stressed the folly of mere political equality as a working-class goal. Vellicus, a tailor associated with Cabet in London, said that without "real and perfect social equality" political equality was "laughable and illusory." Rozier, another barber, argued that "political reform is an *odious fiction* because it conserves the old society" with its "exploitation of man by man" and its "moral tortures." Finally the clockmaker Simar recognized that the workers' exploiters in the economic realm also commanded the instruments of their political oppression.[33]

This banquet had more than symbolic significance in the history of the growth of communism in France before 1848. Its attendance of 1,200 was remarkable. The force of communism had come into public view, and the banquet method of propaganda and agitation was utilized again. Later in the month the Rouennais communists gathered for a banquet, as did a group in Lyons. On March 30, 1841, a communist banquet was broken up by the police in the Parisian suburb of Montrouge. The majority of those arrested were young journeyman tailors.[34] The Belleville event apears also to have had a certain significance for the broader history of working-class agitation in 1840, for, according to Aguet, in bringing workers of various trades together it contributed to the coalescence of the strike movement of August and September.[35] Pillot later attempted to give the strikers a communist ideological orientation, and Martin Nadaud, imbued with communist principles by this time, headed a workers' committee that attempted to coordinate the strikes.[36]

Throughout the year 1840 communism appeared heavily oriented toward violence, and the authorities assumed it to be organized in conspiratorial societies. But in Paris at any rate the only real secret society of any significance was the so-called Travailleurs Egalitaires. It was organized along the lines of Blanqui's societies into basic five-man cells called trades, with higher levels termed

---

[33] Quotations from *ibid.*, pp. 4–14.
[34] Archives de la Préfecture de la Police, Paris, A/426.
[35] Aguet, *Les Grèves*, 195.
[36] "Notes" accompanying the Arrêt de la Cour Royale de Paris du 10 juillet 1841, A.N., BB[18] 1472 dos 6733; Nadaud, *Mémoires de Léonard*, 83.

workshops and manufactories.[37] The organization also called itself simply Les Communistes, however, and thus the association of communism with conspiratorial activity and violence was more or less fixed. The communist committees for suffrage reform were erroneously suspected of harboring the same designs. The assassination attempt of October 15, 1840, seemed to confirm the communist-violence equation, for Darmès apparently had connections with the Travailleurs Egalitaires and was definitely a communist.

The foundations of Cabet's claim to a unique position evolved out of this atmosphere. As the authorities progressively moved to repress revolutionary communism, Cabet emerged as the new major voice of communism with his constant exhortations to pacificism and legalism, to fraternity and class reconciliation. While it is impossible to speak of an Icarian communist movement in 1840,[38] there were pacific communists ready to follow his banner. According to the testimony of Aimée Borel in the trial of Darmès, there existed "two branches of the communists, one of which he did not think was in favor of violent means, the other, the *communistes immédiats,* who wish to overthrow the present government by any means."[39] Borel did not specifically link the former with Cabet and no doubt would have done so had he actually thought Cabet to be the leader of this group. He certainly did not hesitate to name Pillot as the director of the other.

Nevertheless, the legalist principles of the *Voyage en Icarie* were being aired. Cabet himself described his growing influence (as of late 1840) in his typical manner: "Meanwhile, the *Voyage en Icarie* circulated; and, in spite of the efforts of the Babouvists and the new Hébertists who preferred the work of Buonarroti and the precipitancy of Babeuf, a large number of Communists, old and new, adopted the new treatise on Community and pressed its author to publish a newspaper in order to direct them and re-establish union."[40] Pillot also recognized Cabet's importance in his testimony at the Darmès trial (January 1841). In denying the existence

[37] A.N., BB[18] 1472 dos 6735; *Gazette des tribunaux,* July 11, 1841.
[38] I. Tchernoff speaks of an Icarian "sect" as early as 1839 (*Le Parti républicain sous la Monarchie de Juillet* [Paris, 1901], 390). He is reading backwards from the situation in the 1840s.
[39] Cour des Pairs, *Attentat de 15 octobre,* 33.
[40] Cabet, *Ma Ligne droite,* 45.

of a secret society of "communists," he said that the term was used only to express "a principle found in several writings published in recent times, and particularly in a work by M. Cabet, who certainly has more to say on communism than I. . . . As for me, I have always believed that the people who call themselves communists aim only at the propagation of the principles expressed first by Buonarroti, thereafter by M. Cabet, and finally by me, if I have written anything that might be understood."[41] *Voyage en Icarie* was not viewed widely in the press in 1840, but the friends of the people reacted positively. Louis Blanc's evaluation, for instance, was that "This book, the author of which has nobly and courageously marked his place in the ranks of the democratic party, treats . . . those questions most worthy of the attention of serious minds and people of good will. It is worth reading with care, even though one does not have to completely adopt its conclusions."[42]

The real basis of Cabet's notoriety in 1840–1841, however, was his series of brochures on the international crisis, his relentless denunciation of the construction of Thiers' fortifications around the capital, and his ensuing "war" with *Le National* over its support of the fortification plan. His basic thesis was laid down in the *Six Lettres sur la crise actuelle* (Paris, October–November 1840). Thiers' entire stand in favor of Mohammad Ali and war with the powers (of which Cabet, the Jacobin, approved) was merely a ruse to build up a fear psychology in France. Once this was established, Thiers then proposed the necessity of fortifying Paris. These "bastilles" had but one purpose in Cabet's mind: to make Paris into a prison surrounded by the guns of the army, available to repress popular protest.[43]

One of the key developments of 1840 was the support that *Le National* gave to the fortifications. This came as a shock to the entire "patriot" party, for while few doubted that Marrast, Marie, Bastide, and the rest of *Le National*'s clique were not completely popular in their orientation, they were republicans and supposedly

[41] Cours des Pairs, *Attentat de 15 octobre,* 190.

[42] *Revue de progrès,* Oct. 1, 1840.

[43] See Cabet's third letter in the *Six Lettres,* p. 29; Cabet, *Suite de la brochure le National nous perd* (Paris, 1841), 57; Cabet and Dézamy, *Patriotes, lisez et rougissez de honte! Opinions des journaux français et étrangers sur la Question d'Orient* (Paris, 1840), 2; and Cabet and Lahautière, *Biographie populaire de l'armée* (Paris, 1840), 12.

had the interest of the lower classes at heart. Cabet led the attack against them. "Let one read the brochures published recently by M. Cabet, and one will judge the alarm the project to fortify Paris arouses in this courageous citizen, in this indefatigable defender of the rights of the people."[44] It is unnecessary to delve into the details of Cabet's conflict with *Le National* except to note that it was acrimonious and led, finally, to Cabet being challenged to a duel by one of *Le National*'s editors, Thomas. Cabet's argument went directly to the heart of the matter—*Le National* had sold out to Thiers because of its growing fear of social revolution, thus abandoning the heritage of its great editor, Armand Carrel.[45] The bastille issue publicly exposed moderate republicanism's left limits fully for the first time. For Cabet, the conflict broke all links with his old associates of the moderate republican camp. Charles Chameroy, Cabet's chief provincial propagandist, wrote Cabet on October 10, 1841, that "several sincere democrats . . . have told me that they no longer have confidence in you, that you are *mad*, etc. . . . Even in Dijon, your home town, your friends have uttered such comments to me because they say you do not know when to keep your mouth shut."[46]

While Cabet offended the sensibilities of many of his bourgeois friends by his rabid campaign against *Le National,* his popularity among the Parisian workers seems to have soared. A brochure published on July 1, 1841, was supported by 980 Parisians, and other petitions were being circulated in working-class quarters. Cabet was urged to continue bravely his struggle against the "false patriots" of *Le National* and all the *embastilleurs.* "You have courageously torn off their mask: hence their furor! For this is not the least service that you have rendered to the national cause."[47]

To sum up, 1840 was a year of political crisis in France. An

[44] *Revue de progrès,* V (1841), 79. See also Gourvitch, "Le Mouvement pour la réforme," 256, 259–61.

[45] See Cabet, *Le National nous perd par son aveuglement sur les bastilles: Réfutation des ses arguments* (Paris, Feb. 1841), *passim.*

[46] Letter published by Prudhommeaux in his "Un Commis Voyageur en communisme icarien, Chameroy, disciple de Cabet," *La Révolution de 1848,* XXIV (1927–28), 66.

[47] *Protestation des ouvriers de Paris contre le duel, les bastilles, le monopole de la presse et la peine de mort* (Paris, 1841). Firman Favard, later to be Cabet's chief agent in the Parisian working-class milieux, did most of the work in preparing this brochure.

economic depression was just beginning to wane. Numerous protest movements involving both bourgeois opponents of the July Monarchy and workers had grown up. An immense variety of socialist literature had been published. The communist cause had been launched in print and in action. But it came to be associtated in the public mind with violence and secret societies. Cabet, however, avoided all connections with the militant communists and simply allowed the *Voyage en Icarie* and the *Histoire populaire,* with their emphasis on legalism and their denunciations of Babeuf, to circulate. He took the lead in condemning the fortification plan and put the issue in a distinctly social context. Icarian communism was becoming known, but only with the publication of a newspaper in March 1841 would a movement begin to form.

The New *Populaire* and the Rise of Legal Communism

On March 14, 1841, Cabet brought out the first issue of the new *Populaire*. Its publication, he reported, was a response to the demands of a large group of pacific communist workers who were dissatisfied wtih communism's secret-society image. This cadre, largely Parisian in make-up, became shareholders in the Société commandite du Populaire. Many of the shares were subdivided into tenths (*coupons*) so that the poorer promoters of the newspaper might participate in its financing. *Le Populaire,* appearing monthly, thus took its place among the organs representing the interests of the French working classes. At the time, it was the only avowedly communist paper in France, although Richard Lahautière's *La Fraternité* would come out in May and the anarcho-communist *L'Humanitaire* shortly thereafter. Five other Parisian newspapers were aimed at a working-class audience: Cavaignac's *Journal du peuple;* Louis Blanc's *Revue de progrès; L'Atelier* (edited by a group of workers influenced by Buchez' ideas); the vaguely Saint-Simonist *La Ruche populaire;* and the current Fourierist organ, *La Phalange*. Among these papers, *Le Populaire* alone would function not only as a device for propagating a particular point of view, but also as the vital center of a social movement. The office of *Le Populaire,* appropriately located at no. 14, rue Jean-Jacques Rousseau, became the organizational core of the entire Icarian movement; from here Cabet carried on, almost singlehandedly, the vast correspondence of the "Icarian school."

Here also Cabet met with numerous Parisian followers to discuss his doctrine and to organize campaigns for placing his brochures, gathering signatures for petitions, or making inquiries on the conditions of work in various Parisian occupations.

With the passing of the crises of 1840 the authorities kept a close watch over the radical press and diligently prosecuted any group even remotely suspected of conspiratorial activity. Besides the breakup of communist gatherings and the wave of arrests surrounding the Darmès affair, a "war to the death against the press"[48] ensued. Several newspapers were suppressed, including *L'Humanitaire* and another Communist organ, *Le Travail* of Lyons; many others, ranging from the nonpolitical *Courrier des théatres* to *Le Populaire* itself, were brought to trial for press offenses. The investigation of "illicit associations" was equally energetic. A Ministry of Justice report of early 1842 listed thirteen separate prosecutions. Of 187 individuals accused, 137 were condemned for conspiracy.[49] The most important trials concerned the Parisian Travailleurs Egalitaires, which resulted in the conviction of Pillot and seven others, and the "Marseilles plot," a conspiracy touching almost the entire Midi. The Charbonnerie Réformée of Lyons was prosecuted shortly thereafter, further swelling the ranks of communist victims of government action.

It was, therefore, in an atmosphere of severe repression that Cabet launched *Le Populaire*. Preaching probity, moderation, and almost deferential respect for employer and police agent, but offering the heartening alternatives of "civil courage" and the beauties of a communist world, it was favorably received. Each month, for the first seven numbers, 2,000 copies were printed. The authorities found it impossible to prosecute Cabet for any of his writings. Chastened by his experience of 1834 and fully cognizant of the intricacies of the press laws, he made himself untouchable. As early as November 1840 the procureur-général of Paris wished to indict Cabet for his *Six Lettres sur la crise actuelle* but found himself unable to do so in view of Cabet's "antirevolutionary" attitudes. Again, on June 26, 1841, the Minister of the Interior

---

48 *Le Populaire,* Supplément, June 5, 1842.
49 "Associations illicites poursuivies depuis 1ᵉʳ janvier 1841," A.N., BB¹⁸ 1472 dos 6733.

himself, Duchâtel, notified the Ministry of Justice of the appearance of the first four of Cabet's *Douze Lettres d'un communiste à un réformiste,* saying that they were "destined to propagate the dreadful doctrines of the communist sect among the working class" and that their low price made them all the more dangerous. Although he underlined Cabet's description of society as a "stepmother," he and the Minister of Justice agreed that prosecution was impossible.[50] Such evidence demonstrates Cabet's invulnerability; at the same time, this examination of everything he wrote reveals how senseless were the charges of *Le National* that he was "serving the police."[51]

Cabet strove to make communism respectable, to divorce it from the "handful of scoundrels" bent on burning, pillaging, and exciting class hatred whom the *Journal des débats* and other conservative newspapers equated with "the communists."[52] Although he had made his position clear in all his previous writings, Cabet devoted an entire brochure, *Ma Ligne droite, ou le vrai chemin du salut pour le peuple* (September 1841), to outlining his means of effectuating communism in France. Its appearance, only a few days after the Quénisset assassination attempt, was opportune. Summing up his general rationale, Cabet said, "Do you not see the enormous, incalculable evil that such useless acts of violence create for the cause of the people by giving its enemies a pretext to rant about risings, pillages, murders, to make searches, arrests, and seizures, to frighten the Bourgeoisie, strangle the press, etc., etc.?"[53] He then urged the workers to disdain all paths of illegal and/or violent resistance, proscribing assassinations, possession of arms, secret societies, protest in the streets, clandestine press participation, and even banquets. All had proved only to invigorate police repression, even against those involved in manifestly legal activity.

Cabet posed the alternative of passive resistance, which he summed up in the effective phrase, "civil courage." The worker should know the law in detail and demand that any agent of the

---

[50] A.N., BB[18] 1387 dos 1054 and BB[18] 1397 dos 2749. They also failed to find any offenses in his brochures on the Quénisset trial (1841).

[51] Cited by Cabet in *Les Masques arrachés* (Paris, 1843), 26.

[52] *Journal des débats,* Sept. 20, 1841; Grün, *Die Soziale Bewegung in Frankreich,* 336.

[53] *Ma Ligne droite,* 17.

police or the judiciary execute it fully in all contacts. If arrested he should not resist but again exercise his civil rights to the full. In April 1842, Cabet published a comprehensive *Guide du citoyen aux prises avec la Police et le Justice dans les arrestations, les visites domiciliares, la détention provisoire, le secret et devant le Juge d'instruction et le tribunal, après l'acquittement ou la condamnation.* Making good use of his professional knowledge, he outlined the rights of any citizen facing interrogation, quoting extensively from the codes and constitutions, and gave examples of the way police action operated. He advised the worker to respond to questions openly and candidly. "Fear nothing! Have the courage of your convictions! Render testimony to Community, to its morality, its justice, its virtue."[54] He pointed out numerous challenges that a man under investigation might offer to his "persecutors." For example, only the bearer of the arrest warrant had the right to search and the minutes of the investigation had to be written by the same man in the presence of the suspect. Such details were often ignored in the cases involving those without a knowledge of the law. By demanding the letter of the law, the communist worker could do much to discourage police harassment.

Teach yourself the habit of civil courage, more difficult, more rare, and often more useful than militant courage.

The storms will occur of their own accord; we will have to defend ourselves. . . . But in order not to be conquered, crushed, *union* is the first of our necessities. Reformists, communists, democrats, patriots, let us not be foolish enough to lose our cause by vain discussions! Close your ranks! *Union! Union!*[55]

Thus the communist worker should be respectable and forbearing. Here Cabet's overall political strategy is apparent. Communism fights the same battles as the other antiregime elements, and the communist worker, despite his rejection of property, can make himself acceptable to these predominantly bourgeois groups. Then, through the power of his demonstrated "judgement and virtue," he can win the minds of these people to communism. From all points of view, therefore, the proclivity toward violence is absurd. The establishment of Community is impossible without the prior

[54] *Guide du citoyen,* 28–29.
[55] *Le Populaire,* May 20, 1841.

conversion of "public opinion, *la reine du monde.*" "It is said that a revolution is materially realizable only when it already exists morally, when it is generally desirable, when it is in the mind."[56]

Cabet obviously impressed a number of politically conscious workers with such arguments. *Ma Ligne droite* caused a considerable stir among Parisians. A declaration was drawn up by his supporters and signed by 1,600 people. A letter accompanying its delivery shows that Cabet had attracted a number of workers away from secret societies by early 1842:

> We [had originally] adopted the idea of secret societies, which are born of a society that offers to the workers only an existence of misery and humiliation. Ashamed and tired of living for so long in this state of social demoralization we had convinced ourselves to brave the gravest dangers, thinking it possible to put an end to such misfortunes more promptly by force. But soon, persuaded to the contrary by your *ligne droite,* we recognized that *civil* courage is the first that should be employed in order to bring about the triumph of our principles.[57]

Propaganda Techniques and Sources of Appeal

And so Cabet set out to convert France and the world to communism. His agency was almost exclusively the written word. Besides *Le Populaire,* a torrent of brochures, one longer work (*Le Vrai Christianisme*), and several editions of the *Voyage en Icarie* and the *Histoire populaire* flowed from the presses of the Bureau du Populaire. We have already stressed that Cabet must be regarded above all as the propagandist of communism rather than a theoretician. *Voyage en Icarie* was the doctrinal backbone of the movement. Each new edition (there were five between 1842 and 1848) was merely a reprinting. The doctrine was set: theoretical writings thereafter—including *Le Vrai Christianisme*—consisted, in the main, of a repetition or elaboration of ideas set down in the *Voyage.* The great bulk of Cabet's work was concerned, therefore, with propaganda and organization. With single-minded zeal, he gave himself almost entirely to the task of winning supporters. The scope of his efforts is revealed in a report from the procureur du

---

[56] *Ma Ligne droite,* 33. See also his *Comment je suis communiste* (Paris, 1841), 6.

[57] In Cabet, *Procès du communisme à Toulouse* (Paris, 1843), 18.

roi of Saint-Quentin after the seizure of Cabet's papers and records late in 1847:

> The activity displayed by Cabet during this seven-year period is, so to speak, fabulous: the 160 dossiers that are currently in the hands of Justice contain . . . the history of his life since 1841, and, when one examines the enormous files of letters that he had received from his correspondents and his adherents, the answers that he had addressed to all (of which all the rough drafts are in his own hand), when one thinks of all the books that he has written and published to propagate his doctrines, of the work of editing that his newspaper, *Le Populaire,* has imposed upon him, of all the details of administration and book-keeping that he has given himself over to in order to dispatch newspapers and brochures to his correspondents and subscribers, one realizes that every available moment of this man's time during this period must have been consecrated to the fulfillment of his task, to the propagation and triumph of his theories.[58]

Again it is Cabet the activist, the propagandist, rather than the hopeful utopian dreamer who comes to view. In 1845 an article in Girardin's *La Presse* summarized his role: "Communism is a grave symptom of our times; in the domain of ideas, it has eloquent and vigorous defenders; [and] in the domain of facts it has, under the influence of M. Cabet, an active propaganda operating in broad daylight."[59]

The chief instrument of propaganda was *Le Populaire.* Unlike any other paper published in the interest of the working people, it eschewed theoretical matters altogether. Cabet felt that a news-paper intended for working-class consumption had to contain ma-terial of immediate appeal. Theory only made a journal boring and unappetizing. Certainly Cabet did not err in this approach: *Le Populaire* came to have the widest circulation of all popular papers, reaching a press run of 4,500 in 1846. *L'Atelier,* the famous monthly "edited by the workers themselves," had a circulation of about 1,000, few of them from the working class. "It appears . . . that most of its readers were intellectuals or bourgeois democrats

---

[58] From a report of Jan. 17, 1848, published by P. Caron under the title "Cabet et l'Icarie à la fin de 1847," *Revue d'histoire moderne et con-temporaine* (May 1907), 571. The Cabet papers at the IISG and the BHVP are the remnants of this vast amount of material.

[59] *La Presse,* March 10, 1845.

and, in part, even open-minded conservatives who were curious to know what the workers thought." The reasons for its failure to recruit readers among the workers are not hard to find. According to Armand Cuvillier, *L'Atelier* "had against it the gravity and the dryness of the logic of its articles, the moderation of its language that even gave a pale color to its boldest affirmations, its opposition to extreme theories."[60] Such aridity was shared by other papers aimed at a working-class audience. Martin Nadaud found that *La Fraternité,* for instance, "treated social questions from a point of view so elevated that only the best-educated workers could read it."[61] Cabet's paper suffered from none of these disabilities.

Le Populaire was four pages long (with an occasional supplement); its pages and print were larger than those of any other popular newspaper of the day. Rarely did Cabet print an article longer than two columns. The language was always simple, and generous use was made of exclamation points. It had a pleasing appearance and was well printed. These physical features should not be underestimated. *L'Atelier* and *La Fraternité* looked like learned journals by comparison. The slow-reading worker would tend to avoid them almost on this score alone.

Cabet divided his paper into two main sections, the "political" and that "social," and left considerable space for letters from adherents and discussions of the growth and problems of the movement. Occasionally he printed a feuilleton, such as the "Biographie d'un combattant contre la Bastille, Denis Godart" or the novellas about working-class misery by Jenny d'Héricourt under the pseudonym of Felix Lamb. In the political section the director of *Le Populaire* discussed issues of internal and foreign politics. Normally, three or four questions were interpreted through Icarian eyes. The social section reported on police repression, strikes, trials of members of the press and secret societies, and, especially, the conditions of life of the French workers. Occasionally Cabet discussed the social question in foreign countries, notably Great Britain. He also used this section to refute charges made against communism and him personally. Although from time to time he did have some incisive things to say about the social structure and the

[60] Cuvillier, *Un Journal d'ouvriers: "L'Atelier"* *(1840–1850)* (Paris, 1954), 177–78.
[61] *Ibid.,* 179 n. 1.

broad problems of the working class, generalizations were kept to a minimum. Cabet's real forte was to recount hundreds of specific incidents of working-class oppression, stories of murders and accidents, of starving children and fallen women, of moral decay among the upper classes, of the hardships of competition among businesses, of political scandals. These were included in a subdivision called "social disorder." Always tinged with sensationalism, these tales of misery nevertheless represented some of Cabet's best propaganda. Workers recognized situations that they themselves had experienced and saw clear truths about the outward realities of their society. *L'Atelier's* analyses of "industrial privilege" and complex arguments in favor of cooperation and *La Fraternité's* philosophical dissertations could hardly hold the same interest. Cabet would always conclude that the blanket solution was "to proclaim with us the sacred principle of *association solidaire*. None of this in Icaria!"

A few examples suffice to give the flavor of these exposés. In the fifth issue of *Le Populaire,* Cabet reported the instance of a young man caught in the act of burglarizing the flat of a marblecutter, a friend of Cabet. The thief was not turned in by this good Icarian but fed and given money. He was, nevertheless, so remorseful over his act that he later committed suicide. Then there is the tale of a greedy son trying to steal money from his rich father. A third story in this issue is that of a young girl who had secretly become a prostitute to bring in money after her artisan father lost his job. One day she inadvertently propositioned her father; shortly thereafter she killed herself. "And side by side with this misery, we see the mistress of a prince in possession of twelve million—money derived from neither work nor virtue—will it capriciously to a child who lost it all [gambling? speculation?] forthwith."[62] Cabet revealed the pervasive grip of environmentalism on his outlook by including suicides of lovers and sexual crimes among the evils that were to be rectified in Community. Even the effects of floods and earthquakes and the occurence of fires and railway accidents were attributed to the organization (or disorganization) of current society. As Cabet put it, after discussing the terrible devastation caused by an earthquake in Guadaloupe, "[In Icaria] nothing would be neglected to anticipate earthquakes (and floods and fires) and

[62] *Le Populaire,* July 25, 1841.

to repair their ravages; the study of everything concerning these terrible phenomena would be promoted; . . . location of towns and houses would be chosen differently; houses would be constructed differently; for example, they would be made of wood rather than stone, low and isolated rather than tall and contiguous."[63] This explanation at least exonerates him from the charge of attributing magical powers to Icarian social organization!

One of Cabet's favorite propaganda ploys was to emphasize the "persecution" of communists by the government, the press, and the Jesuits. It is possible to extract a veritable Book of Martyrs from the pages of *Le Populaire*. And Cabet did not hesitate to compare the martyrdom of his communist followers (although their possible fate was less dreadful) with that of the early Christians.[64] Many of Cabet's followers were indeed persecuted unjustly. An example is the case of three Parisian shoemakers who were arrested at a rooming house on the pretext that they were thieves. One of them was a known Icarian, but the other two had only been in Paris for three days. The first had several of Cabet's works and a portrait in his possession. They were jailed for fifteen days. On their release, they found that they were without jobs and that their landlord had spread the word around the neighborhood that they were criminals.[65] To stress the fire that communists had to endure, Cabet also printed virtually all criticism of communism and himself. He culled the press for negative comments, often going to ridiculous lengths. For example, when *Le Siècle* made a rather offhand remark about "absurd sects," Cabet magnified it into a purported attack upon himself and devoted a column to refuting it. But in face of persecution and slanders, Cabet's supporters would stand proud and straight: "Courage Communists! Perseverence, union, prudence, wisdom! Let us know how to avoid the faults that furnish the pretexts of our enemies! . . . Let us know how to suffer for [Community], filled with an unshakable faith in its future."[66]

Naturally, Cabet printed any praise found in the press or in letters that he received from workers. The latter especially gave

---

[63] *Ibid.*, April 9, 1843.
[64] For example, see *ibid.*, Nov. 15, 1841, and Feb. 10, 1843.
[65] *Ibid.*, Feb. 27, 1843.
[66] *Ibid.*, April 9, 1841.

the impression of a growing and vital movement; if a letter was written by a group, the number of signatures would be recorded at the end. Another device creating the same effect was a section on "the growth of communism." Each new area in France heard from was noted, as was foreign influence.

The foundations of Cabet's propaganda methods were outlined with disarming frankness in *Le Populaire* of July 13, 1845:

> In general, the worker lacks the primary instruction necessary to read fruitfully. Moreover, he has little time to give to reading. To give him much to read rapidly is to throw his mind into confusion and chaos.
>
> It is better to give him only a small number of simple, clear, and essential books; he can study them carefully and therefore understand them. Let us first make many communists with a small number of essential ideas; all delicate questions will be discussed and decided upon in common later.[67]

Such an approach caused Cabet to make every effort to boil down his doctrine into a few simple slogans. In the second issue of his newspaper he exposed his "Système de la Communauté." If the source of all evil is inequality, the only remedy is complete equality. "The essential principles or characteristics of Community are, for us: (1) *unity* in all; (2) indivisibility in property; (3) equality of enjoyment of the fruits [of the earth] and the products [of industry]. One can even denote Community by a single principle or a single character in saying that it has as its foundation property that is nonindividual but *indivisible, common, social, national*."[68] Three years later Cabet, having found himself challenged on the narrowness of his earlier definition of the "principles or characteristics" of his utopia, incorporated just about every popular catchword then current: "Community is: Fraternity—association—unity—Democracy—equality—liberty—work—organization of work—the triumph of machines—solidarity—mutual aid—universal assurance—order—economy—the triumph of administration—the development of intelligence—the triumph of education, morality, the family, the arts—happiness for all—the ideal of nearly all the Philos-

---

[67] Dézamy attacked Cabet on this score in *Calomnies de M. Cabet* (p. 20). His adversary saw nothing wrong with it: "I persist because it is my opinion" (*Toute La Vérité*, 61).

[68] *Le Populaire*, April 15, 1841.

ophers—Christianity."[69] His communism was everything, therefore, to which the workers demonstrated some devotion. Fernand Rude has stressed Cabet's modernity in this respect: "By the importance that he attaches to a multiform and tireless propaganda, Cabet again announces our times when one standardizes opinion with slogans, when one makes great efforts to make men think in series, and when one practices as a matter of course what is called 'the violation of the masses by political propaganda.' "[70]

A final, and more traditional, technique was his invocation of authority—in the manner of any good lawyer—to support his "client." A seventy-five-page section is devoted to this in the *Voyage en Icarie*. Abandoning all reasonable criteria of selection, Cabet included the names of such unlikely communists as Plutarch, Locke, Montesquieu, and Lamartine. Any famous person who so much as mentions such a word as "equality" or "association" is grouped with such legitimate utopians as Plato, More, Mably, and Morélly. Thus is Napoleon Bonaparte, whose name appears in big letters on page 511, quoted: "The Liberty, EQUALITY, and prosperity of France will be protected from the caprices of chance. . . . The *best* of Peoples will also be the happiest. Happy to have been called by He from whom all emanates to return *Justice,* order, and EQUALITY to the earth, I will face my final hour without anxiety about the opinions of future generations." From time to time in *Le Populaire* Cabet would discover another great man who was a communist. An excellent example of this technique was his commentary on Immanuel Kant in the issue of July 20, 1843. In bold print he began by telling his readers that "the most celebrated German philosopher was a communist." He noted that Kant declared for the Revolution in 1792 and for the abolition of inheritance. Some meaningless verbiage follows. Toward the end of the article—if one gets that far—Cabet admits that "it would be too bold perhaps to affirm that Kant was formally a communist." But since he was a republican and a democrat, he was on the road to communism! Nevertheless, the headline remains and we can be certain that most Icarians who read it informed their friends at the cabaret that "the most celebrated German philosopher was a communist."

[69] *Ibid.,* Oct. 1844.
[70] Rude, *Voyage en Icarie: Deux Ouvriers viennois,* 17.

Enough has been said to recreate the flavor of Cabet's propaganda techniques. Beyond this, he developed three important themes that made his communism palatable to a wider audience. The first was his evident Jacobinism, the second his apparent feminism, and the third his dictum that "communism is Christianity in practice."

Besides his general praise of Robespierre, the chief Jacobin characteristics in Cabet's writings are his bellicose nationalism and his anticlericalism. The former was a constant thread in his writings and was especially manifested by his vision of a war of national defense in the manner of 1793–1794 against the forces of reaction. Moreover, besides an occasional concern that France was falling behind other nations economically,[71] Cabet wrote often on the war in Algeria. Even though he recognized the brutality of General Bugeaud's methods, he never denied the value of acquiring Algeria as a French colony and of colonialism in general. In discussing the course of the Algerian war, Cabet focused on the bravery of the common soldier. On the battlefield, as in the workshop, the *menu peuple* were the backbone of the nation. It was they through whom France would accomplish its "civilizing and democratic mission."[72] Although Cabet was never as effusive on the "Jesuit conspiracy" as was, for instance, Raspail, he took several opportunities to link the organized Church with the forces of political conservatism.[73] The clergy used fear and superstition to make the worker patiently endure the hardships of his lot and accept the hierarchical organization of society. In a society where the workers increasingly rejected Catholicism, there can be little doubt that these sorts of attacks had some influence in winning sympathy for Cabet.[74]

His message to women was a significant new departure, despite

---

[71] See for instance issue no. 1 of *Le Populaire* (March 14, 1841).

[72] *Ibid.*, April 2, June 5, 1842, March 9, 1843, and Aug. 22, 1844.

[73] The following quotation shows that he nevertheless saw a Jesuit conspiracy at work and also the political link: "Nothing is as harmful as the moral teaching, or rather the immorality of their doctrine, which permits all crimes. . . . Since [their return to France in 1814], they have formed a *Secret Society,* a real secret society where the secret is well guarded, which is composed of priestly or long-robed Jesuits and nonpriestly or *short-robed* Jesuits. Among the latter are found public functionaries of all types and men of great influence in Society" (*Le Populaire,* May 11, 1845).

[74] For Cabet's anticlericalism, see *ibid.*, April 15, 1841, June 5, Aug. 7, and Oct. 9, 1842.

certain comments in the *Voyage en Icarie*. It appeared first in the seventh of his *Douze Lettres*,[75] which was later reprinted several times as a separate brochure entitled *La Femme*. His main emphasis was on the virtues and qualities of womankind and the ways women were oppressed in existing society.

> Woman! . . . Ah! if only my pen knew how to express the sentiments of my soul, the admiration, gratitude, affection, respect [that I have] for womankind.
>
> I would paint her as the most beautiful flowers; the most perfect of animate creatures; the masterpiece of Nature, the source, for the man, of his most beautiful inspirations and of his sweetest pleasures; charming him, from the cradle, by her first smile, her first caresses, by the inexpressible grace of her youth; captivating him by her kindness; caring for him and curing him in sickness; standing by him in peril; consoling him in misfortune by her tenderness and devotion; superior to him in patience and in sensibility, his equal in intelligence and in rights.

Only the last line hints at anything more than the idea that a woman exists *for* men. She has definite functions and a definite place because she is a woman. Nevertheless, he decried the current status of woman: "so-called modern society . . . treats the woman as a species of slave," especially the daughter of the proletariat. She must work for her family to survive but under conditions in which she is brutalized, loses her beauty and health, and is threatened constantly by the "plague of libertinage." She is often unable to marry, for economic reasons, and is forced into concubinage or prostitution. But if the degradation of the poor female is severe, the wealthy woman is also oppressed, above all by the legal and economic shackles binding her in marriage. The "advantages of Community" for the woman are obvious. Above all, the economic determinants of female debasement are eliminated. The constitution of Icaria proclaims that "the mass of men owes to the mass of women gratitude, respect, affection." The education of both sexes is equal, as are occupational opportunities. All women in Icaria work, but under the marvelous conditions outlined earlier and only with other women. Regarding relations between the sexes, Cabet felt the Icarian environment would eliminate all license and adul-

---

[75] This letter was published in August 1841.

tery, for these derive entirely from unhappy marriages of convenience in a society dominated by gold.

The Icarian leader totally condemned those communists who (like the editors of *L'Humanitaire*) would seek to abolish marriage and the family: "Yes, Marriage and the Family are, for the woman, the source of a thousand moral pleasures far superior to other pleasures. Yes, Marriage and the Family conform more to the dignity, to the peace, to the happiness of the woman, than her isolation and independence. Yet, it is the woman especially who ought to desire the conservation of Marriage and the Family, purged of all their vices."[76] Middle-class feminists such as George Sand might scoff at such a position, but one must remember that economic privation caused many poor women to postpone or avoid marriage altogether. Cabet's view of marriage was, therefore, more in line with working-class attitudes. He concluded his tract with a long letter from "a daughter of the People" who, in eulogizing the Icarian chief, proclaimed her conversion to Community. Cabet's concern for women won him a number of devoted feminine recruits. Their letters appeared from time to time in *Le Populaire,* and an entire dossier of "letters from women" (so separated by Cabet himself) exists in the collection of the Bibliothèque historique de la Ville de Paris.

Cabet's role in the history of French feminism was equivocal. Later events were to show that, while he gained the support of feminists, he found it difficult even to sanction female suffrage. In *Voyage en Icarie,* despite a general social framework sustaining sex equality, he never specifically said women had the right to vote. Such vagueness remained characteristic. One of his followers, Rabyrin, a teacher in Lyons, published a long article in 1847 on the future condition of women in the proposed Icarian colony. Although he mentioned that they would be able to cultivate their minds and experience "complete emancipation," suffrage and the right to hold office were not discussed.[77] On January 2, 1848, Cabet turned down two women who wanted to join the first group departing for America on the grounds that they would not have the

[76] Cabet, *Douze Lettres,* 49–50, 52, and 57.
[77] "Diverses Opinions sur la femme," *Almanach icarien pour 1848* (Paris, 1847), 136–56.

physical stamina, although he assured them that they were equal in all other respects.[78]

Yet Cabet had given close and heartfelt attention to the problem of female oppression in nineteenth-century society. Moreover, his regular feuilletonist was a woman, Jenny d'Héricourt.[79] He was, therefore, singled out by Jeanne Deroin and Eugénie Niboyet, who edited *La Voix des femmes* in 1848 and launched the French feminist movement, as the principal defender of the rights of women in France. They sent him a eulogy that concluded: "You have courageously raised your eloquent voice in favor of the holy cause of equality for all women as for all men. Be blessed! You and all your generous Icarians and all those who have applauded your noble words. In you, in them, in the sacredness of our cause, we put all our hope."[80] The principal basis for such praise was their belief that Cabet had fully sanctioned female suffrage in a meeting of his revolutionary club on March 29, 1848.[81] This was, in fact, not quite correct. Cabet had spoken at length about the degradation of women and was then pressed from the floor on the question of political rights. Somewhat nonplussed, he finally allowed that perhaps women should be given the vote but that the decision should be up to his audience. Greeted with both yeas and nays, he adjourned the session without taking a definite stand.[82] Deroin nevertheless assumed that this Icarian meeting was a major turning point in the fortunes of her cause and thereafter "began to lay down her program of feminism with vigor."[83] Cabet himself, despite this (somewhat circumstantial) contribution to the early development of political feminism, moved further away from the spirit of the idea.

[78] *Le Populaire,* Jan. 2, 1848.

[79] Héricourt wrote for Cabet under the name of Felix Lamb. I discovered that the two were the same person in a letter that she wrote to Cabet in 1848. Papiers Cabet, Lettres des Femmes, BHVP. Using her pseudonym, she published a novel in 1844, *Le Fils du réprouvé,* 2 vols. (Paris, 1844), a story about a former convict and his problems. Then, under her own name, she published *La Femme affranchie: Réponse à MM. Michelet, Proudhon, E. de Girardin, A. Comte* (Brussels, 1858), the goal of which was "to prove that women have the same rights as men."

[80] "Adresse au Citoyen Cabet," *Le Populaire,* April 2, 1848.

[81] *Voix des femmes,* March 31, 1848.

[82] Societe fraternelle centrale, *Sixième Discours du Citoyen Cabet* (*Séance de 29 mars*) (Paris, 1848), especially 13–16.

[83] A. Ranvier, "Une Féministe de 1848, Jeanne Deroin," *La Révolution de 1848,* IV (1907–08), 324. The author is unaware of Cabet's hesitancy.

By May 1 he was even more equivocal on female political rights.[84] Finally, in the Nauvoo, Illinois, colony women's rights were curtailed both politically and socially. Indeed, women in general became morally suspect. Cabet's former ally, Jenny d'Héricourt, apparently aware of this situation, later attacked him disdainfully. "Another communist sect, that of the Icarians, occupied itself neither with the nature nor the rights of the woman. Its leader, M. Cabet, former procureur-général, was too imbued with the Civil Code, that inelegant paraphrase of the apostle Paul, to think that woman should have political rights or to think that she should not be subordinated to man in general and her husband, good or bad, in particular."[85] In spite of her bitterness toward Cabet personally, Héricourt thought that communism as a doctrine had done more than any other to advertise the "great truth . . . that the liberty of woman is identical with that of the masses." In this sense, Cabet had certainly contributed more than a little, for he clearly made the link even if his own psychological make-up would not allow him to act fully upon it.[86]

The third and most important supplement to Cabet's doctrine was his contention that communism was really Christianity in practice. Although Cabet had earlier alluded to Christ as a great communist forerunner and remarked favorably about the "community of goods" formed by the "first Christians,"[87] he began to stress the Christian-communist link only in the summer of 1842. In the issue of *Le Populaire* of August 7, he commenced a series of "Explanations of the Gospels" in articles cosigned by a certain Charles, who was none other than the Polish communist mystic, Louis Krolikowski.[88] In this series Cabet promised to "examine and explain the

[84] Société fraternelle centrale, *Dixième Discours du Citoyen Cabet*, pp. 6–8.

[85] She did note, however, that the Icarians themselves were much more generous and reported that the great majority said "yes" at the meeting of March 29, 1848 (*La Femme affranchie*, I, 61–63).

[86] It should also be noted that both Jeanne Deroin and Pauline Roland, another active feminist, read Cabet's major works with care. Ranvier, "Une Féministe," 351; Edith Thomas, *Pauline Roland: Socialisme et féminisme au XIX*e *siècle* (Paris, 1956), 140.

[87] *Voyage en Icarie*, 518–19.

[88] Earlier historians have failed to recognize Krolikowski's influence on the development of Cabet's Christian emphasis, at least at that date. Prudhommeaux knew that Charles was the pseudonym that Krolikowski adopted

Gospels to show that the entire philosophy, the entire social doctrine of Jesus Christ and of Christianity constituted, in essence, Community."[89] This, then, was the beginning of a new doctrinal thrust that played an important role during the middle years of the Icarian movement and culminated in the publication of *Le Vrai Christianisme* early in 1846.

While Cabet hoped that both believers and "those who see in Jesus Christ only a philosopher" would heed them, the appeal was to the former. He almost smacked his lips at the thought of the mass of converts to be gained when he wrote, "For those who recognize the divinity of Christ, there is no need to deliberate on the justice and the necessity of the communitarian regime; for it is God who has commanded Community!"[90] Cabet and Charles' main thesis was that Christ foresaw the coming of the perfect life in the terrestrial kingdom, not in the afterlife; that he was, in fact, a social revolutionary. The reason Jesus had been misunderstood for so long was the "necessity of an enigmatic and mysterious style in the Gospels." Christ had to speak in such a way lest the Roman officials and "rich Jews" catch on to his design to create a community of goods in the here and now. Thus the resurrection of Lazarus was a symbol of the uplifting of the masses to material equality.[91] The authors even compared the position of the writers of the Gospels to that of the reformist journalists in contemporary France who must circumvent censorship by means of allegorical language. In actuality, beneath his vague and mysterious verbal shell, "Jesus Christ undertook, against the Roman and Jewish aristocracy, the greatest of reforms or revolutions: the abolition of

---

when he arrived in Paris in 1839. But he was not aware of his contributions to *Le Populaire*. On the other hand, Edmund Silburner and Jan Turowski, who both cite other works on this Polish utopian, think that Cabet and Krolikowski began to collaborate only in 1847, the latter then using his real name. The simple point was that Krolikowski would have jeopardized the stipend he received from the French government's Polish exile fund had he written for a French opposition journal under his own name. The relevant references are Prudhommeaux, *Cabet*, 241 n. 1; Silburner, "La correspondance Moses Hess-Louis Krolikowski," *Annali del' Istituto Giangiacomo Feltrinelli* (1960), 584; and Jan Turowski, *Utopia spoleczna Ludwika Krolikowskiego* (Warsaw, 1960), 168–71.

[89] *Le Populaire*, Aug. 7, 1842.
[90] *Ibid.*, May 8, 1842; see also *ibid.*, July 3, 1842.
[91] *Ibid.*, March 9, 1843.

slavery, the equality and Fraternity of men and peoples, the freeing of women, the abolition of opulence and misery, the destruction of sacerdotal power, and, finally, the community of goods."[92] The core of the entire argument was the answer to the question, "Is the reign of Jesus Christ beyond this earth?" The basic proof was Christ's comment to Pilate: "But *now* my reign is not here." Cabet pointed out that "the priests" long suppressed the "now," which indicates that it would come later, "one day." Thus the perfect life is terrestrial, but in the future.[93] One suspects that this argument won many believing Christians to the Icarian cause. As one of his followers, a wholesale merchant, wrote, "You have done well to revive these ideas, to develop the germ planted by Jesus Christ— which all the efforts of the ambitious of all classes and types cannot destroy!" In general, this modern form of Christian exegesis should be, he said, a great weapon against those who are too blind to see the rationality of Community.[94]

Finally, Cabet's appeal rested in part on his social and economic analysis. While it would be impossible to call him a sophisticated commentator, he did demonstrate a realistic appreciation of the nature of the competitive economy, of the political power wielded by the "aristocracy of wealth," and of the living and working conditions of the working class.

Although Cabet knew very little about "political economy," he had to be aware of the "disastrous consequences of the system of free competition." Workers and capitalists alike are squeezed like grapes under this "detestable regime." As usual his comments arose out of specific situations. For instance, in assessing a wage conflict in a wallpaper factory Cabet professed to believe both workers and employer, asking what else can one expect in the current deplorable organization of society "where industry is nothing more than a battlefield, a cruel arena, where honest workers are devoured and trampled upon, where, at the expense of everyone else, the stockjobbers, dealers, the fat capitalists alone build colossal and scandalous fortunes!"[95] But the stockmarket speculators themselves are also destroyed by the system: "Dissolution continues

[92] *Ibid.*, Sept. 11, 1842.
[93] *Ibid.*, Dec. 11, 1842.
[94] *Ibid.*, Oct. 9, 1842.
[95] *Ibid.*, Nov. 15, 1841.

unendingly in the commercial order. It is not only the merchants and shopkeepers of the first order who succumb, swept away by the torrent of affairs and free competition; it is even (an unbelievable thing!) a crowd of stockbrokers and solicitors, who no longer now hesitate to gamble, at the terrible game of the stock exchange, their honor and their lives along with the fortunes of families."[96] The general picture Cabet offered in dozens of such statements was one of unrelieved economic anarchy governed only by "the law of the strong against the weak." The rich are even allowed to create monopolies in production and distribution while unions and political associations among workers are outlawed: "and one talks of freedom of trade and free competition!" It must all come to an end one day, for "society cannot long exist in a state of war."[97]

The rich dominated politically as well. In the Prospectus of *Le Populaire,* Cabet alluded to the power of the grande bourgeoisie: "When the law is made by one man, or by a family, or by the commissars of 20,000 noble aristocrats, or by the commissars of 200,000 Bourgeois, priviliged because of their money, the millions of men who are forced to obey these laws, whatever they be, are they not slaves rather than free men?" Later Cabet expressed the idea—so often posited by the Fourierists—that a new feudalism, a new hierarchy dominated by the lords of wealth, had emerged during the July Monarchy. Here is a typical remark:

[The Chamber of Deputies] often lacks the number necessary to deliberate. . . . But when it is a question of a railway line, in the concession of which many deputies are always interested, the latter are always right where they should be, thus giving the country the deplorable example of personal interest and egotism. People ask in vain that the rear carriages of a train be covered and enclosed, like the others, so that the poor who ride there will have protection. . . . This request is rejected in the interest of the financial companies the directors of which constitute a new feudalism; and the poor man . . . will be condemned to suffer all . . . the inclemencies of the seasons—a new and revolting example of the barbarous contempt of the opulent for the proletarian![98]

Cabet was clearly cognizant of the general nature of the economomy and of the political control exercised by the "aristocracy of

96 *Ibid.,* Dec. 23, 1841.
97 *Ibid.,* April 16, 1841, and Jan. 30, 1842.
98 *Ibid.,* June 13, 1845.

wealth." But his central concern was the condition of the working classes, the prevalent attitudes of the upper strata of society toward the workers, and the gross inequity of the law with regard to the relative rights of employers and wage earners. Much of the "social disorder" section of *Le Populaire* described the manifold problems of working-class life—low wages, unemployment, long hours, insufferable housing conditions, the impact of machines on craft industries, troubled marital and family relations, and so forth. Some examples of these have already been cited, and it would entail needless repetition to discuss them further. It should also be noted that Cabet made attempts to investigate systematically the conditions of life and work in the various important trades. In 1842 he encouraged workers to send him descriptions of the conditions of work in their trades for publication in *Le Populaire*. Several responded with detailed discussions providing both Cabet and later historians with a wealth of fascinating material.[99] Cabet's concrete education in the life experiences of working people was again extended, and his writing showed an increasingly sophisticated understanding of the world of the worker, a fact no doubt appreciated by thousands of Icarian recruits.

Cabet was especially effective when writing on the disdain shown by the upper levels of society toward the workers. Two examples will illustrate. Speaking to "respectable" society, Cabet charges: "You overwhelm us with injuries, outrages, calumnies, hatred, persecutions, we men of the People, workers, proletarians! You treat us like barbarians, pillagers, men who are depraved! You reduce us to despair . . . while our soul is already tortured by the humiliations of the Fatherland!"[100] Yet look at all we have contributed in the last sixty years. For fleeting moments we have been called heroes, saviors of the nation. We won the revolution of 1830. And what has been done for us since? Nothing: "Are we not therefore abandoned, condemned by Heaven and Earth?" On a more specific level Cabet recounted, with the rest of the radical press, the story of the tragic suicide of Adolphe Boyer. Boyer, a printed connected with several of the editors of *L'Atelier,* had written in 1841 an important work, *De l'Etat des ouvriers et de son*

---

[99] See *ibid.,* issues of Sept., Nov., and Dec. 1842.
[100] *Ibid.,* Oct. 10, 1841. The last line no doubt refers to the recent diplomatic crisis.

amélioration par l'organisation du travail. He had, however, put himself deeply in debt having it published and, in a fit of depression, killed himself in October 1841. Not only the popular press but such publications as the *Revue de deux mondes* brought the shocking story to the attention of the nation, and a sizable subscription was raised for the support of his family. Cabet bluntly commented on this wave of sympathy: "But why does a worker have to kill himself to make people take an interest in him! Why all the indifference toward living workers when one shows such a concern for a dead worker!"[101]

Cabet also constantly stressed the existence of a double legal standard in the treatment of worker and nonworker. Not only was this written into the law, but it was found in law enforcement as well. In one instance, he put the prejudice shown by the Ministry of Justice toward the worker in bold relief. Several workers in a ribbon manufacture were planning to pool what little capital they possessed to create their own workshop. They naturally kept their old jobs until their concern got off the ground. But they were arrested for organizing a union to increase wages and convicted under the Le Chapelier law. "Thus," remarked Cabet, "the masters and the rich can contract any commercial, industrial, or financial organization they wish to make themselves richer (even going to the point of monopolizing and forestalling the market); but poor workers are unable to associate . . . to assure themselves of bread and existence! And this is what they call order!"[102]

What Cabet presents, in sum, is a picture of a society in an advanced state of disintegration, of social anarchy, held together only by the frayed thongs of material interest and the right of the strongest. Thus it is in the realm of total social change that a solution must be sought. To this end, he rejected piecemeal reform, both political and economic. The program of the *Journal de peuple,* which advocated universal suffrage to win social reforms but hesitated to outline a concrete vision of the transformed society, could easily be manipulated, he said, to serve the ends of the power brokers. Trade unionism, reformed *conseils des prud'hommes*

101 *Ibid.,* Nov. 15, 1841. On Boyer, see J. L. Peuch, "Adolphe Boyer, ouvrier réformateur," *Revue d'histoire économique et sociale,* XXII (1935), 121–41.
102 *Le Populaire,* Jan. 30, 1842.

(public arbitration boards), and even worker cooperatives were equally suspect. The crux of his argument was the power of the ruling elite:

Does not the Aristocracy in fact have a thousand ways of neutralizing all the concessions that are extracted from it, and of taking back with one hand what it gives with the other? By the sole power of its monopoly on the products of the soil and of industry . . . all those apparent ameliorations would soon disappear; they would only be a drop of balm in an ocean of sorrows!!! Let us therefore let the system of inequity that oppresses us crumble under its own weight! No props or palliatives! Let us concentrate all our efforts on working for the system of the future![103]

Cabet demonstrated throughout his writings that he considered political action on the part of the working class to be the road to its salvation. But simultaneous with the drive for political reform must be the growth of a commitment to total social reconstruction, to communism. The tactics he endorsed entailed the awakening of working-class political consciousness through communist propaganda and the winning of public opinion to the communist goal. Society would be transformed, root and branch, by a majority of committed communists at the polls. The design was to create a great and overwhelming communist flood, a mass movement.

The Diffusion of Icarianism

From the founding of *Le Populaire* in March 1841 to the trial of several Icarians at Toulouse in September 1843, the movement passed through its formative phase. This period was marked by the diffusion of Icarian principles throughout much of France. Although we have no detailed figures on the circulation of *Le Populaire* during this period, it is clear that there was little change in the total number of subscribers between 1841 and the summer of 1844. The first report on the circulation of the paper appears in *Le Populaire* of June 5, 1844. The first press run (March 1841) was 2,000, but this was cut back to 1,500 beginning with issue number 10 (January 30, 1842).[104] It would appear that at first most of the papers actually sold were purchased by Parisians. But

---

[103] *Ibid.*, Supplément, Oct. 10, 1841.
[104] *Ibid.*, May 8, 1842.

in 1844, 737 copies were sold in Paris while 877 went to subscribers in the departments.[105] These figures suggest that Cabet
lost Parisian support during this period but made it up with
new adherents from the departments. In the long run this provincial success would be the most noteworthy feature of the Icarian
movement.

How was Icarianism originally spread beyond the environs of
Paris? We lack many details concerning the process, but, thanks
to Prudhommeaux, we know that Cabet had an agent named
Charles Chameroy, a traveling salesman for a Lyonnais commercial
house.[106] Chameroy apparently had a moderately good income, but
it was not sufficient to be of any real financial assistance to the
movement.[107] This commercial traveler was originally attracted to
Cabet by the latter's *Histoire populaire.* On November 28, 1841,
Chameroy, having received a friendly letter from Cabet and a copy
of the *Voyage en Icarie,* wrote from Troyes that he had converted
to Icarian communism and that he desired to put himself at Cabet's
service. He would propagate the doctrine as he traveled. Although
his motives are not entirely clear, a letter from "Chaville" (Chameroy's pseudonym) in *Le Populaire* on July 3, 1842, indicates that
his Christian beliefs played a part. "Today, when the Catholic
faith is nearly extinct, the heart of the man who needs belief will
find in communism the way to fulfill his soul; instead of an imaginary celestial paradise, he will find a probable terrestrial paradise."
Five months later he urged Cabet "to report [Christ's] words in
favor of equality and Community."

Chameroy proved an invaluable assistant. His travels took him
throughout France. The following itinerary, reported to Cabet from
Reims on December 31, 1841, renders an idea of the territory he
covered in a four-month period:

Soissons, Jan. 5, 1842	Sedan, Jan. 13
Reims, Jan. 8	Avesnes, Jan. 20

[105] Figures for May 2, 1844, as printed in *Le Populaire* of June 5.

[106] Prudhommeaux, "Un Commis-voyageur en communisme icarien:
Chameroy, disciple de Cabet," *La Révolution de 1848,* XXIV and XXV
(1927–28).

[107] In 1843 he wrote Cabet of his design to marry an heiress in order to
fulfill such a role, but Cabet dissuaded him from doing so because it vio-
lated Icarian ethics. Chameroy to Cabet, Vitry-le-François, Feb. 14, 1843,
ibid., XXV, 152.

Laon, Jan. 30	Compiègne, March 10
St. Quentin, Feb. 8	Melun, March 20
Douai, Feb. 15	Orléans, March 30
Lille, Feb. 24	Montargis, April 10
Arras, March 2	Provins, April 20[108]

Seeing himself as an "advance sentinel of the sacred battalion of Humanity" (Cabet called him his "Saint Paul"), Chameroy moved from town to town contacting known liberals, garnering subscriptions to *Le Populaire* and selling copies of Cabet's major works. Most of his contacts were originally not workers but rather "friends of the people" in Chameroy's own social stratum. He was more convinced than Cabet himself that the wealthy should be converted: "Ah! if the rich and the powerful understood the situation as I do, how they would give themselves over to the enlightenment of the people and strive to know its thoughts." The rich must come to this realization because otherwise the people will rise one day and attack their property. He would, therefore, tell the "store owners, the merchants" of the misery of today and the unjust organization of society.[109] Chameroy sent ahead to people he intended to contact a circular stressing the need for dedicated patriots to give material support to the Icarian cause.[110]

But the drive for bourgeois affiliation was less than successful. As Chameroy resignedly remarked in 1843: "I underline the title *commerçant* (merchant) because, for 99 per cent of the *commerçants,* there exist no political principles. The best form of government [in their eyes] is the one that allows them the most merchandise and procures for them the most benefits in making them pay the fewest taxes; but they find it puerile to involve themselves in politics or in Social Science which, they say, does not concern them."[111] Still, his propaganda somehow found receptive ears among workers in the craft industries. Precisely how this took place on a general level is lost to us.[112] Fortunately, some information

---

108 *Ibid.,* XXIV, 73.
109 *Ibid.,* 74 and *Le Populaire,* July 3, 1842.
110 Prudhommeaux, "Un commis-voyageur," XXIV, 65–66.
111 Letter from Chaville, *Le Populaire,* July 20, 1843.
112 In at least one case—Lyons itself—a submovement was well under way before Chameroy joined Cabet's camp (Chameroy probably came to

concerning the early development of Cabet's following in Reims survives, and this allows one to guess about the process elsewhere. Through an original contact with one of his customers—a local merchant of Reims—Chameroy came to know one of the latter's clerks, a man named Mauvais. Through Mauvais, who had friends among the artisans, initial excitement over the Icarian doctrine was generated. As Chameroy noted in 1843: "I am very happy [with the situation] at Reims. M. Mauvais has made propaganda well above that I had hoped from him. He has put me in contact with citizen Jandon, shoemaker. . . . The latter is very well qualified in terms of his erudition, his subtlety of mind, his elocution. With his devotion to the Icarian cause, he can render us great services."[113] Word thus circulated from friend to friend. We are ignorant as to whether any public presentations of Icarian doctrine took place, but it seems unlikely. Cabet wanted to do nothing to alarm the police. Private conversations and circulation of his newspaper and works seem to have provided the basic avenues of proselytism in the initial stages of growth. Chameroy, early recognizing the need to find other ways to arouse workers' interest in Cabet and his doctrines, contributed an important suggestion: it would clearly aid the cause to publish an "Icarian almanac." Popular almanacs—containing facts and figures on a multitude of subjects, home remedies for common illnesses, practical advice on legal matters, tips to consumers, as well as political and social doctrine —were common in much of Western Europe. Chameroy also suggested that it might be wise to soft-pedal communist doctrine in the almanac in favor of basic democratic principles.[114] Cabet took this advice to heart and in November 1842 brought out the first *Almanach icarien astronomique, scientifique, pratique, industriel, statistique, politique et social.* A new one appeared each year thereafter until 1848. The *Almanach* was immenesly successful. The first issue went through two printings before December 9, when a third was in the making. Cabet justifiably remarked: "This success, which has surpassed our anticipations and our hopes, attests to the

---

Icarianism under the influence of this group). The early growth of Lyonnais Icarianism will be discussed below.

[113] Chameroy to Cabet, Charleville, June 8, 1843, in Prudhommeaux, "Un Commis-voyageur," XXV, 165.

[114] Chameroy to Cabet, Troyes, Nov. 28, 1841, *ibid.,* XXIV, 69–72,

immense progress Icarian communist ideas have made."[115] The following year 8,000 copies of the new *Almanach* were sold and in 1844–1845 10,000.

In the provinces, as Chameroy's propaganda efforts began to have effect, cadres of Icarian sympathizers developed. By the middle of 1842, Cabet was satisfied enough with the growth of his provincial following to talk of choosing "correspondents" of *Le Populaire* in each department.[116] These men, apparently singled out by Chameroy (we know this was the case with Mauvais of Reims), came to play crucial roles in the growth of the Icarian movement. They acted as distributors of *Le Populaire* in their localities, sold Cabet's works, gathered signatures for declarations of support, corresponded with Cabet concerning the progress of his doctrine in their localities, reported disputes among Icarians, discussed general problems of note in their areas, and organized meetings. In short, they were the local leaders of the Icarian movement. There seems always to have been an inner group of Icarian adherents closely connected with each correspondent, and major discussions concerning the best means to propagate their principles and to combat local opponents, as well as the fundamental arguments over Icarian doctrine and tactics, took place within this circle.

The propaganda efforts of the correspondents and their lieutenants is best illustrated by the work of Lyonnais Icarians, where documentation is more abundant. But regional recruitment drives clearly were undertaken elsewhere. In the West, radiating from Nantes, an oval of "Icarian cities," including Rennes, Tours, Niort, and Angoulême, is discernible. Around Niort correspondent Paul Guay traveled to Luçon, Fontenay-le-Comte, Châtillerault, Saint-Jean d'Angély, and La Rochelle. Reims and Toulon served as centers of influence for their departments, while Toulouse sent out tendrils to much of Languedoc. In 1847 authorities discovered Icarian ties among the textile towns of Aisne, dominated by Saint-Quentin. Rémois propagandists had assisted in developing this network. Important groups also existed in the Paris region, especially at Versailles and Choisy-le-Roi; Paris Icarians surely helped in building these cadres. Such clusters of Icarian support no doubt

---

[115] *Le Populaire,* Dec. 9, 1842.
[116] *Ibid.,* July 3, 1842.

were generated by methods similar to those practiced in the better-known case of Lyons.

The basic source for the Lyonnais network are the files of the Ministry of Justice. One would expect the authorities to have been on the alert for such manifestations of "association," and it might be argued, therefore, that the reports of the procureurs-général are not to be entirely trusted. But Chapius, one of Cabet's chiefs in Lyons, wrote personally to his mentor that he had traveled to Givors and Rive-de-Gier for propaganda purposes and to assess the state of the movement:

> Two days ago I returned from Rive-de-Gier and Givors, and I take a moment to inform you of the result of my trip and what I have learned there.
>
> The intent of this tour was to see if I could sell some almanacs; since you already have correspondents there [Boussac and Faure, respectively], I was unable to place many of them. Nevertheless, I am not sorry that I made the trip because I have learned many things about which you should be informed.[117]

This says nothing about the origins of Icarianism in either city, but neither does it indicate that there was anything unusual about Chapius' trip. Moreover, Interior Minister Duchâtel reported that "attempts at affiliation have taken place in the rural communes of the Rhône and in the neighboring departments. One Sr Chappius [*sic*] went to Vienne (Isère) two or three times in the course of the winter."[118]

The Justice files underline the scope of Icarian operations in the region. After the first uprising among the miners at Rive-de-Gier in the spring of 1844 Piou, procureur-général of Lyons, reported that "Troubles of this nature should merit the attention of the authorities all the more since the doctrines of communism tend to penetrate the mines and since people are trying to establish a certain solidarity between the miners and the workers of Lyons. The government . . . cannot take too many precautions with regard

---

[117] Chapius, noting that "your correspondents are not keeping you abreast of everything that is happening," then went on to describe the persecution of Icarians at Givors. Chapius to Cabet, Nov. 6, 1844, Papiers Cabet, VIII, BHVP.

[118] Duchâtel to the Garde des Sceaux, March 31, 1844, A.N., BB18 1420 dos 8195.

to these masses of workers aglomerated at the gates of the second city of the Kingdom wherein numerous elements of disorder exist."[119] He reported later that a "commission" was paid to go to Rive-de-Gier to preach communism during the troubles.[120] By the later months of 1846 the effect of communist propaganda in the coal basin had become a source of concern to Piou. Because of the activities of Bézanac, a man formerly involved in "communist" groups in the Croix-Rousse and Lyons and now on a "visit" to Rive-de-Gier, and Boussac, Cabet's correspondent at Rive-de-Gier, "the invasion of communism into the coal basin is a very grave fact. A dangerous affiliation between the workers of the Loire and those of Lyons has been established."[121] This clearly links an Icarian leader of the Loire with a Lyonnais activist, although we are ignorant of Bézanac's precise ideological credentials.

The second documented thread is the Lyons-Isère relationship. Correspondent Vincent Cöeffé of Vienne was originally a Lyonnais and surely retained his Lyons connections when he moved to Vienne in 1842. We have already seen that Chapius of Lyons made trips to Vienne in 1843–1844. In 1846 the police discovered among Cöeffé's papers a letter from Raffin, an Icarian of Croix-Rousse. This in turn led to investigations of Raffin, Faucon and three other Lyonnais communists. Other letters were found (along with numerous brochures by Cabet and letters from him) linking them with communists elsewhere. At the same time, "one of these letters [found among Cöeffé's papers in Vienne] calls attention to Grenoble as already having a small number of sectarians who make active propaganda." It was also revealed that Rémond of Lyons, an Icarian dissident by that time, was in Grenoble and "has contacted a small number of people who sympahtize with his point of view." Concerning the whole affair, Piou was unable to find any-

[119] Procureur-général de Lyon to the Garde des Sceaux, May 30, 1844, A.N., BB[18] 1438 dos 1219.
[120] Jan. 14, 1845, BB[18] 1428 dos 9580. It is unclear whether this activity was specifically the work of Icarians.
[121] Report of Oct. 27, 1846; for the names of the activists propagating "communism" see the letter of the Garde des Sceaux to the Minister of the Interior, Dec. 10, 1846, A.N., BB[18] 1441 dos 1992. Tristan Duché, a professor who acted as lawyer for the miners tried for strikes and coalitions during this period, is also listed; he was not a communist, however. See also *Le Populaire*, June 27, 1846.

thing demonstrating the existence of an "illicit association"; Cöeffé and Raffin convinced him that the links among their group comprised merely an "intellectual brotherhood," that they "prepare and hasten" social regeneration by these informal ties.[122]

Thus Lyons and other key centers of Icarian strength carried the cause to other towns and cities in France and maintained links with them. The network spread, and a community of interest began to grow. One example is Cabet's story of the funeral of Alphonse Leroy, a Parisian currier and ardent Icarian. The funeral cortege to Père Lachaise was followed by some 200 Icarian mourners. Cabet made it clear that Leroy's shocking death (by accidental asphyxiation) was an *affaire* in the Icarian camp.[123] The most striking evidence of a "party" attitude among the Icarians, however, was the constant flow of petitions and addresses signed by dozens and sometimes hundreds of adherents. The earliest instance was the *Protestation des ouvriers de Paris contre le duel, les bastilles, le monopole de la presse et la peine de mort* of 1841. Ten of Cabet's most enthusiastic supporters circulated this statement favoring Cabet in his conflict with *Le National* and gathered 948 signatures in three days.[124] While all the signatories did not designate themselves "Icarian communists," this was the first use of an instrument that was to be unique to the Cabetists. Since Cabet placed such great emphasis on the conversion of public opinion, he naturally sought to demonstrate that he had a block of support behind him, thus giving greater weight to his general doctrine and specific pronouncements.[125] No other element of French working-class opinion of the day gave such overt proof of its loyalty and cohesion.

The first manifesto giving specific support to Cabet's brand of communism was a piece printed in *Le Populaire* entitled "Des Ouvriers communistes à leurs frères."[126] At press time, it had been

---

[122] Procureur-général de Lyon to the Garde des Sceaux, reports of June 30, July 10, and June 29, 1846, A.N., BB[18] 1441 dos 1992.

[123] *Le Populaire*, Feb. 10, 1843.

[124] *Ibid.*, July 25, 1841.

[125] In his debate with the Fourierists in 1845–1847, he would point to these indications of support and say, in effect, that since he had more supporters, his doctrine was more "scientifically" correct than theirs!

[126] *Le Populaire*, Jan. 30, 1842.

signed by 1,150 Parisian workers. Whether or not it was written by Cabet himself, it manifested a definite *prise de position* on the part of a body of individuals showing their firm adherence to his principles.

It is said that we want to live in idleness. . . . That is not true! We want to work in order to live; and we are more laborious than those who slander us. But sometimes work is lacking, sometimes it is too long, and kills us or ruins our health. Wages are insufficient for our most indispensable needs. These inadequate wages, unemployment, illness, taxes, old age—which comes so early to us—throw us into misery. It is horrible for a great number of us. There is no future, either for us or our children. This is not living! And yet we are the producers of all. Without us the rich would have nothing or would be forced to work to have bread, clothes, furniture, and lodging. It is unjust! We want a different organization of labor; that is why we are communists.

Although they fully agree with Cabet's opposition to those communists who would abolish the family and marriage, they "are discontented because those who are married are miserable for the sake of their wives and their children, for whom they cannot provide an education. And then the majority cannot marry; this wounds us more deeply." They disclaim the epithets "barbarian" and "anarchist" and go on to say: "We do not want misery; we want our rights because we are men and because nature is the mother of all. . . . We want our rights just as the bourgeois who made the revolution of 1789 against the nobles and the clergy [wanted theirs]. But we want unhappiness for no one; we want union among us, equality and fraternity among all Frenchmen. We also want order." They also explicitly deny that they are materialists and point out that there are two kinds of communists, the materialists and the Icarians. "People say that we are materialists, atheists, and that we do not recognize duty. They are liars! We do not want to discuss theology because we do not understand it and because it can never give us work or bread; but we want to live as respectable [*honnête*] people, and we want our duties as our rights." They conclude by vowing to follow Cabet's *ligne droite* and the practice of civil courage.[127]

[127] *Ibid.*

This kind of manifestation of cohesive, if not highly organized, support was echoed again and again as Icarianism spread to the provinces. By August of 1842 Cabet could state that "twelve of the principal towns of France have sent us addresses of adherence expressing the same Icarian convictions." These addresses were full of the personal praise that Cabet liked to hear. Most of them were printed in *Le Populaire,* sometimes with the names and occupations of the supporters, sometimes with their number only. Cabet also made every effort to establish a distinct school of thought. Toward the end of 1842, motivated by the advice of Chameroy,[128] he officially adopted the designation "communistes-Icariens" and employed the adjective "icarien(ne)" in labeling his projects and ideas (*cours icarien, revue icarienne, principes icariens,* and so forth). This no doubt further contributed to the formation of a group mentality among Cabet's followers throughout the country.

Information on the early growth of the Icarian movement is sparse. This lack of evidence in itself suggests that the impact of Cabet in France from 1841 to 1843 was modest. No mention is made of Cabet or his works in the local press in the major centers of later Icarian influence, with the exception of Lyons and Paris. Nevertheless, from the autumn of 1842, primarily because of the work of Chameroy, the Icarian movement was clearly beginning to grow in towns such as Reims, Givors, Vienne, Tours, and Toulouse. An increasing number of correspondents were being chosen, and declarations of support began to be sent to Paris. The title "Icarian" had been adopted. An Icarian movement was taking shape. With the Fourierist journal, *Le Nouveau Monde,* one must "recognize that Communism makes progress, the number of its partisans enlarges, and the book of M. Cabet, *Voyage en Icarie,* circulates in the workshops."[129]

---

[128] Chameroy to Cabet, Lons-le-Saulnier, Aug. 3, 1842, in Prudhommeaux, "Un Commis-voyageur," XXIV, 82.

[129] *Le Nouveau Monde,* April 1843.

3 | Cabet's Political Strategy and Its Consequences, 1841–1845

As the Icarian movement began to coalesce, Cabet inaugurated a general political strategy that agitated the entire socialist camp and especially angered a number of his early working-class followers. Its cardinal principles were unity of the left and Icarian communist regimentation and orthodoxy.

In 1900, Félix Bonnaud, a socialist writer of the Jaurès tendency, published a biography of Cabet stressing his contribution to the doctrine of left-wing solidarity. Cabet was held up as an example for Bonnaud's quarrelsome socialist contemporaries. Bonnaud overstated his thesis, but there is considerable truth to it. The key to understanding Cabet's concept of democratic unity is his oft-repeated contention that all "democrats are communists without knowing it." This implied, of course, that he expected any democrat to follow his own road to communism—but even if repulsed Cabet would not simply declare him an enemy. Cabet still carried with him, then, the ideal of the thirties that all republicans (save possibly the men of *Le National*) were natural allies. Chameroy's initial approach to propaganda—courting bourgeois democrats—and Cabet's belief in class conciliation testify to his consistency in this respect.

More difficult to deal with is Cabet's drive to dominate communism in France. He ruthlessly struck out on his near left and right and simultaneously enforced strict adherence and doctrinal conformity among his working-class allies. One might simply interpret this as a sign of megalomania or ideological rigidity. Both were certainly present in his character. But this fails to take into account Cabet's political acumen. Another plausible explanation is that he wanted to build a solid core of rank and file totally devoted to him, thus increasing his bargaining power in the larger political spectrum.

Seen from this angle, Cabet's general strategy can be discerned. He was certainly a committed communist, and his overtures among noncommunist republicans were undertaken to convert them. But he did not write them off as hopeless muddleheads if they failed to see the light. A unified front of the left was more important. At the same time, it was necessary to clear the field of direct competitors in order to establish his claim to leadership of a major element in this front. As political strategy, such an approach is no doubt debatable, but it is hardly the position of a utopian, in the traditional sense of the word. Cabet understood the politics of power, and unquestionably he sought power himself. His goals had changed since the 1830s, but the mechanisms for reaching them remained essentially the same.

Enemies Within

The most striking feature of the early phase of Icarian development was Cabet's continuing struggle against a diverse army of "enemies." Besides answering the few attacks on communism appearing in the government or reformist press, Cabet refuted or simply railed against other writers who sought to speak to the working class. Significantly, however, he remained silent on (or quietly endorsed) the works of most of the major theorists of the day, such as Louis Blanc, Leroux, Proudhon, Pecqueur, and Laponneraye. He was even deferential to J.-J. Pillot, and he only denounced the Fourierists after they attacked him. His principal thrusts were at fellow communists of lesser influence. Especially bitter were his conflicts with his two former lieutenants, Richard Lahautière and Théodore Dézamy. In the course of these acrimonious struggles, the Icarian party suffered internal tremors of a substantial nature. Cabet rationalized his stance in the name of communist unity, the prelude, in his mind, to general unity of the left. "The four or five recently established communist sheets, instead of uniting against their common adversaries, are trapped and paralysed in an internal struggle, and, by the pretexts that several of them have furnished to the enemies of Community, have done the cause more harm than these enemies themselves."[1] Moreover, "there does not exist a Nation or a People, but only citizens; no party, but only partisans; no Opposition, but only oppponents."[2] An oposition so totally divided could never hope to overcome the current political oppression. And the communists could never hope to dominate (or even participate in) the general reformist movement as long as they remained so deeply fragmented.

Before investigating the factional conflicts of the early forties, it is well to pause briefly to evaluate Cabet's own conception of his role at the time. Its most striking feature was his self-image as a professional "social scientist." This gave him the right to condemn any writer who was not. He compared himself to a physician who, because of his deep knowledge of his field, knew and dispensed the proper remedies for a sick society.[3] His role was "to offer to the . . . workers the tribute of long study, considerable experience, and of limitless dedication in order . . . to guide those to whom the present organization [of society] leaves neither the means nor the time to study it and to understand it." Obviously this meant that the workers themselves had no right to meddle in social theorizing. Cabet made this clear in his brochure against *L'Atelier*. He asked its worker-editors how they could arrogate to themselves the role of professional writers when the greatest part of their lives must be spent in the workshop?[4] Elsewhere he granted that "there is no more merit due me for knowing my metier than for you to know yours"[5] but the message was clear. *L'Atelier* did not bother with a formal reply, simply telling their readers to buy Cabet's brochure and "read it; if you do not laugh yourself to tears, it is because you will have pity for a lost soul."[6]

Concerning how a worker should comport himself in the discussion of social questions, Cabet thought: "If you are modest and reserved, if you speak only in order to respond when one questions you, or to take part in the discussion like anybody else, to submit

[1] Cabet, *Ma Ligne droite*, 1.
[2] *Ibid.*, 36.
[3] *Ibid.*, 10.
[4] *Réfutation des doctrines de l'Atelier* (Paris, March, 1842), 9.
[5] *Ma Ligne droite*, 10.
[6] *L'Atelier*, March 1842.

your opinion or to ask for explanations, you will have no need to ask indulgence and pardon; we will listen to you with benevolence; for, while not having education, you can have some good sense and we know that the ignorant worker can have the germ of genius."[7] The workers should therefore be deferential toward their natural intellectual superiors; their role is to follow and, at best, suggest. Let Cabet, the oracle of science and reason, light their way.

Neither Lahautière nor Dézamy, however, was a worker. Cabet regarded their activities, therefore, as a greater threat to his leadership and to communist unity. In 1840 both these young radicals —already won to communism—had collaborated with Cabet on brochures on the Eastern Question. Dézamy, then aged thirty-two, was already well known in his own right. The twenty-eight-year-old Lauhautière was a less significant figure, although *La Fraternité,* a monthly newspaper that he edited from 1841 to 1843, offered the alternative of "spiritual" communism to an audience of radicals. Through him several of Pierre Leroux's key concepts were absorbed into communist thought.[8]

The split with Lahautière came first and rested upon personal and ideological foundations. Cabet, arguing that their theoretical differences were minimal, saw Lahautière's action as pure spite, noting that he resented being excluded from the editorial board of *Le Populaire.* In April, without Cabet's knowledge, he published a bulky brochure, *La Loi sociale,* and a month later, in order, according to Cabet, to compete with *Le Populaire* and divide communism in France, began, after clandestine preparations, to issue *La Fraternité.*[9] Lahautière himself never spoke in print of the split with Cabet, although some lines in his journal's first number seemed aimed at his former associate: "We do not claim to lead anyone; this dictatorial role suits neither our youth nor our principles. We want simply to erect a platform for propaganda."[10] Despite Cabet's focus on the personal aspect, he also recognized

[7] *Le Populaire,* Sept. 3, 1841.

[8] On Lahautière see Charles Chautard, "M. R. de la Hautière, notice nécrologique," *Bulletin de la société archéologique, scientifique et littéraire du vendômois,* XXI (1882), 271–74, and "Richard de la Hautière," *Dict. biog.,* III, 314.

[9] Cabet, *Ma Ligne droite,* 47–48.

[10] *La Fraternité,* May 1841.

an obvious theoretical incompatibility, speaking with the utmost disdain of "the spiritualist, mystic, metaphysical editor of *La Fraternité,* who speaks incessantly of *God,* of faith, of love."[11] A glance at *La Loi sociale* reveals the significance of Leroux's "religion of humanity" in Lahautière's thought. "The grand master of nature . . . put humanity on the earth as a farmer in order to cultivate and fecundate the earth. We are . . . an association of workers charged with the conservation of visible nature; . . . let us consider humanity as a vast workshop, and let us give to each member of the human association, to each worker, his work, his place, and his wage in an equal and just division."[12] This outlook corresponds closely with Leroux's transcendental socialism, as does the concept of each individual living forever in humanity. "The body is a garment; as humanity changes, progresses, and develops, the bodies of men dissolve in order to make room for bodies appropriate for new needs, for the new practices of humanity. . . . [We] will be compensated for our labors in the future life of humanity."[13] Lahautière's philosophical position was far from Cabet's, and this was no doubt the major reason for the split between them.

But *La Fraternité* rallied other anti-Cabetist communists and not only those of spiritualist proclivities. This was what really upset Cabet, for his aim to command communism in France was thwarted by the paper's existence. He therefore berated and even slandered Lahautière in every possible way,[14] apparently hoping to bury him under abuse.

Of greater importance for the early history of the Icarian movement was Cabet's confrontation with the "left deviationists," the materialist communists, especially as represented by the newspaper *L'Humanitaire* and Théodore Dézamy.

L'Humanitaire, of which two issues appeared in July and August of 1841 before it was suppressed by the authorities, was the most radical journal to see the light of day during the July Monarchy.[15]

---

[11] *Le Populaire,* Oct. 10, 1841.

[12] Richard Lahautière, *La Loi sociale* (Paris, 1841), 62–63.

[13] *Ibid.,* 21–22. To compare this with Leroux's doctrine, see especially Pierre Leroux, *De L'Humanité* (Paris, 1840), I, 244–61, and David Owen Evans, *Le Socialisme romantique: Pierre Leroux et ses contemporains* (Paris, 1948), 52–58.

[14] See *Ma Ligne droite,* 52–55.

[15] Both issues may be found among the Cabet papers (with Cabet's marginal comments) at the IISG.

Militantly describing themselves as communists, its editors (Gabriel Charavay, Jules Gay, Jacques Savary, Charassin, Page, Fombertaux, and, above all, J.-J. May) not only demanded pure communism and proclaimed themselves atheists and materialists but also called for the abolition of the family and marriage (in any form) and of the state. They presented a vision of a world without frontiers and of work without fixed occupations. Total racial intermixture was also part of their dream. Men should travel to the four corners of the earth and taste the full range of physical and intellectual delights that life has to offer. The fundamental goal of *L'Humanitaire*'s editors was to recapture natural man, man in his original goodness and purity.[16] They did not agree with *L'Atelier*'s position that only working people knew their true doctrine; exclusion of this sort was unfraternal—this, at least, they held in common with Cabet. The roots of *L'Humanitaire*'s anarchism were to be found in the *Manifeste des égaux* by Babeuf's associate, Sylvain Maréchal, and the editors devoted a long section to the glory of his memory. *L'Humanitaire* did not speak of the means by which the Eldorado it sought might be established, but it was undoubtedly through violent revolution.

Public reaction to this sheet was heated; the second issue of *L'Humanitaire* was devoted almost entirely to the defense of its doctrine against its critics. In the government press and the newspapers of the moderate republican opposition, the doctrines of *L'Humanitaire* were simply considered to be those of communism in general. Its negative influence was therefore far out of proportion to the actual number of communists who supported it. Its appearance was followed by the Quénisset assassination attempt and publication of another radical communist journal, *La Communautaire,* both of which added fuel to the fire.

Cabet was aghast at this public outburst of ultraradical opinion. His work for the levelheaded and respect-building articulation of the communist cause now confronted vociferous extremism. Aside from questioning the competence of the writers in *L'Humanitaire,* however, his refutation was calm, even conciliatory in tone. Perhaps he feared that some of his adherents would be swept away by

---

[16] *L'Humanitaire,* July 1841. Interestingly, Cabet wrote in the margin beside these remarks, "excess of a good principle," indicating that his immediate personal reaction was not totally negative.

the paper's libertarian dream. "Let us begin . . . by conquering the biases and prejudices that for centuries have forestalled the idea of Community; let us reassure the minds that our enemies seek to frighten; let us avoid especially everything that furnishes a pretext for accusations of debauchery and immorality; let us instead make every effort to make the doctrine simple, clear, easy to understand."[17]

With Dézamy, however, Cabet showed no mercy. Their confrontation developed into a wild bout of personal attacks and empty-headed arguments over doctrinal details. During the first half of 1841, when the younger man was working as a paid employee of *Le Populaire,* the two remained on good terms despite Dézamy's greater militance. After the first few issues, which did not sell as well as Cabet expected, he had to let Dézamy go in order to cut back expenses. Dézamy was generally regarded as a close associate of Cabet—even the men of *L'Humanitaire* identified him as Cabet's lieutenant. But on February 18, 1842, he sent his former mentor a letter expressing his "doctrinal divergence," asking Cabet to print it in the March issue. This Cabet did not do. Shortly after the letter, Dézamy began bringing out installments of his book, *Le Code de la Communauté.* The dam broke in early April 1842, when he wrote:

> The author of the *Voyage en Icarie* . . . had adopted at first without restriction the system of cities and capitals. In the preface to his second edition he admits that one can organize Community with cities or without cities, etc., etc. There are without doubt several other points of his work that after a new examination M. Cabet will hasten to modify in the third edition; for M. Cabet has nothing in common with those shabby people motivated by vanity who hesitate to give up a first opinion when they have knowledge of better solutions. No one esteems more than I the good offices of M. Cabet in this regard.[18]

The irony was unmistakable. This passage motivated Cabet to write a brief brochure entitled *Propagande communiste, ou questions à discuter et à soutenir ou à écarter* (Paris, April 1842).[19] He did not attack Dézamy personally but said that the "young writers" do not understand the ways of propaganda. One does not

[17] Cabet, *Réfutation des doctrines de L'Humanitaire* (Paris, 1841), 7.
[18] Théodore Dézamy, *Le Code de la Communauté* (Paris, 1842), 36.
[19] Cabet made this clear in *Le Populaire,* May 8, 1842.

talk about minor issues like cities or, especially, such touchy ones as the family. Was it not, for instance, "the question of free love that killed the Saint-Simonians?" The two cardinal rules for propaganda were "to simplify" and "to condense."[20]

In the May 8 issue of *Le Populaire* Cabet unleashed a full attack on Dézamy, starting by calmly reviewing the story of their early relationship, then (at last) printing Dézamy's letter, and building to a crescendo by claiming that everything in *La Code de la Communauté* was stolen from the *Voyage en Icarie*—except, of course, the opinions on cities and the family. This set the stage for one of the most scathing personal attacks in the history of polemical writing, Dézamy's *Calomnies et politique de M. Cabet: Réfutation par des faits et par sa biographie,* which appeared in June. Every facet of Cabet's life and work was assessed in the most negative manner possible, from the days of the Charbonnerie, where Cabet was pictured as a coward, to tales of how he failed to publish certain articles by Dézamy and others out of fear that they might outshine him. After calling an assembly of *Le Populaire*'s shareholders for support on July 18, Cabet issued a 112-page personal apologia and point by point refutation of his adversary.[21]

Cabet's various conflicts and struggles during 1841 and 1842 appear to have had a dual effect. On one hand, a number of his original supporters in Paris followed the banners of either Lahautière or the materialists. For instance, of the original ten shareholders responsible for writing and gathering signatures for the *Protestation* of July 1841, only five—Favard, Marinelli, Tessier, Bruère and Bourgeois—figure on the list of forty-six men who supported Cabet against Dézamy by signing to the "Adresse de la commission des actionnaires" that appeared in *Le Populaire* of August 7, 1842. More important, the number of subscriptions in Paris to *Le Populaire* actually diminished during the first three years of its existence.[22] In both *Toute La Vérité* and, especially, *Les Masques arrachés* of 1844, Cabet alluded to "traitors" who had abandoned him. On the other hand, these conflicts solidified Cabet's following. In having to choose sides, communists of the Cabetist

[20] *Propagande communiste,* 7–8.
[21] *Toute La Vérité au peuple ou Réfutation d'un pamphlet calomniateur* (Paris, 1842).
[22] See above, pp. 99–100.

persuasion found themselves more rigidly attached to a specific school.[23] The way now lay open for the development of a stable party in which doctrinal orthodoxy could be enforced. It was no accident that adoption of the title "Icarian" came after all these difficulties.

Working-Class Reactions: The Example of Lyons

The specific effects of such conflicts on the movement can be most clearly seen in Lyons. Unlike most other provincial cities, the "second eye" of France already had an impressive history of conscious working-class action. The great silk manufactory had long dominated the city's industrial life, and the peculiar relations of production—in which some 750 *fabricants* (merchant-manufacturers) put out silk thread to be woven at piece rates by 8,000 *chef d'ateliers* (master weavers) and their 30,000 journeymen—made for a worker unity unparalleled elsewhere in France. The interests of the chefs d'ateliers coincided with those of their journeymen; the former were highly skilled and usually well educated, giving Lyons a body of natural working-class leaders, again unique in the country. The great insurrection of November 1831 is rightly regarded as one of the significant milestones in the struggle for the emancipation of the working man.

Like those of their Parisian brethren the energies of the Lyonnais had been somewhat vitiated by the repression that followed the days of April 1834. But the idea of political engagement as a basis for emancipation had been firmly implanted.[24] It was not surprising, therefore, that after Paris Lyons was the major center for recruitment to secret societies. The Blanquist societies had branches in Lyons, and the Charbonnerie Réformée seems to have had its most important section there. The latter was especially influential in developing communism among the silkworkers, the *canuts*. Indeed the authorities felt that by 1842 there had occurred "a movement of transformation from republican opinions to the adoption

[23] Cabet's own assessment of categories of communists and the need for Icarian orthodoxy is best seen in *Le Démocrate devenu communiste malgré lui ou réfutation de la brochure de M. Thoré intitulée "Du Communisme en France"* (Paris, Sept. 1842).

[24] Fernand Rude, "Le Mouvement ouvrier à Lyon," *Revue de psychologie des peuples* (1959), 230–31.

of the extravagant ideas of communism" among all the secret societies of Lyons.[25] The secret societies, however, never represented more than a fraction of the politically conscious working class. It was ultimately Cabet who turned communism in Lyons into a mass movement. Still, the nature of this development—even in its initial stages—revealed the problems that Cabet's political strategy posed for those who decided to follow him.

The history of the communist newspaper *Le Travail*, which first appeared in Lyons in July 1841, provides an early example of the nature of these difficulties. The essential document is a letter to Cabet from one of the founders of *Le Travail*, Antoine Coignet, a chef d'atelier.[26] Coignet, having read the *Voyage en Icarie*, was already a "partisan . . . of [Cabet's] communitarian principles" and hoped to bring out a paper "in the mode" of *L'Atelier* "but communist." "The idea did not immediately bear fruit" because of a lack of both capable writers and "enough communists of firm conviction." But after a while *"Voyage en Icarie, Comment je suis communiste . . .* came to turn many minds to communist [*sic*]. The *Voyage en Icarie* especially was then a true *sun* enlightening the people. . . . At that time there was not the least dissidence among the communists, division existed only between the communists and reformists."[27] Five silkworkers, Coignet, Beaume, Cathabard, Raymond, and Busque, were elected as editors of *Le Travail*.[28] All of these men were, and remained, ardent supporters of Cabet.[29] The prospectus for *Le Travail, organe de la rénovation sociale* appeared in May, and the Icarian orientation of the editors was clear. Although the paper was run by workers, they did not wish to deepen class divisions but rather sought general fraternity following "the glorious maxim of Christ . . . : 'love one another;

[25] See the final report of the procureur du roi and the attendant documents sent to the Garde des Sceaux on Feb. 8, 1842, A.N., BB[18] 1397 dos 2703.

[26] Coignet to Cabet, Sept. 27, 1842, Papiers Cabet, V, BHVP.

[27] *Ibid.* This was no doubt an exaggeration, but it helps to pinpoint the period of the greatest impact of *Voyage en Icarie* in Lyons—the winter of 1840–1841.

[28] These men are listed at the end of the prospectus of *Le Travail* (Journal no. 5671, Bibliothèque municipale de Lyon).

[29] See Cabet, *Utile et Franche Explication avec les communistes lyonnais sur des questions pratiques* (Paris, Oct. 1842), 19. Léo Busque later emigrated to Nauvoo.

that is the entire law of the Lord.' " They also shared Cabet's economic optimism. "Therefore administer the soil and industry wisely; divide social wealth equitably; call all men to the great banquet of fraternal life, and you will give to each material well-being and moral pleaures unknown to the men most favored by the gifts of fortune, because you will . . . also see your brothers participate in the same happiness." Communism was not only "the last and most complete expression of human reason in the domain of social relations" but also "the veritable Christianity as applied to the relations of life."[30]

But between the publication of the prospectus and the first issue of the paper in June, division broke out within the editorial board. Coignet and two others resigned and a "newly elected" editor said he would "have the color of the paper changed." This man was Louis Blache, a member of the Charbonnerie Réformée. In the July issue, he alone was listed as the *gérant* (manager). Blache was not ideologically opposed to Cabet, but he tended more toward Babouvism and was unwilling to lick Cabet's boots. Since this change, said Coignet, "we have moved from division to division. The spirit of comradship of the secret societies, or intrigue, came to invade our true principles."[31]

The real problem, however, was a split between Cabet's devotees and those sympathetic to his views but unwilling to accept his line concerning competitors. *La Fraternité* had appeared in May, and on May 20 Cabet made his first attack on Lahautière. Coignet had sided with Cabet, but the June 1841 issue (no. 1) of *Le Travail* disapproved. It began by attributing the current division to "personal feelings" and then carried an article entitled *"Le Populaire et La Fraternité."* The editors could not conceive of two communist papers being at odds on basic doctrine, but different organs could express themselves differently, appealing to different types. *Le Travail* simply proposed that Cabet and Lahautière agree to publish their papers at alternative times of the month.[32] The Lyons paper was thus promoting an open forum of communist ideas as

[30] Prospectus to *Le Travail.* As the summation of all philosophy, the editors explicitly stated that their doctrine also drew upon "the love and devotion of Saint-Simonism" and the "rational purity of Fourier."

[31] Coignet to Cabet, Sept. 27, 1842 (BHVP).

[32] *Le Travail*, June 1841.

the proper basis for the growth of the party. It even welcomed *L'Humanitaire* when it appeared.[33]

Before long Cabet placed *Le Travail* among the friends of *La Fraternité* who were against him. Lyonnais communists were in effect presented with a choice of either coming into sheeplike accord with Cabet or being considered his enemies.

Three issues of *Le Travail* appeared, but then it was suppressed in the wake of the Quénisset assassination attempt. In October Blache was linked with the Charbonnerie Réformée. The authorities were unable to prove that *Le Travail* was the "organ of the society" because of incomplete documentation.[34] The editors could only be charged, therefore, with press offenses. After being convicted in February, they appealed their sentence. It is interesting commentary on their open attitude that they first asked Cabet to be their lawyer; only after his refusal did they turn to their alleged ally, Lahautière, who came to Lyons in June of 1842 and won their appeal.

Thereafter, a number of Lyonnais communists mistrusted Cabet's motives, even though they might have been deeply impressed by the *Voyage en Icarie*. Many were also disgusted with the game of personalities. If the Lahautière-Cabet dispute contributed to this attitude, the Dézamy affair further exacerbated it. Both Dézamy and Cabet sent copies of their venomous pamphlets to Lyonnais communists in the hope that they would be distributed. Five communists whom Cabet considered to be his mandatories joined forces to reply to both writers, stating precisely what they thought of these leaders' recent antics and expressing their own feelings about a variety of subjects concerning the working-class movement.

These two letters reveal a great deal about the mentality of at least the Lynnnois working class and constitute important documents among the limited expressions of working-class opinion that have survived from this period.[35] It is impossible to determine how

[33] *Ibid.*, July 1841.

[34] A.N., BB[18] 1397 dos 2703.

[35] Both letters (a copy of the one to Dézamy was sent to Cabet) are to be found among the Papiers Cabet, VII, BHVP, and are clearly the most significant documents in this collection. They are undated, but Cabet states that he received them on Sept. 13, 1842 (*Utile et Franche Explication*, 2). I have published these letters and analyzed their contents in "Deux Lettres

large a body of opinion they actually represented, but one can see in them the origins of attitudes that would characterize a majority of the Lyonnais communists in 1848. One of the authors was Louis Greppo, a representative to the National Assembly from Lyons in 1848 and one of the most famous of the working-class legislators in the Constituent Assembly. The other four were Guillaume Vincent, a bookkeeper; Ginaud, silkworker; Perret, silkworker; and Calandras, worker. We know nothing about Ginaud[36] and Calandras. Vincent became one of the founders of the workers' militia, Les Voraces, which played an important role in the revolution of 1848 in Lyon. Jean-Marie Perret would be elected to the municipal council of La Guillotière in 1848 and then president of the Committee of Public Safety created in Lyons on September 4, 1870.[37]

They began their letter to Cabet by condemning his publication of *Toute La Vérité,* saying that "when a man embraces . . . an apostolate of fraternity, even unjust attacks . . . ought not make him depart . . . from the calmness and dignity that his mission imposes upon him." They then reproached Cabet for his opinion that workers could not be theorists, his use of his own "age and experience" as a means of putting down younger writers, and his dictatorial bearing. "Let all egalitarian doctrines come to light without bitter criticism no matter whether the author is savant or worker, young or old." They reiterated the "open forum of ideas" approach endorsed by *Le Travail.* "But if impatient and hardy minds rush into the high regions of thought and fall into notable errors, it is not necessary to anathematize them, but rather to lead them back to the truth by the power of reason. And, moreover, side by side with their mistakes, perhaps they have along the way gleaned several truths that we would not have discovered in an inferior sphere."

They also criticized Cabet's social theory in two respects. They

---

inédites de cinq ouvriers lyonnais à Cabet et à Dézamy," *Revue d'histoire économique et sociale,* 47 (1969), 529–39.

[36] This spelling is taken from Cabet, *Utile et Franche Explication.* The signature on the letter is not at all clear, and he may have misread it. Could this possibly be Jean-Baptiste Grinand, who, with Joseph Benoit, had been involved in communist secret societies (including Blanqui's Society of the Seasons) in the late 1830s? Perhaps, though the profession of the latter was teacher, not silkworker (*Dict. Biog.,* II, 303–4).

[37] *Dict. Biog.,* III, 515 and 205.

diverged on the issue that had been brought to the fore by the publication of *L'Humanitaire,* the abolition of the family. Without supporting this idea, they felt that Cabet "constitutes the family in a mode in certain respects patriarchal and necessarily individualistic from the point of view of real and complete fraternity." Secondly, and of infinitely greater importance, they disagreed with his attitude toward the bourgeoisie.

We want to speak of your opinion that the bourgeoisie is indispensible to the triumph of democracy. In that, we are not completely of your opinion. First of all, let us define our words. We call bourgeois the man of leisure, the rentier, or better still he who exercises those functions called *high* [*relevée*] and who report fat salaries; as for all those who have to work for a living, we include all of them, whatever be their type of work, under the denomination of the people, in the characteristic sense of the word.

It is unfortunate that they are not more explicit; what about industrialists or the fabricants of Lyons? The following comments seem to throw all the rich into the category of bourgeois, and certainly, the "characteristic" sense of the world *peuple* would not include capitalists:

Do you seriously believe that the first, who exploit the second and who consider this exploitation to be a right, would ever subscribe to any attempt at amelioration, however small it might be? We do not share in our hearts the thought that you formulate thus: "Come to me, follow me, make yourselves men of the people, or I will. . . ." But we believe that the bourgeoisie will always defend the present social order by every means, even the most odious. And do you not see that their egotism leaves them unfeeling and cold with respect to our troubles? Do you not see that these ungrateful and cold masters leave us to die of cold and hunger at the doorsteps of their sumptuous residences, which we have enriched by our sweat? . . . Do not reckon that the bourgeois will ever do anything to alleviate the burden of our misery; let us count only on ourselves, on our own forces and on the power of our ideas that must be spread everywhere in the depths of that immense family of workers; for the people, without the aid of the bourgeois is not, as you say, "a vain word, an illusion, a deception, even a nonentity"; the people has its political and moral education to make or to complete, and, this result attained, you will see if its hand will be unqualified to destroy and to build.

This is a significant statement of class consciousness. The working-man must recognize his enemies and not be duped by dreams of class collaboration.

On the other side of the ledger, however, these workers rejected two of Dézamy's opinions. After reproaching him more severely than Cabet for his role in the conflict, they challenged his negative comments on Robespierre and on dedication (*dévouement*). Their comments on both subjects render important insights into the nature of French working-class political consciousness during the 1840s.

How is it possible, citizen, that the purest and most glorious personification of the revolution, in whom all public and private virtues are summed up, has been, on your part, the subject of bitter blame? How is it possible that the man who proposed . . . great revolutionary measures [and] sacred principles of social order and of public morality, whose entire political life was one long struggle against the enemies of the people, and who finally crowned his noble career by martyring himself for the holy cause of humanity . . . finds in you only a critic who has been deplorably misled? But if the immortal dedication of Robespierre the younger and of Lebas, who wanted to die with him whom you accuse; if that heroic act of virtue unique in the annals of history says nothing to the soul of the oppressors of the people, should it be without significance for you, a sincere republican? But if that is not sufficient for you, will you not believe the testimony of two men whom you venerate as do we, of Babeuf and of Buonarotti [*sic*] . . . ?

But let us speak of dedication. . . . Your first outrage had to have the second as a consequence, the negation of dedication. Dedication, you say, does not have its root in the human heart. Self-preservation is man's pre-eminent instinct and any act of dedication is a sacrifice of the human *me*. Dedication . . . is like an attack of fever that can carry us to heroic acts but that does not have to be preached, and under no circumstances has it the right to our veneration. There is the sense of your words. Ah citizen! What a condemnable error! and how grievous would the future be if such a doctrine could find some credit.

They were, in fact, condemning Dézamy's deterministic materialism. They range themselves decidedly on the side of human volition in the processes of history, a stand inherent in any moral outlook endorsing the primacy of fraternal dedication. They continued:

But if we wished to appeal to history, we would find acts of well-considered dedication, of existences entirely given to dedication. What name do you give to the action of a man who sacrifices his life for the happiness of his fellow man when he knows that his death will be clothed in eternal oblivion. . . . With us, you long for the moment when the holy insurrection of peoples will break out . . . , and you come to deny dedication? And where, then, are you going to find those men who will have to run first to a certain death if you preach the grievous doctrine of personal interest? Oh, such an ungodly [*impie*] doctrine might seduce a few gutless philosophers, a few men of arid and cold heart; but among the people, with fire in its soul, with its noble and generous instincts, it will never implant itself.

These words provide remarkable proof of the emotional zeal that animated the spirit of many working-class militants in the 1848 era. *Robespierre, dévouement:* these symbols were emblazoned on the heart of the people, and to deny them was sacrilege.

In October 1842, Cabet published a reply to his five critics, his *Utile et Franche Explication avec les communistes lyonnais sur des questions pratiques.* The issues had already become a public one in Lyons because the five had read their letters in open meetings. This indicates that the dissidents were actively trying to win the communist element to their side, but it is not clear whether they wished to form an anti-Icarian communist party in Lyons. From what they had said to both Cabet and Dézamy, however, it would appear that they were determined to go their own way. Whatever the case, Cabet virtually excommunicated them. "I cannot keep from remarking that these five signatories pose as Savants, as Doctors, as infallible Geniuses, and that they speak to me and treat me as if they were my masters, my directors, my commandants, my fathers, my tutors, and my judges."[38] What they did, of course, was to treat him as their equal. How dare they? The main doctrinal question at stake was their working-class exclusivism. This Cabet simply rejected, citing the great services made to the growth of communism by nonworkers (Voyer d'Argenson was the example he cited).

But his fundamental grievance remained their unwillingness to submit to his leadership. He also suggested that many Lyonnais militants wanted to take the lead of the working-class movement

[38] Cabet, *Utile et Franche Explication,* 5–6.

away from Paris.[39] It was only "at the price" of "conducting my pen" that "they will propagate my writings and continue to pay me the tribute of GRATITUDE and *fraternal* ESTEEM." Cabet revealed again that his guiding principle of party organization was unquestioning obedience to him. His final decision, therefore, was "to put an end to all relations, whether with the five signatories, or with the Commission of correspondence [of which only Calandras and Perret were members], and to ask [all Lyonnais communists] for an accounting of the execution of my mandate."[40]

These events in Lyons shed light on the process by which a distinct Icarian party was formed. On September 27 came the decision to take the title "communistes-icariens." Conditions in Lyons seem to have remained in flux, and Cabet was not at all sure whom he could trust. In a long letter to Chameroy on October 28, 1842, he asked whether "the man called Chapius" was "not in accord with the others."[41] As it turned out, Chapius was loyal and became Cabet's correspondent for Lyons. Cabet then issued the following warning to his new agent in an open letter in *Le Populaire:* "This conformity of opinions is the rigorous condition of our relations. If you were not sincerely an Icarian communist, I would not give you my confidence. If you deceived me, it would be a type of treason . . . ; but I do not have the least anxiety in this regard."[42] A letter of support from Lyons dated July 20, 1843, bore 553 signatures (in the name of "five thousand"). Significantly, they declared that "the multiplicity of communist journals" could only harm the cause by creating "competition" and that the bourgeoisie "will end up by appreciating and adopting" communism.[43] The proportion of Lyonnais communists represented by this figure is difficult to estimate, but one piece of evidence allows us to guess that Cabet's support was far greater than the others'. One of Cabet's

[39] *Ibid.,* 28. This apparently had some basis in fact. Among the documents relating to an insurrection in the Midi (March 23–24, 1841, at several towns in the Vaucluse and at Marseilles), was a letter, seized in Lyons, stating that "the patriots of the Midi are getting tired of following the impetus of Paris; they propose to join with Lyons in isolating themselves from Paris." A.N., BB[18] 1391 dos 1559.

[40] Cabet, *Utile et Franche Explication,* 19 and 28.

[41] Prudhommeaux, "Un Commis-voyageur," XXIV, 149.

[42] *Le Populaire,* April 9, 1843.

[43] Cabet, *Procès du communisme à Toulouse* (Paris, Sept. 1843), 20.

adherents in Lyons wrote him in late September or early October 1842 that "the five signatories, knowing that I was going to respond to this letter, have just crowned their hostility by convening a meeting of 130 persons. . . . Nevertheless one assures me that the great majority of the Lyonnais communists are Icarian communists."[44]

The other side recognized Cabet's victory. Joseph Benoit, who was in league with Greppo, explained the whole development in his memoirs. In 1838 he, Grinand, and Perret had belonged to the central committee of the Blanquist Société des Familles at Lyons. They made contact with the radical notary's clerk, Félix Blanc, who "had made a succinct analysis of the doctrine of Babeuf drawn from the book of Buonarotti [*sic*]." They also participated in the Saisons and continued their cooperation thereafter in a Société des Egaux. In 1840 or 1841 they were joined by Louis Greppo. They were essentially Babouvist and revolutionary. Benoit maintained that this early phase of communist development in Lyons was begun and sustained by the workers themselves and that its leaders, all workingmen like himself, Greppo, and Perret, were loved and esteemed. But many workers began to think that their education was insufficient and their experience too limited for men from their own ranks to serve as their guides. Thus it was that the "writers," such as Blanc, Leroux, Proudhon, and especially Cabet, began to hold sway in Lyons: "These foreign voices," noted Benoit, "immediately acquired a great superiority over [ours]." With regard to Cabet and the conflict of 1842, Benoit painfully recalled that "When we attempted to refute several articles of his doctrine that seemed to be contrary to the sound ideas that we wanted to have triumph, people answered us: he knows more about it than you do, he has studied, he was a Deputy and public prosecutor." This did not stop them, but "Our rejoinders could not weaken the good opinion they had of men clothed in titles superior to ours." Thus, "Cabet took a good number of adherents away from us."[45] This shows the effectiveness of Cabet's allegation that

---

[44] Cabet, *Utile et Franche Explication*, 26.

[45] Benoit, "Confessions d'un prolétaire," ms. 302, Bibliothèque municipale de Lyon, 77, 81–83. This manuscript has been printed since my research was done. Edited by Maurice Moissonier, it was published by Editions sociales, Paris, 1968. Page references are to the original.

"simple workers" could not deal with "great theoretical problems."
But his emphasis on the futility of secret-society organization had
an impact as well. Sébastien Commissaire, discussing his conversion
to Icarianism, pointed out something Cabet never tired of repeat-
ing: "These societies were secret only for the public; the prefecture
had its agents who informed it on the acts and deeds of the affiliates to such an extent that there was nothing less secret than these
supposed secret societies. In reality they were only snares by which
the government could operate a razzia when the needs of politics
demanded that it arouse the specter of anarchy."[46]

Thus by mid-1843 the dominance of Cabet among the Lyonnais
communists was being established while his opponents floundered.
Benoit and his friends faced "several conflicts in our little society,
conflicts that led to dissolution." Although accord was reached
among them later, Benoit himself gave up active politicking, limit-
ing his activity to writing articles for *La Fraternité* and *La Tribune
lyonnais*.[47] The July 20 Icarian Manifesto consolidated Cabet's
triumph.

The Lyons situation thus gives us a detailed account of how
Cabet's dominion within the communist camp began to grow. The
summer of 1843 appears to have been the vital period in this
process. Shortly thereafter there occurred an event of great importance in advancing the fortunes of Icarian communism while
simultaneously seeming to prove the validity of his left-wing unity
thesis.

"The Triumph of Communism at Toulouse"

From August 21 to August 31, 1843, twelve men, eight of them
Icarians, were tried before the royal court in Toulouse on a conspiracy charge. All were acquitted, although two others, Jacques
Imbert[48] and Albert Laponneraye, were convicted in absentia. The
trial marked the turning point in the history of the Icarian movement.[49] After this date support for Cabet grew, slowly at first, then

---

[46] Commissaire, *Mémoires et souvenirs* (Paris and Lyons, 1888), I, 78.

[47] Benoit, "Confessions," 88.

[48] Imbert later became a close associate of Marx in Brussels; see *Dict.
Biog.*, II, 362–63, and Walter Haenisch, "Marx and the Democratic Association of 1847," *Science and Society* (1937–38), 83–102.

[49] Cabet thought this to be the case and used the terms that head the
present section. See *Le Populaire*, Oct. 1, 1843.

rapidly after mid-1844. The struggle with competitors also sub-
sided measurably. The trial became a minor cause célèbre for the
entire left because—besides the communists implicated—prominent
republicans of the area and one of the leaders of the recent abortive
republican insurrection at Barcelona, Abdon Terradas,[50] were involved. The influential radical newspaper of Toulouse, Félix Paya's
L'Emancipation, carried on a veritable crusade in defense of the
accused, and the most prominent republican of the Haute-Garonne,
the current deputy for Toulouse and future commissaire for the
provisional government in 1848, Jacques Joly, defended Terradas.
Joly summarized the significance of the trial for the emergence of
Icarian communism in his concluding remarks. Speaking to the
government, he said, "You have picked a fight with communism;
but the dispute has been settled to its profit. It is henceforth an
accepted idea that the Icarian theory is seductive."[51]

The affair began with a wave of investigations and arrests in
February and March shortly after a banquet in Toulouse held in
honor of a group of exiled Catalonian revolutionaries from Perpignan. The thirty-four individuals present included Terradas, head
of the junta, several of his compatriots, and republicans and communists from southern France. The banquet had been organized
by Cabet's agent at Toulouse, Adolphe Gouhenant, and was presided over by Albert Laponneraye, then working in the Midi to
sell Cabet's (and his own) works. The authorities claimed that this
gathering was the preliminary meeting of a conspiracy designed to
foment a general insurrection in the Midi. Allegedly Gouhenant led
this secret society, and Laponneraye was the agent of a central
committee in Paris.

There was some justification for the authorities' suspicions. In
1841, Toulouse had been the scene of armed resistance to the plan of
the Minister of Finances, Humann, to redistribute the tax burden in
order to equalize assessments among departments, arrondissements,
communes, and individuals, while increasing net revenue at the same
time. His circular on the subject was badly worded and implied that
fiscal agents would be prowling everywhere, undermining local pre-

---

[50] Tarradas was former mayor of Barcelona and editor of two republican
newspapers, the *Huracan* and the *Republicano.*

[51] Quoted from the trial record in *Le Populaire,* Nov. 12, 1843.

rogatives.[52] Although popular resistance occurred in many parts of France, developments in Toulouse were of most consequence. In July both the new prefect and the procureur-général were forced to leave town as the workers of the Faubourg Saint-Etienne and the bourgeois of the National Guard stood shoulder to shoulder against the census that would determine the redistribution. *L'Emancipation* railed bitterly against the tyranny of Paris.[53] Although the attempt to block the plan failed in the end, the Toulouse insurrection forced the resignation of Humann and created widespread popular mistrust of the July Monarchy while simultaneously bringing workers and middle-class republicans into close relations. The government also uncovered several radical associations, including a Toulouse section of the so-called plot of Marseilles, but failed to gain convictions.[54] Toward the end of this eventful year the procureur-général, Niceas Gaillard, remarked wearily in writing to his superiors: "despite all I have been able to tell you, you do not have even an approximate idea of the local difficulties."[55]

It is thus not difficult to understand Gaillard's belief that he had uncovered an insurrectionary plot when he rounded up the Terradas banquet participants. Greater plausibility was added in light of the background of its organizer, Gouhenant. Adolphe Gouhenant, a painter whose talents were apparently never appreciated,[56] was born in Flagny (Haute-Saône) in 1805 and spent some time in both Lyons and Paris before coming to Toulouse in 1840. He is typical of the few bourgeois who followed the Icarian banner. He was a practicing Swedenborgian and perhaps simply saw Icaria as his New Jerusalem; while working as Cabet's correspon-

[52] On the tax census, see E. Regnault, *Histoire de huit ans, 1840–1848*, 6th ed., II (Paris, 1883), 131–50, and F. Ponteil, "G. Humann et les émeutes antifiscales en 1841," *Revue historique*, CLXXIX (1937), 311–31.

[53] P. Paul, "L'Agitation républicaine à Toulouse et dans la Haute-Garonne de 1840 à 1848," in J. Godechot, ed., *La Révolution de 1848 à Toulouse et dans la Haute-Garonne* (Toulouse, 1948), 43–49.

[54] A.N., BB18 1472 dos 6733 and A.N., BB18 1391 dos 1559.

[55] Gaillard to the Garde des Sceaux, Nov. 4, 1841, A.N., BB18 1398 dos 2824.

[56] The *Dict. biog.* lists his occupation as *peintre ouvrier*. This is incorrect. Both Cabet and the procureur-général of Toulouse recognize that he painted pictures for a living. Indications of his lack of financial success may be seen in several references of the procureur-général of Toulouse in his reports to Paris. A.N., BB18 1409 dos 6143.

dent he also sought to win converts to his religion. As he put it, his fundamental aims were "to accomplish a moral and religious mission and to organize labor."[57] He was drawn to the ritual and secrecy of the compagnonnage, but felt that the organic spirit of each trade should be extended to a general brotherhood of all compagnons.[58] To his penchant for mysticism Gouhenant added a vivid, if somewhat undisciplined, imagination. There is the story, for instance, of a monument that he proposed to build on the Terasse de Fourvières in Lyons in 1831. It would have been "at once an observatory, lightning rod, and study hall." So impressed was he with his design that he went to the Duc d'Orléans, then busily stamping out all vestiges of the insurrectionary spirit in Lyons after the revolt of the canuts, to ask for assistance while he completed his project.[59] A letter to *L'Emancipation* that Gouhenant smuggled out of prison after his arrest in 1843 is indicative of the kind of exaggeration to which his emotions led him.

After sixty days of solitary confinement . . . of the most rigorous secrecy . . . without any kind of communication . . . without news . . . without pens, without paper, without a stub of a pencil . . . without books, without anything that could arrest or fix my ardent imagination, a thousand times more active in isolation than out in the world; completely deprived of air and nearly of light; forced to endure the cold or die asphyxiated, and in a little closet of six or seven square feet, one half occupied by the cot and the other by a common chair, the table, and the modest water jug; my forces were at an end. But, fearing nothing, and bolstered, furthermore, by an irresistible force, that of the soul, I followed at every point the impulses of my heart, which was righteous.[60]

[57] "Copie d'un rapport adressé, le 8 mars 1843, au Procureur-général du Procureur du roi," A.N., BB[18] 1409 dos 6043.

[58] Cabet, *Procès des communistes à Toulouse,* 44.

[59] G. Marty, *Etienne Cabet et le procès des communistes à Toulouse en 1843: Discours prononcé le 4 décembre 1927, a la rentrée solonnelle de la conférence des avocats stagiaires* (Toulouse: Mazières et Laporte, 1928), 47. This study is drawn almost exclusively from the Archives départementales de la Haute-Garonne and was undertaken because the Toulouse trial was a legal landmark; the decision not to allow Cabet to defend Gouhenant because he was not a member of the bar of the Haute-Garonne, though justified by article 295 of the Criminal Code, had never occurred before.

[60] *L'Emancipation,* April 6, 1843. From all indications it is unlikely that any of this is accurate, though Gouhenant may have imagined it to be so. See Procureur-général de Toulouse to Garde des Sceaux, April 9, 1843, A.N., BB[18] 1409.

The romantic character of this man may also be seen in Cabet's own description of him:

His face is imposing and severe, his hair long and curly, his beard blond and full, his eye mobile, indicating an artistic and impressionable organization. His large forehead, pale and calm, reveals passions presently smothered. His speech is elegant, easy, and precise, as that of a man who has studied and reflected a great deal. His clothing, of black velvet set off by polished wristbands and a white collar, gives him the character of a man of the Middle Ages.[61]

All this would seem to describe a high-strung, inwardly turbulent nonconformist.

The judiciary had stronger reason to suspect Gouhenant than an appreciation of his personality, however. A prosecution witness claimed that in the wake of the conflicts over the tax census at Toulouse Gouhenant had asked him to join an insurrectionary movement that would seize power there and then march on Lyons.[62] Moreover, a report of a "secret agent," dated January 20, 1843, said that Gouhenant, along with two workers, Rolland and Saganzan, had recently organized a secret society called the Organization méridionale with sections in various cities.[63]

This secret report was in fact written by the president of the banquet of January 15 (this is stated in the report itself)—that is, by Albert Laponneraye. Although it is surprising that this was not revealed in 1848, the evidence supports the identification. Laponneraye was known to be in financial trouble in 1842. Then he disappeared totally from the political scene, after January 1843, until he surfaced once again as editor of the *Voix du peuple* of Marseille in 1848. Finally, a letter of February 16, 1843, from the procureur-général of Toulouse to Paris says, in its "most specially confidential part": "I have every reason to believe that the Minister of the Interior was not ignorant of M. Laponneraye's trip [to Toulouse] and that this man, at first and for too long associated with the criminal intrigues of the parties, sincerely and on his own ac-

[61] Cabet, *Procès du communisme,* 51.
[62] A.N., BB[18] 1409, "Rapport." See also Cabet, *Procès du communisme,* 68–69. A letter fom André Callet, a Lyonnais revolutionary, was also found in Gouhenant's apartment.
[63] Paul, "L'Agitation républicaine," 50.

count remains in or has reentered them since as a secret agent of the superior administration."[64]

But, *mouchard* or not, Laponneraye was not around to testify at the trial. The government therefore had to base its case on circumstantial evidence alone. Using a list of subscribers or potential subscribers to *Le Populaire* found in the possession of Gouhenant, the justice officials made over fifty household searches (including one to the office of *Le Populaire* itself) during February and March and, after an unduly long imprisonment, brought twelve defendants to trial beginning on August 21. Besides Gouhenant, seven others were professed Icarians: Jean-Marie Dubor, a printer from Agen, aged 27; Resplandy, a traveling drug salesman, 34; Dufour, a retail merchant of church ornaments from Saint-Frajou, 38; Perpignan, a shoemaker in Toulouse, 25; Jules Balguerie, a student at Toulouse from Agde, 23; Rolland, a master stonecutter in Toulouse, 48; Saganzan, a Toulousain woodworker, 46. (Cabet said of the last two: "These two workers, both of great size, can give an idea of the working masses in their force and their confidence."[65]) The other four defendants were Terradas, aged 34; Bruneau Cucsac, an artist who denied his communism even though several of Cabet's brochures were found at his residence, 34; and two prominent political republicans, the lawyer Lucien Lamarque of Condom, 28, and Manein, "ex-commandant of the National Guard of Valence," 35. On the first day of the trial Cabet had demanded to be admitted as the lawyer of Gouhenant, Dubor, and Perpignan but had been turned down. He thereupon wrote letters to Parisian papers and *L'Emancipation* of Toulouse expressing the injustice done to him and his party. This situation, when added to the concern already aroused by the supposed hardships of the prisoners, made the Toulouse affair an example of martyrdom in the name of the entire left. Cabet, who had intended to use the trial as a forum to advertise his cause, found that the republican press and Jacques Joly were doing it for him. The fact that he was silenced at the trial probably had a greater impact than if he had

[64] A.N., BB[18] 1395c. It is interesting that the justice officials were not supplied with information concerning the agents provocateurs of the Ministry of the Interior. This letter was misplaced in the cartons on the census struggle of 1841 and is revealed here for the first time.

[65] Cabet, *Procès du communisme*, 52.

spoken. The jury, in part motivated by the injustice of Cabet's denial and by the inadequacy of the government's case, acquitted the twelve on August 31.

The crowds at the trial were, according to the procureur-général, "always large" and in sympathy with the defendants; the audience consisted largely of workers from the Faubourg Saint-Etienne. *La France méridionale* reported that "never have the avenues around the Palais been so . . . crowded." The news of the acquittal "was received by the crowd outside with cries of 'Vive le jury.' "[66] These citations support Cabet's assertion that "the entire city applauded the decision; joy is universal."[67] After the trial Cabet, who stayed until September 15, was introduced around Toulouse and in neighboring towns by the triumphant Gouhenant. "His name, his ideas have become a little more popular among [the workers] and he left carrying 300 to 400 subscriptions or promises of subscriptions to his newspaper, *Le Populaire*." Cabet claimed that he had gained 150 new subscribers in the area as a result or the trial.[68] Thus, the victory at Toulouse had an important impact in developing the Icarian cause in southwestern France. For Cabet, it appeared even more significant than that: "Yes, Communism . . . has passed the Rubicon; once cast into the world, it will make its way. . . . Whatever lot the future prepares for us, there will be found martyrs ready to look it in the face and to bring about, by their dedication, the triumph of the idea that is destined to be the salvation of humanity."[69]

Moreover, his political strategy seemed to be bearing fruit. The whole gist of the Toulouse development was toward republican-communist coalition, and workingmen and bourgeois radicals appeared to be pursuing similar democratic goals. Simultaneously, the Toulouse trial provided further evidence of Cabet's growing hegemony over communism in France. Unfortunately the internal

[66] "Dépêche télégraphique de Toulouse," Sept. 1, 1843, A.N., BB[18] 1409; Procureur-général of Toulouse to the Garde des Sceaux, Aug. 21, 1843, A.N., (BB[18] 1409); Marty, *Cabet*, 26.

[67] Cabet, *Procès du communisme*, 94.

[68] Copy of a letter from the Prefect to the Minister of the Interior of Sept. 18, 1843, quoted in Marty, *Cabet*, 57; Cabet, *Procès du communisme*, 94.

[69] *Le Populaire*, Nov. 12, 1843.

contradictions of both these aspects of his strategy were beginning to emerge as well.

Conflict and Consolidation in Lyons

Cabet sought to capitalize on the Toulouse victory by making a personal unity plea to Lyonnais communists when he stopped in Lyons on his way back to Paris. His prestige had never been higher, and conditions in Lyons were favorable. Chameroy wrote on September 3: "I have now been at Lyons for three weeks. I have seen several communists; all demand union. People ardently wish that you would come through Lyons."[70]

Cabet arrived later that month and met with deputations of communist workers at his hotel. He also attended small dinners at various places in Lyons and the Croix Rousse.[71] The workers who met with Cabet were, according to the procureur-général, of "diverse associations," and "their first conversations with Cabet passed in recriminations." They "were not successful in reaching agreement on several points that have divided them for some time." At later meetings, however, striking developments occurred. In a confidential report of October 2, 1843, Piou revealed that Cabet had apparently abandoned his antirevolutionary position, although "nothing ought to be attempted . . . during the lifetime of the king." But "the moment of his death" would be an opportune time for "an armed rising."[72] Three weeks later the procureur-général concluded that "the effect of this declaration was to rally to him the entire communist party, which has nearly completely absorbed the other secret associations."[73] Needless to say, the Garde des Sceaux informed Duchâtel that "this information calls for very careful surveillance of the moves of Sʳ Cabet and his party."[74] If accurate, it means that Cabet was less opposed to revolution than

[70] Chameroy to Cabet, Lyons, Sept. 3, 1843, in Prudhommeaux, "Un Commis-voyageur," XXIV, 168.

[71] Procureur-général de Lyon to the Garde des Sceaux, reports of Sept. 11, 16, 19, 21, and 22, A.N., BB¹⁸ 1415 dos 7135. Some of these documents were printed by G. Bourgin in the *Revue socialiste*, XLVI (1907), 519–41. I have followed the originals here.

[72] *Ibid.*, reports of Sept. 24 and Oct. 2, 1843.

[73] *Ibid.*, report of Oct. 22, 1843.

[74] *Ibid.*, undated letter sent with a copy of the report.

historians have thought. Moreover, Engels, writing in the *New Moral World* on November 4, 1843, said, "Even the Icarians, though they declare in their publications that they abhor physical revolution and secret societies, even they are associated in this manner and would gladly seize upon any opportunity to establish a republic by force."[75] The allegation about secret societies is unconvincing, but the "word" may have circulated through clandestine channels in October that Cabet had revised his stand on revolution. Finally, Sébastien Commissaire, though he did not mention the incident of 1843, let drop an interesting phrase implying that Cabet's ultimate goal was revolution: "[Cabet] and his adherents agitated in the open. The doctrine was propagated by brochures and the newspaper, *Le Populaire*. They had no need of secret societies in order to prepare for taking up arms."[76] Perhaps none of this should be a surprise. In the thirties, and as late as 1839 in his manuscript "Note à X," Cabet had consistently maintained that he thought a great popular revolution by the overwhelming majority of Frenchmen was not out of the question.

At any rate, the visit of September appeared to have been a success. It was widely reported in the Lyons press, and the *Globe* said that "the illustrious M. Cabet, the chief of the communists, the high priest of the Icarian religion," saw about 800 workers during his visit.[77] Cabet praised himself handsomely in *Le Populaire* of October 1 and November 12, though in the latter he denied a "pernicious" story then circulating that he had taken a revolutionary stance.

The major result of Cabet's propaganda of 1842–1843 and his visit in September seems to have been to break up or ennervate the secret societies. We have already pointed out that Benoit's group was dissolved at this time. More important evidence is provided by Duchâtel's letter to the Minister of Justice of March 31, 1844. After listing the various secret societies currently operating in Lyons, he said:

Thus on the whole . . . the political Societies in the Rhône still

---

[75] "Progress of Social Reform on the Continent," in *Marx-Engels Gesamtausgabe,* Erste Abteilung, Band II (Berlin, 1930), 440.

[76] *Mémoires,* II, 98.

[77] Quoted in *Le Populaire,* Nov. 12, 1843.

. . . have frightening enough means at their disposal, especially if they base themselves on the reciprocal sympathies of the diverse portions of the working class and on the conflicts of interest that exist between the weavers and the fabricants, between the masters and the workers.

However, . . . you know how many of these affiliations are characterized by weakness, by human respect, and with mental reservations of prudence at the moment of action. . . .

In placing oneself in this point of view, one recognizes in this state of things, as compared to the past, a notable improvement, at least with regard to the city of Lyons.[78]

There can be little question that Cabet had some influence on this development.

The Icarian movement reached something of a high point in Lyons during the fall and winter of 1843–1844.[79] By mid-summer of 1844 it was again beset by troubles, problems that necessitated a second visit by the Icarian chief in July. The origins of these difficulties are somewhat obscure, but several suggestions can be made. Commissaire recalled that in 1844 "a schism was produced at Lyons among the partisans of Icarian communism; one side wanted to establish this new state by violence; the others, as well as their chief, Cabet, put all their hope in pacific propaganda."[80] The revolutionaries argued that the system of education under the monarchy made it impossible to triumph through propaganda alone. Hence a revolution was necessary in order "to establish a dictatorship in the interest of the masses in place of a dictatorship in the interest of a small number, a family, or a single person."[81] Apparently, Cabet had thought it tactically advisable to moderate his position once again. The antagonism between the two wings reached bitter proportions with "the revolutionaries [calling] the

[78] A.N., BB[18] 1420 dos 8195.

[79] A polemical battle that Cabet waged with a Catholic writer in Lyons named Horace Fournier de Virginie probably also raised Cabet's stock there. See *Le Populaire*, Aug. 19, 1843; Fournier, *Lettre sur le communisme adressé à M. Cabet* (Paris and Lyons, 1843). Cabet, *Le Gant jeté au communisme par un riche Jesuit, académicien de Lyon* (Paris, Feb. 1844); and Fournier, *Petit Livre d'or de l'ouvrier français* (Lyons, 1844).

[80] This indicates that the union brought about by Cabet's alleged "revolutionary" talk was fleeting, but since this current situation was *within* the Icarian party it appears that some unity had been previously effected. Commissaire, *Mémoires*, I, 98.

[81] *Ibid.*, 100.

pacifics cajolers [*endormeurs*], and the pacifics [calling] the revolutionaries hotheads whose doctrines would lead to annihilation." Another question was at stake as well, however, that of liberty within the movement and in Cabet's projected society. Concerning the latter, many rejected the manifest regimentation in Icaria.[82] But more important, the ghost of Greppo and his friends stalked the movement; they had, in 1842, complained of Cabet's will to direct all. In April 1844 the same problem arose when Cabet desired to impose, officially, the title Icarian on his following. The spirit of independence so evident in Benoit, Greppo, and their associates emerged among many of the Icarian sympathizers themselves. Mme Buisson, a sometime flower shop worker who had illusions of being the poet laureate of Icarianism, presented the loyalist side in a verse "concerning a quarrel over the word Icarian," in which she argued that the title would distinguish them clearly from proponents of "riots" and "secret meetings." The final line of the poem, "please do not speak ill of me," was aimed at renegades who obviously had begun to do so.[83] In May and June 1844 there were new rumors that secret-society activity was on the move again.[84]

At that very moment Flora Tristan, a new and persuasive voice for working-class unity, came to Lyons. At first, she had "little success. . . . The [workers] disdain her utopias and refuse to hear any any other doctrine than that of communism." They said to her, "You are a Phalanstérienne [Fourierist], go back to the Phalanstériens; we intend to remain communists." But later on, although she made only minor progress among the communists, other workers began to take an interest in her.[85] Commissaire was even more positive when he categroically stated that "her trip to Lyons was a great success."[86] And given the fact that his experience was largely confined to the communist group, she probably made some inroads there as well. Thus within the splintering Icarian group, Tristan's

---

[82] *Ibid.*, 98–99.

[83] She sent a copy (handwwritten) to Cabet, which is now to be found in the Papiers Cabet (X), BHVP.

[84] A.N., BB[18] 1420 dos 8133.

[85] Procureur-général de Lyon to the Garde des Sceaux, May 18, 19 and June 23, 1844, A.N., BB[18] 1420 dos 8133. If anything, Tristan was a Saint-Simonian.

[86] *Mémoires,* I, 109.

ideas, particularly her emphasis on the workers acting and thinking for themselves, probably found willing listeners at this time of doubt about Cabet's heavy hand in the movement.

Cabet arrived in Lyons on July 21, 1844 in order to heal the rift. As before, he met with workers in small groups, attending as many as five meetings a day. Although he stayed on until August 6, he was not ultimately successful in his mission; the questions of revolution and liberty could not be ironed out. With regard to the latter, Cabet characteristically antagonized some of his audience when, after they had pressed him on the apparent lack of personal freedom in Icaria, he said that he did not claim to have found a completely perfect mode of social organization, but if they did not like it why did they not produce a better one?[87] Toward the end of his stay Cabet was greeted by the news that the dwelling of his new correspondent, the tailor Faucon,[88] had been invaded by the police. They had discovered his large stock of Icarian pamphlets and books. The Minister of Justice then told Piou to sequester them in the hope that he could find something that might get a conviction before a Lyons jury. Piou was no more successful than the censors in Paris; he remarked bitterly about Cabet's ability to keep seditious statements out of his brochures even though the total effect was completely "disastrous."[89]

This "persecution" may have had an effect upon the situation in the Icarian party at Lyons. If even the pacifists are not safe, they may have reasoned, why fear a firmer stand? Perhaps such thoughts contributed to what was probably inevitable anyway; in late 1844 secret-society activity picked up markedly in Lyons.[90] But the Icarian loyalists demonstrated a renewed determination to remain (at least publicly) pacifist and to show their civil courage. On August 22 there appeared in *Le Populaire* an "address to the Parisian Icarians" from the commission that Cabet had appointed

[87] On the failure of the mission, see *ibid.*, 99–100, and *Le Populaire*, Aug. 22, 1844.

[88] Chapius, the first correspondent, was a loyal Icarian but apparently too pressed by his work and rather weak-willed. Cabet had decided to replace him as early as September 1843 (see Chameroy letter of Sept. 3, cited n. 70 above) but with the triumph of that month apparently thought it best to keep him on.

[89] Report of Aug. 8, 1844, A.N., BB[18] 1423 dos 9801.

[90] Commissaire, *Mémoires*, I, 101–2.

during his visit. They promised their loyalty and willingly signed their names:

Barre, chef d'atelier	Gluntz, tailor
Begou, chef d'atelier	Heustache, chef d'atelier
Berodiat, pastry cook	Joinon, hatter
Chapius, chef d'atelier	Razuret, silk weaver
Coignet, chef d'atelier	Regnier, chef d'atelier
Crevesec, master bootmaker	Troillet, tailor
Faucon, tailor	Vernay, netmaker
Garçon, folder	

Yet even this group was not solidly behind Cabet. By the end of the year new threats to the unity of the movement had been manifested. The leaders of the renegades were Frédéric Garçon and Jean-Joseph Razuret. There had already been some indication that "Garçon and his friends" were not slavishly devoted to Cabet,[91] although things were patched up enough for Cabet to appoint members of Garçon's group to the commission in July. On October 31, however, Chapius informed Cabet in a confidential letter that a split had arisen among the members of the commission: "We . . . shall be forced to part company." Someone named Maggiolo[92] had succeeded in alienating Garçon, Razuret, Crevesec, and Coignet from Cabet, and the situation had been aggravated by an apparently vicious letter from the Icarian leader to Maggiolo. The latter was trying to induce subscribers to quit *Le Populaire* and support a journal that he, Garçon, and their allies would publish.[93]

This move was a serious one. On November 9, Poncet, a friend of Chapius, warned Cabet that Rémond had come to see him "to ask me if I wanted to take subscriptions to this newspaper, which should appear very soon and which is destined, he told me, to back up [*seconder*] *Le Populaire*. All that I tell you is correct." He also noted that Mme Buisson supported the Garçon paper.[94] This paper never appeared, but the whole situation shows the depth of

---

[91] Cabet to Chapius, July 13, 1844, Papiers Cabet (VIII), BHVP.
[92] I have been unable to find out anything more about Maggiolo—a bourgeois who owned a business (*maison*) of some kind—than is exhibited in this letter. He is not even mentioned in Benoit's "Confessions."
[93] Chapius to Cabet, Oct. 31, 1844, Papiers Cabet (VIII), BHVP.
[94] Chapius to Cabet, Nov. 9, 1844, *ibid.*

the new split in the Icarian party. Coignet had been one of the early friends of Cabet in Lyons, being the strongest advocate of Icarianism on the editorial staff of *Le Travail*. Mme Buisson only six months before had defended Cabet against those who balked at taking the title Icarian. Rémond was a propagandist for Icarianism in the Isère and elsewhere. Both Garçon and Razuret had been more independent, but even they had willingly become commissioners. The latters' defection—separation is perhaps a better term, for they retained an essentially Icarian outlook[95]—was certainly of major importance because both were towering figures in the working-class movement in Lyons in 1848 and later. What had precipitated this new schism? One can hardly avoid the conclusion that it was mainly due to Cabet's will to dominate. None of these people was inclined toward secret societies; they were probably no more revolutionary than Chapius, Faucon, or Poncet.[96] It seems probable that Maggiolo's sin was simply that he had position and might become a rival to Cabet at Lyons. Although the Greppo affair was a case with deeper ideological foundations, there was a real similarity between the current situation and the earlier confrontation. And what did Cabet do about this new schism? In typical fashion, he proceeded to rant against his enemies, slandering Maggiolo especially in *Les Masques arrachés*. The split was apparently definitive. Razuret, at any rate, did not use the title Icarian in any of his several communications to the *Tribune lyonnaise* in later years. What had developed was an anti-Cabet Icarian element in Lyons.

Detailed information of the Icarian movement at Lyons fades after 1844. Despite the fact that declared Icarians continued to defend their cause and worked actively on projects assigned to them by Cabet, it would seem that this gap in the material on the

[95] See, for instance, Razuret's long letter defending communism in the *Tribune lyonnaise* (Oct. 1846). Although he does not call himself an Icarian, the doctrine presented is Icarian in its substance. The only specific mention of Cabet is praise for his "transitory regime"; but he repeats Cabet's historical survey of the growth toward Community, and the whole essay is permeated with Christian allusions. If he divided at all from Icarianism, it was on the question of machines, which he saw as competition (at least under the existing organization of society.)

[96] Garçon and Razuret would become deeply involved in the cooperative movement in Lyons before and after the revolution of 1848.

Lyons movement corresponds to an actual state of stagnation. Joseph Benoit was probably not exaggerating greatly when he said:

> In the beginning, Cabet detached a good number of adherents from us; but gradually they came back to us, repelled by his dictatorial ways and his exclusivism. There remained with him only a small number of simple but devoted men who were noteworthy for their exemplary conduct. They were fanatics of good faith, having a blind confidence in Cabet and a naïve faith in the Icarian communist idea . . . and many went to experiment in America where they inevitably encountered numerous deceptions, which were fatal to many. But with others, their faith would be lively and persistent enough to continue their work in the midst of nearly insurmountable obstacles.[97]

Undeniably, however, Icarianism had a deep and continuing influence in Lyons. Cabet's doctrine had made its way into the general corpus of communist thought. The label "Icarian" might be avoided, but Icarian principles and slogans were evident. The forum for the presentation the of communist opinion was *La Tribune lyonnaise,* the quasi-Fourierist monthly newspaper edited by Marius Chastaing.

Chastaing himself introduced the subject of communism in his paper in May and June of 1845. In one article he criticized the disciples of Babeuf and Buonarroti for their conspiratorial activities, implicitly comparing them to the Jesuits in terms of organization and methods.[98] In another, however, he defended communism against charges recently made by Cormenin in *Feu, Feu!* (Paris, 1845).[99] The first communist writing to appear in *La Tribune* responded to the conservative *Gazette de Lyon,* which had warned that the frightening growth of communism in France and Europe could only be countered by government action to alleviate proletarian misery. The *Gazette* attacked communism doctrinally, saying that all communists wanted temporary marriages, proscription of the liberal professions, and "to force the banker to make shoes and hats."[100] Two articles, each signed by Razuret and Rémond along with individuals from the Benoit camp, refuted the *Gazette.*

[97] Benoit, "Confessions," 83.
[98] *La Tribune lyonnaise,* May 1845. Bibliothèque municipale de Lyon, no. 5651.
[99] *La Tribune lyonnaise,* June 1845.
[100] *Gazette de Lyon,* July 14–15, 1845.

The former Cabetists had joined a wider communist front that coordinated the interests of so-called pacifics and violents.

The first article challenged the three points made by the *Gazette,* saying, with Cabet, that under communism "marriage will remain as it is but removed from any mercantile idea." Cabet had been challenged before on the "liberal professions" question and had stressed strongly that "the arts" were important to communist life; the writers of this article said the same thing. As for the third question, they admitted that some *oisifs* must fall by the wayside under communism but not by violent means.[101] The second article (this one also signed by Benoit himself) was more revealing because the doctrine of the group was presented more fully. Christ was the greatest of all communists. Fraternity, the human act of brotherly love, is the crowning ideal that will make communism possible; it will emerge victorious over egotism and act as the basic social cement to assure liberty and equality. Moreover, "Any intelligent and conscientious democrat is necessarily and inevitably a communist; but the only democrat deserving of the name is he who gives the example of social virtues by love of work, purity of morals, respect for his fellow man, dedication to the cause of the oppressed and of all humanity." To bring about this "social revolution, the moral obligation is instruction in common; to work to make the evils that cause the exploitation of some by others and the happiness that will be born of universal solidarity understood [implying revolution by propaganda]."[102] Much of this contradicted Dézamy's materialist communism; specifically, the praise of dedication repeated the objection made by Greppo and his friends to Dézamy in 1842. But Cabet was everywhere in evidence—Christ as communist, the importance of the ideal of fraternity, and especially the notion that any true democrat is a communist.

Doctrinaire Icarianism also broke into print in 1845. André Poncet criticized both the *Gazette* and Chastaing's Fourierism in a brochure called *Réponse communiste-icarienne à la Tribune lyonnaise* (Lyons, October 6, 1845). Although not of great interest in terms of content, this brochure is unique in the Icarian movement, being the only separate work by a French Icarian produced during the July Monarchy that was not directly ordered and censored by

---

101 *La Tribune lyonnaise,* Aug. 1845.
102 *Ibid.,* Oct. 1845.

Cabet.[103] Poncet's main emphasis was on challenging Chastaing's rebuttal of communism, and in rather typical Cabetian fashion he said little more than "you are wrong" and recapitulated the doctrine.

In general, except for repeated praise for Cabet, employment of the term Icarian, and a greater stress on pacifism, there was little doctrinal difference between this work of an Icarian loyalist and the articles in *La Tribune*. The point, then, that Benoit neglected to mention in his comments on Icarianism in the later forties is that while he may have won numerous Icarians back to his side the general tide of communism in Lyons shifted significantly toward an acceptance of many tenets of Icarianism.[104] Finally, Benoit himself, former secret-society member and revolutionary that he was, said in his memoirs—in line with Cabet—that he did not desire the revolution of 1848 because he felt that the working class was not yet "ready to profit from it."[105]

Yet even in 1845 a shadow was being cast across the Icarian movement. While Cabet's general strategy of left-wing unity and personal control within the communist camp seemed to be producing results, the growing rigidity of the Icarian party and the noticeable defections of loyalists already anticipated a problem that would reveal how unrealistic it was. Events later that year would show that the social-republican left could not abide communism; shortly thereafter the depression of 1846 would revitalize the revolutionary communists. Cabet and his party would ultimately find themselves isolated. Instead of a communist mass movement fortifying the far left of a unified social republican opposition in France, Icarian communism gradually evolved into a semireligious sect. But before relating this story we must analyze the movement at the height of its power, in 1845 and 1846.

[103] The *Protestation . . . contre le duel* of 1841, the *Actionnaires du Populaire: Biographie de M. Cabet* (1846), and L. V. Maillard's *Les Villageois* (1847) were all produced under Cabet's watchful eye.

[104] This may also be noted in other communications to the *Tribune lyonnaise*. See especially its numbers of Dec. 1845, Oct. 1846 and Dec. 1846. Auguste Morlon, a Fourierist who wrote often in *La Tribune*, attempted in 1847 to develop a doctrine that would combine Fourierism and Cabet's communism.

[105] Benoit, "Confessions," 90.

4 | Bases of Icarian Adherence

During the middle forties Icarian communism had come to France. But the energy and political skills of its master alone do not explain its success; Stein was no doubt correct when he said that the emergence of communism was the "response of a whole class, the expression of a whole social situation" in the context of "the contradictions within industrial society." What was the constellation of social, economic, and cultural factors that gave rise to and shaped the development of the Icarian communist movement? In answering this central question we must explore the worlds of the Icarians themselves. Who were they, what did they want, and how did their life experiences push them toward communist sympathies?

Such questions are admittedly difficult to answer even when addressed to the political proclivities of our contemporaries. The methodological arguments of political sociology attest to this. Moreover, much of the best work on the problem in a historical framework has been through electoral analysis. But most Icarians could not vote, and even when they did, as in 1848, it is impossible to sort them out from the rest of the electorate. Quantitative analysis and the use of sophisticated correlational techniques are therefore denied us. Instead we must use "soft" data—drawn from correspondence, the press, and other contemporary writings in which Icarians are revealed to us—and relate them to our general knowledge of the social, economic, and moral universe of French working people during the 1840s. In short, while some Icarians speak of their paths to communism; while others pinpoint social ills influencing their decision; while much concrete evidence on specific occupational and local economic difficulties can be adduced as well—we must still exercise that gratifying luxury left to historians, the use of the imagination.

General Perspectives on the Movement in France

The difficulties involved in attempting to gauge the numerical support given to any social movement at any time are many. But in France under the July Monarchy, where formal political organizations were officially proscribed, the problem becomes almost insurmountable. While statistical rigor is impossible, the estimates presented below are based upon more extensive evidence than has ever before been marshaled and render what seems to be an adequate impression of the scope of the Icarian communist movement.

In 1844 and 1845, Cabet's growing influence began to provoke comment. Police and the public at large identified him as the "chef des communistes," thus indicating his position within the still fragmented communist camp.[1] Both Eugène Sue, the socialist novelist, and Eugène Pelletan, the moderate republican journalist, could agree that by 1845 Cabet's influence among French workers was equaled only by that of Louis Blanc. In the same year Karl Grün said that Cabet had already amassed the largest active backing of any contemporary European theorist. Two years later the strength of Icarian communism was undeniable. The bourgeois newspaper, *L'Industriel de Champagne* reported that in comparison with Babouvism, Fourierism, and Saint-Simonism, Cabet's doctrine united the most adherents and had "established profound roots in France." Proudhon, a hostile critic, provided a very rough numerical estimate late in 1844: "Socialism does not yet have consciousness of itself; today it is called communism, the communists number one hundred thousand, perhaps two hundred." Dr. Desmoulins, an associate of Cabet at Tours, set the number of Icarians at 100,000 at the same time.[2]

An important index of the numerical strength and growth of

[1] A letter from one of Cabet's followers, Boitel, noted that the police in his commune had referred to Cabet in these terms. Boitel to Cabet (fragment), Aug. 21, 1844, Papiers Cabet, VIII, BHVP. By 1845 such terminology had become habitual in official correspondence and the press.

[2] Sue praised Cabet as the man "whose truly Christian heart gives such a pacific, fraternal, and moral character to the just demands of the communists." (From *La Démocratie pacifique*, quoted in *Le Populaire*, March 1845. In late 1844 and early 1845 *Le Populaire* was dated by month only.) For Pelletan's remarks, see *La Presse*, March 10, 1845. Grün, *Die Soziale Bewegung*, 333–36; *L'Industriel*, Dec. 16, 1847; Pierre Joseph Proudhon, *Correspondance*, II (Paris, 1875); Desmoulins, letter in *Le Populaire*, Oct. 1844.

Icarianism after 1843 is provided by the circulation figures of *Le Populaire* (see Table 1).[3]

To determine the relevance of these figures in estimating the overall size of the movement we must investigate the relationships between circulation and numbers of readers, those influenced by readers, and actual converts. The cost of many single subscriptions was shared by several individuals. For example, in June 1846, Cabet reported that three orders of the previous month had been shared by ten, twelve, and fifteen workers respectively. Moreover, one of the facets of French working-class culture during this era was the public reading and discussion of the radical press during Sunday afternoon gatherings at the cabarets.[4] There were other means of spreading the word. For example, Sixte Boile, a barber in the working-class district of Vienne and an ardent propagator of the Icarian faith, told the police in 1846 that "I put my newspaper [*Le Populaire*] on the bench; those who wait their turn read it and find it quite good."[5] Local meetings were also organized by Icarians to advertise their cause with readings from *Le Populaire* and Cabet's other works.

As for the actual ratio between the number of papers sold and the number of adherents, we can make only rough estimates. Cabet set the figure at about one to 25; late in 1843 he declared that with a total circulation of 1,900 he had 50,000 reader-followers. This may not have been unduly optimistic. At Autun, for instance, there were 21 subscribers in August 1846, while an "address of affiliation" made the previous March was signed by 203 declared

---

[3] The figures recorded here are all drawn from *Le Populaire*, 1844–1848. Unfortunately there is no corroborative evidence. The "Dossier *Le Populaire*," A.N., F[18] 403, concerns only the newspaper edited by Cabet and L.-A. Pagnerre from 1833 to 1835; A.N., F[18] 569 dos 996 contains reports on the publishing activities of Cabet's agent in France, J.-P. Beluze, from 1852 to 1856. If one doubts the validity of Cabet's figures, he should remember that *Le Populaire* was a Société commandite par actions and that circulation and sales figures were given in the paper as a continuing report to the shareholders. The details (such as those presented in Table 2) could be challenged easily—and never were—by any of Cabet's dozens of opponents. He may have been overbearing, suspicious (even paranoid), and obstreperous, but he was scrupulously honest about day-to-day affairs.

[4] *Le Populaire*, June 27, 1846; Nadaud, *Mémoires de Léonard*, 99.

[5] Cited in Fernand Rude, "L'Arrondissement de Vienne en 1848," in Rude, ed., *La Révolution de 1848 dans le départment de l'Isère* (Grenoble, 1949), 236.

Table 1. Circulation figures of *Le Populaire*

Date	New subscribers	Total printing
October 1843		1900
April 1844	92	
May	57	
June	58	2000
July	62	
August	70	
September	85	2200
October–November	200	
December		2400
February 1845	130	
March	150	2600
April	149	2700
May	84	
June–July	83	
July–August	115	3000
September	80	3100
December	138	3200
January 1846	136	3200
February	115	3200
March	89	3300
April	104	3400
May	163	3500
June	102	
July	78	3600
August	120	3600
October	172	
November	142	4000
December	102	
January 1847	117	
February	80	
March	115	
April	185	
May	306	
June	334	
June 27–July 18	143	
July 18–August 15	168	
August 15–October 3	311	
October	254	
November	253	4500
December 5–January 9, 1848	341	
January 9–January 23	380	5000
January 23–February 13	350	

Icarians in the name of a total, it was said, of 500. The following year, Laty, the correspondent for Autun, reported that he had sold 600 copies of the *Almanach*. In Givors 400 copies of the *Almanach* were sold, even though the number of subscribers to *Le Populaire* was only 24. At Vienne, Vincent Cöeffé, the correspondent, estimated the total Icarian force at 400 to 500, but only 62 subscriptions were held by Viennois. In 1847 the *Journal de Reims* stated that there were 49 Rémois subscribers to Cabet's paper but that it "influences 1,200 to 1,500" individuals. A ratio between subscribers and Icarians of about one to 20 seems reasonable and is consistent with the general estimates we have already cited.[6] Other data, while not very helpful in establishing a total figure, contribute to an appreciation of the scope of the movement. *Le Populaire*'s subscription for a medal for novelist Eugène Sue in 1846 produced 7,151 individual contributions, while 3,492 gave to Cabet's collection to assist the Polish revolutionaries during the same year. When *Le Vrai Christianisme,* Cabet's last important book, appeared in 1846, 2,000 copies wwere purchased in 20 days. As already noted, 8,000 copies of the 1843 *Almanach icarien* were sold, and the 1844 issue had 10,000 buyers.[7]

In comparison with *L'Atelier,* the readership of *Le Populaire* was massive. The former never had more than 600 regular subscribers before 1848, and the total number printed reached a pre-revolutionary maximum of 1,050 in 1847.[8] Circulation information on *La Ruche populaire* and *La Fraternité de 1845* is vague, but neither appears to have claimed more than 1,000 readers before 1848. In fact, *Le Populaire*'s readership can only be compared with the circulation of the major reform journals, whose subscribers were largely bourgeois. The mean number of copies of *Le Popu-*

[6] It might be argued that the regular readers of *Le Populaire* were not all adherents of Icarian doctrine. This is probably true. We shall see that Cabet lost subscribers during a conflict with Ledru-Rollin in 1845–1846, most of them no doubt previously sympathetic reformists. But the highly doctrinaire nature of the movement and Cabet's stress on loyalty make it likely that non-Icarian readers of his newspaper comprised only a small percentage. Sources for the foregoing figures are: *Le Populaire,* Oct. 1, 1843, March 26, July 26, Aug. 28, 1846; *Journal de Reims,* Dec. 4, 1847. See also Appendix 1.

[7] *Le Populaire,* Sept. 27, June 26, Oct. 31, 1846; Grün, *Die Soziale Bewegung,* 336.

[8] Cuvillier, *Un Journal d'ouvrier,* 177–79.

laire printed in 1846 was 3,500, while for *La Réforme* it was 1,860, for *La Démocratie pacifique* 1,665, and for the influential *National* 4,280.[9] To be sure, these journals were all dailies, but even so, such figures are impressive evidence of the breadth of Cabet's movement. When we couple this statistical information with the great agitation and concern on the left raised by the emigration proposal of 1847 and with the clear importance of Cabet and the Icarian groups in Paris and several provincial centers in 1848, it is clear that Icarian communism was a social movement of major significance.

Perhaps more important than the total number of Icarians in France was the geographical extent of the movement. By August 1846 there were subscribers to *Le Populaire* in seventy-eight departments. Table 2, which appeared in *Le Populaire* on August 28, 1846, pinpoints the locations of Icarianism, although its later presence in towns such as Saint-Etienne, Le Havre, Mirecourt, and Luçon are not indicated. Several facts immediately strike the eye. Above all, twenty-two cities (including the Parisian suburbs) account for 76 per cent of the total number of subscribers in France.[10] Essentially, Cabet had no rural following at all, and, although two or three letters printed in *Le Populaire* may have come from "villagers," the weakness of Icarianism in basically agricultural departments and the urban concentration of subscriptions in those that might qualify as largely agricultural make this clear. (When Cabet realized that he needed farmers in his American Icaria, he had L.-V. Maillard, one of his lieutenants, write a brochure called *Les Villageois* [1847] to apeal to peasants directly for the first time.) Among the twenty-two cities, modern industry was dominant in only three: Rouen and Mulhouse, where mechanical cotton spinning had become a major source of employment, and Rive-de-Gier, in the heart of the principal coalmining region in France during the July Monarchy. In several others, industrialization was beginning to have an impact, notably in the Parisian suburbs and in Reims, Givors, and Vienne. In Paris the commercialization—especially the growth of "ready-made" production—of

[9] See J.-P. Aguet, "Le Tirage des quotidiens de Paris sous la Monarchie de Juillet," *Schweizerische Zeitschrift für Geschichte,* X (1960), 216–86.

[10] Albi, Autun, Bordeaux, Givors, Grenoble, Lyons, Marseilles, Mulhouse, Nancy, Nantes, Paris, its suburbs, Périgueux, Reims, Rive-de-Gier, Rouen, Toulouse, Toulon, Tours, Troyes, Versailles, and Vienne.

Table 2. Subscribers to *Le Populaire*, 1846

Department (city)		Subscribers
Ain		7
Aisne		17
Laon	4	
Vervin	2	
St.-Quentin	2	
Allier		6
Alpes (Hautes)		1
Alpes (Basses)		2
Ardèche (all at Annonay)		12
Ardennes		8
Sedan	4	
Rethel	3	
Aube		16
Troyes	14	
Aude		26
Carcassonne	9	
Narbonne	3	
La Grasse	4	
Bouches-du-Rhône		41
Marseille	27	
Aix	13	
Calvados		8
Charente		12
Angoulême	9	
Charente-Inférieure	2	
Cher		2
Corrèze		1
Côte-d'Or		14
Côtes-du-Nord		2
Creuse		2
Dordogne		76
Périgueux	54	
Thiviers	6	
Doubs		11
Besançon	8	
Drôme		4
Eure		17
Evreux	6	
Eure-et-Loir		8
Chartres	4	
Finistère		3
Gard		6
Nîmes	4	
Garonne (Haute)		154
Toulouse	136	
Gers		8
Gironde		13

Table 2. Subscribers to *Le Populaire,* 1846 (cont.)

Department (*city*)	Subscribers	
Bordeaux	8	
Hérault		14
Montpellier	5	
Béziers	5	
Cette	3	
Ille-et-Vilaine (all at Rennes)		16
Indre		5
Indre-et-Loire		26
Tours	21	
Isère		86
Grenoble	16	
Vienne	62	
Jura		1
Landes		1
Loir-et-Cher		2
Loire		40
Rive-de-Gier	16	
Loire-Inférieure		95
Nantes	94	
Loiret		7
Pithiviers	4	
Lot		4
Lot-et-Garonne		20
Agen	11	
Nérac	6	
Maine-et-Loire		3
Manche		1
Marne		54
Reims	49	
Marne (Haute)		5
Mayenne		2
Meurthe		28
Nancy	24	
Meuse		8
Moselle		3
Nièvre		9
Nord		1
Oise		22
Méru	11	
Orne		3
Pas-de-Calais		6
Calais	5	
Puy-de-Dôme		14
Clermont	4	
Thiers	3	
Pyrénées (Basses)		9
Bayonne	7	
Pyrénées-Orientales		11
Perpignan	4	

Table 2. Subscribers to *Le Populaire*, 1846 (cont.)

Department (city)		Subscribers
Rhin (Bas)		2
Rhin (Haut)		40
Mulhouse	26	
Belfort	6	
Massevaux	5	
Rhône		303
Lyon	256	
Givors	24	
Saône (Haute)		7
Saône-et-Loire		38
Autun	21	
Sarthe		9
Le Mans	4	
Seine-et-Marne		1
Seine-et-Oise		81
Versailles	28	
Seine-Inférieure		72
Rouen	61	
Sèvres (Deux)		34
Niort	24	
Somme		5
Tarn (all at Albi)		29
Tarn-et-Garonne		5
Var		70
Toulon	54	
Brignoles	10	
Vaucluse		1
Vendée		3
Vienne		3
Vienne (Haute)		6
Vosges		14
Yonne		6
Total		1,707
Paris		952
Banlieue		86
Subscribers in France		2,745
Sold au bureau and by correspondents		ca.700
Total sales in France		3,445
Foreign subscribers		94
Total sales		3,539
Exchanges and free copies		49
Total circulation		3,588
Press run		3,600

older craft industries was moving apace. Lyons was dominated by the silk industry, which exhibited a highly capitalistic putting-out system of production marked by intense social antagonism. Traditional craft industry held sway in the other towns where Icarian communism showed strength and this preponderance correlates with the occupational structure of the movement. The virtual absence of Icarians in the rapidly industrializing cities of the Nord, such as Lille and Roubaix, indicates that one of the general rules of the social impact of industrialization holds for Icarianism as well: the new factory proletariat is normally passive and without political consciousness during the initial phase of industrialization.[11]

A majority of Cabet's subscribers were provincial. In some cities, such as Reims and Vienne, Icarian communism was the first doctrine of social reform ever to gain wide currency among the working classes. In many cases the proportion of Icarians to the total number of workers was much higher in provincial cities than in Paris. For instance, at Vienne, where the total number of workers was about 7,000, there were 62 subscriptions to *Le Populaire*—a ratio of about 110 to one; in Paris the figures were 342,000 and 962, or a ratio of 350 to one.[12]

The social status of Icarians can be gauged roughly from their occupations. It has been possible to identify the jobs of 497 declared Icarians (see Table 3). From this information some projections about the occupational structure of the entire movement can be made.

Table 3. Occupations of Icarians

Occupation	Number	Per cent
Tailors	89	18
Shoemakers and bootmakers	82	17
Cabinetmakers	28	5.5
Hatters	14	3
Weavers	37	7
Building trades workers	41	8
Mécaniciens	13	2.5

[11] See especially André Lasserre, *La Situation des ouvriers de l'industrie textile dans la région lilloise sous la Monarchie de Juillet* (Lausanne, 1950), 226–27.

[12] The figures on total numbers of workers are drawn from Rude, "L'Arrondissement de Vienne," 216, and Chambre de Commerce de Paris, *Statistique de l'Industrie de Paris* (Paris, 1851), 38.

Table 3.   Occupations of Icarians (cont.)

Occupation	Number		Per cent	
Locksmiths		11		2
Jewelers		10		2
Printers, lithographers, binders		7		1.5
Spinners		2		0.5
Diverse occupations		90		18
Total workers or artisans				
(status unspecified)		424		85
(a) In traditional crafts	379		76	
(b) Possibly in modern				
industry*	23		4.5	
(c) In food and service				
industries†	22		4.5	
Masters and chefs d'atelier				
(specified)		11		2
Petty bourgeois				
(shopkeepers and clerks)		17		3.5
Commercial bourgeois‡		19		4
Professional bourgeois§		23		4.5
Rentiers		1		—
Peasants		2		0.5
Grand totals		497		99.5

* Included here (despite the lack of precision): *mécaniciens, fondeurs, fileurs, ouvriers en limes,* a *raffineur,* and a *gazier.*
† Included here and not calling themselves *marchands: boulangers, bouchers,* a *patissier,* a *charcutier,* a *crémier,* a *garçon de café, blanchisseurs, coiffeurs, conducteurs de dilligence,* and *jardiniers.*
‡ 8 *marchands and commis;* 8 *fabricants,* 3 *négociants.*
§ 4 lawyers, 3 physicians, 2 teachers, 7 writers, artists, or students, and 7 from diverse occupations.
SOURCES: The principal sources for table 3 are: (1) the list of shareholders and their occupations printed at the end of Cabet's brochure, *Les Masques arrachés* (Paris, 1844); (2) additional names in a similar list supporting the *Biographie de M. Cabet* published by the Actionnaires du Populaire (Paris, 1846); (3) "addresses d'adhesion" with names and occupations from Nantes, Tours, Reims, and Périgueux appearing in *Le Populaire;* (4) a short list of correspondents that appeared in *Le Populaire* on Dec. 25, 1846, plus additional correspondents whose occupations are given in various issues of *Le Populaire,* the *Almanachs,* Cabet's brochures, and the local press (25 persons altogether); (5) the Lyon Commission (*Le Populaire,* Aug. 22, 1844) and other Lyonnais Icarians whose occupations I have discovered in a wide variety of sources (29 persons); (6) new names appearing on addresses and personal letters protesting Cabet's arrest and trial for "swindling" early in 1848 (Cabet, *Notre Procès en escroquerie* [Paris, 1849]); (7) new names on a list of members of the Société pour fonder l'Icarie, formed late in 1847 (*Le Populaire,* Oct. 17, 1847); and (8) additional persons drawn from a host of archival and printed documents concerning the Icarian movement. This collection has been made on the basis of name and occupation. No person has been counted more than once. The largest number of names and occupations come from the years 1843 and 1847, thus encompassing both the earlier and later phases of the movement. I have been reluctantly forced to reject one source, a long list of correspondents compiled by the procureur-général of Saint-Quentin from Cabet's files in preparation for his trial in January 1848, since there is no indication of how many were actually Icarian adherents and how many were in correspondence with Cabet for other reasons. For this list, see Pierre Caron, "Cabet et l'Icarie en 1847, document inédit," *Revue d'histoire moderne et contemporaine,* 8 (1907), 569–85. See Appendix 2 for the complete occupational list.

This table is admittedly an approximation, being based not on a random sample but on a collection of all the individual Icarians whose occupations are known and necessarily dependent on the nature of the sources. Three major sources, two lists of shareholders of *Le Populaire* (1844 and 1846) and one list of members of the Société pour fonder l'Icarie (1847), while excellent in that they include affiliates at three different stages of the movement, are somewhat misleading in two respects. First, Parisian trades are overrepresented; about 50 per cent of the people counted in the table were Parisians, while only one-third of *Le Populaire*'s subscribers were from Paris or its suburbs. Second, since it cost money to become a shareholder or to join the Icarian colony, better-paying occupations are no doubt overrepresented. Moreover, we lack long lists of supporters (with their occupations) from Vienne, Rouen, Mulhouse, or Lyons; hence textile workers—especially weavers— are probably underrepresented. Then there is the problem of the craft status of the many traditional artisans affiliated with Icarian communism. How many were masters and how many wage-earning journeymen (or other variations)? We do not really know. A man who lists himself as a *cordonnier,* for example, could well be a master shoemaker. At the same time we know that Cabet, desiring that the movement seem as respectable as possible, indicated the highest status possible for his followers. Overall, it is probable that the number of masters listed is too low, but there can be little doubt that a large majority of Cabet's artisan followers were *ouvriers.* In any case, the income differentials among master, chef d'atelier, wage-earning worker, and an *ouvrier* working on his own account without receiving wages was often not very great in the tailoring, shoemaking, and weaving trades (although there might be a great range from one type of establishment, product, or town to another). This is a complex problem that cannot be fully sorted out on the basis of only such summary occupational designations as *tisserand* or *tailleur*. Finally, I suspect that workers in modern industry are underrepresented, though not by a great deal. Icarianism showed some strength in towns where factory industry and mining had made important inroads; since we have little occupational information from these cities, the number of spinners, for instance, indicated here is probably not completely accurate.

Two technical problems should also be mentioned. *Menuisier*

might indicate either a furniture maker working on common woods
—as opposed to the higher status *ébéniste*—or a woodworker in
the building trades; there is no way of distinguishing between the
two (only two menuisiers indicated their connection—one in each
occupation). I have therefore divided the twenty-four menuisiers
equally between the two trades. The same question arises with
serruriers (locksmiths), who might be true locksmiths, stovesmiths,
metalworkers connected with the building trades, or machinists
(*mécanicien* and *serrurier* could connote the same occupation).
One cannot deal with this problem systematically.

It is clear from Table 3, whatever its shortcomings, that Cabet's
adherents were overwhelmingly recruited from the working class
as it was defined in the 1840s. In contrast, the other great "school"
of the day, the Fourierists, seems to have attracted mostly well-
educated professionals.[13] Within the Icarian group, four-fifths of
the working-class element came from trades dominated by handicraft artisans, and among these tailors and shoemakers alone constituted two-fifths. The latter were among the most populous
trades in France and particularly in Paris. But 40 per cent of the
Icarian workers came from these trades, a figure that far outstrips

[13] No detailed study of the Fourierist movement during the 1840s has yet
been made, but most indications sustain the judgment of Sébastien Commissaire that "The phalanstère scarcely found any partisans in the working
class" (*Mémoires*, 92). Duveau (*1848*, 241), who quotes Commissaire to
this effect, notes, however, that Fourier was fairly well known among working-class leaders. Anthime Corbon, *Le Secret du peuple de Paris* (Paris,
1863), 99–108, says that both Fourierism and Saint-Simonism were much
less popular with the lower classes than was communism. Finally, the government was less likely to attack Fourierist than communist groups precisely
because it recognized the former's social composition. Of the four documents
concerning Fourierist public lectures that I have found in A.N. series BB[18]
(Justice), two note that they were attended by the respectable classes and
were allowed to continue until their completion (lectures given by Jules
Duval and Victor Hennequin at Limoges and Grenoble in 1847). But Victor
Considérant spoke to assemblies "composed largely of workers" in Saint-
Quentin in 1845, and the lectures were apparently suspended. The other
document, concerning a lecture held in Lyons in 1847, does not mention
the social composition of the audience or the outcome. That the authorities
were complacent about Fourierism is indicated by the fact that the mayor
of Limoges, with the approbation of the prefect (who attended the first two
meetings), allowed Duval to give his lectures in the Palais de Justice. Later
in 1847, however, Duchâtel, Minister of the Interior, instituted a general
policy to forbid Fourierist public lectures in light of the "present crisis."
A.N., BB[18] 1434 dos 619A, 1451 dos 3660 and 3636.

the proportion of tailors and shoemakers working in Paris (twelve per cent in 1848).[14] Cabet drew poorly from the "aristocratic" crafts, such as printing and jewelry making (despite the overrepresentation noted above). These were occupational groups that were more interested in economic action and moderate political pressure within the existing social framework and that gave support to *L'Atelier,* Ledru-Rollin, and even *Le National.*[15] The building trades gave only moderate support to Icarian communism; while they constituted 12 per cent of the worker population in Paris in 1847–1848, only 10 per cent of Icarian workers were in the building trades, and a large majority of these were provincials. This fact tends to support the oft-repeated assertion that Parisian builders, if they were to take a political position, would line up with the proponents of violence. Still, Icarian communism made an impact among these men. A Parisian mason reported in 1846 that pacific "communism has recently made considerable headway among the workers in the building trades; . . . there are few workshops that do not seriously discuss [it]."[16]

The lack of petty-bourgeois support reveals that there was little sans-culottism in Icarian communism. The line had been well drawn during the July Monarchy; the grocer and the stationer, the fruit lady and the baker could easily rally to social republicanism, but communism was not the society of small property holders, not Robespierre's *république des jouissances;* it was instead a world in which they would have no function at all and in which they could no longer look down their noses at those whose only property was their hands. The same type of argument assists in explaining what appears to be the small number of master artisans in the Icarian ranks.

Finally, these data clearly indicate the meager following that Cabet found among bourgeois occupations. This was a heartbreaking experience for him for he had expected that he could count upon the good will of the propertied classes, that they could be rationally convinced of the happiness for all to be found under communism. As we shall see, this failure to win adherents among the bourgeoisie caused Cabet to recognize the deep antagonism

---

[14] Chambre de Commerce de Paris, *Statistique,* table 28.
[15] See Cuvillier, *Un Journal d'ouvriers,* 179–81.
[16] *Almanach icarien pour 1846* (Paris, 1845), 180–81.

that existed between the working class and the bourgeoisie in France at the time and that would ultimately face him with the bitter choice choice between the promotion of working-class revolution and escape.[17]

Economic Change and the Lives of French Workingmen

Most Icarians were working men and women. In the forty-eight era, however, the terms working class and proletariat, while well integrated into the parlance of the day, did not evoke the same image that they would later in the century. The great majority of those included under such rubrics were not factory or mine operatives but individuals plying hand crafts. With the exceptions of textile spinning, certain aspects of the metallurgical industries and mining, and a few specialized industries such as papermaking and sugar refining, little mechanization had taken place in France by the 1840s. But economic modernization meant more than the modernization of industry. Indeed, a case might be made that the key changes before the Second Empire derived less from new technology than from more efficient business practices and more careful exploitation of traditional labor resources. For instance, the sophistication of management and marketing procedures and the concentration of ownership maintained the place of Lyons silk in the world market, and the growth of standardization and a putting-out system developed a mass market in clothing and furniture during the forties. Even in the common textile industires, the employment of low-paid rural hand-loom weavers did as much to make them economically viable as the mule-jenny. Moreover, an increasing divsion of labor and local specialization characterized the progress of many industries yet untouched by the factory system. Economic progress without mechanization was by no means unique to the French industrial revolution. A high degree of efficiency and productivity was achieved, for example, in the English Midlands hardware industry in a handicraft technical framework that lasted well into the industrial era.[18] As we shall see, Icarian recruits were

---

[17] See below, Chap. 5.

[18] W. G. B. Court, "Industrial Organization and Economic Progress in the Eighteenth Century Midlands," in his *Scarcity and Choice in History* (New York, 1970), 235–49. My remarks about general economic change in France are drawn from a wide reading in secondary and primary materials. Among the latter, the "Enquête sur le travail agricole et industriel" (A.N.

drawn overwhelmingly from crafts that were affected less by direct industrialization than by its side effects.

Few historians today would contest the thesis that conscious militance in the early industrial revolution was to be found largely among artisans.[19] If militance existed in large-scale industry a further significant factor was the age of the working-class community and the continuity of its traditions.[20] Indiscriminate discussion of artisan militance is meaningless, however. The artisans of France were splintered in numerous ways and were less homogeneous than the working class of later years. There was a veritable hierarchy of crafts, recognized by most artisans themselves and by society at large. Pride in craft and corporate traditions, perhaps admirable qualities when viewed from the more atomized perspective of the twentieth century, saw to it that intercraft antagonism remained a fact of life even after the abolition of the guilds during the French Revolution. This antagonism was exacerbated by the continuation of the ancient compagnonnage, which not only promoted mistrust and violent conflicts among the crafts but also preserved a ritual character seriously undermining its practical work in defense of journeymen's interests. Only in the 1840s did Agricole Perdiguier and other reformists seek to build unity and bring syndicalist ideals

C943–969) is unquestionably the most important. The major general studies of economic growth in nineteenth century France are listed in the bibliography. See also Christopher H. Johnson, "The Revolution of 1830 in French Economic History," in John Merriman, ed., *Essays on the French Revolution of 1830* (forthcoming).

[19] See especially the assessments of Peter Stearns, "Patterns of Industrial Strike Activity during the July Monarchy," *American Historical Review,* LXX (1965), 383–90; Patrick Kessel, *Le Prolétariat français avant Marx* (Paris, 1968), 194–358; Maurice Agulhon, *Une Ville ouvrière au temps du socialisme utopique: Toulon, 1815–1851* (Paris, 1970); Rémi Gossez, *Les Ouvriers de Paris;* Livre premier; *L'Organisation, 1848–1851* (La Roche-sur-Yon, 1967); and E. P. Thompson, *The Making of the English Working Class* (London, 1963).

[20] The classic example here is the nature of strike activity in Lodève as opposed to Lille. Despite a certain amount of Luddism, Lodévois textile workers, whose roots went back several generations, struck during the July Monarchy in times of prosperity and exhibited a high degree of organization and discipline. The only strike in Lille during the July Monarchy occurred in 1839, in the depth of a depression, and took on the character of an urban jacquerie. Stearns, "Strike Activity"; Frank Manuel, "L'Introduction des machines en France et les ouvriers: La Grève des tisserands de Lodève," *Revue d'histoire moderne,* X (1935) 209–25, 352–72; Lasserre, *La Situation des ouvriers.*

into this institution.[21] But the compagnonnage included only a minority of journeymen, most of them in the building trades. Another factor breeding intercraft resentment was the bifurcation between licensed workers and those whose skill was not certified under public law. The skilled crafts with strict apprenticeship regulations fell into the former category, and therefore income differentials further magnified the sting of legal inferiority. Among the numerous advantages of certification was the fact that the only official institution of the age specifically authorized to deal with employer-worker disputes, the conseils des prud'hommes (comprised of an equal number of elected representatives from each side), allowed only licensed workers to participate.[22]

While such divisive forces remained important, during the July Monarchy the changing structure of the economy began to reduce their significance. One can discern the first steps in the "proletarianization" of the diverse groups of artisans, at least in the larger cities, and a growing realization on their part—often masters and workers alike—that they had a common foe, the capitalist entrepreneur.

Corporate relations within the crafts varied considerably from one to another. In this transitional economy nearly every type of small-scale industrial structure was represented. Direct-sale consumer production was largely carried on in small workshops that normally doubled as retail outlets. Representative here were such trades as blacksmiths, wheelwrights, harnessmakers, tailors, shoemakers, locksmiths, and cabinetmakers. But in large urban centers, two trends were apparent by the forties. First, while the small master with one or two journeymen still predominated, larger shops, employing a dozen or more individuals, were moving into the market and drawing the wrath of small masters and increasingly bitter resistance from their own workers. Second, ready-made production (*la confection*), controlled by huge putting-out firms, was now in serious competition with made-to-order work, especially in the clothing trades. Both trends increased the division of labor, thereby reducing the diversity of skills possessed by any single worker and routinizing his workday more thoroughly. Large tailor

[21] See Briquet, *Agricole Perdiguier*.
[22] See Maurice Bouvier-Ajam, *Histoire du travail en France depuis la Révolution* (Paris, 1969), 85–86.

shops, for instance, were hierarchically organized, with cutters holding pride of place over a team of sewers, some of whom (a much resented fact) were women. But trousers were often put out for sewing to extremely low-paid piece workers working in their own quarters. In the world of confection all work save cutting was put out to much larger numbers of pieceworkers or sometimes to small shops that had failed as made-to-order retailers. "Sweated labor" arrived on the scene long before the cheap Singer sewing machine circled the globe.[23]

The social relations of production within these crafts depended, therefore, on scale and organization. In small shops, older, familial relations were no doubt paramount. Thus for a majority of artisans in these trades, antagonism between master and worker was minimal. Indeed, because of the growing competition from larger outfits and the generalized overcrowding of traditional crafts that marked the thirties and forties,[24] they drew closer together in common defense against the more clearly capitalist elements in their crafts, the big masters and especially the confectionneurs. Small shops as a whole tended to sympathize with the grievances of wage earners in larger concerns. Perhaps the most oppressed elements among the traditional consumer production crafts were those who worked on their own. Often a master's certificate was meaningless here, although it might bring in better-paid work than was garnered by the independent journeyman. In either case, their normal role was that of a pieceworker at the mercy of the merchant-manufacturer and his commissioned agent (*commis*). Luckier ones might become subcontractors, who hired temporary labor and divided (unequally) the piece rates paid by their suppliers. But they in turn—quite literally—became class traitors. *Ouvriers en*

---

[23] Little modern research has been done on these important issues. A summary may be found in Henriette Vanier, *La Mode et ses métiers: Frivolités et luttes des classes, 1830–1870* (Paris, 1960), 59–63, 75–105. With particular reference to sweated labor, see Albert Aftalion, *Le Développement de la fabrique et le travail à domicile dans les industries de l'habillement* (Paris, 1906), 20–27, 51–54. The best analysis of confection in its early phase is Lémann, Négociant confectionneur, *De L'Industrie de vêtements confectionnés en France* (Paris: Paul Dupont, 1857). See also *Le Journal des tailleurs* Nov. 21, 1830; Feb. 16, March 1, April 1, May 1, 1831; July 1, 1832; Feb. 16, Nov. 1, 1833; Jan. 1, 1835; Feb. 16, 1857; May 1, 1841; and Chambre de Commerce de Paris, *Statistique*, 36–46, 285–305.

[24] See Bouvier-Ajam, *Histoire du travail*, 122–23, and below, nn. 72–76.

chambre (people working in their own residences) comprised a majority in many trades and were often lost in contemporary analysis—and in historical discussion. Perhaps this is in part because, as in the famous *articles de Paris* trade (including paperflowers, umbrellas, and other accessories), so many of them were women and foreigners.[25] Among shoemakers, the independent worker was often truly independent; he carried his bench directly to the house of the customer. But as we shall see in the tale of an Icarian, this guaranteed neither a sense of fulfillment nor bread.

In general, then, the working world of the traditional artisan was in flux during the July Monarchy and rumbling with discontent from a variety of sources. The most evident trend was toward capitalist, if not industrial, forms of organization that tended to homogenize this great mass of artisans and turn their sights toward dismantling the emergent system. *Communauté*—in the general sense of solidarity, in cooperation of production (perhaps the strongest urge in this age), or in communism itself—drew its first breath from the new set of circumstances besetting them.

Other important forms of artisan productive organization included artisan "factory" production, the old-line putting-out system, and the peculiar structure of the building trades. The first comprised all hand industries where fixed capital costs were too great to be defrayed by a man with little more than his skill to offer. Included here would be a variety of metallurgical crafts not yet converted to modern methods, the carriage trade, tannery, pottery, glassmaking, brickmaking, and the like. Workers in such industries were often better paid even than many masters in the consumer crafts, but, unless itinerancy marked their life style (as with the glass blowers),[26] their pride, literacy, wage-earning status and concentrated numbers often placed them among the most self-conscious workers of the era.

If rural domestic workers are included, putting-out operations, especially in textiles, probably took up more man-hours in the mid-nineteenth century than any other form of production except agri-

[25] On resentment against women in the clothing trades, see Vanier, *La Mode*, 78–82.
[26] See Joan Scott, "The Glass Workers of Carmaux," in S. Thernstrom, ed., *Cities in the Nineteenth Century* (Cambridge, Mass., 1971).

culture.[27] (Because of the composition of the Icarian group, however, the problems of the rural outworker must be by-passed.) Among urban putting-out systems, the Lyonnais silk industry was no doubt the most famous. The chef d'atelier, a master weaver employing several compagnons, owned his looms and sometimes his own workshop as well. Yet he was at the mercy of the fabricant, who provided him with the silk thread and paid him piece rates (to be divided among his compagnons and himself) for the finished product. The exploiter in this case was clearly the fabricant; although the interests of the chefs and their compagnons were sometimes at odds,[28] the composite group of masters and workers (the *canuts*) formed a common front against him. The hand-loom weavers in cotton and the weavers, combers, and carders in wool provide another case in point, but here one does not find the elaborate substructure of production that existed in Lyons. Normally the corporative status of these men made little difference because of the individual or small-group nature of their work. A commis, employed by the cloth merchant, distributed the yarn (now usually spun in factories) to the single weaver and paid him piece wages for his work. The comber's and carder's situation was usually identical; he received the raw material and returned it to be spun. The abuses accompanying this system were legion. In the Tourcoing-Roubaix area, for example, wool combers were granted only a 4 per cent loss in weight due to evaporation on the materials they received, combed, and returned to the mill owners. This was reasonable, but they were not allowed to contest the weight declared by their employers upon return of the goods. It was esti-

[27] There can be little doubt that the putting-out system increased, both in numbers of employees and in scale of enterprise, during the first half of the nineteenth century. The great development came in rural hand-loom weaving in response to the massive demand for weavers created by the mechanization of spinning. Everywhere in France where textile production had previously been established—save in linen areas of the west and some woolens enclaves in the Midi—a boom in domestic outworking was perceptible. Often, however, it meant replacement of old fabrics by new, which caused short-term local displacements (for example, *sayettrie* by *nouveautés* in woolens). On this whole question, see the careful assessment of Maurice Lévy-Leboyer, *Les Banques européenes et l'industrialization internationale dans le première moitié du XIX° siècle* (Paris, 1964), 66–115.

[28] See Fernand Rude's discussion of this in connection with the rising of November 1831 in *Le Mouvement ouvrier à Lyon depuis 1827 à 1832* (Paris, 1945), 499ff.

mated that combers lost as much as 5 per cent of their pay because of underweighing.[29] Deductions made for allegedly sloppy work were a chronic problem for weavers of all sorts. The merchant-manufacturer had the final word on such matters, and the chilling phrase "dock this man ten centimes an ell," was heard all too often.[30] Urban textile outworkers were among the most militant of the early industrial era in most West European countries. All the pressure of the emergent economic system, from both organizational and technological sources, weighed upon them.

In the building trades the workmen were almost entirely journeymen. Their direct superior was not normally a master in the craft but either a *contre-maître* [foreman], a salaried employee of the building contractor, or, more often, a marchandeur, who hired men after agreeing to a contract price for a project with the entrepreneur. Subcontracting was one of the great abuses afflicting the building trades and would be the subject of a major decree of the provisional government in 1848. These job-bosses might be master masons, carpenters, and so on, but not necessarily. In any case, since the worker-employer ratio was quite high (twenty-five to one for the Parisian masons for instance)[31] and because the entrepreneur could not always be on the job, there was little similarity between the relations of production of the building trades and those of traditional crafts. Builders' wages were generally below those of the factory artisans but higher than outworkers. But builders had the rigorous training of the former and perhaps an even higher estimate of their skill. They lived in a rough-and-tumble world, moved about a great deal, and were faced with seasonal unemployment that often forced them to seek other work (or return to their home country in the winter). Especially in Paris, there was probably no other group of more worldly workers, and they tended to be politically sophisticated.[32]

Thus, though France's development toward industrialization was slow and the number of factory proletarians small during the

---

[29] Enquête sur le travail agricole et industriel, Nord, Tourcoing, Archives départementales du Nord (Lille), M 547/1.

[30] R. J. Bezucha, "The 'Pre-industrial' Worker Movement: The *Canuts* of Lyon," in Bezucha, ed., *Modern European Social History* (Lexington, Mass., 1972), 102.

[31] Chambre de Commerce de Paris, *Statistique*, 83.

[32] Nadaud, *Mémoires, passim,* exemplified this clearly.

first half of the nineteenth century, the vast class of artisans, the supposed appendage of another era, was itself undergoing a transformation in which the bourgeois merchant capitalist was emerging as the real employer. Modern relations of production were developing despite the continuation of the traditional tools and processes of production. Rather than being simply eliminated by technology —though this obviously occurred—many artisans, master and worker alike, came under the dominion of an entrepreneurial, but commercial, bourgeoisie. The real antagonist of the cabinetmaker was not the owner of the furniture factory, for his competition at this point was negligible, but the dreaded commis.[33]

To speak of a working class with a reasonable community of interests is, therefore, not impossible. Differences existed, to be sure: between artisan and factory worker, between journeyman and master, and perhaps above all among crafts and even within crafts between the factions of the compagonnage. But by the 1840s the French working class was a much less amorphous entity than it had been fifty years before. Certainly when Flora Tristan preached the doctrine of working-class solidarity she was not just talking to the factory workers but to all working people subordinated to the domination of capital.

Simply to note the objective social forces engendering working-class homogeneity is not to explain the emergence of the social question and of working-class consciousness during the 1840s. Economically, the first half of the nineteenth century in France was, despite the appearance of modern industry, a depressed period. According to Labrousse and others, the long secular trend of rising prices and relative prosperity came to an end in 1817. Prices fell, but wages and employment more so. This was coupled with fairly rapid population growth. The forties saw a revival of the general economic fortunes of France, but workers' earnings were caught in a classical price-wage squeeze.[34] Moreover, in the case of many traditional occupations, now beleaguered by economic modernization, wages fell even further. Such global economic problems found their day-to-day expression in widespread working-class misery. The conditions of working-class existence need no general elucida-

[33] Chambre de Commerce de Paris, *Statistique,* 160.
[34] See the graph on p. 38 of E. Labrousse, *Le Mouvement ouvrier et les théories sociales en France de 1815 à 1848* (Paris, 1948).

tion here. The overwhelmingly pessimistic views of such contemporaries as Ange Guépin, Bigot de Morogues, Louis Villermé, and even Adolphe Blanqui and of historians from Emile Levasseur to Georges Duveau, Louis Chevalier, and Maurice Agulhon suffice to defend the simple conclusion that a majority of French working people were poorly fed, miserably housed, and inadequately clothed.[35] Moreover, they were largely unprotected from unemployment due to sickness, accidents, weather, or the vicissitudes of the market. Savings institutions were in their infancy, and workers' paltry attempts at self-help—the mutual benefit societies—were often mistrusted by the authorities and broken up on suspicion of being secret societies or trade unions. Scattered examples of employer paternalism can be found, and a few priests preached the "eye of the needle" sermon, but, at least internally, this was the age of laissez-faire. In the minds of the ruling class drink was a more important source of misery than low wages.[36]

The law, in the name of freedom of contracts, prohibited trade unions and indeed any unauthorized association. Only one piece of social legislation was passed between 1815 and 1848, the Factory Act of 1841, and even it remained unenforced.[37] The workingman could not vote at any level, and given the laws on caution money, it was made difficult for him even to read political information favoring his interests.[38] The law forced many workers to carry a *livret,* a little booklet in which his previous employer could discuss his qualities (and opinions) to pass on to the next. More serious perhaps was the fact that employers often made sizable advances

[35] See Guépin, *Nantes au XIXᵉ siècle* (Nantes, 1835); Bigot de Morogues, *De la Misère des ouvriers et de la marche à suivre pour y remédier* (Paris, 1832); Villermé, *Tableau de l'état physique et morale des ouvriers employés dans les manufactures de coton, de laine et de soie,* 2 vols. (Paris, 1839); Adolphe Blanqui, *Des Classes ouvrières en France* (Paris, 1849); Emile Levasseur, *Histoire des classes ouvrières et de l'industrie en France,* II (Paris, 1903); Duveau, *La Vie ouvrière en France sous la Second Empire* (Paris, 1946); Chevalier, *Classes laborieuses et classes dangereuses* (Paris, 1958); Agulhon, *Une ville ouvrière.*

[36] Although I have not made a statistical tabulation on this question, I have been struck by the many responses to question 26 of the Enquête sur le travail of 1848 (A.N. C 743-C 769) emphasizing that temperance was the key to overcoming working-class misery.

[37] Kessel, *Le Prolétariat,* 331–32.

[38] Irene Collins, *The Government and the Newspaper Press in France* (Oxford, 1959), analyzes with care the high cost of journalism.

to workers upon hiring them and then recorded the debt in the livrets (which the employers kept in their possession).[39] There is no need to expand upon the obvious consequences of such an abuse. Under the aegis of laissez-faire, the law skirted most subjects of potential industrial dispute. Weight and quality rules, abolished with the guilds, were now the whim of the boss and—a much rued fact—the retail merchant. And what if a worker should want to lodge a legal grievance? Conseils des prudhommes existed in only seventy-one cities in France as late as 1850,[40] and their usefulness was doubtful given their composition. Even if all contremaîtres, chef d'ateliers, or licensed workers resisted bribes offered by employers' representatives, the public official who presided had the tie-breaking vote. The cost of litigation was exhorbitant, and even should a worker be so bold as to take his boss to court, article 1,781 of the Criminal Code blandly noted that, in cases where an outside witness was lacking, the word of a master would be accepted over that of his man.

Adeline Daumard suggests, in her masterpiece on the Parisian bourgeoisie, that the French social structure may have been less open during the July Monarchy than at any other time since the collapse of the old regime. She demonstrates not only that the bourgeoisie rigidified internally but that access to it, even on its lower levels, decreased. For example, in 1820 10 per cent of all clerks in Paris were the sons of artisans or wage-earning workers, while the figure had dropped to 6 per cent in 1847. But the door remained open to the sons of land-owning peasants, especially among the medium-income shopkeepers, where 35 per cent at both dates came from such a background. This must have frustrated workers all the more. To be sure, considerable social overlap existed between the petty bourgeoisie and the working classes, but even here 1820 death records show that 37 per cent of the children of petty bourgeois had become wage-earning workers, while the number had risen to 45 per cent by 1847. Such data indicate that the July Monarchy, far from being the promised era of opportunity for working people, actually witnessed downward social mobility.[41]

[39] See the important dossier, Enquête sur les avances aux ouvriers (1850), A.N., F12 2354.

[40] From a list in *ibid.*

[41] Daumard, *Les Bourgeois de Paris au XIXᵉ siècle* (Paris: Flammarion, 1970), especially 125–66.

Yet the workers had been taught for fifty years that liberty and justice had come to reign in France because of the heroic acts of their forefathers. The Great Revolution had abolished oppression. Then, in 1830, Parisian workers went to the streets to defend liberty anew—and won for themselves and France a regime perhaps more insensitive to their cry for social justice than any before or since. But a few Parisians, then Lyonnais, then increasingly workers all over France began to sense the significance of their power after 1830.[42] They listened, wrote a little, and often acted with purpose in defense of their rights and interests. The revolution of 1830 was a great milestone in the history of working-class consciousness in France for it provided a concrete example of the workers' potential political impact and a concrete lesson on the wiles of (at least) the grande bourgeoisie. The Lyons risings, the rue Transnonain, social republicanism, secret societies, Robespierre, Babeuf, Raspail, Cavaignac, Buchez, Buonarroti, Blanqui, Cabet himself—the Pantheon of the thirties was now lodged in the hearts of a sizable minority of workers. Such expectations in face of such injustice and misery, of such bewildering economic change! Here were the ingredients of the social movement of the 1840s, and of the revolution of 1848. In such a framework men and women began to opt for communism.

Icarians Speak

What did Icarians say about themselves, their society, and the factors that brought them to communism? That we have any information at all is an unusual blessing. The workingman leaves few traces of his opinions and attitudes, and one method of getting at the working-class mind—the use of police records—is largely closed to us in this case since few Icarians were arrested.[43] We must rely heavily, therefore, on the communications sent to Cabet. A number of the extant manuscript letters Cabet received show the immense effort that was required of many a worker if he was to write at all, let alone express himself in a meaningful fashion. The

[42] The basic study of French workers during this period remains Octave Festy, *Le Mouvement ouvrier au début de la Monarchie de Juillet* (Lyon, 1908).

[43] In any case see Richard Cobb, *The Police and the People: French Popular Protest 1789–1820* (London, 1970), 3–57, for a discussion of the relative value of police evidence and informers' reports from earlier years.

handwriting is often strained, grammar and spelling are incorrect, and punctuation is sometimes nonexistent. Cabet, if he printed the letters, would usually correct punctuation and orthography, but occasionally he printed one as he received it—not to embarrass the sender but to capture more faithfully the voice of the common worker who had come to communism.

One should, therefore, not expect sophisticated phraseology or analysis from the pens of Icarian communists. Yet most were aware of their oppressed condition, and most saw in Cabet's doctrine the true road to happiness. The following letter from J . . . , aged twenty-nine, a Parisian woodworker in the carriage trade is typical of hundreds of communications sent to Cabet:

Paris September 27, 1841

Citizens,
Excuse me if I take the liberty to write you. I have seen with pleasure that you take an interest in the people, principally in the uneducated worker who has good ideas but who cannot express them owing to his ignorance. I am of this number and I want to instruct myself in the ways of Community. Yes, citizen, I am a communist because I want the well-being of my brothers, I am a communist because I have no other ambition than to do good. In my mind Community is the finest thing that could exist. With it, pride, ambition, avarice, tyranny will fall; without Community the people will always be cast into the abyss into which they are plunged every day; without Community no happiness for the people. To have this moral Community, education is necessary for us, children of the people; well, citizen, it is to you that I address myself for my education; as you see I still do not have much education.[44]

Several general themes emerge from Icarian correspondence. Most letters mention the workers' misery and exploitation, but only a minority reveal a full consciousness of the power of a united working class. The latter were usually written during the years 1845–1846, indicating a possible trend in this direction.

In 1842 "a worker in another large city" hoped that *Le Populaire* would become a weekly, because

it could give the PARIAHS of the social order the advice they need; we

[44] *Le Populaire,* Supplément, Oct. 10, 1841.

would also have a greater chance to say a few words about our situation, we who are at the mercy of the *exploiters* in a city where mercantile egotism is carried to the highest point. While there will always be some work available here the *bad organization of labor,* coupled with the hardheartedness of the monopolizers, will always cause the worker . . . to go to die in the poorhouse if a Social Reform does not occur, . . . if the rich refuse to hear the voice of humanity.

Louis Mauvais of Reims considered that, in comparison to the employers of today, "the slaveholders [in the colonies] are philanthropic friends of humanity, for at least they nourish their slaves. Oh Christ, is it for such results that you died on the cross!!"[45] A greater sophistication is to be found later on; experience and propaganda led to a firmer resolve. A letter from Annonay early in 1846 echoed Sieyès: "The worker realizes that he ought to be something, he who is the force and wealth of the nation." Nineteen Rouennais supported Icarianism because it promoted their just claims on society. They had to speak out "when each day is marked by a violation of our rights, when all our relations, whether with our masters or with public functionaries, are acts of authority that wound our dignity." And who can doubt the power of a united working class? In the opinion of a group of Parisian Icarians, should a class "struggle" occur, "the bourgeoisie, egotistical, cuning in trade [but] contributing nothing to the production of its wealth, would not even try to fight against the strong arms of the producers."[46]

Such social analysis, however, is less in evidence than the simple vision of a peaceful, untroubled, and prosperous life to be had in Icaria, without concern for the complexities of current society or the potential problems of Cabet's utopia. "Community unites within it everything that man could desire in order to make the Golden Age live once more, to make a veritable paradise," said a young female Icarian from Lyons. Several followers in Toulouse thought Icaria was a real place and wanted to know how to get there. Others saw the doctrine as a kind of "balm" or "consolation" akin to a fairy tale or romance. It also made "new men" out of some affiliates. A draftsman wrote that he had "cursed my social position

---

[45] *Ibid.,* May 8, June 5, 1842. Cabet later wrote an article expanding on the last point and was attacked for being in favor of slavery!

[46] *Ibid.,* Jan. 24, May 29, 1846, Nov. 22, 1845.

and the entire society" seeing only gold as the road to happiness; he was "not really alive"; but Cabet's writing "cast a healing balm on my senses . . . by showing me the cause of the evils of which I only saw the effects."[47] The therapeutic effect of Cabet's doctrine cannot be doubted, but it involved a clear danger—that the balm of the Icarian dream might undermine the resolve to create it in reality. Shortly before her death, Flora Tristan labeled Cabet an *endormeur*, claiming that he entrapped his followers in a fantasy world while the real purpose of working-class agitation was to consolidate resistance against the capitalist regime. Although there was no love lost between Tristan and Cabet, her statement had some basis in fact.[48]

Some workers became Icarians after comparing several "systems," or at least through a genuine intellectual effort. The *Voyage en Icarie* was normally the work that finally brought such people to communism. This is an interesting phenomenon, because it shows that there existed a kind of market place of socialist ideas from which some workers rationally chose the most appealing wares. A letter from A. Barbier, a woodworker in the building trades, is particularly interesting for the intellectual biography it presents of a thoughtful workingman. Barbier arrived penniless in Paris at the age of fourteen but was lucky enough to find a master who taught him his trade and sent him to a Protestant school, where he learned "to love others as I would have them love me." He originally learned of socialism from a "worker who seemed to meditate often on the life of man." Barbier thus came to see some basic contradictions: "Why here the rich, overflowing with the pleasure of the glittering life and all the gifts of nature, and there are unhappy poor, denied all wealth, crouching in the corner . . . humiliating themselves by supplying the affluent with the wherewithal of their existence? Why this difference between beings of the same nature

---

[47] *Ibid.,* Oct. 10, 1841. For some of the many examples of this attitude, see also the issues of Sept. 3, 1841, Oct. 9, 1842, March 9, 1843, and Jan. and Feb. 1845, Supplément.

[48] In her personal journal, she said: "M. Cabet has done much harm to the workers. He has paralyzed all desire for action in them; today the workers see only the reign of Icaria—resting there, fascinated, before this vision. They wait instead of working actively to prepare this happy reign." Quoted in Jules Puech, *La Vie et l'oeuvre de Flora Tristan* (Paris, 1925), 140, n. 2.

and capable of the same intelligence?" These preliminary thoughts were fueled by the heartlessness of most masters and by wages that were becoming "more and more insufficient because of the large number of workers who, out of need, work at any price." Then Barbier discovered Cabet and the *Voyage en Icarie.* It was as if a "new dawn" had broken, for it gave concrete direction to his resentment. It was thus that he gravitated from Saint-Simonism to Icarianism.[49] Frédéric Olinet, eventually a participant in the American colonization, remarked in his memoirs that in Lyons three writers, Leroux, Proudhon, and Cabet, were the dominant influences among the "partisans of socialism." But "the doctrines of the last, clearly defined in the *Voyage en Icarie,* exerted a different kind of enticement for them than the vague ideas of the other two masters, from whom they derived no image that could be easily grasped." Sébastien Commissaire, recalling his Icarian days in the mid-forties, also stressed the impact of the *Voyage en Icarie:* "This book, written in a simple style, in a way that could be understood by any intellect, had found numerous admirers in the working class. It was a plan of social organization, and in order to make it understood M. Cabet had imagined a society organized *en communauté,* living in an imaginary country to which he had given the name Icaria." The perfection of this new society had an overpowering effect on Cabet's working-class readers. "It was more than was needed to capture the imagination of the poor workers who suffered, who were uneasy about their future and that of their children, and who saw no possibility of bettering their lot."[50]

Working people also responded to particular elements of Cabet's appeal. The civil courage theme was fundamental in the thinking of many. Nearly all the declarations of support printed in *Le Populaire* and in Cabet's brochures stressed pacific means. The place of pacificism as a factor in the growth of the movement has been demonstrated in previous chapters. But the voice of an Icarian wife from Lyons reveals the ramifications of this message. Cabet reconstructed his conversation with her in the *Almanach* for 1846.

[49] Barbier to Cabet, Nov. 2, 1847, Papiers Cabet, BHVP. For other examples see Cabet, *Toute La Vérité,* 42; Cabet, *Utile et Franche Explication,* 26–27; Sordaliet to Cabet, Nov. 27, 1845, BHVP; *Le Populaire,* June 6 and 13, 1847.

[50] Frédéric Olinet [Job], *Voyage d'un Autunois en Icarie* (Autun, 1898), 18; Commissaire, *Mémoires,* I, 96–97.

The question asked was why so many women were devoted Icarians.

It is very simple; before Icarian Communism appeared, our husbands were nearly all in secret societies, . . . neglecting their work, spending all their money, always uneasy and upset, often arrested and prosecuted; and we were always abandoned, always in misery and anxiety. Since Icarian Communism, on the contrary, everything has changed; our husbands have renounced secret societies, and we no longer fear those dreadful searches, those terrible arrests, that ruined us in the past; they take us with them to their meetings with their friends to discuss things; the women thus find themselves meeting together along with their husbands and their children.[51]

Another important factor in the adherence of some Icarians was Cabet's long-time reputation as a defender of the working-class cause. Several remembered his role as editor of the republican weekly, *Le Populaire de 1833;* one correspondent called him the "oldest veteran of French democracy."[52] The most interesting comments on this score were made by Dubeau, a Parisian cabinet-maker living in the Marais: "I have followed your steps in the progress of socialism for quite a long time. . . . You were my guide in 1834. I read all your pamphlets; I followed you to the Chamber to defend our sister, Poland; my heart grieved to see you seated upon the bench of the accused, and I saw your calm bearing on hearing the sentence which pronounced the infamous penality; . . . I have thought about you in exile, writing the social document that will give the world an earthly paradise." He went on to say that in his mind only two men, Cabet and Raspail, were worthy of the love of the workingman, the latter because he cures the body and Cabet because he is "the doctor who cures the soul."[53]

Even before Cabet allowed the religious message to overwhelm the rest of his doctrine, in late 1846, the Christian-communist equation was powerful. Numerous letters agreed with the worker from Méric who testified before the procureur du roi, "Certainly you know that Jesus Christ identified with the poor. . . . Jesus Christ was a communist; our communism is the same thing as Christianity in its purity." Many spoke of the "holy doctrine" and

[51] *Le Populaire*, Nov. 13, 1842; *Almanach icarien pour 1846.*
[52] *Le Populaire*, May 20, 1842.
[53] Dubeau to Cabet, July 26, 1847, Papiers Cabet, XII, BHVP.

of Cabet as the "apostle of communism." Although we shall return to this when discussing the growing sectarian nature of the movement, one point should be noted here. While numerous working-men were convinced by the Christian-communist link, this emphasis was responsible for the adherence of nearly all Cabet's bourgeois followers. Dr. Desmoulins of Tours; the former merchant Laty of Autun; Finet, an Angoulême merchant; Dr. Rabyrin, a teacher from Lyons; Charles Chameroy, a traveling salesman; the journalist Adolphe Elléna of Toulon; these and many other middle-class figures in the movement saw it as the core of the doctrine. The group of Icarians at Nancy was strongly influenced by Chameroy's propaganda and had a heavy bourgeois representation; the forty-one Nanciens ("many of whom are fabricants") who declared their support in January 1846 said the major reason for their affiliation was that communism was the "doctrine of Christ." The best expression of the significance of the Christian-communist equation in bringing about bourgeois adherence was made by a salesman-merchant from Toulouse:

Enemies [say] that our doctrines suit only men without wealth and without social position, as if a man, simply because he possesses much, were incapable of having a heart which is generous, compassionate, and susceptible to sentiments of justice and humanity toward his brothers! Do they not know, these enemies of the truth, that communism is nothing but Christianity returned to its primitive purity? . . . that Chrisianity is the . . . precept, and communism the immediate consequence, that is to say, the practice, of this . . . precept? And that a faith without works is a dead faith . . . ? Thus one cannot really be a Christian without being a communist. . . . [In reading communist thought] I found myself face to face with the principles that had lulled me in my youth, that is, with that great and sublime doctrine that Christ had confirmed with his blood.

And despite Cabet's blatant anticlericalism he even won over a priest, who promised to proselytize within his "social class."[54] We have no idea of his success. By and large, however, priests were ardent opponents of communism, especially after Pope Pius IX specifically condemned the doctrine in 1846.[55]

[54] The foregoing citations are to be found in *Le Populaire* of June 5, 1844, Jan. 24, 1846, July 12, 1843, and Jan. and Feb. 1845, Supplément.
[55] In an encyclical "letter on doctrines" of Nov. 1846, the pontiff declared

Finally, there was Cabet's special message to women. A good many individual women wrote of their support. Of the 2,135 people who signed addresses condemning the arrest of Cabet late in 1847, 390, or 18.3 per cent, were female.[56] Some of his female correspondents saw *La Femme* (1842) as the central aspect of his entire message. A schoolteacher from "a town in the Alps" felt that the sex equality preached by Cabet was the way to the "salvation and perfection of the world." A market saleslady of Angoulême said, "What happy women are the women of Icaria." She was doing everything in her power to "Icarize" her "neighboring marchandes." She concluded by saying that she was rather embarrassed that a mere woman should interest herself in such profound matters— deference to be sure, but an awakening of real significance.[57]

To generalize about why people became communists from these statements of Icarian opinion would be impossible, but they do serve as a point of departure in the attempt to build a composite picture of the Icarian movement. To add further to this picture we must now investigate the trades and locales that rallied most strongly to Cabet and examine, where evidence permits, the specific socioeconomic conditions generating Icarian support.

Occupational Problems

Everywhere in France, but particularly in Paris, tailors, shoe-makers, and cabinetmakers flocked to the Icarian cause. Workers in these occupations shared some important characteristics. All were artisans of the old guild tradition. Their crafts required con-siderable skill and were plied almost entirely by hand. Conse-quently a tradition of pride in workmanship was very strong among them. Some of the ébénistes of the Faubourg Saint-Antoine in par-ticular were "labor aristocrats" of the highest order. Their reputa-tion as the European style leaders in furniture production was well established, and M. Baudin, the rapporteur for the international exposition of 1844 re–emphasized the fact: "Since our competitors agree, we can say [without boasting] that furniture of all types

communism to be "unnatural" and "immoral." Cabet responded: "Would the Pope thus be anti-Christ?" (*Le Populaire*, Dec. 25, 1846).

[56] Calculated from letters and lists in Cabet, *Notre Procès en escroquerie* (Paris, 1848).

[57] *Le Populaire*, Sept. 5, 1847, Oct. 31, 1846.

made in Paris is executed with greater taste and greater solidity than anywhere else in the world."[58] Paris had a similar reputation in clothing as well. In both the clothing and furniture trades, although the great majority of the workers were not involved in high fashion, attitudes of pride in workmanship filtered down into nearly all echelons of the crafts. A. Audiganne, in his excellent study of the French working class, underlined the self-esteem and the great concern for quality evident in these trades.[59]

The structure of these industries still exhibited guild forms of organization. Apprenticeship was rigorously observed. Among the shoemakers, it lasted for three years and, as in the old days, the apprentice was unpaid—in fact the master normally required the parents of the aspiring shoemaker to pay an initial fee.[60] A similar situation obtained in the tailoring and furniture trades, although apprenticeship in the latter was longer. As already noted, all three crafts were typically organized in small units of production. In 1848 the most elaborately subdivided industrial group in Paris was the clothing trade, with an average worker-employer ratio of 3.08 to one. This was almost three workers per employer less than the next industry (articles de Paris, 5.82 to one).[61] While the ratio in the general category of furniture was 6.33 to one, among the ébénistes and menuisiers the ratio was 4.72 to one.[62] One of the authors of the Chamber of Commerce inquiry of 1848 remarked that the subdivision in the cabinetmaking industry was dictated less by conditions of production and technology than by its practitioners' desire for independence and artistic individuality. The common practice of quitting a larger workshop to set up on one's own almost always worked to the financial detriment of the person who did so.[63]

[58] Office du Travail, *Rapport sur l'apprentissage dans les industries de l'ameublement* (Paris, 1905), 92.

[59] *Les Populations ouvrières et les industries de la France,* 2d ed. (Paris, 1860), I, 289.

[60] See "Revue industrielle," *Le Populaire,* Aug. 7, 1842.

[61] Chambre de Commerce de Paris, *Statistique,* 36. The overall average in Paris was 5.28 to 1. Of the 29,216 "entrepreneurs d'industrie" in the clothing trade, only 6 per cent employed (thus not including apprentices) 10 or more workers, while 28 per cent employed between 2 and 10; 66 per cent employed one or none.

[62] Nine per cent employed 10 or more, 45 per cent 2 to 10, and 46 per cent one or none (computed from figures given in *ibid.,* 157).

[63] *Ibid.,* 72.

Among the males in these trades in Paris the vast majority knew how to read and write; the cabinetmakers were 96 per cent literate, the tailors 94 per cent, and the shoemakers 92 per cent.[64] The fact is that most skilled artisans during this period were literate. Of all the Parisian male workers on whom the Chamber of Commerce gathered such information in 1847–1848, 87 per cent could read and write. Only in textiles (where semiskilled former peasants predominated among the adult males employed) was the literacy rate (73 per cent) lower than 83 per cent.[65] In general, the trades providing the heaviest Icarian following showed higher literacy rates than the average for the entire male working-class population. This tends to confirm subjective impressions. I have run across only one Icarian who did not know how to read and write,[66] although there were surely others.

Beyond the factor of high rates of literacy, conditions of work in these crafts allowed for a greater amount of time on the job for reflection and discussion of political questions. Although the work required considerable attention, it was quiet and sedentary. In discussing the life of needleworkers the author of a section of the Chamber of Commerce inquiry noted the unusual propensity toward political involvement among this group and attributed it in part to this factor.[67]

Among the many problems affecting tailors, shoemakers, and cabinetmakers alike during the July Monarchy, the overcrowding of their crafts, especially in Paris, drew much attention. To ply one's trade in Paris was the goal of many an artisan, not only because of the higher wages involved but also because one had "arrived" as a professional if he could make his way in the style center of the world.[68] Equally significant was the influx of foreign workers, particularly from Germany, that occurred during the July Monarchy. Some, like Wilhelm Weitling, came for political reasons, but the bulk of them were attracted by higher wages. The competition, among masters and journeymen alike, became increasingly

[64] *Ibid.,* 159.
[65] *Ibid.,* 68.
[66] See the letter from a Lyons worker writing for his illiterate Icarian friend, *Le Populaire,* Aug. 30, 1847.
[67] Chambre de Commerce de Paris, *Statistique,* 66.
[68] *Ibid.,* 50.

intense as the July Monarchy progressed.[69] During the 1830s especially the influx of foreign workers in cabinetmaking "led to quar-
rels between the journeyman ébénistes of [French and German]
origins. The employers, to bring about tranquility, were obliged to
compose their workshops entirely of Germans or of Frenchmen."[70]
It also meant that wages would suffer. Although a complete wage
series for these trades during the July Monarchy do not exist it
should be noted that in 1847, among all the Parisian industries,
clothing was the lowest paying with a daily average piece wage of
3.34 francs.[71]

If overcrowding and resultant competition presented grave difficulties to the workers (and masters) in these three trades, the rise
of the ready-made business was equally injurious. Before the July
Monarchy, shoes, clothes, and furniture had been almost entirely
made to order for the individual consumer. The great expansion
of the new practice dates from around 1840.[72] It was directly connected with the burgeoning number of artisans in the trades since,
in face of competition, many masters and independent journeymen
found that they had no choice but to go to work for a merchant
who would supply them with their raw materials. What were the
effects? Above all, confection was considered degrading, for it took
the individuality out of workmanship.[73] The tailor or cabinetmaker
who was forced to go into ready-made production suffered from
a disquieting sense of lost dignity.[74] Among the ébénistes the degradation of manufacturing in advance for sale to merchants was especially felt. Many of them, to avoid conforming to the specifications
(usually meaning a reduction in quality) and the economic author-

[69] Louis Chevalier, *La Formation de la population parisienne au XIX*
siècle (Paris, 1950), 115. Chambre de Commerce de Paris, *Statistique,* 50,
underlines the "harsh competition" existing in the clothing trade, as do many
other contemporary sources.

[70] Chambre de Commerce de Paris, *Statistique,* 159.

[71] *Ibid.;* this figure includes the many seamstresses of Paris whose wages
were exceedingly low, however.

[72] Chevalier, *La Formation,* 115.

[73] Office du Travail, *Rapport,* 87. Chambre de Commerce de Paris, *Sta-*
tistique, 54.

[74] This no doubt contributed to the pervasive significance of dignity and
professional pride in worker attitudes, which is underlined by Armand
Cuvillier in his discussion of the "Idéologie de 1848" in his *Hommes et*
idéologies de 1840 (Paris, 1956), 227–45.

ity of the hated commis, would fashion pieces to their own taste and attempt to sell them *à la trôle* (from the old verb *trôler,* meaning to go here and there). They would carry their finished work from their quarters in the Faubourg Saint-Antoine over to some busy commercial street, such as the rue du Temple or the rue de Cléry, and offer it to passers-by or perhaps to a shopkeeper for resale. "Often they wander around until the evening without selling a thing; then, tired from carrying a considerable load since morning, forced now to head for home, and afraid to return without the money so often necessary to live and to pay the primary materials already purchased on credit, they are obliged to let the piece go at a very low price."[75] One can appreciate the pressure, however, to give in to confection; a succession of days like this would mean not only heartbreak and little profit but also the loss of much valuable time that might otherwise have been spent at the workbench. Thus while ready-made production might be professionally degrading, while it might shackle the master and journeyman alike to a merchant capitalist, while it might mean lower pay, economic necessity pushed tailors and cabinetmakers into it. Look at the bright side, advised a liberal writer in the inquiry of the Chamber of Commerce: as a worker in confection, you do not have to worry about the mid-winter and summer slack times; "the commis comes to visit all year round!"[76]

The problem of confection also had an impact in the provinces, but from another point of view. Much to the dismay of the local tailors, traveling salesmen carrying ready-made clothes visited provincial cities. At Grenoble this occasioned outright violence. In November 1843 a salesman set up a shop in the market square displaying ready-made apparel, sold a few items, and moved on. The tailors of Grenoble petitioned the mayor to take "measures that would preserve them from such dreadful competition." They were not heeded. On April 22 of the following year three clothes stalls were erected. A group of tailors surged into the square, pillaged the goods, and destroyed the stalls. They were arrested and finally tried in August. The court let them off, since they had already spent some months in jail; but the muncipality made no move to relieve

[75] Chambre de Commerce de Paris, *Statistique,* 160.
[76] *Ibid.,* 54.

the problem (nor could it, of course).[77] Cabet commented upon this incident and, although sympathizing with the tailors, condemned their action, comparing it with the futility of breaking machines. Furthermore, he said, addressing himself to the tailors, if one of you should happen to become a clothes merchant, "would he hesitate to compete with his former comrades?" Of course not, because this is what the present system demands. Interestingly, the first news of adherence to Icarianism in Grenoble arrived the following year.[78] It seems clear that confection created psychological and material conditions that would make communism appealing not only to independent journeymen but to masters as well.[79]

Technological change also influenced the lives of these men. For the cabinetmakers, a certain amount of competition was provided by the installation of a few furniture factories in Paris, the largest being the much-hated Krieger mill, established in 1846. Furthermore, new machine tools in woodworking were being developed that were priced beyond the pocketbooks of the smaller shop owners and the independent craftsmen, thus allowing the more well-to-do enterprises to underprice the poorer ones. In the late thirties a cheaper method of shoe construction, using nails and rivets instead of screws, was developed. Those who suffered were the poorest shoemakers, who found the cost of purchasing the new equipment necessary for the changeover too high.[80]

The shoemakers faced a special problem during the July Monarchy. On January 25, 1808, a group of journeymen shoemakers applied for membership in the compagnonnage. They were not recognized by the other professions but proceeded to organize their corporation in this manner anyway, setting up a *Tour de France,* creating centers for lodging (*mères*), and arranging for the placement of workers on the circuit. By no means all of the shoemakers became members, but a sizable minority of journeymen were compagnons. As newcomers and as men in a trade requiring less than artistic skill, they were rejected by the twenty-seven other pre-Revolutionary compagnonnages, and considerable antagonism was

[77] Reports of April 23, and Aug. 12, 1844, from the procureur-général of Grenoble to the Garde des Sceaux, A.N., BB[18] 1421 dos 8243.
[78] *Le Populaire,* May 2, 1844, and Oct. 18, 1845.
[79] See n. 23 above.
[80] Office du Travail, *Rapport,* 86–87; Chevalier, *La Formation,* 116.

shown toward them. Jean Briquet, whose knowledge of the compagnonnage is unparalleled, describes the shoemakers as "pariahs" within the organization. Numerous brawls took place between shoemakers and members of other professions: at Toulouse in the late thirties several fights between carpenters and shoemakers; at Avignon the murder of the shoemaker Bédoin; at Lyons in 1833 the torture (a cross sliced on the back with a knife) of a young shoemaker by several stonecutters—such was the lot of many a compagnon cordonnier.[81] Surely such difficulties added to the despair in this profession.

We conclude this discussion with a description of the life of journeyman shoemakers presented by one of Cabet's adherents, Coriot, in the "Revue Industrielle" appearing in *Le Populaire* in October 1842. After the difficult period of apprenticeship, they spent two or three years as *semainiers,* working for pittance wages doing odd jobs for various shop-owning masters, hiring themselves out on a week-to-week basis. Then the bulk of them "begin to work on our *pièces,"* that is, they made shoes on their own. They normally registered with a central depot and would go out on call at the homes of their clients. Coriot complained of the time lost in traveling there by foot, indicating that it was preferable to work in a shop. He claimed that the usual piece rate was 2.25 francs and that one pair of shoes per day was the normal output; in good times the shoemakers earned 15 francs per week.[82] Unemployment was rife, and Coriot cited cases of up to eighteen months without pay. But seasonal unemployment (mid-winter and mid-summer) was bad enough; during these periods a shoemaker incurred heavy debts and then, when work picked up again, was often obliged to

[81] Briquet, "La Signification sociale du compagnonnage," *Revue d'histoire économique et sociale,* XXXIII (1955), 324. Office du Travail, *Les Associations,* I, 134–41.

[82] The Chamber of Commerce enquiry discovered that of the 13,495 male shoemakers in Paris, 5,870 (or 44 per cent) made less than three francs per day while 7,582 (or 56 per cent) earned from 3 to 5 francs; only 43 men made more than 5 francs per day. Shoemakers were less well paid than tailors; the respective percentages for the latter were 15 per cent, 84 per cent and 1 per cent. For the more affluent ébénistes the figures were 8 per cent, 90 per cent, and 2 per cent. The figures for all Parisian workers show that both tailors and shoemakers were below average, while the cabinetmakers were slightly above average; the aggregate percentages were 14 per cent, 81 per cent, and 5 per cent.

work eighteen hours a day to pay them off. Such a schedule destroyed a man's health, and the writer claimed that by the time a shoemaker was twenty-five or thirty he was in permanent bad health. Despite their difficulties, most shoemakers married (usually around the age of thirty) and, he remarked dolefully, began to produce "the children of the poor." Normally, their situation became increasingly burdensome even if the wife worked. By the age of forty or fifty the shoemaker was "used up, damning the society that made him live and work like an animal to stay alive."[83]

In summary, it would appear that the principal socioeconomic bases for the fact that nearly half of the recorded members of the Icarian movement were tailors, shoemakers, and cabinetmakers were material misery and the loss of professional status. The problems of overcrowding and competition, the challenge of confection, technological change, and professional jealousy within the compagnonnage all contributed to these conditions. Misery as such, some social historians would claim, often leads merely to apathy. Such may have been the case with the new factory worker and, to a lesser extent, with the mineworkers. But these groups possessed neither the long-standing traditions nor the high degree of literacy of the tailors, shoemakers, and cabinetmakers. When threatened, men in these trades had a greater propensity to fight back, to seek solutions. Yet the very nature of their trades—the fact that their members were settled and usually married, that they were "reflective," and that they were rarely physically robust—made it unlikely that they would depend upon violence to alter their conditions. Cabet's pacific communism, which stressed the patient courage so amenable to the mentality of these workers but which nevertheless promised a total transformation of their lives, emerged as the answer many of them sought.

Another important element partly explaining the heavy recruitment of Icarians among these crafts was disappointment with trade union and strike activity. Until 1840 tailors, especially, were at the forefront of economic action both in Paris and in the provinces. The Société philanthropique des ouvriers tailleurs, founded in Paris in 1831, was one of the most active and well-coordinated "societies of resistance" organized during the July Monarchy and established connections with groups in Lyons, Marseilles, and

[83] *Le Populaire,* Oct. 9, 1842.

Nantes. Though it was repressed in 1833, there is evidence of continued union organization among tailors through the thirties. Besides their attempts to protect their own craft, tailors promoted broader union interrelationships and also tended to mix republican politics with their syndicalist ideals. In 1840, the tailors inaugurated the great strike movement that convulsed Paris in August and September. They saw their own efforts destroyed as the prefecture sided with the masters and did nothing to break up the latters' coalition while arresting the leaders of the journeymen. Moreover, the total repression of the entire cross-craft movement in September appeared to close the door on efficacious action through union organization. Similar official action was taken in Toulouse and other provincial centers. Even mutual benefit societies became suspect thereafter.[84]

Thus the journeymen tailors initiated the great strike movement of 1840, fought valiantly to gain their demands, but succumbed to defeat when the power of the government was turned against them. This experience must certainly have convinced some of them that the real arena of working-class action was political. The situation was therefore ready-made for the impact of Cabet's doctrine. Economic action was blocked; political interest was already in existence; communism had been introduced to them at Belleville; but pacificism was an ingrained trait of their trade: in such circumstances, many a Parisian tailor would pick up the recently published *Voyage en Icarie* and read it attentively late in 1840. And indeed, figuring prominently among the workers who signed the *Protestation* of July 1, 1841—most of whom had no doubt been among those urging Cabet to bring out *Le Populaire*—were numerous tailors, including some of the movement's chief figures, the Favards (father and son), Giraud, Ducreux, Aron, Crozat, and Oudin. All these men were members of the central commission of shareholders of Cabet's newspaper. Moreover, one of the important leaders of the tailors in 1840, Pierre Wahry, became an Icarian sympathizer and in 1849 would assist Krolikowski and Hermann Ewerbeck with the editing of *Le Populaire* after Cabet's departure

[84] O. Festy, "Dix Années de l'histoire corporative des ouvriers tailleurs d'habits (1830–1840)," *Revue d'histoire des doctrines économiques et sociales*, V (1912), 116–99; A.N., F⁷ 3886, Bulletin de Paris, Nov. 7, 1832; Aguet, *Les Grèves*, 194–99; A.N., BB¹⁸ 1398 dos 2824.

for America. Late in 1840 he wrote a proposal for a large-scale tailors' cooperative. The plan was later discovered by the police, and Wahry was condemned to two years in prison for trying to form a secret society.[85]

Parisian shoemakers went out on strike late in July 1840, but a commission of arbitration was quickly organized and the conflict over wages was resolved in the shoemakers' favor although their full demands were not met. Even so, because a majority of journeymen worked on their own, this settlement touched only a small number of men in the trade and among them the quarrel concerned only the piece rates for low quality shoes.

The cabinetmakers of Paris were apparently not involved in the strikes of 1840. In fact, there was little union activity of any type in this profession during the entire July Monarchy. It seems, therefore, that among the three crafts, only in the case of the tailors can it be argued that the futility of union and strike activity was a fundamental cause of worker interest in Icarian doctrine. But in broader perspective, the suppression of the great strike movement of 1840 had a profound impact on the collective mentality of the Parisian workers. Aguet agrees with Martin Nadaud that these events were of crucial significance in turning the workers irrevocably against the government of the July Monarchy and in making visible "the growing division between the worker and bourgeois classes."[86]

Conditions of Life and the Development of Icarianism in Several Centers of Influence

Further understanding of why workers became Icarians may be gained from a discussion of working-class conditions in some of the major centers of Cabet's influence. The previous analysis has necessarily centered upon Paris because of available information and the preponderance of Parisians among the Icarians whose occupations we know. But one of the principal characteristics of the Icarian movement was its strong provincial impact. In many cases, such as in Vienne, Reims, and Périgueux, Cabet's doctrine was the first social ideology to have any significant influence on the local working

---

[85] Festy, "Dix Années," 196; *Le Populaire*, May 20, 1841. The *Dict. biog.* (III, 526–27) does not mention Wahry's connections with Icarian communism.

[86] Auget, *Les Grèves*, 225.

class. Although the decision is somewhat arbitrary, eight cities can be identified as the principal centers of Icarianism. Taking four factors into consideration—number of Icarians in relation to total population, impressionistic contemporary estimates of Icarian influence, demonstrated cohesiveness of the local Icarian group, and the importance of individual Icarians in the politics of the revolution of 1848—Vienne, Reims, Lyons, Nantes, Niort, Périgueux, Toulouse, and Toulon, approximately in that order, were the cities where Cabet's doctrine made the greatest headway. In August 1846 they accounted for 48 per cent of the number of provincial subscriptions to *Le Populaire*. They shared no particular economic similarities. Toulouse and Périgueux were regional administrative and trade centers with almost exclusively artisan industrial populations. Niort played a similar role but also supported important chamois and glove manufacture. The port of Nantes was in decline and, despite the appearance of factory production in the early nineteenth century, the industry of the city remained largely artisanal. Vienne and Reims were cities in which the woolen industry predominated without making them, like Lyons, essentially mono-industrial; in both, modern industrial production had become an important factor and threatened artisan stability. Toulon, stimulated by the growth of its naval arsenal, experienced a real industrial revolution in the first half of the century. There were other important Icarian towns. In the west sizable groups of Icarians were to be found in Tours, Rennes, Luçon, and Angoulême. Rouen and, later, Le Havre were Norman cities where Cabet had an impact. Icarian elements developed in Saint-Quentin and several nearby towns, as they did in Charleville in 1846 and 1847. Cabet and Chameroy tried hard to develop a following in Nancy but with only moderate success. By and large the industrial towns of the east, like those of the north, remained relatively immune. Such was not the case, however, with the important center of musical instrument manufacture, Mirecourt (Vosges). In the Lyons area, because of the active proselytism by Icarian faithfuls from that city or from Vienne, several towns, including Givors, Annonay, and Grenoble, built up significant groups. The coal basin of the Gier was "infected" in 1846 and 1847. Aside from Toulouse and Toulon, the south was largely unaffected by Icarian communism.

Lyons, Vienne, and Reims deserve the greatest attention. These were the cities where Icarianism probably made its greatest impact, and we are fortunate that the secondary literature on the social history of each is at least adequate.

There can be no doubt about the influence that Cabet exerted on the workers of Lyons during the 1840s. As we have seen, Lyons was second only to Paris in the number of subscriptions (256) to *Le Populaire*. In March of 1844, Minister of the Interior Duchâtel wrote to the Minister of Justice: "As for the *Icarian Communists,* it is impossible, because of a lack of real organization in this society, to fix their number exactly. It is believed, however, to be not less than one thousand individuals at Lyons."[87] Eight hundred thirty people contributed to the subscription for the medal for Eugène Sue in 1846, and 1,800 signed the petition protesting Cabet's arrest in 1847. The analysis of the vicissitudes of Icarianism offered above and the assessment of interested contemporaries such as Benoit, Commissaire, and Olinet demonstrate its profound impact. Modern historians agree. Maximillien Buffenoir stressed that Icarian communism found the greatest following of any communist doctrine during the forties.[88] Jean Gaumont went beyond this, stating that while Fourierism was the dominant social ideology in Lyons during the late thirties and early forties, Icarianism "got the upper hand over the Fourierist propaganda of Regnier and his friends, and henceforth it was to guide the workers in the revolutionary period."[89]

Economic conditions at Lyons were not markedly different during the 1840s from what they had been during the heroic period of working-class activity in the early thirties. If anything, they had probably improved. Although wages may have been down somewhat from the earlier period, employment was probably more regular. In general, Dr. Villermé's judgment that the workers of Lyons were among the best off in France seems correct: "For a long time, but especially in the last twelve years, their physical, moral, and intellectual state has progressively improved . . . and

[87] Letter of March 31, 1844, A.N., BB[18] 1420 dos 8195.
[88] "Le Communisme à Lyon de 1834 à 1848," *Revue d'histoire de Lyon* (Sept.–Oct. 1909), 350–56. This article fails to utilize Prudhommeaux or the BB[18] series at the A.N. Nor was the manuscript material now at the BHVP available to him.
[89] Gaumont, *Histoire générale de la coopération* (Paris, 1924), I, 353. As we shall see, the last part of this statement is overdrawn.

I affirm . . . that the workers here, among all our great manufacturing towns, are more laborious, more sober, more intelligent, and, in certain regards, no less moral than the other workers taken en masse."[90] The 30,000 silk looms that dominated the industrial life of the urban agglomeration were located in old Lyons, Les Brotteaux, La Guillotière, and especially the Croix-Rousse. Still, Lyons boasted other important trades; aside from those necessary for providing the city with the essentials of life—including, naturally, a large clothing industry—Lyons exported other goods besides her fine silks, above all hats (the hat industry was fading, however, throughout the July Monarchy). But because of the preponderance of one great industry there was little conflict among the various corporations in the town, and the workers in other trades joined their efforts with those of the canuts. This phenomenon was certainly in evidence in the great rising of November 1831.[91] Thus, socially, Lyons presented a picture of a remarkably homogeneous working class. And it was one whose common interests were recognized. As a result of the acerbic conflict in the silk industry that had exploded in violence in 1831 and 1834, the Lyonnais working class had achieved a degree of social and political consciousness perhaps not equaled even in Paris. Within the silk industry, at least, the bases for antagonism between the fabricants and the canuts had increased during the July Monarchy. Not only had the workers failed to get the wage schedules they fought for in 1831 and 1834; in addition a concentration of economic power occurred during the thirties and forties. Although we do not have the figures for the period of the July Monarchy itself, from 1830 to 1860 the number of fabricants fell from 750 to 450.[92] Moreover, the need to house the bulky Jacquard loom and cheaper rents had, during the first half of the century, caused many silk workers to move to the suburbs.[93] Increasingly their living space was separated from that of the bourgeois in a ghettoization process that was becoming common in other large cities as well.

Many workers of Lyons had, as a result of the defeat of 1831,

[90] *L'Etat des ouvriers,* II, 336.
[91] Rude, *Le Mouvement ouvrier à Lyon depuis 1827 à 1832,* 357ff.
[92] Georges Duveau, *La Vie ouvrière sous le Second Empire* (Paris 1946), 179.
[93] Bezucha, "The 'Preindustrial' Worker Movement," 99.

begun to look beyond the narrow confines of their own professional concerns and thought in terms of a more general transformation of society. Republicanism made headway among them, and in 1834 many fought in the name of the social republic. Even before the insurrection Saint-Simonism captured the minds of some of the canuts and remained a force in Lyons down to 1848.[94] And Lyons was almost unique in France in that Fourierism won a large number of converts among workers there during the 1830s.[95] Even in the following decade, Joseph Regnier's *Echo de l'industrie,* Fourierist in its orientation, and *La Tribune lyonnaise* under the quasi-Fourierist Marius Chastaing competed as the two major voices of the workers. Finally, of course, neo-Babouvism was especially influential among the silk workers. Thus, like Paris, Lyons was well conditioned for the introduction of Icarian ideas.

Many historians have remarked on the unique spirit that characterized the workers of Lyons. First of all, at least a portion of them were extremely well read. "Lyons," in the words of Fernand Rude, "became an ardent center of enlightenment for workers who inaugurated their endeavor of liberation.[96] Besides this intellectual elevation, another, less explicable, aspect of the Lyonnais spirit must be stressed. "Between the Croix-Rousse and Fourvière," wrote Michelet, "in this valley of work, there is a core of social mysticism, of tenderness, and of furor." Jean Jaurès also underlined the mystical outlook of the Lyonnais worker, attributing it to the fact that François Joseph l'Ange, a revolutionary precursor of the cooperative idea and a man of great long-range influence in Lyons was by origin a Westphalian and familiar with the doctrine of Weishaupt's *Illuminati.* Gaumont, who cites Jaurès, admits the influence of l'Ange (though he doubts that he was a Westphalian) but points out the impact of mesmerism and Freemasonry in the eighteenth century as well.[97] Moreover, the religious orders were quite influential in Lyons and, although many workers had become strongly anticlerical by the nineteenth century, the mystical tradition here may have been of importance. The great Lyonnaise historian Justin Godart remarked that while it was "not religious,

[94] Rude, *Le Mouvement,* 266–72.
[95] Gaumont, *Histoire générale,* I, 115.
[96] Rude, "Le Mouvement ouvrier de Lyon," *Revue de psychologie des peuples* (1958), 236.
[97] Gaumont, *Histoire générale,* I, 77–80.

Lyons was *mystique.* Lyonnais mysticism served the cause of co-operation and of all projects of social reform."[98] But Michelet also stressed the polar qualities of tenderness and furor among the Lyonnais workers. These are by no means incompatible if one realizes that the furor, their explosiveness, was manifested only when all conciliatory means had failed; then, precisely because of the restraint normally ruling them, they could erupt in violence of an order without parallel among the working population in France. The tenderness demonstrated by the worker of Lyons was reserved especially, for his fellow laborer. This quality goes a long way to explain why the mutual-aid societies movement in France should have been born in Lyons. Another aspect of the spirit of the Lyonnais worker was his almost puritanical sobriety and seriousness. His violence, as noted, was never without purpose, and simple disorderliness was foreign to his nature. While he shared with his Parisian counterpart a willingness to take the larger view of his problems and the idea of working-class fraternity and mutual aid, he did not have the latter's "irresistible taste for dissipation and spending, [his] ardent thirst for pleasure, [nor his] passionate love of change [for its own sake]."[99] Godart, echoing Villermé and many others, praised the Lyonnais weaver, "that admirable worker, a man of real technical value [to society], of a resistance that is astonishing, of a sobriety that is stupefying even though he is incessantly in the shadow of misery."[100]

These comments about the mentality of the Lyons worker are of relevance in understanding the reasons for Cabet's growing ascendancy in the working-class movement there during the forties. There was a marked propensity to avoid violence, and Cabet's alternative of civil courage jells with the inherent characteristics of sobriety and patient determination. Moreover, the mysticism of the Lyonnais worker may well have found satisfaction in Cabet's increasing emphasis on the connection between communism and Christianity. But other factors, the Lyonnais workers' independence of mind and strong sense of self-worth, also made them among the most critical Icarians in the movement. We have already witnessed

[98] "Les Origines de la cooperation lyonnaise," *La Révolution de 1848,* III (1904), 337.
[99] Audiganne, *Les Populations ouvrières,* I, 283.
[100] Godart, "Les Origines," 411.

some of the consequences of this outlook for Cabet's political strategy.

In proportion to a total population of around 14,000, the Icarian communist movement at Lyons' neighboring city to the south, Vienne, was the largest in France. Although only 25 signatures appear on the first declaration of support in March 1845,[101] in September of the same year 72 signed a protest against Ledru-Rollin and 87 "in the name of 300" declared their devotion the following February. There were 62 subscribers to *Le Populaire* in August 1846; 200 gave money for the Sue medal, and the same number signed a protest, published in *Le Populaire* on September 26, 1847, against the anticommunist remarks of the Fourierist Victor Hennequin. Finally, 180 Viennois Icarians signed a declaration protesting Cabet's arrest in 1847. Fernand Rude, who has studied the history of Vienne during the 1840s in great detail, states that while Babouvism and Fourierism had some impact in the city, it was "above all Icarian communism" that dominated the flow of social thought; he agrees that its following in the later forties was between 400 and 500 workers.[102]

The leader of the Icarian group at Vienne was Vincent Cöeffé. Born in Lyons in 1790, he made shoe forms for a living. He became a convert to Icarian communism in 1840 and was probably involved with the group that put out *Le Travail*. Two years later he moved to Vienne, possibly motivated by the desire to spread the Icarian faith.[103] Economic conditions there during the 1840s were conducive to the growth of the movement. The major industries in Vienne at this time were woolen cloth production (*la draperie*) and metallurgy. Both were located in the narrow gorge of the Gère where 80 hydraulic machines provided much of the power. "Various factories and workshops employed about 7,000 workers, of whom more than 4,600 were in the woolens industry and nearly 1,000 were in metallurgy. If it is impossible to speak . . . of

---

[101] Unfortunately, we only have the names of these men: Cöeffé, Fey, Sodot, Colomb, Jean L'Héritier, Chaudier, Bergeron, L'Héritier *ainé*, Vinçon, Allard, Charre, Marcheval, Malosse, Guillaume, Saucy, Berriand (C.), Drevon, Franc, Picolet, Tillet, Robert, and Jean Baptiste Roche (three others are not named).

[102] "L'Arrondissement de Vienne en 1848," 231. See *Le Populaire*, July 26, 1846.

[103] See Rude's Introduction to his *Voyage en Icarie: Deux Ouvriers viennois*, 20.

monoindustry, the preponderance of the woolens industry is clear: 1,514 male workers, 1,890 females, and 1,220 children under sixteen worked in 316 workshops."[104] By 1840 spinning at Vienne was almost completely mechanized. The only significant development during the July Monarchy was the increasing size of the machines: "after 1840, the humble mule-jennies of 60 spindles began to be replaced by powerful machines of 120, 140, and soon 200 spindles with automatic winding and twisting." These changes had effects upon employment conditions but were little more than passing inconveniences. More important was the progressive introduction of carding, shearing, and teasing machines. As early as 1819 there had been a major outburst of Luddism against the new shearing devices, and agitation continued intermittently until 1848. The situation of the weaver was also altered. Although power looms would not be set up in Vienne until 1861, the first Jacquard looms were introduced in 1833, and "after 1840 they knew a growing vogue."[105] Undoubtedly this technical change injured the fortunes of the weaver operating the older one-man hand-loom. The Vienne draperie was organized into numerous workshops, often vertically integrated. There were few independent weavers. Most worked in shops where the master owned several looms or in larger factories where the entire process of production was carried out under one roof. By and large, conditions of existence for the bulk of those in the woolens industry were not pleasant during the July Monarchy. Although wages seem to have been relatively stable, they were extremely low. The average wage of a male spinner was 2.20 francs per day, while weavers made 1.90 francs. These figures compare unfavorably with workers in metallurgy, glass blowers, and tanners, whose daily wages usually exceeded three francs.[106] A report of the 1840s stated that, while a single man could live well enough on these wages, if he were "married and had a family, he could hardly provide for the most urgent needs of his family unless his wife received wages also."[107] Although we know the occupations of only a handful of Viennois Icarians, two were involved in the

---

[104] Rude, "L'Arrondissement de Vienne," 216.

[105] Pierre Léon, *La Naissance de la grande industrie en Dauphiné* (Paris, 1954), II, 502, 504, and 506, and Rude, "L'Arrondissement de Vienne," 232.

[106] Rude, "L'Arrondissement de Vienne," 219 ff.

[107] Quoted in Léon, *La Naissance*, II, 751.

draperie. The most important of them was Gagnière, a weaver, who would be one of the leaders in the great strike in the industry in 1848.[108] It may be assumed that he and Boussu, a trimmer on a carding machine, had many fellow Icarians in their trade.

Rude stresses that Viennois working-class consciousness heightened considerably during the July Monarchy and especially after 1840. There were close links with Lyons militants. Already in 1834 the insurrection in Lyons had stimulated "some effervescence" in Vienne. Moreover, Vienne was one of the major stops on the Tour de France. Both the compagnonnages and mutual benefit societies tended to become "veritable societies of resistance." During the 1840s there were several strikes in Vienne; those of the shoemakers in 1841 and the weavers in 1842 were perhaps the most important. By 1848 eight cooperative associations had been legally authorized. Beneath all this activity ran a strong spirit of working-class solidarity, forged in part by deep traditions of conviviality and confraternity. Popular culture here centered on the cafés, and the Viennois workers were renowned for their penchant for song and poetry.[109] Icarianism no doubt benefited from and strengthened these elements of the working-class mentality.

If Lyons and Vienne should be ranked as the first Icarian cities of provincial France, Reims was not far behind. Reims was one of the first places to be affected by the propaganda of Charles Chameroy. Only in 1844, however, do we have evidence of a real Icarian group in Reims. Three Icarians wrote Cabet in July of that year that the doctrine was spreading rapidly due to their propaganda efforts.[110] In November the first declaration of support arrived. The twenty-three signatories believed that the present society could not long continue "without dreadful catastrophes that would make it fall again into its primitive state." They opposed violence and secret societies and emphasized that "our doctrine is purely evangelical, and we recognize only Jesus Christ as our master."[111] By 1846 the Icarian presence was being noted with fear by the local press. The *Revue de Reims* claimed in Febuary that "the working class is Icarian communist, not Fourierist." In July a

---

[108] Rude, "L'Arrondissement de Vienne," 402.
[109] *Ibid.*, 221, 323–35.
[110] *Le Populaire*, July 12, 1844.
[111] *Ibid.*, Nov. 1844.

powerful Catholic sheet, the *Journal de Reims,* launched a five-column attack on communism. In this article it quoted a speech by the deputy from the arrondissement of Reims, Léon Faucher (a prominent conservative republican in 1848), who said that the growing influence of communism should be understood as a warning to the bourgeoisie to extend their hand downward "if they do not want to lose their power." At that time there were 54 subscribers to *Le Populaire* in Reims, and 214 persons had donated to the subscription for the Sue medal. Later that year Cabet proudly reported that the busy Rémois Icarians had placed 200 *Almanachs* and gained 20 new subscribers to *Le Populaire* in a single month. Late in 1847, the *Journal de Reims* estimated that among "the poorest workers," Cabet influenced 1,200 to 1,500 individuals.[112] Finally, the Reims protest against Cabet's arrest at the end of the year was signed by 443 Icarians, more than any other provincial city with the exception of Lyons.[113]

Nine of the twenty-three signatories of the first address from Reims were woolens workers. In that day, Reims was the major woolens manufactory in France, and, according to contemporary observers, it grew rapidly during the July Monarchy.[114] Out of a population of 44,000 in 1846, almost 15,000 were connected with the woolens industry while only 2,000 helped manufacture the great champagnes of Reims.[115] The Rémois draperie was not nearly

[112] *Revue de Reims,* Feb. 1846; *Journal de Reims,* July 31, 1846, and Dec. 7, 1847; *Le Populaire,* Dec. 25, 1846.

[113] The only negative opinion about the importance of Icarianism in Reims comes from the worker-poet Gonzalle, who remarked that "the communist party, which was believed to be all-powerful by the number of its adherents and by its influence on the working class, was in reality only a small handful of individuals whose pacific propaganda was exercised only on a restricted circle of converts and friends." Gonzalle, however, was an enemy of the Icarians in 1848 and entered into something of a power struggle with them for control of the communist club and its newspaper. This in itself indicates that the Icarians were stronger than he claims. Gonzalle, "Souvenirs de la révolution à Reims" (1860), quoted in R. Chéramy, "L'Année 1848 dans le département de la Marne," (1946), MS 1511, Bibliothèque municipale de Châlons-sur-Marne.

[114] Chéramy, "L'Année 1848," 7.

[115] Marc Vincent, "La Situation économique et la condition des travailleurs dans le département de la Marne d'après l'enquête de 1848 sur le travail agricole et industriel," in G. Laurent, ed., *La Département de la Marne et la Révolution de 1848* (Châlons-sur-Marne, 1948), 92–93; Chéramy, "L'Année 1848," 6.

so streamlined as that of Vienne. One reason why Vienne made the transition to mechanized production easily was accessible water power; in Reims mechanized spinning necessitated the use of steam. While some steam-powered spinneries were built in the city or its suburbs, the main development was the rise of hydraulic mule-jenny spinning in villages outside Reims near fast-flowing streams, especially the Suippe and Vésle. This change, coming rapidly in the thirties and forties, set off a chain reaction that ultimately made the weaver's lot in Reims a harsh one. There was an immediate demand for unskilled labor in the small communes. The peasants who formerly provided much of the thread for Reims were largely unwilling to seek factory employment; hence there was an influx of cheap Belgian and German labor. But these outworkers in the countryside still needed the extra money, and many of them switched to weaving heavy cloth, the traditional staple of Reims itself. Since the peasant-weavers, working only part time, would accept lower wages than the Rémois hand-loom men, the latter faced a grave peril. Simultaneously, however, the Jacquard loom came to Reims, and the city was becoming—during the July Monarchy—the great center of the fine, patterned product of the Jacquard revolution.[116] Numerous Rémois weavers were caught in the middle, and one can hypothesize that many of them flocked to the Icarian banner. Mechanization in the countryside was also injuring the hand-spinners, combers, carders, sorters, and shearers of Reims. In general, as the industrial revolution began to take its toll at Reims wages fell across the board. In all areas of woolen production, daily wages fell drastically during the July Monarchy. For instance, the weaver in merinos (utilizing the old one-man hand-loom) made 2.25 francs in 1831; but this rate gradually declined until in 1846 he could count on only one franc. Even the more favored Jacquard weaver was crushed by the wage squeeze; in 1837 he made 4 francs, but the crisis of 1837–1839 (apparently) caused his wage to drop precipitously to 2.75 francs in 1840, and by 1846 it had declined by another franc. The male spinner, however, only saw his wages drop from 2.50 francs to 2 francs over the same period.[117]

[116] Vincent, "La Situation," 93–95.
[117] See the table in Georges Boussinesq, "Reims à la fin de la Monarchie

The major industry in Reims, although progressing by standards of economic growth, was thus experiencing a transition of great magnitude, producing undeniable hardships for the workers. Moreover, tailors were facing the familiar problem of ready-made goods. Theirs was one of the most plaintive cries in 1848 as they damned "the competition of the confectionneurs who, having much capital, impose very onerous conditions of work on their workers, who, being without resources, are obliged to submit to them."[118] All in all, a strong case can be made for the advance of sheer misery as the basis for Icarian adherence in Reims—much more so, certainly, than in Lyons or even Vienne.

Rémois Icarians stressed that they "recognize only Jesus Christ as their master" and generally appeared more impressed by the Christian-communist equation than most of their brothers elsewhere. Reims, where Joan of Arc had led Charles VII to be crowned, and where another Charles had more recently exercised his thaumaturgical powers, was one of the great strongholds of the Catholic Church in France. Boussinesq and Laurent, in discussing the Restoration, said, "To tell the truth it seems that the history of Reims, in this period, is uniquely the history of religious ceremonies."[119] Yet the only manifestations connected with the revolution of 1830 were attacks on religious establishments by the Rémois lower classes.[120] Such a blend of Christian feeling with anticlericalism was always a powerful reagent in the chemistry of Icarian conversion.

Icarian communism developed deep roots in the lower Loire Valley and the west, stretching as far south as Périgord. Its capital was at Nantes, and its appeal there seems to have been especially strong among the very poor.[121] *Le National de l'Ouest* reported in 1844 that *Le Populaire* was much more popular than *L'Atelier*. Icarians themselves claimed that Cabet's paper was the "organ of

---

de Juillet et pendant la periode révolutionnaire de 1848," *La Révolution de 1848*, XIX (1922–23), 321.

[118] Vincent, "La Situation," 92.

[119] Georges Boussinesq and Gustave Laurent, *Histoire de Reims depuis ses origines à nos jours*, II, *Reims moderne*, Book 1 (Reims, 1933), 448.

[120] *Ibid.*, 486–96.

[121] Pedron, Cabet's correspondent at Nantes, reported significant progress in 1844 but was distressed that so many converts could not afford to subscribe to *Le Populaire*. See *Le Populaire*, July 12, 1844.

the workers" and that it had more readers than *La Réforme*. With its 94 subscribers as of August 1846, the Nantes group was the fourth largest in France and, in a city of 94,000 people, was proportionately on a par with Reims and Vienne as a center of influence. *Le Breton* estimated Cabet's following to be 600; "communism" it said, "is in the air." Icarian influence radiated from Nantes to Rennes and Tours and south to Niort, Angoulême, and Périgueux. Paul Guay, correspondent at Niort, was an especially active local propagandist and appears to have borne the message to Luçon, Saint-Maixent, Fontenay, and Châtillerault. In Niort it was said that "most of the workers in the city . . . are imbued with the ideas of communism." Nantais Icarians were linked with brethren in Angoulême, and there were contacts between Périgueux and the capitals of both Charente and Deux-Sèvres.[122]

Unlike Paris or Lyons, Reims or Vienne, there is little to indicate that basic economic change had much to do with the rise of Icarianism in this area, with the exception of the declining leathergoods center of Niort. Instead, previous union organization and its repression by the government and the preoccupation of the judiciary and ministry of the interior with the threat of legitimism in the west need emphasis. While textiles, shipbuilding, sugar refining, and distilling underwent progressive development in Nantes itself in the 1830s and 1840s, occupations claiming Icarian support, such as tailoring and shoemaking, experienced no major changes with the probable exception of the rise of ready-made production. But these crafts were noted, both in the early thirties and the late forties, for the significant poverty of their journeymen.[123] Most

[122] See *L'Atelier*, Aug. 1844; *Le Populaire*, Nov. 1844; E. B. LeBent, "Notes pour servir à l'histoire de la Révolution de 1848 dans les départements," Archief Cabet, IISG (LeBent was a Nantais friend of Ange Guépin); *Le Breton*, Oct. 25, 1846; and Procureur-général de Poitiers to the Garde des Sceaux, April 2, 1845, A.N., BB[18] 1428 dos 9580. On Guay's regional activities, see similar reports of April 3, 1845, BB[18] 1451 dos 3524 (March 5, 1847), and M. Faucheux and L. Moreauzeux, "Les Débuts du communisme en Vendée: L'Affaire Madeline," *Etudes: Bibliothèque de la Révolution de 1848*, XV (1953), 79. One hundred and twenty-four Niort Icarians signed an "adresse d'adhesion" printed in *Le Populaire*, Nov. 22, 1845. The police found correspondence from Angoulême to Nantes that made them consider fleetingly the possibility of prosecution for secret-society activity. Procureur-général de Rennes to the Garde des Sceaux, Dec. 24, 1847, A.N., BB[18] 1441 dos 1992.

[123] See Ange Guépin, *Nantes au XIXᵉ siècle*, 481–90, and Georges Cre-

other important towns in the west were almost untouched by industrial change, maintaining their traditional roles as centers of exchange for regional products. Périgueux was typical. Its major economic improvement during the July Monarchy was the construction of a new road that facilitated departmental commerce. Nailmaking by hand served a fairly wide market but it did not employ many men. The few entrepreneurs who attempted to create large units of production failed. In general "the ambitions of commerce were limited to the satisfaction of the immediate needs of the city population and of the large clientele of the countryside. Pots and pans, agricultural tools, grain and seed, clothing, shoes—these were above all what were sold on the market." The known professions of Périgueux Icarians reflect this situation: two diligence drivers, a bootmaker, a hatter, a woodworker, a painter-decorator, a waiter, a nailmaker, a founder, a barber, and a pharmacist. Pépin, Cabet's correspondent, was a mirrormaker. About the only factor with material implications that changed significantly was population; between 1800 and 1860, Périgueux grew from 5,733 to 14,778 people.[124] Urban demographic increase was significant elsewhere in the west and appears to have resulted from structural change in rural areas; its effect in the towns was to overburden the more easily accessible craft industries such as weaving and needlework. Such was the case at Tours, where distraught weavers made up over a third of the Icarian group.[125] Overcrowding notwithstanding, material pressures do not seem to have increased markedly in most Icarian centers in the west during the 1840s.

On the other hand, these towns witnessed one of the most important early movements of working-class association in France. And, of great significance for our purposes, this movement was organized and developed by journeyman tailors. The Société philanthropique des ouvriers tailleurs, created in Nantes in October 1833, encouraged branches at Tours, Rennes, Bordeaux, and other larger cities of the west and even developed links with Marseilles and Toulon. But its key centers were Nantes and Niort. While most such

---

veuil, "La Condition ouvrière et la crise de 1848 à Nantes," *1848 et les révolutions du dix-neuvième siècle* (1948), 39–61.

[124] Gérard Lavergne, *Histoire de Périgueux* (Périgueux, 1945), 142–43.

[125] *Le Populaire*, Jan.–Feb., 1845.

organizations were broken up by the policy of resistance in 1834, this one lived on secretly until 1839. The principal focus was upon practical trade unionism: aid to the aged and infirm, death benefits, and strike activities, often supported by funds from branches in other cities. It also thought of itself as a "model for future races" in the "achievement of universal fraternity," since it sought the ultimate association of all workers, beginning at the local level. It was explicitly republican, and the authorities even suspected that it aimed at social revolution.[126] There is a striking similarity between the foci and extent of the Philanthropic Society and of the Icarian movement in the west. In Nantes, twenty of the eighty-eight Icarians whose occupations are known were tailors, including Pedron, the local leader. After the suppression of the Philanthropic Society in 1838–1839, these politically aware tailors, now disillusioned with economic action and secrecy, probably rallied to nonrevolutionary communist politics and utilized their lines of contact to spread the doctrine.

Curiously, Icarianism, harassed by the authorities from its inception almost everywhere else, was not even investigated in the west until 1847. Perhaps it was simply not taken seriously since the government thought, quite rightly, that the great danger in this area came from the potentially legitimist countryside. Even in the towns, the emergence of communist groups was not viewed with great alarm. For instance, the procureur-général of Poitiers was confident (mistakenly so) "that in the city of Luçon the doctrines of communism are generally rejected by the good sense of the population, that they have no future there."[127] The combination of a relaxed official attitude toward communism and the repression of effective and widespread trade unionism among tailors may have been more significant than economic change in the emergence of Icarian communism in the west of France.

Niort, however, provides an exception, for during the first half of the nineteenth century its economic life was disrupted. The Niortais Icarians met often among themselves and with members (both republican and legitimist) of other groups opposed to the

---

[126] Festy, "Dix Années," 166–99.
[127] Report of Dec. 24, 1846, A.N., BB[18] 1441 dos 1992. On the fear of legitimism, see reports of Apr. 3, 5, 1845, A.N., BB[18] 1428 dos 9580.

government.[128] There were 24 subscribers to *Le Populaire* at Niort in 1846; the year before, 124 individuals (their names were not given) had signed a declaration of adherence.[129] The guiding spirit of the Icarians at Niort and throughout its region was Paul Guay, a shoemaker. Precisely how he came by his communist opinions is unknown, but he was a native of Deux-Sèvres and therefore had not, like Cöeffé at Vienne, been indoctrinated elsewhere before settling in the center of his activity. Possibly the old Nantes-Niort links of the late thirties in the tailors' Société philanthropique had been maintained, providing the original channel of dissemination. Although we have no direct evidence of specific Icarian connections between Nantes and Niort, we do know that the Nantais communists were in touch with Icarians as far away as Angoulême;[130] it is likely, therefore, that the much shorter Niort-Nantes link existed. Guay was an ardent propagandist for the Icarian cause. His leadership is well demonstrated by the investigations of communism in the Vendée in 1847, in which he was arrested and arraigned in Fontenay-le-Comte on a charge of leading a secret society embracing three departments.[131] Guay ran unsuccessfully for the constituent assembly in 1848; in 1851 he was involved in revolutionary activity following the coup d'état.[132]

Until the end of the eighteenth century, Niort ranked among the most prosperous small industrial towns in the kingdom, largely because of its chamois and glove manufacture, the products of which were sold mainly to the military. But the revolutionary and imperial armies, to cut costs and "democratize" their structures, increasingly abandoned the use of chamois pantaloons in the cavalry and soft leather gloves in all branches, substituting cheaper woolen and cotton products. Niort, whose climate and waters were ideal for the delicate process of chamois production from calf, sheep, goat, and deer skins,[133] struggled through the first decades of the

---

[128] Procureur-général de Poitiers to the Garde des Sceaux, Apr. 2 and 3, 1845, A.N., BB[18] 1428 dos 9580, and March 5, 1847, BB[18] 1451 dos 3524.

[129] *Le Populaire*, Nov. 22, 1845.

[130] Procureur-général de Rennes to the Garde des Sceaux. Dec. 24, 1847, A.N., BB[18] 1441 dos 1992.

[131] M. Faucheux and L. Morauzeux, "Les Débuts du communisme en Vendée," 79. See A.N., BB[18] 1441 dos 1992.

[132] *Dict. biog.*, II, 308–9.

[133] On the industry and its localization in Niort see "Rapport de M.

century, trying to develop a civilian market for its chief product. It also pursued a market in leather products, especially shoes, because the residue of the fish-oil mixture used to prepare chamois was much sought after as an ingredient of tanning oil. Neither campaign was very successful. In 1832 shoemaking was in disastrous shape, despite the fact that the number of shoemakers had remained stable.[134] But the twenties and early thirties brought a brief period of hope for these complementary industries when the North American market seemed to be opening up. Niort gloves were establishing a reputation in Philadelphia, New York, and Boston. Then came the Bank crisis and the depression of 1837 in the United States. In the late 1830s, Niort had become desperate. Said the prefect in his biennial report on the economy during the second half of 1837: "No one [in chamois and gloves] has worked for a long time; every evening the streets are filled with unfortunates who beg. The resources of charity, while immense, are nearly used up, and the authorities find themselves strongly embarrassed in such a state of prolonged misery."[135] Whereas the normal number of indigent families in Niort was around 500, some 2,200 received relief in the first half of 1838, and the bureau of public assistance complained of inadequate funding throughout 1839 and 1840.[136] The years 1839 through 1843 saw fifteen bankruptcies in Niort with a non-recovered debt of 544,000 francs, a period of collapse in the nineteenth century comparable only to that of the Second Republic.[137] After a brief, hope-instilling revival in 1842, the chamois and leather industries of Niort, which together employed nearly half the industrial population of the city and stimulated other local crafts, languished for the rest of the July Monarchy.[138]

One of the principal local trades was tailoring. Already suffering

---

Petit-Crétal sur la chamoiserie de Niort" (1852), A.N., F¹² 2266, and André Greffé, "La Ganterie niortaise: Etude géographique d'une survivance industrielle dans le Centre-Ouest," (unpublished Diplôme d'études supérieres de géographie, 1949), Archives Départementales (A.D.), Deux-Sèvres, Ms F n.a. 1220.

[134] Prefect's report of Jan. 25, 1852, A.D., Deux-Sèvres, 10 M 17/1c.

[135] *Ibid.*, report for second half of 1837.

[136] A.D. Deux-Sèvres, 2 X 115, Bureau de Bienfaisance; secours à domicile.

[137] A.D., Deux-Sèvres, 10 M 17/2 Faillites.

[138] Enquête sur le travail agricole et industriel (1848), Cantons de Niort, A.N., C 966.

from the depressed conditions of the general economy, tailors there, as elsewhere, began to confront the problem of confection, but this time with an even more galling twist, prison production. A petition of 1848 expressed their grievances (and their generosity):

> The shops selling ready-made clothing are destroying the existence of the signatories. . . . They believe it is their duty to submit to you their fears for the future hoping always that a new order of things will bring them the work they require and the tranquility necessary for order. They are doubly unhappy in their inviolable silence for they are not ignorant that a large part of the ready-made clothing comes from prisons. But, as fraternal workers, they have never protested against this burden that weighs on them and that allows the unfortunates to die less slowly in the prisons.[139]

While there are several indications that middle-class paternalism vis-à-vis the workers of Niort was accepted with deference,[140] the troubles of the late thirties seem to have stimulated popular political radicalism. As in Toulouse, the census of 1841 was vigorously resisted. For example, in the rue St.-Jean, a street with a socially diverse population, 191 out of 290 houses refused to allow the census takers past their threshholds.[141] The forties witnessed increasingly a phenomenon also apparent in Toulon—bourgeois democrats speaking out vigorously in defense of the workers and their problems. In 1846, Antoine Baugier, a liberal lawyer who had led the census fight and then a struggle against religious educational dominance in 1843, became provisional mayor. The circumstances of his selection are indicative of the political situation in Niort. The municipal council refused to endorse any government candidate to the office, and the prefect was unwilling to formalize the power of any of the opposition candidates. The July regime allowed this curious situation to continue largely due to the good relations that the local elected officials had established with the worker population. Baugier, who on taking office declared his unequivocal support for "organization of labor," guided Niort through the

---

[139] A.D., Deux-Sèvres, 11 M 19/13a. Petition from 46 journeymen tailors to Maichain, provisional commissar, March 6, 1848.

[140] See especially Rosélia Roussiel, *La Fille d'un proscrit* (Paris, 1848), 31–47.

[141] A.D., Deux-Sèvres, 4 M 6/13, copy of *l'Echo du peuple*, Aug. 28, 1841.

trauma of the crisis of 1846–1847 without once jeopardizing this faith.[142] Such bourgeois radicalism was not mere paternalism but an evident response to growing working-class political concern. Yves Toul has demonstrated that Niort and its environs saw the development of a variety of radical and socialist movements during the 1840s. Besides the Icarians, there were a number of eclectic ideological strains, including those focusing on the peasantry, such as Jacques Chabot's newspaper, the *Oeil du peuple,* and the social populism of Claude Durand of Mauzé, the composer of the famous *Chant des vignerons.* This lower-class impulse had a profound effect on the way elections took place: "The electoral committees presented the most moving and magnificent spectacles one could imagine. The working and popular masses, while deprived of the right to vote, took part by their collective will and their supportive demonstrations in the great electoral battles; the fire of their contact and interaction heated and inflamed the soul of the privileged and restricted elections."[143] Niort politics in this period thus gives an impression of real worker participation even if their social betters still called the final shots.

The roots of Icarianism in Niort are not difficult to understand. A collapsing traditional manufacturing base whose skilled and proud workers faced the relief rolls, considerable suffering in other trades of known Icarian potential, a history of union militance among the tailors, widespread circulation of radical and socialist ideas, and a local politics combining a meaningful lower-class input with intelligent middle-class management—all contributed to its success.

In the South, the most important center of Icarianism was Toulouse.[144] There were 136 subscribers to *Le Populaire* in Toulouse in 1846. In January 1848, 180 individuals signed the protest against

[142] On Baugier, see M. Chabaudy, *Vie de feu: Antoine Baugier* (Niort, 1864), and Yves Toul, "Les Origines des mouvements ouvrier et socialiste dans les Deux-Sèvres," *Bulletin de la Société historique des Deux Sèvres,* II (1961), 383–407.

[143] Chabaudy, *Antoine Baugier,* 43–44.

[144] There were also 27 subscribers to *Le Populaire* in Marseilles in 1846, and 115 protested Cabet's arrest in late 1847. But this is a small number in comparison with the total population, and there is no indication that the Marseilles Icarians had any great influence on the working class. In 1848 they were of little importance in the revolutionary movement.

Cabet's arrest in the name of "1,000 Icarians." Surprisingly, however, we know very little about the movement in Toulouse; the indications are, too, that it declined significantly in the two years before the revolution. And in 1848 itself, no Icarian was prominent in revolutionary politics. Still, the mere size of the movement and the fact that the Toulouse trial initiated the ascendent phase of Icarianism in France make it necessary to examine briefly the possible economic bases of the Icarian response there.

The bulk of Cabet's adherents in Toulouse were probably artisans in the traditional trades, although we know the precise professions of only three of them, a shoemaker, a master stonecutter, and woodworker. The central fact in the economic history of Toulouse during the July Monarchy was its striking population growth. In 1831 the population was 59,630; by 1846 it had reached 94,236. It is unlikely that consumer demand increased as quickly as the population. An underclass of poverty-stricken migrants from the Pyrenees and the surrounding countryside accounted for a large proportion of this growth. Many of them sought to enter lower-skill artisan trades, thus depressing the wages of native craftsmen. Those who failed to do so provided little stimulus to the economy at all. In these classic conditions of overpopulation, the specter of misery touched much of the working-class population. Housing shortages further aggravated the situation. In the working-class neighborhoods of east-side Toulouse, the population doubled from 1820 to 1851, while the number of houses increased by only 10 per cent.[145]

A large Icarian contingent existed in Toulon (54 subscribers in 1846, 229 signatures on the protest of January 1848) under the direction of Frayssée, a locksmith. Icarianism first penetrated the traditional crafts of the city and, in conjunction with social republicanism and other varieties of socialism, made its way to the workers in the great military shipyards as the 1840s progressed. Maurice Agulhon's brilliant study of Toulon[146] provides sufficient information to assess the possible bases of Cabet's influence. The pertinent economic factors were not dissimilar from those of

[145] Jean Coppolani, *Toulouse; Etude de géographie urbaine* (Toulouse, 1954), 132. The foregoing analysis based on figures presented in this excellent work, pp. 111–33.
[146] *Une Ville ouvrière.*

Vienne. This southern pocket of the French industrial revolution witnessed rapid modernization, especially in the metallurgical trades. Rapid shifts in production techniques both within and outside the arsenal produced reverberations in all crafts. Commercialization of tailoring and shoemaking and extremely heavy competition from prison and poorhouse labor were also significant.[147] A special factor lending cohesion to the indigenous Toulonnais working class was the influx of many skilled and even more unskilled laborers to the booming city during the July Monarchy. Total population increased more rapidly here than in any other major city in France during the first half of the nineteenth century. Politically, Toulon resembled Niort in some respects. The interaction between bourgeois democrats and workers was intense—especially, in this case, because both saw the "outside" port and military authorities as a common foe. This led to a situation in which the Toulon working class, favorable to the White Terror in 1815, rapidly moved from right to left by a process of social imitation. The patronage of conservatives was broken by what Agulhon terms "a democratic patronage."[148] Bourgeois initiative and leadership played a fundamental part in the emergent "red" consciousness of Toulon workers. This was less the case perhaps with Icarianism than with Saint-Simonism, but the atmosphere of bourgeois-working class alliance surely assisted in the implantation of Cabet's conciliatory communism.[149]

Several other cities in France were facing economic difficulties that might have contributed to Icarian growth. The town of Mirecourt in the Vosges, in which at least fifty-four Icarians were to be found in 1848, was the seat of an important musical instrument manufacture. Julien Chambry, an organmaker and Cabet's correspondent, reported in 1846 that the wages of workers in this trade had undergone "an incredible diminution" over the previous twenty years. Also, as we have seen, Lyonnais communists propagandized among the workers of the coalmining region of the Gier and in the town of Givors. In the latter, an important Icarian group already existed as early as 1842 under the leadership of Faure (possibly

[147] Cantons de Toulon, Enquête sur le travail agricole et industriel, A.N., C 968.
[148] *Une Ville ouvrière*, 332.
[149] *Ibid.*, 199–265.

the knifemaker Joseph Faure, who was to be provisional mayor of Givors in 1848);[150] there were 24 subscribers to *Le Populaire* there in 1846, and 150 contributed to the Sue medal collection. At Rive-de-Gier and Saint-Etienne the period of rapid Icarian development came in 1846 and early 1847. The entire coalmining region was faced with the oppressive power of the great monopoly, the Company of the Loire, and in 1845 the miners (joined in Saint-Etienne by the ribbonmakers) broke out into open revolt against it. These problems probably contributed to the growth of Icarianism in the region. Finally, there is the question of Icarianism at Rouen. There is a woeful lack of information on the impact of Cabet's doctrine there. All we know is that sixty-one Rouennais subscribed to *Le Populaire* in 1846 and that Cabet was satisfied enough with the work of his correspondent, Caudron (a shoemaker's tool merchant), to undertake the publication of *Le Populaire* as a weekly in Rouen (to avoid the large security deposit required in Paris) in 1847. The occupational breakdown of the Rouennais Icarians is unknown; there is, therefore, no way of telling whether the modernization of the textile industry was an important economic factor behind Icarian conversion.

How can one summarize the bases of Icarian adherence? Quite clearly (and naturally), economic difficulties played an important role. We have seen that the main occupational groups that lent support to Cabet were facing hard times during the July Monarchy and that, for the most part, the cities in which Icarianism had the greatest impact had sizable element being pressured by economic or demographic problems. Furthermore, there were a few clear statements that the Icarians in particular cities were miserable in material respects.[151] At the same time, Icarians were not drawn from the flotsam and jetsam of society. Almost all worked in established trades and were literate. These trades were largely of lesser rank in the social scale of the artisans of France. There were few workers in the modern sector of the economy, although in many cases Icarians were threatened by modern economic forces, be it

---

[150] *Dict. biog.*, II, 172. The possibility is strengthened by the fact that the Icarian Faure is described by Cabet as a "conseiller municipal" at Givors in 1844 (*Le Populaire*, June 5, 1844).

[151] Another example is a letter of 1847 from twenty-one Icarians at Amiens who say they are all "very poor." *Le Populaire*, April 18, 1847.

confection or the dislocations caused by factory production. Many Icarians, however, reacted to something more than the pangs of their stomachs. Although in general one must agree with Daniel Stern that most of those grouped around Cabet were "of simple mind, respectable men who were attracted by the benevolent morality and paternal tone of a teaching that took nothing from either science or philosophy,"[152] embracing communism did require some intellectual effort. Whatever the main idea bringing men to Icarianism—recognition of capitalist oppression, the Christian message, or the description of life in Community—the response for many came only after reading and reflection. But in terms of both impersonal stimuli and conscious motives, one is faced with a bewildering diversity of bases of Icarian adherence. Is it, then, fruitful to speak of a "typical" Icarian? Perhaps, but only if the Weberian concept of the ideal type is applied with the full rigor he theoretically attached to the term, that is, as a description that applies to no Icarian in particular but that brings together the dominant features of Icarians' experiences, conditions of existence, and attitudes. The ideal-typical Icarian would seem to have been: (1) a poor journeyman artisan in a traditional, urban craft threatened less by technological change than by modernized business practices; (2) a person who was literate and possessed some propensity for a theoretical consideration of his situation; (3) a Christian, if not a supporter of the institutional Church; and (4) a family man of middle age who had already endured considerable hardship and who was frustrated by his own lack of mobility in a society that made equality of opportunity one of its chief values.[153]

[152] Stern, *Histoire de la Révolution,* II, 166.

[153] The last characteristic is admittedly impressionistic, since we know the age of only a small number of Icarians. Yet only three of these were younger than thirty in 1845, and an examination of personal letters to Cabet suggests that most of his correspondents had behind them considerable experience in the trials of working-class life. The family emphasis, which Cabet made for doctrinal purposes, seems to have been in line with the realities of the Icarian party. The large number of women in the Icarian camp and the nature of Icarian group life provide further evidence. Finally, the large number of families that emigrated to America indicates that most Icarians were between thirty and fifty and were married.

5 | From Movement to Sect, 1846–1847

One of the more interesting facets of utopian socialism in general was its nearly inevitable tendency toward religiosity and sectarianism. If a movement grew up around the doctrines handed down by the master, it pushed on toward becoming a "church" rather than a "school." Thus Saint-Simon published his *Nouveau Christianisme* in the year before his death, and on Christmas day, 1829, Père Enfantin, Père Bazard, and the rest formed their Saint-Simonian Church. The "family" then located themselves first in an old hotel on the rue Monsigny and later in more spacious quarters (without the schismatic Bazard and under *Le Pape* Enfantin) at Ménilmontant.[1] If Fourier himself did not take on a religious posture (unless it might have been as Behemoth),[2] his disciples in the forties thought him to be a manifestation of the Second Coming: "first came Jesus Christ, then Fourier." Robert Owen, after the New Moral World was announced, became increasingly messianic, and a recent work by John F. C. Harrison has emphasized the sectarian nature of the later Owenite movement.[3]

The problem is more complex with Cabet and the Icarians. Among all the utopians of the nineteenth century, he had a sense of political reality and a thirst for concrete political power that makes one wonder if he should be placed in this category at all. The success of the movement in part depended upon Cabet's realism, and his mastery of propaganda techniques was almost out of

[1] See Charléty, *Histoire*, 57ff.
[2] F. Manuel discusses Fourier's megalomaniacal urge to punish France and the world in *The Prophets of Paris* (Cambridge, Mass., 1962), 245–48.
[3] *Quest for the New Moral World: Robert Owen and the Owenites in Britain and America* (New York, 1969). Millennial strains were never absent from Owen's thought, to be sure, but after 1834 the trend became more pronounced; see pp. 132ff.

place in the nineteenth century. But in 1845 and 1846 his political strategy, which was relatively consonant with his general theory of class conciliation and his personal desire for authority, went awry. The reason was that Cabet had not properly understood either the nature of social relations in France or the mentalities of many of his followers. He did not consciously try to build a sect, nor did he ever seriously portray himself as a Messiah. But when repulsed by such bourgeois social democrats as Ledru-Rollin, who feared the implications of communism, he saw his class-conciliation plank decay. Simultaneously revolutionary Babouvism revived as the economic crisis of 1846 descended upon France. And when Cabet's most devoted followers began to view him as a kind of prophet he allowed himself to be swept away by the tide, ultimately choosing to create a communist New Jerusalem across the seas. How this process occurred is the subject of this chapter.

Icarian Organization and Culture

How was the Icarian movement organized, and what degree of internal cohesion did it possess before the sectarian development set in? Because of the restrictions set by law, the Icarian group could not be organized in any formal manner.[4] Thus the only visible form of organization centered on the publication and distribution of *Le Populaire*. This turned out to be a fairly efficient means of maintaining unity. Strictly speaking, *Le Populaire* was a legal business enterprise. It formed a société commandite, and its shareholders, largely recruited from the working class, met on a regular basis. Although they dealt with business problems, the main purpose of their meetings was to discuss practical and doctrinal issues.

A commission of from ten to twenty Parisians handled the details of Cabet's many special projects, prepared certain works in the name of the entire Icarian party, directed shareholder and subscription campaigns, advised Cabet on day-to-day affairs, and reported the sentiment of Parisian workers. The commission had no formal structure, but one man, Firman Favard, emerged as its de facto director. He was a tailor and became Cabet's son-in-law in 1846.[5] The commission provided Cabet with a group of devoted

[4] That is, without government consent. The Law on Associations of 1834 effectively destroyed the possibility of formal radical organization.

[5] Martin Nadaud was very impressed by Favard, a "superb young man

agents without whom the development and management of a movement would have been impossible. Its occupational composition
mirrored that of the Icarian party as a whole.[6]

A kind of kitchen cabinet also figured in the direction of the
movement. Its members advised Cabet on major policy decisions
and on theoretical questions. Unlike the commission, all, with the
exception of Favard and J.-P. Beluze, a cabinetmaker, were bourgeois. It included Hermann Ewerbeck, who also served as Cabet's
correspondent to German-speaking allies, Louis Krolikowski, Berrier-Fontaine in London, and the peripatetic Charles Chameroy.
All influenced the decision-making process within the movement.
Two merchants, J.-B. Robillard and L. V. Maillard assisted in the
publication of *Le Populaire* and the *Almanach,* as did Favard
and Beluze.

The basis of the nationwide organization of Icarianism was the
system of local correspondents. These agents took subscriptions
and sold Cabet's other works, keeping a stock of his books and
pamphlets on hand. They distributed *Le Populaire* from their homes
or shops when the bundles arrived each month; made collections,
such as the one to finance a ceremony in honor of Eugène Sue;
organized petitions; held periodic meetings; and in general oversaw
the movement at the local level. Above all, they were Cabet's link
with his huge following in the provinces. They reported the progress
and difficulties of the movement, circulated addresses of support
for signature, and felt the pulse of their communities. Normally
one man could handle the job in any one area, although in Lyons
a commission, similar to that in Paris, assisted the correspondent.[7]
All the correspondents reported directly to Cabet. Thus, while such
missionaries as Faucon and Guay might be responsible for carrying

---

who, due to his studies, had deep knowledge on all social questions"
(*Mémoires de Léonard,* 175).

[6] Of the members of the 1846 commission, Aron, Favard, and Ducreux
were tailors, Ducoin a shoemaker, Desty and Julin bootmakers, Beluze (who
replaced Favard as chief after the latter's death in 1847) and Guérin cabinetmakers, Bapsubra a hatter, Prudent a jeweler, Simon a clockmaker, Guéni-
chet a pianomaker, Coutellier a machinist, Montagne a filemaker, Dumotier
a weaver, Nadaud a mason, Maillard a merchant-commissions agent, Robillard a wealthy merchant in the bakery trade (he was also an elector), and
Leroy a leather merchant. Actionnaires du Populaire, *Biographie de M.
Cabet* (Paris, 1846).

[7] See above, pp. 138–39.

the Icarian message to towns in their region, no hierarchical network was allowed to develop, for this would have smacked of secret-society organization. Moreover, it would have reduced Cabet's control over the movement.

Ultimate sovereignty within the movement rested fully with Cabet. The structure of Icarianism both reflected and accentuated his authoritarian position. While the shareholders had some formal influence in purely business matters, their votes on all other issues had no binding power, and the rank and file in Paris and the provinces had no direct structural influence whatsoever. A man could give up his subscription and denounce Cabet, but positive democratic avenues of pressure were nonexistent. The law, of course, would have viewed such procedures as manifestations of "unauthorized association." In effect, Cabet's power benefited from the repressive political system he so often decried.

Still, it would be incorrect to think of the Icarians as a constellation of atoms revolving around a single center. As the movement matured, the bond among its adherents deepened, especially on the local level. While he and his advisers sometimes suggested areas in which group activities might be undertaken, Cabet seemed hesitant to follow through on them.[8] His attitude toward intense local relationships within his party always remained equivocal, whether for fear of the police or of losing his power we cannot say.

Whatever the leader's position on this question, a local group life and relative cohesion among Icarians grew. The bulk of our information concerns Lyons, and the most valuable commentary on the nature of Icarian gatherings and relationships comes from Sébastien Commissaire.

The Lyonnais Icarians formed several groups, of which the most important met at the home of M. Garçon, rue Saint Rose, in the Croix-Rousse. I often attended these meetings, which were composed of men, women, and children. Evenings there passed agreeably. We recited fables. We sang politico-socialist songs that were, for the most part,

[8] Instruction societies, libraries, "a great society for moralization and temperance," and a "judicial council" to advise workers on their legal rights were all proposed in *Le Populaire* during 1842 and 1843, but none of them was instituted. These proposals (and an apology for not having acted on them) were listed again in the September 24, 1844, issue of the newspaper.

written by young Icarians. We discussed all sorts of political and social questions. It was an excellent way for men to get used to public speaking. To please the women and children, the evenings usually ended in playing games.[9]

With these few words one is carried to the heart of Icarian life. Perhaps the most interesting remark is the reference to fables and songs composed by Icarians themselves. This means that a kind of Icarian culture existed. We are fortunate that one of these "fables" has survived (though we do not know whether its author, B. Turgard, was a Lyonnais). Entitled "Le Rocher, la source et le vieillard," the manuscript is located among the Cabet papers at the Bibliothèque Historique de le Ville de Paris.[10] The story begins in the depths of a great promontory, overlooking a sunbaked and barren plain, where "a tiny spring, of crystal waters, had just been born." Blocked by the massive cliff, the rivulet asked "to continue my way, for such is my destiny." But the cliff haughtily refused its passage, deaf to the entreaties of the spring that its waters could make the fields below green again—"I will cover the great meadow with flowers, vines will cling to your sides: Utopia!" The insensitive stone replied only with mocks and threats. Then an old man appeared and, with one blow, opened up the great rock and spring flowed forth.

> Et soudain prairie et coteau,
> Etant arrosés du ruisseau,
> Se couronnèrent de verdure. . . .
> La source à l'onde pure
> Est le socialisme.
> Le roc c'est l'ignorance et égoïsme.
> Le vieillard aux effets puissants,
> Le temps.

Some Icarian songs also survive. A worker from Niort who had moved to Paris, Charles Tessier, composed a "Chant communiste, dédié à M. Cabet" and sent it to Cabet with a letter on June 1, 1844.[11] In the letter he stressed that songs were a marvelous means

---

[9] Commissaire, *Mémoires,* I, 97–98. Garçon split with Cabet in late 1844, so Commissaire is referring to an earlier period.

[10] Papiers Cabet, XV (undated), BHVP.

[11] Tessier's handwritten version may be found among the Papiers Cabet, VII, BHVP.

of propaganda, especially among those for whom reading was difficult. They would also increase Icarian solidarity. The last stanza
of his song epitomizes the spirit that he hoped to generate.

> Le temps n'est pas si loin qu'on peut le croire,
> Où les Trésors dont vous vous emparez,
> Même à vos yeux ne vaudront pas la gloire,
> En beins communs vous les réunirez.
> Vos noms, qu'alors on aura soin d'inscrire,
> Passeront grands à la postérité:
> Avec bonheur nous irons les relire,
> Nous qui voulons *sagesse* et *liberté*.

The songs of the "young Icarians" of Lyons were probably not so
polished but undoubtedly expressed similar thoughts. Commissaire
noted that since the affairs he was describing were "extralegal,
every time the police came around it was necessary that we play
innocent games."[12] Thus a certain amount of danger and excitement remains; the old secret-society atmosphere was not entirely
absent.

Sunday outings into the countryside were also popular in Lyons.
Unlike the more serious evening gatherings, these picnics were
largely for pleasure. "Friends were invited; everybody got to know
one another; the young people danced; finally, we enjoyed ourselves the more because no one spouted off there." Thus did
Frédéric Olinet, a later emigrant to Nauvoo, pass many Sundays.[13]
Garçon and Lardet, two Icarian leaders in the earlier stages of the
movement at Lyons, opened their homes to those who wished to
set up night schools for adults of both sexes. Finally a formal society, known as the Bibliothèques, was created in Lyons in 1843.
Subdivided into groups of fewer than twenty persons, who met
periodically to discuss socialist and radical works they had read,
its members paid dues in order to build up a library and created a
lending service for nonmembers. The government attempted to link
the Bibliothèques with a group of militants found to possess an
armory in 1844 but could not prosecute; this Icarian subassocia-
tion lived on thereafter and no doubt helped to spread the doctrine
in Lyons.[14]

[12] *Mémoires,* I, 98.
[13] Olinet, *Voyage,* 18–19.
[14] The relevant documents are: Procureur-général de Lyon to the Garde

Although the Icarian group at Lyons may well have been the most active in France, similar confraternities probably existed elsewhere. After the emigration announcement Cabet became less guarded about discussing such activities; numerous reports of banquets, fetes, and outings were printed in *Le Populaire*.[15] Since the examples from Lyons all date from before 1847 and were not reported it stands to reason that a local group life existed in other centers earlier as well.

There are many other indications of the bond that existed among Icarians. We have already seen that Cabet put heavy stress on doctrinal conformity within the movement; the adoption of the title "Icarian" in 1843–1844 was an attempt to bring greater cohesion to his following. The gathering of signatures for the addresses of adhesion was another means of creating a feeling of unity. How did all of this affect the attitudes of the individuals involved? Did Icarians feel a deep loyalty to the doctrine and a real sense of confraternity? Two examples, both from 1845, suffice to show that they did. The first concerns a worker in Rive-de-Gier who was fired from his job because he subscribed to *Le Populaire* (or so he said); rather than renounce the Icarian doctrine, he moved from his home town and sought work in Lyons.[16] The second story shows the feeling of brotherhood among Icarians. Two Parisian workers who did not know one another came to the aid of a drunken old woman who had been ridiculed and thrown into the gutter by some young toughs. After they had chased away her tormentors, the two discovered to their astonishment that they were both Icarians. This common bond immediately brought them into a fast friendship.[17]

Icarianism was indeed a movement with clear, if informal, organization, intercity connections, a local group life, and even a culture of sorts. There was still little, however, to suggest a sectarian nature.

---

des Sceaux, Sept. 20, 1844, A.N., BB[18] 1423 dos 8701; *Le Populaire*, Sept. 28, Oct. 1844; Cabet, *Les Masques arrachés*, 41–44; and Commissaire, *Mémoires*, I, 105–6.

[15] See, for instance, reports of Icarian banquets and festivals at Reims, "in the Alps," and at Rennes and of "outings" at Lyons itself in *Le Populaire*, Sept. 12, Oct. 17, and Nov. 28, 1847.

[16] *Le Populaire*, Jan. and Feb., 1845, Supplément.

[17] *Ibid.*, Aug. 16, 1845.

Sectarian Tendencies, 1845–1846

But a close analysis of the movement from the fall of 1845 reveals a trend in which the two dominant characteristics of sect formation—an exclusive fellowship of true believers and a strong religious, even millenarian, emphasis—become more evident.[18] In examining this trend, one is also exploring the factors leading to its most striking result, the announcement on May 9, 1847, that an Icarian "model nation" would be created in America. After this decision the sectarian nature of Icarianism became obvious and Cabet himself, who did not initially desire such an outcome, acquiesced in his new prophetic role. This entire development could be labeled "the Icarian tragedy," but such an emotional response would obscure the deeper social and cultural forces that in large measure determined its course. The story unfolded in three, fairly distinct, phases: the struggle with *La Réforme* and the noncommunist social republicans, which produced a growing emphasis on Icarian exclusivism (September 1845–Spring 1846); the publication of *Le Vrai Christianisme,* a period marked by a rising sense of religious purpose and a new veneration of Cabet within the Icarian camp (Spring 1846–Spring 1847); and the emigration decision and its aftermath. The first two phases will be examined in this section and the dénouement in the following one.

A preliminary question must be confronted: Beneath his outward posture of practicality and political realism, did Cabet actually harbor Messianic desires—was his goal all the time to gather a sufficient number of brethren to create a communist kingdom in the wilderness? If so, much of the analysis that follows would be academic; the traditional image of Etienne Cabet, archutopian, would appear valid. Undeniably, Cabet was self-centered, vain, and authoritarian. But, at least until 1847, one is hard-pressed to find in him a religious enthusiast, much less the Messiah of the

---

[18] Harrison, summarizing the work of Bryon R. Wilson as it applied to Owenism, defines a sect as "a small religious group, in which membership is voluntary and limited to persons having certain special convictions or experiences in common. A rejection of the values of society, and withdrawal or separateness from the world, together with an expectation of some form of adventism further typify the sect. A mission to preach the Kingdom, an emphasis on fellowship (brotherly love), and allegiance understood as 'belief in the truth' are also commonly found." *Quest for the New Moral World,* 135.

Second Coming. Furthermore, there is strong evidence that he rejected community-building out of hand until early 1847.

As noted earlier, Cabet began in 1842 to stress that communism was nothing more than "Christianity in its primitive purity." Yet this was hardly tantamount to a personal religious conversion. Christ was a man, a great philosopher, having no divine attributes. There is of course this interesting comment in *Voyage en Icarie:* "Do not forget that Moses announced a reformer awaited down through the centuries in all the East; that Jesus Christ manifested the *good news* of the arrival of this reformer and predicted the future coming of another Messiah."[19] Would this perhaps be Etienne Cabet? We have no way of knowing. But this is the only sentence in all of his writings indicating a possible Messianic impulse. In comparison with Weitling or the "prophets," such as Albrecht or Barmby, Cabet was as foreign to such self-images as was John Stuart Mill. He specifically rejected any prophetic role. When Fournier de Virginie called him a "false prophet," Cabet protested "I have never had any pretention of passing myself off for a Prophet"; rather, he was one who "devotes his life to Truth."[20] Personally Cabet was a deist, and he said so on many occasions. Dr. Desmoulins of Tours tried to convince him of the divine origins of Icarian doctrine, but Cabet replied, "I thank you for your wishes and your efforts for my conversion and my salvation. But I pity you as much as you pity me, for none of your arguments has convinced me in the least. . . . Since you were an unbeliever until 1841, I can certainly still be one today."[21] He denounced the historical church. "In our mind the Catholic faith has offered great dangers, it has had deplorable results; for if it was a source of consolation for the unfortunate, it was also the sword and buckler of tyranny, which it made all the more audacious by restraining all desire of resistance among the oppressed."[22] Traditional Catholicism had thus been the opium of the people. John Minter Morgan, the English utopian and designer of the Christian Commonwealth communities, was disappointed that Cabet's work was "all mixed up with political matters. . . . He pretends to no faith in the

[19] *Voyage en Icarie,* 532.
[20] *Le Populaire,* Aug. 19, 1843.
[21] Cabet to Desmoulins (draft), May 8, 1843, Papiers Cabet, V, BHVP.
[22] *Le Populaire,* Oct. 10, 1842.

Christian Religion, but classes it with all other religions of the earth as having one common origin—the ignorance and superstition of the ruder stages of society."[23] About the only real indication we have that Cabet toyed with presenting a religious and Messianic image of himself dates from after the emigration call, when he circulated a portrait of himself accompanied on the opposite flap of the hinged lithograph with a picture of Jesus. This is reported by the procureur-général, who saw it, however, simply as a means of raising money, since Cabet was selling the little album "for a high enough price."[24]

On the other hand, Cabet did maintain friendly relations with socialists of mystical or prophetic inclinations. The "prophet" Albrecht translated his *Crédo communist* into German; Krolikowski was his close collaborator; Pierre Leroux was about his only close friend among the major socialist thinkers;[25] and he himself lauded Abbé Châtel's Eglise catholique française and railed against both the suppression of this Christian socialist movement and the condemnation of the newspaper of Châtel's ally, Baudelier, *La Religion naturelle.*[26] Cabet warmly greeted Emile Brée's *Almanach-Catéchisme,* which had strong religious overtones, and was in turn praised by this worker-turned-publicist as a modern Thomas More whose followers were "plebian Saint Johns playing the parts of worthy precursors of the future Messiah, a man of the people."[27]

How was Cabet regarded by his followers? Was there a current of opinion that saw him in saintly or Messianic colors? Among his Parisian adherents Cabet was known personally and well liked, but no religious adulation came his way. Martin Nadaud's impression was perhaps representative.

Cabet was a man of rare dedication and of a force of character rarer still; from 1832 [*sic*] at the time of the publication of his first newspaper, *Le Populaire,* Luquet, Druand, and I were attached to him. . . .

[23] *Letters to a Clergyman on Institutions for Ameliorating the Conditions of the People* (London, 1846), 119.

[24] Procureur-général d'Amiens to the Garde des Sceaux, Nov. 29, 1847, A.N., BB[18] 1441 dos 1992.

[25] Louis Leroux, Pierre's son, attested to their relationship in a letter to Beluze of June 20, 1870. Archief Cabet, IISG.

[26] *Le Populaire,* June 5, Dec. 11, 1842, June 10, 1843.

[27] Advertisement for Cabet's *Almanach icarien pour 1843* in the *Almanach catéchisme* 2d ed. (Poitiers, 1843). On Brée, a figure not reported in the *Dict. biog.,* see A.N., BB[18] 1408 dos 5802 and 1434 dos 667.

Learning of his return in 1839 . . . we went to see him. . . . . He welcomed us in such a courteous manner, even though we were dressed in work clothes, that from that time until 1848 I attached myself firmly to this worthy defender of the people. I rarely missed attending the meetings that were held each Sunday in his salon on the rue Jean-Jacques Rousseau. . . .

[One day in 1842] he had us come to his residence. . . . He had just finished shaving and still held his towel and razor in his hand. He shooks hands vigorously with each of us; then he seemed to be moved with joy to see so dressed so nicely; "Ah! messieurs," he said in a serious manner, "if your adversaries could see you now, you would disarm their criticisms; your appearance, your demeanor are those of the best brought-up people." Never had I seen him smile so much; his handsome face, usually serious, gentle, and delicate, was radiant with satisfaction.[28]

Although Nadaud's attitude was deferential, there is nothing here to indicate that Cabet was anything more than a good and great man in his eyes.

Cabet was regarded as "père" by his followers. Sébastien Commissaire of Lyons presented this picture of Cabet:

I had the pleasure of seeing this sincere friend of the people. . . . His face was . . . marked by an air of kindness that put the most humble person at ease; his dress was quite simple; his language was that of one who had faith, of an apostle convinced of the excellence of his ideas; his entire person breathed an air of bonhommie that caused his followers to call him *le père Cabet*. . . . This word includes all other appellations for the workers. . . . It indicates not only the admiration but the love the workers show for their friends.

Do not think that the people is extravagant with this title. This would be a great error, even though it gets enthused easily; I have only seen two men given this name in my time, M. Cabet and M. Raspail.[29]

"Father," therefore, as normally employed by the French workers, did not have any religious connotations. Still, Commissaire regarded Cabet as an "apostle," and the term father was rarely used until 1846, when the sectarian trend became discernible. Add the

---

[28] Nadaud, *Mémoires,* 173–75.
[29] *Mémoires,* I, 98–99. Commissaire goes on to note that Bugeaud received it from his soldiers.

constant adulation of the Icarian leader (although largely in secular terms) and it becomes clear that, especially in the provinces, he
already possessed an image that bordered on the religious. This,
however, proves nothing about his own designs.

Cabet clearly rejected the traditional utopian device of model-
community building, especially if it would involve leaving France.
He was aware of the possibilities and limitations presented by the
creation of experimental communities even at the time of his conversion to communism during his London exile. In speaking of
Robert Owen in *Voyage en Icarie,* Cabet praised Owen's thought
and his generous soul but felt that he had wasted precious funds
that could have been used for propaganda purposes on his communitarian experiments.[30]

In the second issue of *Le Populaire,* Cabet was more explicit:
"We think that Community is easier to create the larger the country, the more numerous the People, the more powerful the industry;
we think that a small-scale attempt would have no chance of success and that the unfortunate results of a partial experiment could
prove nothing against a large-scale attempt."[31] In July 1842 Cabet
cautioned against emigration of any kind, saying that "Europeans
cannot take too many precautions and too many guarantees before
leaving their homeland to carry themselves to a distant, unknown,
and completely different land." Two months later he enunciated his
fundamental objection to socialist experiments overseas in reference
to the Fourierist Brazilian colony: "Emigrations . . . deprive the
popular cause of a great number of defenders whose dedication
would have been more useful to it in the midst of the crises that
are coming." He reiterated the same arguments in the *Almanach*
for 1843.[32]

At about the same time, however, Cabet mentioned two schemes
for the creation of a "practical attempt." In November 1842 he
alluded vaguely to the possibility of using governmental resources
and convicted criminals "to transform a department into a Community, or to attempt a large Community in a colony."[33] But this
single sentence was a part of an article on prison conditions, and

[30] Cabet, *Voyage en Icarie,* 519.
[31] *Le Populaire,* April 18, 1841.
[32] *Ibid.,* July 3, Sept. 11, 1842, and *Almanach icarien pour 1843* (Paris,
Dec. 1842), 95–96.
[33] *Le Populaire,* Nov. 13, 1842.

the idea remained dormant. He also suggested public initiative in carrying out the program. Moreover, *Le Populaire* of February 10, April 9, and June 10, 1843, contained renewed attacks on overseas experiments. In the last he denounced the Fourierist promoters of the disastrous scheme to create a phalanstère in Colombia in these terms: "There is the country where these unfortunates have gone to establish themselves [this follows a description of the Colombian climate and terrain], without knowing it and without sufficient information, refusing to listen to all contrary observations! And to complicate their misfortune, division broke out among them, so that these emigrants could think of nothing but returning to their homeland."[34]

But in 1843 Cabet also toyed with the only serious proposal for an experimental community he ever made, which appeared in the *Almanach* for 1844 under the title "Petite Communauté des dévoués" and was repeated in *Le Populaire* on May 2, 1844. The nature of the organization can best be described as a laboratory of communism. A small core of individuals (no more than twenty) should associate themselves to form a "single soul" devoted to the principle of "Christian fraternity." Around this core would be two groups, "paying guests" and "worker guests," who would stay for three months in order to practice various aspects of communitarian life and to drink deeply of Icarian doctrine. The "dedicated" would consist of eight to ten writers, five or six workers, and five to seven "others" (rich and generous donors). Cabet was purposely vague on the precise organization of the community because the major aim was to try diverse methods, study the results of each, and publish the findings.[35] The community, to be located in Paris or nearby, would also serve to propagandize the Icarian cause: "All their writings and all their acts will excite all classes to reciprocal benevolence, to union, to concord, to the practice of true Christianity and fraternity."[36] The community was, therefore, conceived as part of his overall program of propaganda and was certainly not seen as the first in a series of localized communitarian cells that would

[34] *Ibid.*, June 10, 1843.
[35] Cabet presents this point of view with special clarity in a letter of July 3, 1844, answering the objections made by the Société démocratique française of London in their meetings of May 6 and 13, 1844. Archief Cabet, IISG.
[36] *Le Populaire*, May 2, 1844.

multiply and eventually engulf France; unlike Fourier or Raspail, Cabet was totally opposed to such decentralization.

The last mention of this scheme came on July 12, 1844. In *Le Populaire* of that date Cabet printed a letter from the Société démocratique française of London questioning the efficacy of any such enterprise. He remarked that their apprehension was well founded, given the numerous failures of such undertakings, but indicated that he was not yet ready to give up the idea.[37] Nevertheless, his later silence on the issue suggests that, in reality, he may have been convinced by their arguments.

Cabet made two other statements after July 1844 on the question of partial Communities. In the heat of a controversy with the Fourierist journal, *La Démocratie pacifique,* he reacted to their charge that he was afraid to test his system with an experiment, saying that he had not yet had the opportunity and advising them, therefore, not to decide that the realization of communism would lead only to "disorganization and anarchy" before "an experiment on our part."[38] This isolated comment was the most outspoken avowal of a desire to create an experimental community to appear in Cabet's writings before May 1847. The circumstances reduce its importance, however. At this point Cabet was locked in a furious duel of words with the chief organ of Fourierism. His failure to follow up the remark suggests that it was more a technique of argumentation than a statement of intent. Furthermore, it was contradicted by his comments of September 27, 1846, when he pointed out that experience demonstrated the futility of attempts to construct partial communities and reiterated the necessity of propaganda in order "to multiply the number of men capable of the common life."[39]

Although all of this indicates that Cabet's attitude toward experimentation was not completely consistent, the weight of the evidence points to the conclusion that he was generally opposed to emigration and wary of communitarian experiments. This should hardly be surprising since the whole thrust of his program was conceived in a Jacobin framework. A highly centralized Community of the

---

[37] *Ibid.,* July 12, 1844. The original may be found in the Archief Cabet, IISG.
[38] *Ibid.,* Aug. 16, 1845.
[39] *Ibid.,* Sept. 27, 1846.

entire French nation was the Icaria of Cabet's dreams. Moreover, the foregoing citations comprise nearly the entire body of his comments on experimentation and emigration. That they are so few in number provides further proof of Cabet's lack of interest in such questions before 1847. Further corroboration may be found in the fact that in criticizing Cabet's emigration plan, *La Fraternité de 1845* reminded him of his declarations against precisely what he now intended to do.[40]

Then, in the course of 1846 and 1847, a major reorientation took place within the movement. Growing Icarian exclusivism and religious enthusiasm overtook practical political work and culminated in a dramatic reversal of Cabet's general strategy, the emigration decision. His acerbic conflict with *La Réforme* late in 1845 acted as the catalyst, for in the course of this debate it became clear that his program of left-wing unity, class conciliation, and a pacific mass movement was inherently defective. As this realization dawned on him he swung first toward a position bordering on that which Marx and Engels were formulating at that very moment; then, recognizing that the uniqueness of his communism, the very core of his rationalistic system, was threatened by the doctrine of class struggle, he gathered the faithful, unleashed the millennial imagery, and finally decided to abandon European politics altogether.

To understand this development, we must isolate the major issues upon which his tactical dilemma turned. Four interrelated phenomena were involved: (1) Cabet's changing attitude toward the bourgeoisie and the possibility of class collaboration; (2) his enunciation of the principles of working-class solidarity; (3) his proposition that capitalist concentration actually paved the way for the socialization of the means of production; and (4) his concept of revolution.

The first two are so closely interconnected that they are better dealt with simultaneously. As Cabet despaired of bourgeois collaboration, he increasingly invoked working-class solidarity. In his writings of 1841–1843, his well-known position in favor of class

---

[40] *La Fraternité,* May 1847. Interestingly, this Babouvist paper, under the guiding spirit of Dézamy, spent much more time in 1845 and 1846 discussing experimental projects and was clearly more positive with regard to their usefulness than was Cabet.

collaboration and his trust that the bourgeoisie would rationally comprehend the necessity of communism were fully and repeatedly expressed. "Yes, the proletarian should have no fatal illusions; the People can make no conquest without the cooperation of a part of the Bourgeoisie; it is nothing without the latter, it will be nothing without it; and nothing is more antipopular than separation and exclusion between the workers and the bourgeois who, heart and soul, are devoted to their cause."[41] He spoke also to the bourgeoisie:

> Do not close your eyes to the growing diminution of wages of the worker, to his lack of work, to the high prices of the food of the poor, to the augmentation of taxes, to misery, to the concentrated despair of which the explosion would be most terrible! Respect the human dignity of these proletarians who . . . are actually your brothers! Be compassionate, humane, just toward these workers whose arms nourish you, dress you, house you, of whom a large number merit your esteem by their virtues, and who all merit your benevolence and your concern because they are the victims of a tyrannical social organization that refuses them education . . . without even assuring them work and bread! Be just by love of justice and of humanity! Be so at least out of prudence and interest well understood! For it would be folly to forget that "the hungry stomach has no ears" and that "no one listens less to reason than the desperate!"[42]

Numerous other examples of such appeals could be presented, for they represent the "orthodox" Cabet. Nor can there be any doubt about the sincerity of his position. As we have already seen, Cabet disavowed followers who were unwilling to support his views in favor of class collaboration.[43]

As late as February 1845, Cabet was still intent upon making the bourgeoisie see the error of its ways; this was the date he published the brochure of "un prolétaire"[44] called *L'Esclavage du riche,* in which the author tried to demonstrate that the bourgeois is enchained by his property and haunted by the fear of losing it to such an extent that his misery is equal to that of the worker whom he oppresses. Can the rich actually prefer a "life of hate" to one of

---

[41] Cabet, *Réfutation des doctrines de l'Atelier* (1842), 10–11. See also *Ma Ligne droite* (1841), 37.

[42] Cabet, *Toute La Vérité* (1842), 111.

[43] See above, Chap. 3.

[44] This was none other than Aloysius Huber (or Hubert), who was to proclaim the dissolution of the Assembly on May 15, 1848.

love and fraternity?[45] Cabet fully embraced the message of this "remarkable" work. That May he warned Europe that a "storm" was brewing, not only because of political tyranny but especially due to "the vices of the *social* organization, egotism or *individualism* which serves as its base, competition, the universal development of machines and of industry joined to an iniquitous distribution of the public wealth, the diminution of work and of wages, and growth of misery, and the despair of the masses, and the resistance of the Conservatives." The only means to avoid the imminent cataclysm was through "the union of minds and in the unity of efforts" among all democratic reformers, bourgeois and proletarian alike. But he was no longer sure that sufficient time remained, for the specter of social war hung heavy over Europe. Still, consonant with his strategy, he counseled that all communist workers must continue "to extend a fraternal hand to all sincere Democrats."[46] But this was Cabet's final effort; in September, Ledru-Rollin and *La Réforme* rejected Cabet's plea for democratic cooperation.

In the past, *Le Populaire* and *La Réforme* had been on fairly amicable terms, even working together on certain schemes. The most important of these was the great petition for suffrage reform promoted by *La Réforme* in 1844; many Icarians helped to gather signatures. Moreover, in at least one city, Rouen, an association existed that solicited subscriptions and shares for the two newspapers simultaneously.[47] In *Les Masques arrachés* of 1844, whenever he was not slandering his former associates, Cabet would curry favor with the bourgeois radical left, especially Ledru-Rollin. It was thus a rude shock when, in a speech at Le Mans, the latter roundly condemned communism and quoted Robespierre in his support.

The Icarian leader discussed this turn of events at length in *Le Populaire* of September 19, 1845. As well as presenting Bounarrotist arguments that Robespierre was a harbinger of communism, Cabet stressed that Ledru-Rollin's denunciation of the communists

---

[45] *L'Esclavage du riche* (Paris, 1845), 14.

[46] Cabet, *Le Cataclysme social, ou conjurons la tempête* (Paris, May 1845), 3–4, 21.

[47] Procureur-général de Rouen to the Garde des Sceaux, April 23, 1844, A.N., BB[18] 1421.

was a shattering blow to the movement of democracy, for he was cutting himself off from a large segment of the working class. Cabet then called on all communists to redouble their efforts and gird themselves for the prospect of going on alone.[48] The following month Cabet pointedly labeled *La Réforme* "an organ of the bourgeoisie." To leave no doubt about his meaning, he reminded his readers of the betrayal of the proletarians by the bourgeoisie in the revolutions of 1789 and 1830. In essence, *La Réforme* had sold out to propertied interests.[49]

Some of Cabet's friends, especially those who knew him in the thirties, thought that the foundations of the rift were shallow. Right-thinking men of the bourgeoisie should not be inimical toward communism, nor should Cabet be disturbed by the revolutionary tone of *La Réforme* in light of his own past.[50] But Cabet quickly moved on to prepare a tract unveiling a new attitude toward the bourgeoisie. In *Salut par l'union ou ruine par la division, la paix ou la guerre entre le Populaire et la Réforme* (November 1845), he still entertained the hope that *La Réforme* would come to appreciate communism but made it clear that he was unwilling to compromise any of his principles by moving toward it. There was no middle ground between "individualism and communism," and *La Réforme* appeared to have opted for the former. He closed with a section entitled "Attitude du peuple envers la bourgeoisie." Workers might still make the bourgeoisie "the offer of fraternal alliance."

But let us be firm! If the Bourgeoisie persists in rejecting us, it is necessary to resign ourselves to being rejected. Let us then close our ranks; let us march separately on our own side. Only instead of forming the avant-garde as before, let us form the rear guard and the reserve army; let us allow the Bourgeoisie to engage itself, and we will throw ourselves in only to decide and to direct the victory to our profit as to its.

The last phrase, of course, shows that Cabet had not fully embraced the concept of class antagonism. But this brochure warned

[48] *Le Populaire,* Sept. 19, 1845.
[49] *Ibid.,* Oct. 18, 1845.
[50] See especially a letter of Nov. 10, 1845, from "un détenu politique," Papiers Cabet, BHVP.

the workers that they could no longer trust the bourgeoisie. Furthermore, while it had revolutionary overtones, let there be no mistake: "We shall no longer be dupes and will no longer burn our fingers to pull the chestnuts from the fire for [the bourgeoisie] to eat without leaving any for us!" Finally, "The Bourgeoisie, which is only a privilege and a kind of caste, can disappear and will disappear before the principle of equality and fraternity, while the People cannot perish."[51] Cabet seemed to be reclassifying the bourgeoisie, removing it from among the useful elements in society. This implied a marked departure from the past.

The situation evoked a variety of reactions among Icarian sympathizers. A letter from Chaville (Charles Chameroy) pointed out that the split was causing "reformists" to cancel their subscriptions to *Le Populaire,* but "your true friends will not abandon you."[52] In a letter supporting Cabet, "five ex-members of a reformist committee" quoted Robespierre's famous dictum that existence is the first of human rights; this proved that communism was the logical conclusion of the thought of "this incorruptible friend of the people." Eleven workers from Nantes were convinced that "Ledru-Rollin has sold out to the bourgeoisie." Seventy-two Vienne workers were astounded that Ledru-Rollin could say what he did in light of the fact that "Christ was a communist." But twenty proletarians who labored together in a Parisian workshop squarely faced the central issue:

The communists do not want to destroy; they want to re-establish Society on true bases; they do no separate their cause from that of the People; universal fraternity is their end; they are *pacific,* and are conscious of their power; they will know how to use it when the time comes; but words will not satisfy them; the fine language of a man has little value for them; they consider only his acts; if society became . . . separated into two camps, if there were a struggle, the victory would not be in doubt: the bourgeoisie, egotistical, skillful in the wiles of trade, impotent as to the production of the wealth it amasses, would not try to struggle against the strong arms of the producers; and the latter, while less polished than the former, have qualities that the others do not have; they have a heart to love and feelings to render compas-

[51] Cabet, *Salut par l'union,* 50 (all quotations).
[52] *Le Populaire,* Oct. 18, 1845.

sion, not by sterile grimaces but by action in the care of their unfortunate brothers, in taking on what is necessary and receiving the pittance that marks the compensation for the great actions of man.

This was why "the workers are communists." We have already quoted part of this letter in Chapter 4. In a temporal context it has even greater meaning, because it was by far the strongest language that Cabet had allowed to appear in print up to this point. These Parisian workers' class solidarity and disdain for the bourgeoisie coincided with Cabet's new mood very well. A letter from Périgueux bearing twenty-one signatures identified *Le Populaire* as the organ to unify all workers: "We say . . . to all our brothers: Let us all regard ourserves as *solidaires;* let us tighten our links further and let us rally around our *Populaire;* let it become henceforth the common center to unite all the Workers; it is our guide and our defender!"[53]

"Henceforth": here was the key to the new atmosphere being generated within the Icarian movement. The break with *La Réforme* meant that bourgeois collaboration no longer seemed likely. Communism could only be a working-class movement. On November 16, 1845, a meeting of the "General Assembly" of the shareholders of *Le Populaire* met in Paris in an air of "unanimity and enthusiasm." The decision was made to promote the "closing of ranks" and to emphasize general working-class solidarity based on communist principles. Cabet stated that the "high level of the decisions taken opens a *New Era* in the history of communism."[54]

Throughout the following year Cabet continued to emphasize the need for working-class solidarity and to warn workers that to trust in the bourgeoisie was sheer folly. In December 1845 he printed an article by Julien Chambry, his correspondent at Mirecourt. "Proletarians, our existence is a tissue of misery and of slavery; . . . from our earliest years we are exploited, sometimes the prey of greedy and inhuman men who get fat on our sweat and who, not content with enriching themselves to our detriment, disdain us and commit outrages against us!!!"[55] The only alternative to this "system of exploitation of man by man" was commu-

[53] *Ibid.,* Nov. 22, 1845 (both letters).
[54] *Ibid.*
[55] *Almanach icarien pour 1846* (Paris, 1845), 179–80.

nism, to which he called the "proletarians" to rally. No appeal whatsoever was made to the exploiters to mend their ways.

Le Populaire of April 25, 1846, took up the grave issue of the Loire miners' revolt, in which several workers were killed by royal troops. Though saddened by the violence of the workers, Cabet viewed the uprising as the natural outgrowth of intolerable exploitation: "The numerous companies that exploit the coal miners meet together, associate themselves, combine and concentrate, buying even the railway and the canal in order to corner the market, . . . in order to dictate the law to everyone, to lower the worker's wages, to raise the price of coal, to enrich themselves at the expense of the workers, the industry, and the public: What cancers are egotism and cupidity!" Such is the power of the bourgeoisie when in coalition. A month later, Cabet presented the antidote. No longer can "pleas to the rich" be expected to accomplish anything; only in the spirit of "fraternity and solidarity" among the workers themselves will the road be opened to the new organization of society.[56]

The idea expressed in the word "solidarity" was relatively new in 1846. Flora Tristan popularized it in her great and passionate work, *Union ouvrière* (Paris, 1843). After the *Réforme* affair, worker unity and solidarity became repeated themes in Cabet's writings as well. His most forceful statement appeared in the *Almanach* for 1847. He was discussing the compagnonnage, decrying its internal conflicts as well as its regional antagonisms. If this continues, "the Workers will always be persecuted, oppressed, unhappy. Misery will come to an end only when the spirit of fraternity and solidarity becomes universal, when . . . all the workers of a department, all the workers of France, even all those of Europe come to understand fully that they are brothers, that they have a common interest, that they ought to aid one another and all sign a petition to demand justice and their rights."[57]

There is no question here of declaring solidarity beyond the working class; nothing about fraternity of all men, only of all workingmen. The only thing dividing Cabet from Marx and Engels a year later was the last clause. This was, of course, a significant difference, and Cabet's refusal to sanction class conflict, even

[56] *Le Populaire*, May 29, 1846.
[57] *Almanach icarien pour 1847* (Paris, 1846), 135–36.

though the development of his thought would seem to demand it, provides the foundation for the thesis presented here that petition rather than violence evolved into escape rather than revolution.

But, one might reason, if the bourgeoisie was without real sympathy for the plight of the working class, could such moral action have any effect? Experience showed that when faced with workers whose faith in the true doctrine of the working class, communism, was unshakable, the radical bourgeoisie would join the conservatives. In December 1846 such a situation arose in Niort, in the selection of officers of the National Guard. Cabet understood the issue.

Does the Bourgeoisie call itself Democratic and Popular only with ulterior motives and on the tacit condition that the People choose it to lead? Does it invoke equality only against the Aristocracy without tolerating it for the People? Are the words People and Democracy in its mouth and under its pen only snares to lead the People to serve as its instrument? Is it always ready to combine with the Conservatives rather than consent to treat with the Worker as equal to equal?[58]

Yet Cabet could not bring himself to draw the logical conclusions: that the interests of bourgeoisie and proletariat were almost entirely contradictory, and that their antagonism was built into the social disorder of contemporary France. In the midst of his reassessment of class relations, Cabet was still searching for signs that a reconciliation of interests was possible. Indeed, he found one in the victory of the Anti-Corn Law League in England. He held it up as a symbol of the fruits to be gained from class collaboration. If only the bourgeoisie of France could see the light.[59] Moreover, while he was warning the workers not to trust the bourgeoisie, he himself was corresponding with Alphonse de Lamartine, by then a powerful voice of middle-class democracy, about a loan of 30,000 francs to help convert *Le Populaire* into a weekly. Although Lamartine turned him down, the request itself illustrates Cabet's equivocal stance.[60]

Cabet's primitive discussion of capitalist concentration, however, further revealed the erosion of his earlier optimism. He presented

[58] *Le Populaire,* Dec. 25, 1846.
[59] *Ibid.,* Feb. 26 and Aug. 28, 1846.
[60] Three original drafts of letters dated Aug. 31, Sept. 17, and Oct 1, 1846, from Cabet to Lamartine exist in the Cabet papers at the IISG.

no iron law of capitalist development but nevertheless articulated the opinion that the transiton to Community would be facilitated by the monopolization of the means of production in the hands of a few "fat capitalists." The first manifestation of this idea was tucked away in *L'Ouvrier,* a brochure published in June of 1844. His argument on concentration was integrally connected to the multiplication of labor-saving machinery: "It was also said that railways and steamboats were impossible; but machines revolutionize everything, and these machines, which make social reorganization necessary by inceasing the misery of the workers, make Community easy by increasing production. There is nothing more to do than decide upon an equitable division of the products."[61] Cabet's most pointed statement on this phenomenon came in *Le Populaire,* a year later when, after reprinting part of an incisive article in *La Revue indépendante* on concentration (with special reference to the impact of confection on the clothing industry), he made this significant comment:

Financial, industrial, and commercial concentration is one of the principal features of the epoch and a significant movement over the last several years.

And this movement can only continue to grow in a rapid progression.

And it is this that will lead to Community; for, on one side, in ruining all the little manufacurers, it makes a great social reform necessary; and on the other, in concentrating the workshops, the stores, the mines, the railways, etc., etc., it shows the economies and the power of concentration, of association, of unity, and prepares the ways of Community, which is nothing but the most vast association and the most complete concentration, but in the interest of all.

Realized in the interest of a few while ruining the mass of men, concentration is a calamity; but realized in the common interest on the basis of fraternity, concentration, which would then be called Communism, is the greatest of benefits for Humanity.[62]

Cabet even seemed to be saying that a sort of determinism was operating in the evolution of capitalism.

On October 30, 1846, he repeated: "The wealth, not just of France but of all Europe [the direct reference was to the great financial houses of Baring and Rothschild], will end up being con-

---

[61] Cabet, *L'Ouvrier* (Paris, 1844), 40–41.
[62] *Le Populaire,* July 13, 1845.

centrated in the hands of a few individuals, the great capitalists."[63] Such an estimate had more meaning for Cabet by this time since his view of class relationships now saw little hope for reconciliation of interests. In this new framework his idea of concentration became an argument against concern about bourgeois support. Together, his willingness to give up the quest for bourgeois collaboration and the idea of concentration evoke the image of a new Cabet. Sobered by bourgeois rejection of his doctrine, he seemed to realize that communism could have meaning for the working class alone. Sophisticated by the daily study of capitalist society, he had found within it an economic basis for its own transformation.

Thus illuminated, what should be his tactics? Should he continue to try to build working-class support while capitalism devoured itself, waiting until the bourgeoisie was small enough to be eased from economic and political power? Such a course would imply continued propaganda on the same old pacific and legalistic basis with the aim of creating a great international communist mass movement. But one thing must have bothered him: even assuming that the bourgeoisie became greatly diminished, it would still have the wherewithal, because of its great financial power and political dominance, to put up a solid wall of oposition against any movement, no matter how strong numerically, that would not resort to violence. Would mere words batter down this wall?

In the course of the polemic that Cabet was involved in with the Fourierists in late 1845 and throughout 1846, his adversaries repeated with telling force that mere propaganda, indeed even the actual democratic installation of a communist regime, would not be sufficient to pry the bourgeoisie loose from its property. The capitalists would inevitably fight to the death.[64] (This was why the pacific Fourierists felt that some rights of private possession had to be maintained in the phalanstère.) The weakness of Cabet's response indicates that he might have half-believed their arguments. If Cabet was convinced that the bourgeoisie would fight—and, as we have seen, much of his experience in 1845 and 1846 seemed to point in this direction—then logically his stand should surely

[63] *Ibid.,* Oct. 31, 1846.

[64] Examples of this argument may be found in *La Démocratie pacifique,* Nov. 2, 1845, and Dec. 6, 1846.

have been to orient the movement toward the prospect of violence. Icarian communism would have to become revolutionary.

But it did not. We have seen that Cabet was somewhat more disposed toward revolution than Prudhommeaux cared to admit. His "Note à X" of 1839, the Lyons affair of 1843 (despite his apparent reversal shortly thereafter), and several of the comments quoted above indicate this. Still, Cabet remained pacific; the only revolution he might possibly sanction would be a grand movement on the order of 1789 or 1830. Indeed, his new attitude toward the bourgeoisie made him more cautious about even this kind of revolution. As he said in announcing the emigration, even if a revolution should succeed, "its results would not be for the People, but for the Bourgeoisie."[65]

And so we find Cabet, in the spring of 1846, caught in the greatest dilemma of his life. His grand strategy of left-wing unity, rooted in the republican politics of the thirties, had run aground in the mire of a rapidly changing society. Theory and practice no longer meshed. But his reputation had been made through the concepts of legalism, pacifism, and civil courage. To opt for class struggle, to sanction working-class revolution, to endorse economic determinism was to throw in his lot with the materialists, to admit that Dézamy was right all along. So let praxis be damned. Cabet (at least at this point) allowed the utopian element in his personality to triumph. There was, after all, a way out. Jesus Christ had shown the world the immense power of passive resistance and moral arguments over the minds of men. He had done so with a relatively small number of fervent disciples. Could not his example light the way through the darkness of modern social evils? Let the Icarians become like the first Christians. Descend into the catacombs if necessary, but retain your faith in the future of man and one day you will re-emerge into a new dawn.

Thus while Cabet wrote of bourgeois chicanery and proletarian solidarity he also propagated the Christian message and the concept of the Icarian brotherhood. And this thrust proved to be the modus vivendi by which he maintained theoretical consistency—and the leadership of the largest communist contingent in Europe.

[65] *Le Populaire,* May 9, 1847.

But it also turned the Icarian movement into the Icarian sect. This is not to say that Cabet alone was responsible for such an evolution. While many of his followers responded enthusiastically to his new assessment of social relations, many others had already demonstrated the dominance of the Christian-communist equation over their minds and their willingness to accept Cabet as a kind of high priest. From mid-1845, even before the *Réforme* crisis, Cabet found it necessary to excuse himself in *Le Populaire* for delaying publication of *Le Vrai Christianisme*. The announced purpose of this book was to prove that Christ's grand design was nothing less than a communist society on earth. He was receiving numerous letters, some of which bordered on chiliastic exaltation, in favor of making Christianity the core of his doctrine. This religious ingredient in the movement was criticized by Proudhonists and materialist communists. A minor polemic on this issue coincided with the struggle against *La Réforme*. Already, in early 1845, Philippe Collier, a Proudhonian from Marseilles, had sent Cabet a letter (which he dared him to print) closing with the words, "to the reverend father don Quixote, Icar, infallible Pontiff of the Romanesque Icaria."[66] But the real blows were dealt by a materialist communist called Legré, who termed Cabet's followers sheep, and by Dézamy, who attacked what he thought to be a religious dictatorship: "How can [Cabet] believe that he is strong enough to accomplish this immense task [creating a communist society] all by himself? . . . The time of prophets is past; each must bring his part of the edifice of the future. . . . Let it be known that the people does not have to await the coming of a Messiah to embrace this sublime doctrine."[67]

Such charges were of course denied by Cabet. But the response from his followers was curious. Instead of protesting their independence and secularism, many of the "manifestations" of early 1846 inadvertently strengthened the arguments of Cabet's atheistic opponents. *Le Populaire*'s shareholders in Lyons were typical, calling Cabet "the living martyr of our epoch."[68] "Père" seemed to have found a new meaning; dozens of letters now gave it a semireligious flavor. For instance, twenty-four Icarians from

[66] Printed in *ibid.*, May 11, 1845.
[67] *La Fraternité de 1845*, Jan. 1846.
[68] *Le Populaire*, Feb. 26, 1846.

Toulon wished to "say with Christ, forgive them [Cabet's attackers] Father, for they know not what they do."[69]

Then on May 26, 1846, Cabet announced that his *Vrai Christianisme* was finally ready and proceeded to install Christianity at the heart of his doctrine: "Forward therefore, Communists! Let us take again the principles of Christ! Let us be his disciples and his soldiers! and we shall be sure to march on the road of Progress, of triumph, and of salvation. Let us invoke the doctrine of Jesus! for our communism is manifestly, incontestably, the same thing as true Christianity, or at least, of all the old and new doctrines, the one that comes closest to it!" One might think that at this point Cabet had decided to take the great leap, the transformation of his doctrine into a sincere religious enthusiasm; but his definition of God remained deistic: "The *God* of Christianity is not a God of superstition and ignorance, of privilege and oppression; it is the God of Nature and of Reason, the God of intelligence and enlightenment, the God of Liberty and Equality, especially the God of the Poor to save them from misery, and the God of the oppressed to deliver them from oppression." The true religion was one of love and concord, of "the human personality, of the dignity of man, of his independence and his liberty." By and large, Cabet's religious rhetoric remained rational, although he did occasionally lapse into semimysticism—for example, "If you have Faith, you will appease the tempest and you will walk on the waves. And then you will emerge from the Shadows to pass into the Light, from Death to pass into Life, from the Reign of Satan to pass into the Reign of God, which will give the Human Race eternal life with eternal felicity." The variation of tone was no doubt designed to satisfy both the humanists and the fundamentalists among his followers.[70] *Le Vrai Christianisme* itself, although mainly devoted to explaining the Bible in rational terms and showing why allegorical language had to be used, was still filled with emotion-packed sentences, such as, "This will be a Perfect People, a Holy Nation, the pure of heart, imitators of God, without sins, without crimes, and without vices."[71] In playing to both the true believers and the "intellectual Christians," it would seem that Cabet caught more of the

[69] *Ibid.*, March 26, 1846.
[70] *Ibid.*, May 26, June 27, 1846.
[71] *Le Vrai Christianisme*, 313.

former and, in addition, brought out the latent millennial enthusiasm of many of his older followers. By June of 1846 the Icarian group in Toulon was comparing Cabet to Christ: "You imitate, by your dedication, this Christ whose maxims you adopt; like him you identify yourself with the poor and the oppressed; like him you preach the most sublime morality that the heart of man can form; like him you expose all the attacks of the Pharisees of the century and of the Priests who crucified him." For the rest of the year and in early 1847 Cabet continued to exhort the workers of France; his new work sold well, and his followers replied in kind by avowing their Christian-communist faith to Cabet, the "dear and venerated father of the poor and the oppressed." While his followers in Vienne would "go on their knees before no mortal" and the Toulousains agreed that "the age of prophets had passed," there began to occur in 1846 a vague but perceptible shift toward seeing Cabet as the martyr and apostle of a religious faith.[72] If we also recall Benoit's comments about the rigidification and total devotion of the shrinking loyal Icarian group in Lyons, a new picture of the Icarian party begins to emerge. The movement was becoming a sect.

In the course of 1845 and 1846, then, the logic of Cabet's position on the bourgeoisie had driven him to appreciate the potentiality of class conflict. Yet to sanction class conflict as the basis for working-class emancipation contradicted the tactics upon which his reputation rested. *Le Vrai Christianisme* was winning favor throughout the movement and gaining new converts, most of whom were workers; moral appeal therefore still had some power. But both the estrangement from bourgeois democrats and the religious emphasis had had one effect in common. When Cabet had said "close our ranks" in October 1845 he was talking to the entire working class; but (as was always his assumption) the working class was coterminous with the communist potential, and therefore, to his followers, Cabet's call was also for a closing of the communist ranks. The conflict with *La Réforme* thus stimulated rigidifica-

---

[72] *Le Populaire,* June 27, 1846; J. Clémence to Cabet, March 6, 1847, Papiers Cabet, VIII, BHVP. For reactions to *Le Vrai Christianisme* and for Cabet's increasing use of Christian catchphrases (for example, "Communism can only say: I am the resurrection and the life," *Le Populaire.* Aug. 28, 1846), see *Le Populaire* during these months.

tion and sect formation. Villified by the bourgeois radical press, Icarians would "march separately on our own side" in the name of the entire working class. The "true" message of Christ then further strengthened their sense of uniqueness, even of martyrdom. In this framework, we can begin to understand why the "Father" Cabet might begin to think of colonizing. The loyal band was there, but the drive to win men of all classes had failed. The only way that France might possibly become Icaria at this moment would be through a Buonarrotian coup d'état. Perhaps Icaria might be built there in the future by means of a great communist revolutionary working-class movement prepared to fight the class struggle when the army was big enough, but—an exceedingly important consideration—that would be long after Etienne Cabet was in the grave. Neither of these alternatives was acceptable for practical, doctrinal, and personal reasons. Thus the only way to keep Icarianism alive, and perhaps to see it conquer the unbelieving world some day, was to carry the band off to some uninhabited terrain, to flee from the great dilemma that the problem of class antagonism had posed.

Allons en Icarie!

Events during the months of late 1846 and early 1847 pushed Cabet toward this option. The bad harvest of 1846 created the basis for a severe economic crisis,[73] and the ensuing high price of bread and unemployment induced an attitude of desperation among large segments of the French working class. Icarians were hardly immune; the situation increased the inclination of some of them to seek revolutionary solutions.

In late 1846 communism in general was expanding apace. Although somewhat alarmist, the press often mentioned the communist phenomenon. Said the quasi-republican *Siècle:* "Take guard; communism is invading the populations of our large cities. . . . Lyons, for instance, is possessed by communism. And the ardor that it excites . . . is such that when one enters a workshop, one sees the worker sitting between his work and his brochure, with one eye on his loom and the other on his book."[74] *L'Ardour de*

---

[73] See Ernest Labrousse, "Panoramas de la crise," in Labrousse, ed., *Aspects de la crise et de la dépression d'économie française au milieu du XIX*e *siècle, 1846–1851* (La Roche-sur-Yon, 1956).

[74] *Le Siècle,* Sept. 13, 1846,

Bayonne estimated that communism held the allegiance of one-third of the workers in the large industrial towns of France. The Catholic organ in Lyons, *La Guillotière,* warned its readers of the "immense" spread of communism in recent months, and the *Propagateur de l'Aube* connected this growth with the increasing misery of the working class. The Fourierists noted in February 1847 that "everywhere the progress of communism irritates its enemies and excites their calumnies."[75] The government viewed the situation with apprehension. Officials became anxious; the mayor of Saint-Gervais informed the Minister of Justice on February 20, 1847 that 60,000 Parisian communists were ready to revolt. Duchâtel, apprised of this, found no grounds for the report but did not hesitate to say, "All the same, it is true that the number of workers perverted by the evil doctrines of communism is very considerable in Paris."[76]

The question, however, is whether Icarianism was expanding as rapidly as the outwardly revolutionary communist elements. Two incidents indicate that it was not. At Tours a sizable group of Icarians was drawn into an association inspired by the irrepressible Auguste Blanqui, currently at the local hospital recovering from the brutal hardships of his imprisonment at Mont-Saint-Michel. Cabet, disturbed by this development, wrote a brochure disclaiming his renegade followers.[77] A letter from Cabet's agent at Tours, Dr. Desmoulins, points up the problem facing pacific Icarianism. There was a feeling among many there that Cabet wanted "to capsize the revolutionary bark forever." He went on to say that the dissidents believed that the publication of *Le Vrai Christianisme* was a mistake because it re-emphasized moral ap-

---

[75] For these citations see *La Démocratie pacifique,* Aug. 28, 1846, and Feb. 20, 1847; *Le Populaire,* Nov. 27, 1846 and Feb. 22, 1847.

[76] A.N., BB[18] 1441 dos 1992.

[77] After a minor bread riot, several Icarians (and others) were incarcerated and charged with conspiracy. The principal government witness, Houdin, drew Blanqui's name into the trial and charged that he had organized the group as a secret society. See the *Gazette des tribunaux,* April 3 and 29, 1847, and Anon., *Les Communistes de Tours: Persécutions de police à Blois* (Paris, 1847) (Bibliothèque Nationale, Lb[51] 4338). The pertinent archival sources are A.N., BB[21] 5028 and Archives départementales de Loir-et-Cher, 3 UI 42 (Audiences correctionelles de 26, 27, 28, 29 avril 1847). See also Cabet, *Le Voile soulevé sur le procès communiste à Tours et Blois* (Paris, 1847).

peal and pacifism. Imagine Cabet's reaction to Desmoulins' concluding words:

> You ask me why there might be a plot against you? The reasons for it are quite simple: you are the single obstacle preventing the communist party from becoming terribly revolutionary overnight, and revolution is as fascinating as it is easy to make—in the imagination. However, many of the most restless among us are already in favor of revolutionary means while today such means appear to you to be completely inopportune. Thus, there is certainly a motive for plotting against your influence.[78]

The same issue was posed by Madeline affair at Luçon. On February 13, 1847, a placard condemning the historical church and its priests was posted near the cathedral. It had been written by a communist. While avoiding revolutionary provocation, the author's language was strong. Madeline, a weaver, was accused of having posted it. He was an Icarian connected with Poupineau, *Le Populaire*'s Luçon correspondent, and twenty-five Icarians were arrested and interrogated. In the ensuing trial, however, the government failed to make its case, and the accused were acquitted on August 25, 1847. While final proof is lacking, the authors of an excellent article on the affair are of the opinion that Madeline might well have been responsible for the placard.[79] If so, this is another example of Icarians acting less prudently than Cabet wished them to.

These incidents set the problem facing Cabet in bold relief: if he continued to promote legalism, would he not face the possibility of losing large segments of his following to revolutionary communists? While he never admitted such losses, an analysis of the circulation figures of *Le Populaire* reveals a significant subscriber turnover during the winter of 1846–1847. New subscriptions came in at the previous rate, but Cabet stopped reporting total circulation figures. He did not do so again until a year later, when the increase shown was only 500 (see Table 1 in Chapter 4). It appears that while the Christian message brought new adherents to Cabet, the economic crisis and its attendant radicalization caused offsetting cancellations. The timing of his rather sudden decision to emigrate

---

[78] Desmoulins to Cabet, Nov. 26, 1846, Papiers Cabet, BHVP.
[79] Faucheux and Morauzeau, "L'Affaire Madeline," 74–76.

thus begins to make sense. The Luçon affair took place in February 1847, and the Tours trial commenced in March. At that moment, Cabet began to shape his preliminary plans for the emigration. Moreover, he later admitted that the Tours affair affected his decision to leave France, that he had concluded then that "we will never be able to reform the entire world all at once nor stop those . . . who compromise Communism; . . . this is one of the main reasons causing us to cry *allons en Icarie!*"[80]

On May 9, 1847, Cabet revealed his "great secret" in *Le Populaire*. Under the heading "Workers, let us go to Icaria!" he stated that since the persecution of Icarian communism in France was so intense it was necessary to follow the words of Jesus Christ: "If thou art persecuted in one city, get thee thence to another." Only by departing from the old and degenerate Europe will we be able to find "our dignity as men, our rights as citizens, and Liberty with Equality." As "the New Hebrews," the Icarians would "conquer the Promised Land, [create] a new Paradise on Earth." We shall be the advance battalion, "the congregation of Humanity."[81] The project was not designed as a small experiment. Rather the goal was to find an area, somewhere in America, large enough to build a "veritable Communist nation." Thus between 10,000 and 20,000 Icarians should be prepared to get the task under way. It was to be a mass emigration, and Cabet promised to take the lead personally. In twenty years, the first generation of communists would be formed, the first communist state would be in existence, and, on seeing the success of the new way, the world would follow. Thus, from the outset, Cabet rejected the Owenite or Fourierist utopian experimental program. The idea of "showing the world" was there, of course, but the Icarian leader, true to his Jacobinism, could only conceive of "large-scale Community."

The announcement came out of the blue. Although Cabet had spoken of a "great secret" in the weekly issues of *Le Populaire*[82]

---

[80] Cabet, *Le Voile soulevé*, 24.

[81] *Le Populaire*, May 9, 1847.

[82] Cabet had finally realized his dream on April 4, 1847, when he began to print *Le Populaire* on a weekly basis at Rouen. He and the main office remained in Paris, however. Caudron, his correspondent in Rouen, took on the duties as gérant (see *Le Populaire*, April 4, 1847).

since April 18, there had not been a single word in print that he was giving any consideration to such a turnabout. The Icarians were as surprised as everyone else in Europe when the news broke. Pressed by inquiries, Cabet found it necessary to remark briefly on the gestation of the emigration idea. He was in a difficult position because of his past comments against such actions. Still, he implied that he had been giving the matter thought for a while.

With everything, with the harvest . . . as with childbirth, it is necessary that the fruit be ripe.

Three years ago, two, one, we had wanted to begin nothing [of this order].

Since then, we have been consulted, even solicited, concerning emigration projects.

A month ago, with the famine and the misery, with the universal malaise, with the stormy clouds of the future, with the immense progress of communism, finally with the persecutions that have menaced it, the wind seemed favorable to attempt a great emigration in order to realize Community, and we hoped to bring together one hundred thousand emigrants.[83]

The only information we possess concerning Cabet's preparation for the announcement is an exchange of letters with Berrier-Fontaine in London during April 1847. On April 13, Berrier, at the end of a letter concerned with other matters, simply said: "Do not think of colonizing. There are too many dissolvent causes at work in society today for one to flee from it." It had taken him a month to reply to the proposal Cabet had made to him, so we may assume that Cabet's decision was made in late winter. Moreover, the rather offhand manner of Berrier's response suggests that Cabet remained unsure of his intentions even in March. Only on April 20 (the date of the first word of a secret to be announced later in *Le Populaire*) did Cabet make it clear that his mind was "almost made up because it will be the only means to avoid the persecution that is being prepared."[84] Shortly thereafter a letter from Michelot in the name of the Société démocratique de Londres informed Cabet that a "great majority" of the society disapproved of his plan. Berrier only wrote Cabet personally the day following the

[83] *Le Populaire*, May 23, 1847.
[84] Cabet to Berrier (draft), April 20, 1847, Papiers Cabet, BHVP.

announcement, but his analysis no doubt reflected the position of his fellow exiles.[85]

> The result of our meditations is a profound conviction that a small-scale experiment will not succeed. Several good minds have attempted it and have failed. In the present state of civilization, would others be more fortunate or more skillful? Even if successful, what impact would be made on the vices of the current social order and on the preconceived notions of the larger society? . . .
>
> If you would fail, and I believe that you would, then what harm to the cause.

All of this—along with Cabet's comment in *Le Populaire* of May 12 that he had decided only "a month ago" that conditions called for the emigration—is good evidence that the decision itself was made quite rapidly.

Cabet's public rationale for the emigration proposal, "communist persecution," had a specious ring to it. Unquestionably Icarians had been harassed in recent months. Cabet listed five categories of persecution then in effect: by the clergy, by employers, by the government, through the hostility of the press, and through the calumnies of the revolutionaries. He gave several examples of each. One priest in Champagne had forbidden his parishioners to read *Le Populaire,* another had burned the *Voyage en Icarie.* Julien Chambry of Mirecourt had been fired from his job because he was a communist. Poupineau of Luçon, Cabet's correspondent, was currently under arrest, and *Le Populaire* had been troubled constantly by the Rouennais officials. Many newspapers had attacked Cabet and Icarianism; the communists were accused of causing the grain shortage, and Icarians were confused with the materialists. Finally, *La Réforme* and *La Fraternité* ("revolutionaries") hated Cabet.[86] In fact, such persecution was mild when compared with a past that had included action against the Bibliothèques, Cöeffé's harassment in Vienne, the legal prejudice shown against three Icarians in Givors,[87] the Toulouse trial, and dozens of other inci-

[85] Berrier to Cabet, May 10, 1847, Papiers Cabet, BHVP. The earlier letter is lost. Cabet mentions it in a note to Berrier on April 23 (draft).
[86] *Le Populaire,* May 9, 1847.
[87] See Chapius to Cabet, Nov. 6, 1844, Papiers Cabet, VIII, BHVP.

dents.[88] To be sure, the government had intensified its drive against Cabet in 1847. Delessert, Prefect of Police, wrote Duchâtel on January 19 that the "writings of the socialists," because they "mislead the working class by painting at once an exaggerated tableau of its miseries and a picture of happiness that would arrive by social renovation," deserve "particular attention and the most active repression by the judiciary authorities."[89] Taking his cue, Duchâtel, on learning of the forthcoming weekly publication of *Le Populaire* at Rouen, told the Minister of Justice on March 25 that since "this publication, designed to appeal to the popular passions, can only have a dangerous effect," the latter should inform his procureur-général in Rouen "to proceed against this newspaper every time it appears to put public peace in danger." The prefect would be asked to give all cooperation necessary.[90] This document was sufficient to convince Pierre Angrand that the persecution thesis was valid. "Cabet thinks that his newspaper, the fruit of his labor and the expression of his faith, is condemned. It is then that the cry, 'Allons en Icarie,' is issued."[91] The fact is, however, that after attempting to prosecute Cabet and Caudron for irregular handling of the manager position, the authorities realized that they had no case.[92] Cabet knew this and in the May 9, 1847, issue of *Le Populaire* let it be known that they were safe from prosecution. *Le Populaire* was brought to trial later, on another charge, but was exonerated.

The most important refutation of the persecution thesis, however, is that "persecution causes progress," a phrase Cabet even used in the same issue that he declared the emigration! It was as true now as it had ever been. On April 11 he had said that there existed "a vast system of persecutions on the part of the priests, the privileged, and the government; but have no fear! Persecution will double our energies, accelerate our progress, and render the triumph of our doctrine more prompt and more certain."[93] In the

[88] Cabet himself felt that such "martyrdom" served to advertise the cause. See especially *Le Populaire,* July 26, 1846.
[89] Published in J. Taschereau, *Revue rétrospective* (Paris, 1848), 95.
[90] A.N., BB[18] 1451 dos 3598.
[91] *Étienne Cabet et la République de 1848* (Paris, 1948), 27–28.
[92] Duchâtel to the Garde des Sceaux, May 3, 1847, A.N., BB[18] 1451 dos 3598.
[93] *Le Populaire,* April 11, 1847.

issue of May 9 itself several of his examples of persecution were followed by proof that communism was aided by them. A man in Toulon had been arrested and then lost his job because of his Icarian beliefs; nothing daunted, he spent his new-found free time to proselytize in the department, winning new converts. At Louviers an employer had blacklisted the *Almanach,* but this act got many of his non-Icarian workers interested in the doctrine. Fires and placards had been blamed on the communists in Nantes, but they "are confident that the general persecution will only strengthen communism." And Poupineau of Luçon saw the failure of the police to pin anything on him as evidence of the eventual triumph of Icarian communism; he told the judge himself that it would take "an awfully large prison" to put away all the communists.

Even after the announcement Cabet could not resist showing how persecution made for progress. The police were certainly assiduous enough—they even surveyed a "communist" funeral in Lyons[94]—but the Icarians were not hurt by it. Chambry of Mirecourt demonstrated such courage and perseverance that his employer was convinced of his fine character and agreed to take him back (a story widely circulated in the Vosges). In September an Icarian physician, Dr. Paumier, was arrested (as were twenty-three of the patients in his office) at Maronne. The effect was to make the government the laughingstock of the area and to increase interest in Icarian doctrine. In the department of the Indre—an area of little Icarian support heretofore—one of the few communists there was interrogated by the subprefect and released; thereafter, the "whole town" was talking about communism.[95] Finally, in December, Cabet's own office was searched by the police, and a case was prepared against him charging him with heading a secret society organized in the form of a newspaper business. Although the authorities soon realized that it was impossible to prosecute him on this charge (they then changed it to one of swindling),[96] this development made Cabet the most famous man on the left for a brief time; all the radical papers condemned the action because they feared the same thing might happen to them. The point is obvious; if persecution does not end in full repression it serves

[94] A.N., BB[18] 1441 dos 1992.
[95] *Le Populaire,* May 30, Sept. 26, and Nov. 28, 1847.
[96] See below, pp. 257–58.

only to advertise the cause of the persecuted. Cabet often cited the early Christian experience to this effect. The *Tribune lyonnaise* summed up the whole situation when it said, in September 1847, that it might be able to understand the emigration call if the Icarians were horribly persecuted, like "the Protestants after the Revocation," but "far from that, its propaganda is the order of the day, it acts freely on opinion by means of both the press and associations. What more could [Cabet] desire?"

Reception of the Emigration Call

How was the news of May 9 received by the left in France and Europe and by the Icarians? The procureur-général at Rouen put the immediate non-Icarian reaction to the "great secret" in a nutshell when he said that at Rouen (where the news broke first) the Fourierists were for it and were "all disposed to follow Sr Cabet," while the reformists were enraged and accused him of "being paid by the government." Others were saying that he was "devoured by ambition." In any case, passions were clearly aroused over the announcement.[97] The Fourierist newspaper, *La Démocratie pacifique,* although at odds with the Icarian leader on other questions, welcomed the call, and several Fourierists decided to become Icarians.[98] As for the reformists, they universally condemned Cabet for abandoning the struggle in Europe, saying that he had probably been paid off by Louis-Philippe or Nicholas I, calling him a coward, and designating his followers "runaways, deserters, or traitors."[99] Later in the year, the editors of *La Réforme* even organized a campaign to oppose the emigration. Their approach was interesting. Rather than simply denouncing Cabet, they tried to show sympathy for communism and even said that Ledru-Rollin's denunciation of it in 1845 at Le Mans had been a "blunder." But

[97] Report of May 7, 1847, A.N., BB^{18} 1441 dos 1992; apparently local distribution took place before the date on the newspaper.

[98] See, for instance, the long letter from "Junius," editor of the Fourierist monthly, *La Satyre sociale,* in which he said he would like to participate in the emigration (*Le Populaire,* May 23, 1847). Junius then spent a great deal of time attempting to work out a doctrinal modus vivendi between the two "schools," which appeared in many issues of *Le Populaire* in 1847. For other examples see *Le Populaire,* Aug. 5, Oct. 24, and Nov. 2, 1847.

[99] Such is Cabet's own summary of their attacks on him, *Le Populaire,* June 20, 1847.

they tried to convince the Icarians that Cabet was leading his people away in order to play the dictator of Icaria. Icarians must stay
in Europe to await the "great day."[100]

Most objections to the emigration decision, however, came from
those more closely connected with communism. The most influential—judging from Cabet's attempts to refute it—was a brochure
written in June by a man named D. Marcelino Prat. We know
nothing of Prat save that in the brochure he called himself a communist.[101] He wrote "to draw the attention of our coreligionists
to the danger of the proposition of M. Cabet." He began with
Cabet's motives, implying that Cabet wished to spirit away a loyal
group in order to satisfy a desire for power. This opinion was
strengthened in Prat's mind by the fact that "Everyone has the
presentiment of a revolution," especially because of the extent of
working-class misery. "And it is this moment that you choose to
carry off from France her purest children, her most intelligent and
devoted patriots." Prat was also concerned about the future of
communism, saying that he feared exile would destroy the fire of
communism in the emigrants themselves and ruin the movement in
France. Moreover, if Cabet himself decided to go the French working class would lose its only effective voice. The author then predicted that the colony would fail. What government would be willing to cede an area large enough to sustain a million people?
Finally, Prat summarized his central argument: "It is upon Europe
that the world has its eyes fixed. From France especially, it awaits
its regeneration. How have you been able to deceive yourself, you,
M. Cabet, one of the veterans of Democracy and . . . one who
has never lacked perspicacity?"[102]

Others took up some of the same themes. Adrien Delaire, a
Parisian cabinetmaker and socialist militant, stressed that the Icarians were deserting their fatherland and their cause:

[100] This information is to be found in a report to Cabet from his correspondent at Reims, Butot, who had received a visit from one of the reformists. Though he did not believe the latter's stories, he still judged him
to be a "good, wise, and sincere Democrat." One wonders how many Icarians
this impressive gentleman actually won away from Cabet. See *Le Populaire*,
Oct. 31, 1847.

[101] *A M. Cabet à propos de son projet d'émigration en Icarie* (Paris,
1847).

[102] *Ibid.*, 3, 4, 6, and 8.

Quoi! la discorde est en nos rangs,
Enfants de notre belle France!
Quoi! vous secondez les Tyrans,
Vous retardez indépendance!
Pour obtenir un triste résultat,
D'un intrigant vous suivez la bannière.
Mais Dieu punit l'enfant ingrat
Qui laisse succomber sa mère.[103]

An anonymous brochure attacked the nature of Icarian society, seeing it as a repressive despotism marked by a soulless puritanism.[104] As might be expected, the bitterest attack came from Dézamy in *La Fraternité*. The author became very emotional (a rarity in this newspaper), saying that he and his group would "stay by their post; to abandon it would be to desert the cause of our brothers in order to realize an egotistical happiness." To run away before persecution is a betrayal of the cause and sheer cowardice. Finally, who does Cabet think he is? Has he considered the immensity of the task of creating a new and totally different society, especially in light of "the insufficiency of your powers"? "Oh blindness, oh temerity!" The only objection he added to those of Prat was that the habits and morality of the present generation were not far enough advanced to allow the full establishment of communitarian life. Cabet replied in the usual manner, asking the editors of *La Fraternité* for their pedigrees as thinkers and blustering rather than arguing. For once, they responded in kind. After noting the vacuity of Cabet's comments, they indulged in a polemic of real brilliance, finally concluding that Cabet was the "Bugeaud of socialism."[105]

The provincial socialist press commented as well. The *Voix du peuple* of Toulouse found it astonishing to see "a journalist pose as Moses in the nineteenth century."[106] The most important statement, however (in view of its great influence on the Lyonnaise working class), was made by the *Tribune lyonnaise*. Chastaing had hesitated

---

[103] Delaire, *Aux Communistes sur leur départ pour l'Icarie* (Paris, 1847), IISG.

[104] *Voyage de M. Mayeux en Icarie: Ses Aventures curieuses dans le pays de M. Cabet* (Paris: Bonaventure et Ducessais, 1847).

[105] *La Fraternité de 1845,* May, July, and Aug., 1847; *Le Populaire,* July 18, 1847.

[106] Quoted in *Le Populaire,* July 18, 1847.

to make any comment at all but was pressed by many workers to do so. He praised Cabet at length for his past contributions to the working-class cause but then said flatly, "We condemn the appeal made by M. Cabet to his coreligionists." After demonstrating his mistrust of the persecution thesis, he argued incisively on the difficulties of creating "a new social order" and the service that such a retreat did "the enemies of revolution." He compared the idea to the futile crusade of Peter the Hermit and then appealed to Cabet's vanity: "M. Cabet ought to give some consideration to himself; he has an honorable place in France, a useful and glorious role to fulfill, and we recall to him that Rome thanked Fabius for not having despaired of the Republic. If the doctrine of communism is true it will triumph." Finally he spoke to Icarians' patriotism: "For the time being, we say to the workers: indeed, your lot is unhappy, but your emigration would be a kind of suicide. One does not abandon his mother even if she is unjust. . . . Stay to defend her against the aristocracy, stay to propogate not only communism but all worthy doctrines; let your hearts remain united whatever be your banner so that the apologists of tyranny will tremble before your compact and united masses."[107] This declaration had an effect in Lyons. In November Auguste Morlon, one of many Lyonnais motivated in part by Icarian ideas, if not a Cabetist, remarked, "I approve of your [*La Tribune*'s] reflections on the emigration project to Icaria, and you have, in this respect, been the mouthpiece for a large number of enlightened communists."[108]

Abroad, the bulk of the negative reactions came from the growing coterie of Marx and Engels. On July 11, 1847, Jacques Imbert's newspaper, *L'Atelier belge,* after saying that Cabet's contribution to the maturation of the French working class was "inestimable," disagreed—in Marxist fashion—with his utopian plan and especially with the emigration: the latter "destroys all the good you have done."[109] Although Berrier-Fontaine agreed to assist Cabet in his plan, his friends in the Société démocratique and their allies among the German exiles in London disapproved entirely: "Your emigration project finds a great deal of opposition here." Still, Cabet should "not believe that the democrats of the Société

[107] *La Tribune lyonnaise,* Aug. 1847.
[108] *Ibid.,* Nov. 1847.
[109] Quoted at length in *Le Populaire,* July 18, 1847.

française are your enemies; far from it—they just have their own manner of judging the emigration."[110] Then on September 20, 1847, the Arbeitersbildungsverein and the Société démocratique sponsored a great banquet at German Hall to celebrate the founding of the First French Republic. Friedrich Lessner noted later that the Germans had spent "a whole week" discussing the matter of the emigration with Cabet[111] (who was in London making arrangements for the purchase of land in Texas) in mid-September. At the banquet they gave their verdict. Karl Schapper condemned the exodus disdainfully. George Julian Harney and Ernest Jones, Chartists, Fraternal Democrats, and communists as well by now, were there also. The latter, while calling Cabet a "great man," denounced his emigration project.[112] The same line was followed by the *Kommunistische Zeitschrift* in its first number, in September 1847. The author, probably Engels himself, praised Cabet's struggle "in the cause of suffering humanity" but accused him of abandoning the working people, leaving "the field to the religious obscurantists and exploiters."[113] It seems likely, given the sympathy previously shown Cabet by the London exiles, both French and German, that the emigration plan opened the way fully for their shift to Marx and Communist League.[114]

What happened to the Icarian movement as a result of the new direction taken by its master? The subscription statistics of *Le Populaire* indicate the extent of the upheaval that occurred between November 1846 and November 1847. Comparison of new subscriptions with change in total printing shows that over thirty per cent of Cabet's subscribers in November 1846 were no longer with him a year later and that nearly half the subscribers in November 1847 were new.[115] This information is extremely valuable because

---

[110] Berrier to Cabet, July 15 and Aug. 20, 1847, Papiers Cabet, BHVP.

[111] Lessner, *Sixty Years in the Social-Democratic Movement* (London, 1907), 11.

[112] All this is dutifully recorded by Cabet in *Le Populaire*, Oct. 3, 1847.

[113] See D. Ryazanoff, ed., *The Communist Manifesto* (London: Martin Lawrence, 1930), 295. He translates the article in Appendix E.

[114] This issue is not mentioned in Ernst Schraepler, "Der Bund des Gerechten: Seine Tätigkeit in London," *Archiv für Sozialgeschichte,* II (1964), 5–29. For more details on this and related problems, see Christopher H. Johnson, "Notes on the International Influence of Etienne Cabet," *International Review of Social History* (forthcoming).

[115] See Table 1 in Chap. 4.

it verifies what could otherwise be only a raw guess; that the emigration announcement was widely opposed by Icarians despite Cabet's talk of universal enthusiasm and acceptance. To be sure, the hardships caused by the economic crisis[116] and the resurgence of revolutionary communism probably cut into Cabet's following as well. But since the numbers of new subscriptions from November 1846 to April 1847 (when *Le Populaire* became a weekly) were rather modest in comparison to those of May and later (499 as against 1,849), and since Cabet does not seem to have reduced the total printing during the earlier period, we may assume that the central factor in the changing composition of the Icarian movement was the emigration announcement and that most of the losses of old Icarians (as well as the gains in new converts) were due to it.

Other evidence shows that many Icarians (or Icarian sympathizers) disapproved of the emigration. The propagandist for *La Réforme* mentioned above told Butot flatly that in his travels he had discovered Icarians in "many towns" (he specifically mentioned Nantes, Tours, and Lyons) who censured the new development.[117] If this source is not to be trusted, there are other indications, most of them to be found in the pages of *Le Populaire* itself. The most important was the formal protest from twenty-eight Nantais Icarians who felt that the "struggle for popular rights" had to be fought in France. Cabet pretended that these men were not really Icarians but "ultras" trying to discredit the movement. This was not the case with four of them, at least; Vieille, Ragand, Méjot, and Paris all appear on the list of Nantes Icarians printed in *Le Populaire* of January and February 1845. Furthermore, a fawning address signed (says Cabet) by 200 Nantais Icarians spoke of their "misguided brothers."[118] On July 25 Cabet made the revealing statement that the "revolutionary communists" were trying to compromise the Icarians and the emigration by calling

---

[116] Butot, writing from Reims early in the spring of 1847, told Cabet of the "frightful" impact of the depression there; "misery paralyzes all our efforts" (*Le Populaire*, April 11, 1847). See also D. Carrel, a Parisian worker, to Cabet, Nov. 18, 1847, Papiers Cabet, VIII, BHVP.

[117] *Le Populaire*, Oct. 31, 1847.

[118] *Le Populaire*, July 4 and Aug. 29, 1847; Berrier-Fontaine to Cabet, July 15, 1847, Papiers Cabet, BHVP.

themselves Icarians. One wonders if the majority of these were not in fact Icarians who condemned the project. The negative reaction in Lyons seems to have been quite strong, despite M. Buffenoir's statement that "the enthusiasm is so great among the Icarians at Lyons that no one is disheartened, and even those who remain have the hope of leaving some day."[119] This should read: "Among the *Cabetist* Icarians." In addition to the statement of Morlon in *La Tribune lyonnaise,* quoted above, a short note sent to *Le Populaire* by J. J. Razuret, one of the leaders of the anti-Cabet Icarians, objected to the departure because, "We believe that a revolution is near, or that the governors will be forced by circumstances to make profound and rational reforms."[120] The declaration of support for the emigration from Lyons represented the views of only the narrow clique of Cabetist Icarians and not the much broader general current of Icarian opinion there. Several other Icarian repudiations of the emigration plan in general were allowed to appear in *Le Populaire*. For example, the Swedish group wrote Cabet that it might be nice to go to Icaria but they did not want to be considered "fugitives"; and a French adherent (who praised Cabet so highly for other things that Cabet simply had to print his letter) firmly objected to Cabet's "leaving the field of battle."[121]

On the other hand, the positive response from the Icarians in France during the summer of 1847 was significant. We need not delve very deeply into the numerous "receptions of the secret" that rolled in from the various Icarian centers. The theme of pure and simple escape was overwhelmingly evident. New converts were won by the announcement. Some Fourierists came over but so did a few revolutionary communists.[122] Many letters, without designating their writers' former political opinions, spoke of new people gained to the cause because of the emigration idea. In one town there used to be only ten or twelve communists, but now there were more than sixty; big gains were reported in Toulon; "everybody" in Périguex was talking about the emigration; "many new adherents"

[119] Buffenoir, "Le Communisme à Lyon," 357.
[120] *Le Populaire*, Nov. 21, 1847.
[121] *Ibid.,* Jan. 23 and Oct. 10, 1847.
[122] *Ibid.,* May 23 and Oct. 31, 1847.

joined in Nancy.[123] For the first time, peasants showed an interest in Icarianism.

There are some interesting facts to be noted in the nature of these declarations of support. For one thing, an unusual number were individual letters, and, when groups were involved, the number of signatures was not often printed at the end. For instance, the number of Lyonnais who supported the emigration was never given, while 1,300 people signed the address condemning Cabet's arrest in late 1847. In the few instances where numbers were presented, some (but not all—see Appendix 1) were much smaller than those on other addresses. For example, only 99 people (who apologized for the tardiness of their response) signed the "reception" from Reims[124] whereas 443 supported Cabet in January 1848.

Cabet thus seems to have deliberately misrepresented the "great enthusiasm" that his call supposedly generated. He also grossly overestimated the size of the group he expected to lead to America; only sixty-nine men participated in the first departure. This was an advance party, to be sure, but according to the agreement Cabet had made with an American land company, he was to have as much land as his men could build homesteads upon and therefore the more emigrants, the more land for Icaria. Also, a curious turnabout occurred about a month after the announcement; Cabet began to emphasize that what Icaria needed was "quality rather than quantity."[125] Is this an indication that he knew what the real situation was? Another problem enters the picture here. To become an emigrant one had to make a preliminary "contribution" of 600 francs.[126] Numerous communications complained about this sum and indicated that special arrangements should be made for poor Icarians. Cabet never changed his mind on this matter although naturally he would allow a wealthier colonist to subsidize a poor one. Most writers on the subject felt that some kind of discrimination was involved and agreed with the poor Parisian locksmith who

[123] See *ibid,* especially in the weeks immediately after the emigration announcement.

[124] *Ibid.,* July 11, 1847.

[125] *Ibid.,* June 20, 1847.

[126] *Ibid.,* May 23, 1847. This was to apply for the first departure only and would be reduced later. Cabet obviously had visions of the first departure being quite a sizable one however.

said (reminding Cabet of the many times he had emphasized that the only property owned by a worker was his skilled hands) "my titles are in my work."[127] Rare indeed was the poor man who agreed with Poublain (another Parisian worker) that the fee of 600 francs had not dulled his enthusiasm in the least.[128] The most devastating comment on the implied discrimination of the contribution (and our best single piece of direct evidence showing widespread disaffection shortly after the emigration announcement) was made by F. Lechapt, a Parisian worker:

You have said . . . that your revelation was received everywhere with tears of joy because no doubt those who can leave with you have alone manifested this sentiment; but if those whom you abandon knew or dared express their thought, this joy would soon be no more than a drop of rosé beside a torrent of sorrows! The well-beloved of Jesus had thought they saw reborn in you their divine father, and their hearts bled with despair at the idea that they could have been deceived! They would want to conceal their unhappiness; but they could not erase from their memory these words, so heartrending for them, "We will set a minimum social contribution which will be, perhaps, for the first departure, 600 francs per adult." From that they concluded that the doors of Icaria would forever be closed to them and that in losing their liberator they lost with him all of their brothers who, by the influence that their fortune and their talent give to them over the blind masses, would alone be able to pull them out of the abyss into which they are forced each day!

He went on to reiterate that Cabet's departure would bring about a "retrograde movement" in France and even chided Cabet for wanting to go to enjoy the pleasures of Icaria when important work remained in Europe. He concluded with an alternative plan under which poor workers would work off their fee in Icaria rather than seek out some rich benefactor in France.[129]

Greater disillusionment was in store for many Icarians. On September 19, 1847, Cabet published the "Contrat social ou Acte de Société pour la communauté d'Icarie: Explication préliminaire,"[130]

[127] *Ibid.,* July 25, 1847.
[128] Poublain to Cabet, Nov. 13, 1847, Papiers Cabet, III, BHVP.
[129] F. Lechapt to Cabet, May 27, 1847, Papiers Cabet, III, BHVP. Cabet did not publish this letter.
[130] In *Le Populaire* of that date.

wherein he proposed, quite simply, a dictatorship under the "gé-rant-directeur," Etienne Cabet. Because of the "necessity of harmony, unity, and celerity, it appears to us that a single directorship is absolutely required; it will be so much more useful because it will have all moral responsibility." This dictatorship would last ten years, but its powers would derive solely from the associates. The dictator might be removed if he lost this confidence, although no indication of how this would take place was given. He would direct everything in the colony and approve every applicant who wished to join. Cabet spoke of elections but gave no hint of what they might concern. And "adherence [to this constitution] will be an election." If no one approves of it, it will be void; but if all "or a mass" show their approval, then an election for the director-ship will have been made! The "Contrat social" was in the form of a business organization, a Société en nom collectif, and hence under the protection of French law. A curious form indeed for the society of the future! In such a society money, once deposited, cannot be withdrawn (although Cabet mentioned "aid" that would be given to those having to return to France because of health or other problems). In a very brief concluding section (no. 16) Cabet spoke of the "rights of the associates": "all are electors"—but the question remained, electors of whom or what? How were elections to be organized? Icaria was to have universal suffrage, but it would be as meaningless as the same right accorded to the citizens of the Second Empire.

On October 10 a meeting of the new society's shareholders took place, which dutifully approved the plan. On October 1, however, Cabet had received a letter that challenged every facet of this "constitution in the form of a commercial contract," though the letter was not published until October 24, well after news had been spread of the shareholders' decision. This long communication, from Jean-Baptiste Millière, a lawyer who had previously considered himself an Icarian sympathizer,[131] made all of the obvious

---

[131] In 1848, Millière was one of the leaders of Barbès' Club de la Révolution; later he fought the reaction of the closing years of the Second Republic. Exiled until 1859, he returned to do battle against the tyranny of Napoleon III, serving finally as manager of *La Marseillaise,* founded by Henri Rochefort in 1869. He was elected deputy to the assembly at Bordeaux in February 1871 but later returned to Paris and adhered to the Commune. On May 26, 1871, although he had no official post in the Com-

objections, saying that "Your Icaria would be a sort of degenerate daughter of the old society," an "absolute monarchy" (Millière even compared Cabet to Louis XIV). Cabet retorted that this charge was incorrect since he would always base himself on "public opinion" (as interpreted by the leader—the "totalitarian democrat" is quite evident here). Millière also asked Cabet at least to have an election among his followers for the leadership position. Everyone knows who would win, but not to do this would "establish a precedent that could have a fatal influence on later decisions." To this maxim of democracy Cabet replied, "Since the election will be certain, incontestable, why bother with it?" Although he did not do so Millière might have reminded Cabet of what he had said to Thoré five years before: "And it is the Icarian principle that its communitarian constitution be submitted to the discussion and deliberation of the entire People."[132] More recently (May 30, 1847) he had invited objections and suggestions with regard to the system laid out in the *Voyage en Icarie;* it is, after all, neither "a Code nor a Constitution but only a project open to discussion."

A few "addresses of support" for the "Contrat social" were printed in *Le Populaire* in later months, but overall the Icarians were curiously silent on the question. One of the very few letters in which objections were raised that found its way into print came from an "old patriot" of Toulouse named Chaudurie. He had originally planned to join the emigration but now, because of its despotic constitution, would not. Although Cabet answered benevolently, he said, in effect, that it was a pity, "We shall miss you."[133] The paltry number of supportive declarations and the limited participation in the first departure indicated that the constitution iced the cake: the emigration was rapidly becoming an experiment with a great deal in common with Robert Owen's New Harmony fiasco.

We do not know the extent to which the Icarian movement was reduced in size in 1847, or even definitely that it was. But a change in composition was manifest, and a new spirit of greater exclusiv-

---

mune government, he was summarily executed after being forced to his knees before the Panthéon by Captain Garçin (*Dict. biog.,* III, 110–20).

[132] Cabet, *Réfutation du Dictionnaire politique* (Paris 1842); he was referring to Thoré's discussion of Babouvist ideas on dictatorship.

[133] *Le Populaire,* Nov. 28, 1847.

ism and greater submission to the will of the leader developed among those Icarians who remained loyal. This does not mean that Cabet's influence among those who openly or tacitly disapproved of the emigration was dead. Icarianism lived on, if Cabetism retreated. Two Icarian movements existed side by side in 1847—one in the form of a community of principles without slavish devotion to the leader, the other, increasingly, in the form of a religious sect. The two would coalesce again in 1848 as the early revolution submerged the emigration project and Cabet became one of the great popular voices. But after the anticommunist storms of April and May 1848, the goal of emigration re-emerged, most Icarians (and many Cabetists as well) moved into new avenues of activity, and a tiny sect, with eyes focused on America, was all that remained of the Icarian communist movement.

This sect, if visible on the horizon in 1846, came into its own after the emigration project was announced. The strong Christian, if not Catholic, impulse that still animated many French workers in the 1840s,[134] stirred by the frustrations of misery and the vision of an earthly paradise, burst into full flame. Nearly all of the "receptions" carried some religious allusion. A declaration from Périguex is typical: "Yes, let us leave this worm-eaten and gangrenous society! . . . Apostles of the social regeneration, let us go to place the first stone in the edifice announced by Christ . . . for we shall leave behind life in the tombs in order to be born again in the promised land and under the sun of enlightenment."[135] Cabet was described in a variety of ways; he was the "New Moses," the "dear and worthy apostle of Christ," "the faithful imitator of

---

[134] François Isambert has stressed this point. "One even sees a change of reference come about progressively during the July Monarchy. More and more, at least at Paris and Lyons, it is Christianity that is invoked as the religious base of which the Catholic Church is only a particular denomination"; "L'Attitude religieuse des ouvriers français au milieu du XIX⁰ siècle," *Archives de sociologie des religions,* VI (1958), 21–22. The term "dechristianization," used by many scholars, creates the impression of a rejection of the Christian religion altogether. Upon careful reading, of course, it becomes clear that the decline in church attendance, canonical marriage, and general respect for the sacraments means only a rejection of the historical church. See Joseph Moody, "The Dechristianization of the French Working Class," *Review of Politics,* XV (1958), 46–69. An apology is due Professor Moody for my misguided criticism of this study in the *American Historical Review,* LXXVI (1971), 686, n. 123.

[135] *Le Populaire,* May 23, 1847.

Christ," and even "the new Messiah."[136] The words of Justine B. of Nantes show the new meaning "père" had gained. "Oh, our father par excellence who prepared the paradise for all humanity, . . . let us follow [him] who wishes to lead his children, and to share their pains and their hardships. . . . My blood, my life belong to him!"[137] Pierre Rivard, a Parisian journeyman tailor, was joining the emigration because he wanted "to realize the goal of Christ —let the mountains crumble and the valley fill." Another worker, identified only as R . . . , specifically compared Cabet to Christ: "Our epoch has many analogies with the one when God sent Christ to save humanity, and we must honor with our sympathies he who dares in our day to undertake a similar mission."[138] In reviewing these voices of the new Icarian atmosphere it is difficult not to agree with Proudhon, who, observing the movement and Cabet's utopia even in 1846, remarked: Icarians are to be like "oysters attached side by side, with neither activity nor feeling, on the rock of fraternity."[139]

Cabet had a very practical matter to deal with during the summer of 1847. He had announced the great Icarian emigration but had no idea where the Promised Land was to be. Assuming that the English communitarians like Goodwin Barmby and Robert Owen might be more knowledgeable about possible locations, especially in America, he asked a somewhat reluctant Berrier-Fontaine to approach them for assistance.[140] Berrier passed along most of the work of Charles Sully, a young French bookbinder and "zealous Icarian" living in London. Barmby, though fully approving of Cabet's plans,[141] proved to be of no help, but T. W. Thorn-

---

[136] The last was rare. See for instance *ibid.*, Oct. 17, 1847.

[137] *Ibid.*, Aug. 22, 1847.

[138] *Ibid.*, July 25 and Dec. 5, 1847.

[139] Proudhon, *Système des contradictions économiques, ou Philosophie de la misère* (1846) reprinted in C. Bouglé and M. Poysset, eds. *Oeuvres complètes de P.-J. Proudhon*, II (Paris, 1923), 282. Here is Proudhon's reaction to the emigration: "Expatriation!—to go to America, to *Icaria!* . . . *Quelle blague!* Such is what an old fool can come to! I have no positive reason for accusing him of having sold himself.—But this is to do the things of the government!" (*Carnets*, ed. Pierre Haubtmann [Paris, 1961], II, 98).

[140] Information in this paragraph is drawn largely from two sources that Prudhommeaux did not use, Berrier-Fontaine's correspondence with Cabet in 1847, held in the BHVP, and the Owen Papers (University of Wisconsin microfilm 1,090).

[141] A glance at Barmby's *New Tracts for the Times, or Warmth, Light,*

ton, an old friend of Cabet's and an Owenite, brought Sully and Owen together.[142] Out of these contacts, land for the Icarian "nation" was found in Texas. An American land agent named Peters had previously been discussing a possible transaction with Owen and the latter passed the information on to Cabet. The total area comprised 10.5 million acres of virgin soil located between the Red River and the forks of the Trinity. More important, the land would cost nothing—each married man could claim 320 acres and each bachelor 160. All they had to do was to set up a homestead by July 1, 1848. Through Sully, Cabet told Peters sometime in August that he was interested. But Peters, supposedly an ardent socialist,[143] had neglected to tell the Icarian chief about one small detail. His company served as homesteading agent for only one-half the land, distributed in one-mile checker-board squares across this vast tract. The State of Texas owned the rest. Moreover, the Peters group was willing to concede only half the territory they controlled to homesteaders, planning (as was the state) to sell their portion at a later date.[144] Cabet discovered these facts when he came to London in September. What kind of a community could be created out of noncontiguous chunks of prairie land?

No evidence exists to explain Cabet's decision, but, incredibly, he made up his mind to accept Peters' offer anyway. None of this was known to his followers and when he made the electric announcement on November 14, 1847, that Icaria would be in Texas, he uttered not a word about the distribution problem.[145] At the same time he made known the names of the avant garde, told his followers that Sully was already in the United States making preliminary arrangements, and that he personally would stay behind in France given the many arrangements for future departures that had to be made. These tragi-comic developments took place in an atmosphere where the suspicions of some and the enthusiasm of others of his followers heightened daily.

---

and *Food for the Masses* (London, 1843) shows the basic similarity between his and Cabet's communism. Barmby, however, posed as a true prophet, 1843 being the Year I of the regeneration.

[142] Owen Papiers, piece #1472 and Thornton to Owen, Aug. 6, 1847, #1497.

[143] *Ibid.*, Peters to Owen, Nov. 2, 1846, and June 7, 1847.

[144] See Prudhommeaux, *Cabet*, 226–29.

[145] *Le Populaire*, Nov. 14, 1847.

Cabet had already been busy preparing the enrollment of Icarians in France for the emigration. He published information on the many socialist and religious communities that had been created in America and elsewhere, statistics on current emigration in general, and reports on other experimentalists such as John Minter Morgan. On the practical level, he set up "commissions of admission" to the colony in Paris, Nantes, Mirecourt, Périgueux, Lyons, Vienne, Rouen, Albi, Tours, Saint-Etienne, Sedan, Toulon, and Choisy-le-Roi.[146] Each aspirant registered with the correspondent in his town and was then screened, first by the commission and finally by Cabet.[147] The information about the participants was then used in planning the schedule of future departures. It is not known how many colonists signed up prior to the revolution.[148] It seemed, in November and December of 1847, that the only concern in the Icarian movement was the emigration. Contests were announced for the best design of Icarian clothing and for the Icarian national anthem; letters anticipating the joys of Icarian existence were sent to *Le Populaire;* plans concerning minor details of the colony and blueprints of inventions were submitted; and the drive to recruit farmers was begun.[149] The Icarian sect, turning in upon itself, seemed to have become a recruiting society for the emigration.

Then an event occurred that brought Cabet and the Icarians back into the national limelight. In mid-December Cabet was interrogated by the police; two weeks later his papers were sequestered in connection with the alleged conspiratorial activities of one of his followers in Saint-Quentin, the weaver Dumotier.[150] In the course of the investigation, Cabet's agents in most of northern and northeastern France, including Butot of Reims, were investigated and their dwellings searched. On January 9, 1848, Cabet reported to all France (his letter appeared in most of the important opposition newspapers in Paris as well as *Le Populaire*) that his office

[146] Caron, "Etienne Cabet et l'Icarie," 885. The list of towns was found among Cabet's sequestered papers.

[147] *Le Populaire,* Sept. 5, 1847.

[148] The registration forms, if they were available, would be invaluable for analyzing the movement. Unfortunately they are not to be found among the known holdings of Cabet materials.

[149] Before the publication of Maillard's *Les Villageois* (Jan. 1848), propaganda for rural France was inserted in the *Almanach icarien pour 1848* (published in Nov. 1847), 131–36.

[150] A.N., BB[18] 1456 dos 4655.

had been ransacked by Department of Justice officials and that he faced trial for heading a secret society. This news aroused the fear of the entire opposition press that they might be next. Icarians (and here we assume many anti-Cabetists and antiemigration Icarians) responded with the greatest output of supportive declarations in the history of the movement.[151] The authorities soon discovered that there was no incriminating evidence to be found among all the pounds of papers squestered and changed the charge to one of "swindling," saying that the contributions Cabet was taking for the emigration amounted to a mere hoodwinking of the workers. The case was still pending when the revolution broke out.[152]

At the same time, preparations for the departure moved along as well, and on February 3 the 69 Icarians of the advance party, dressed in black uniforms and singing the specially written *Chant de départ,* waved goodbye to Cabet and 450 others on the wharves of Le Havre and sailed for New Orleans. They would be met by Sully and would soon cut the first furrows of the communist nation by the Red River.[153] They reached their destination on the very day that the people of Paris initiated the greatest simultaneous wave of revolutions in the history of Europe. Two days before, Cabet, witnessing the banquet campaign, thinking that the crafty M. Thiers was attempting to engineer another 1830, and despairing at having to take a position, concluded that there was no hope for the future in the Old World; thus, "en avant en Icarie!"[154]

In the final analysis, the entire movement displayed two contradictory trends. On one hand, men deeply influenced by Cabet increasingly rejected his authority, his pacifism, his religiosity, and/ or his simple utopian concepts of social constructionism. In effect, they followed the logic that Cabet himself suggested in the course of his debate with *La Réforme*—the recognition of bourgeois-

[151] These appeared in *Le Populaire* during Jan. and early Feb. and were later reprinted in Cabet's brochure defending himself against charges brought by disillusioned Icarians in 1849, *Notre Procès en escroquerie.*

[152] On the Saint-Quentin affair see: A.N., BB[18] 1456 dos 4655, 1441 dos 1992, and 1451 dos 3598 (including the report printed by Caron); all issues of *Le Populaire* of Dec. 1847, Jan. and Feb. 1848, and the *Journal de Reims,* Dec. 12, 1848 (for Cabet's visit to that city in connection with the affair).

[153] *Le Populaire,* Feb. 6, 1848.

[154] *Ibid.,* Feb. 20, 1848.

working-class antagonism—without losing the basic idealism, the belief in dedication, that marked his outlook. On the other hand, clusters of Icarian true believers, impressed by the ephemeral New Jerusalem that Cabet promised overseas and by the Christian-communist equation, and possessing a semi-Messianic view of their "father," insulated themselves from the outside world. After a brief flirtation with the idea that the revolution of 1848 might make France the Icaria of their dreams, they encased themselves, in dwindling numbers, in an exclusive fellowship devoted to the realization of the saintly kingdom in the wilds of America. That the sectarianization of Icarian communism destroyed its viability as an influential movement is beyond doubt.

Such a process was virtually inevitable. It is useless to blame Cabet and Krolikowski alone for the emergence of an Icarian sect. The flood of chiliastic responses to *Le Vrai Christianisme* and to the call for emigration adequately demonstrate the deep well of working-class religious enthusiasm that their words had tapped. In broader perspective, the most striking aspect of this development is that the social consciousness of a long-oppressed class cannot form solely on the basis of immediate experience but at first integrates values lodged deep in the traditional culture. Materialism and belief in the class struggle were largely foreign to this culture. Christianity was not; nor, thanks to the French Revolution, were such Jacobin concepts as dedication, virtue, and dignity. Neither, of course, was a certain amount of working-class deference to the alleged intellectual superiority of its bourgeois "betters." As we have seen, the Christian element, always present in Icarian doctrine, served to draw into the movement most of the bourgeois who became Icarians during its early period of growth. Bourgeois, such as Desmoulins, Laty, Chameroy, and Krolikowski exerted great influence on Cabet, the former lawyer, procureur-général, and deputy. For most of his working-class followers (at least the Cabetists) this influence was accepted as natural, given the normative framework of their social attitudes. The specific source of the Christian emphasis was bourgeois, and sectarianism developed in part as a response to bourgeois ideology. Regenerated, "true" Christianity thus tied a working-class movement to a basic element of preindustrial Western culture and tended to patch over the increasingly evident gulf between class interests in French society.

6 | Cabet and Icarian Communism in 1848

In some respects, the revolution of 1848 was an anticlimax in the Icarian story. The movement had been transformed by the events of 1846 and 1847. Loyal Cabetists focused on the emigration, and Cabet's major preoccupation in the months before February 1848 was the preparation for the first departure. But as the revolution unfolded, both sectarian Icarians and the broader spectrum of more independent communists influenced by Cabet tended to co-alesce, returned to the political arena, and played important roles in the upheaval. For a while it seemed as if Cabet himself had forgotten the colonial enterprise. His voice was among the most pop-ular (and the most practical) on the radical left in the early months of the revolution. Once again we see the Cabet of old: the politician, by a quirk of history, could re-emerge. The contrast with the sectarian pontiff of Icaria of late 1847 could not have been greater. Yet in the end, social forces beyond his control (or at least beyond his predisposition to assess accurately) threw him back again into the clutches of the utopian dilemma; to be a com-munist was to be the enemy of the property-holding and the re-spectable. The choice remained to fight or to run away.

The Communist Specter

Historians of Marxism have often contended that the opening line of the *Manifesto* was either a figment of the authors' imagina-tion or an exaggeration to frighten the bourgeoisie. The latter may have been true to an extent, but, as Oscar Hammen has ar-gued,

When Marx, in 1848, speaks of the "specter of communism" that haunts Europe, he thus enunciates a verifiable fact, at least with regard to France and Germany. There existed, at mid-century, a generalized feeling of fear or hope before the prospect of an uprising of the masses —having a complete reorganization of human society as its probable outcome. During the forties "communism" became, in revolutionary circles, the social theory par excellence, the formula more and more accepted as the ultimate end, the perfection to arrive, for society.[1]

In the case of France, the existence of the communist threat and a "generalized fear" of it on the eve of 1848 can hardly be doubted. In January 1848 *Le Corsaire,* an influential paper of the moderate opposition, said, "Today, not only the word [communism] but the thing is on all lips, under all pens, the subject of hope for some, terror for others."[2] The government tried valiantly to root out communism in 1847—and with good reason. Communism was growing as a force in the popular imagination as the economic crisis deepened. In 1847 and early 1848 incidents involving Icarians received widespread attention. In Lyons "communist discussions" enlivened the pages of *La Tribune.* Joseph Rey, the old Owenite, sought to harmonize relations between "the two major schools of the day," communism and Fourierism. In Paris two major trials, that of Coffineau and the "materialist communists" and that of "les bombes" (communist militants whom agents-provocateurs Chenu and La Hodde had encouraged to manufacture munitions), marked the summer of 1847. Communists in Alsace were arrested for alleged connections with grain riots.[3]

The press heralded the presence of communism; *Le Siècle, La Réforme, La Démocratie pacifique, Le National,* and *L'Atelier,* as well as such government sheets as *Le Journal des débats,* spoke of communism on many occasions in 1847, and two avowedly communist papers, *La Populaire* and *La Fraternité,* advertised the cause in broad daylight. Communism crossed the pages of the provincial press as well. Cabet cited many of these articles in *Le Populaire* throughout the year. In Reims and Périgueux especially,

---

[1] "1848 et le 'Spectre du Communisme,'" *Le Contrat social,* II (1958), 199–200.

[2] Quoted in *Le Populaire,* Feb. 6, 1848.

[3] See J. Rey, *Appel au ralliement des socialistes* (Paris, 1847); *Gazette des tribunaux,* July 14, 15, and 17, 1847 (on the materialist communists); and Oct. 8, 10, 13, and 17 (on the *procès des bombes*); Félix Ponteil, "L'Agitation ouvrière dans le Haut-Rhin en juin-juillet 1847," *La Révolution de 1848,* XXVIII (1931–32), 155–67.

Cabet's communism received considerable attention. We have already noted the opinion of the *Industriel de la Champagne* that "Communism has thrust down deep roots in France"; the *Journal de Reims* could not understand why so many workers attached themselves to Cabet; and the *Echo de Vésone* (Périgueux) had a running battle with some of its Icarian readers on the question of pacific versus materialist communism.[4] The power of communism was evident. Lamartine, following Ledru-Rollin and Arago, felt obliged to declare his opposition to communism at a banquet in Autun in December.[5] On the other hand, Ledru-Rollin was so impressed with communism by 1847 that he changed his tune and tried to ingratiate himself with its followers, while at the same time opposing the escapism of Cabet's emigration scheme. Victor Hennequin, in his long tour to advertise the Fourierist cause early in 1847, failed to make any converts among the communists and wondered why communism made "so much greater progress" than his own doctrine.[6] The voice of the Jesuits, *L'Ami de religion,* predicted that this "widespread sentiment among the masses" would bring about "social revolution" unless the government did something to improve the lives of the workers.[7]

But was the "specter of communism" more significant as a fear among the conservatives and the property owners or as a manifest reality? The evidence presented above makes it clear that communism was indeed an important phenomenon in 1847 and that no one was more important in making it so than Cabet. But at the same time ridiculous comments, such as "This thief Cabet and his entire band of communists are monopolizers of wheat; it would be well to take these communist brigands, cut them into pieces and burn them,"[8] show that the communists were becoming scapegoats as well. An article printed in both *La Patrie* and *Le Commerce* in December 1847 explicitly played down the communist menace, first citing Metternich's charge that communists were responsible for the rising of the Polish landlords in Galicia and then blaming much

---

[4] See the *Industriel de Champagne,* Dec. 16, 1847; *Journal de Reims,* Dec. 12, 1847; and the *Echo de Vésone,* Nov. 24, 28, Dec. 8 and 19, 1847.

[5] See *Le Populaire,* Dec. 12, 1847.

[6] *La Démocratie pacifique,* quoted in *Le Populaire,* April 11, 1847.

[7] Article quoted in full in *Le Populaire,* Aug. 22, 1847.

[8] Overheard by a worker and reported to Cabet; *ibid.,* Nov. 6, 1847.

of the agitation over communism in France on the government, which sought to obscure the sad political and economic state of the nation. Such an approach, said the article, works wonders because "it frightens people where they are most easily frightened in this materialistic epoch—in relation to their property." Communists were there, to be sure, and the greater force is probably with the pacific variety, but this threat is not overwhelming and would be nil if the government would reform.[9] In fact, communism flowed into the history of the revolution of 1848 both as a real force and as an exaggerated fear, and Cabet, despite the fact that he was more interested in news from America than in the approaching upheaval in France, was at the heart of both elements of the story.

The revolution of 1848 caught Cabet off guard. One of his central arguments justifying the emigration was the hopelessness of the political situation in France. Yet in three days—as in 1830—the regime was overthrown. And on the fourth day, in sharp contrast to the earlier revolution, the capital rang with cries of "Vive la République."

What had Cabet done during the new *trois glorieuses?* The only source is the series of accusations made by the rich Parisian trunk merchant, Gosse, who had become a supporter of the Icarian cause after the emigration call but split with Cabet when the emigration idea faded as the revolution developed. His comments were published by Cabet in *Réalisation d'Icarie No. 3.* We can reconstruct the situation by noting what Cabet does not deny. On the evening of February 23, Cabet moved in with Gosse because he feared arrest. He was, therefore, not among the combatants. The two finally ventured out late in the afternoon of February 24, when they traversed several barricades and made their way to Belleville. Gosse claimed that throughout their journey Cabet was petrified with fright; Cabet blamed his distress on his painful rheumatism.[10] Cabet returned that night to his office on the rue Jean-Jacques Rousseau and began to outline the position that he was going to take on the recent events.

[9] *La Patrie,* Dec. 11, 1847, and *Le Commerce,* Dec. 23, 1847. Blaming the communist specter on the government may be somewhat out of line. A perusal of the letters of Louis-Philippe and Guizot to Duchâtel during 1846 and 1847 reveals that neither even mentioned communism, let alone tried to make it a scapegoat. A.N., 2 AP 7 and 8 (Papiers Duchâtel).

[10] See Cabet, *Réalisation d'Icarie No. 3* (Paris, July 24, 1849), 41ff.

One can easily imagine what passed through his mind that evening. His utopian project overseas had been launched; he had committed himself fully to it and planned to depart for the colony himself at a later date. But now all was changed. Perhaps Icaria could be constructed in France. Perhaps they would make him a minister.[11] But to what extent should he, a pacific communist, identify with the revolution? Should he support the largely bourgeois provisional government? Should he demand that preparation be made immediately for the transition to a communist regime? His answer was published the following day as the first special issue of *Le Populaire*. His "Manifeste aux Communistes Icarians" was among the first proclamations from the socialist camp and was posted all over Paris.

"Quelle Révolution!" The people of Paris, he said, had undone eighteen years of unkept promises in a single stroke. The creation of a republic seemed to be assured. And, most important of all, Icarians should support the provisional government, "which declares itself to be republican and democratic, which proclaims national sovereignty and the unity of the nation." Cabet listed the demands of the communists, which included the right of association, individual liberty, freedom of the press (abolition of caution money and the stamp tax), "especially the guarantee of all the rights and of all the interests of the workers, the formal recognition of the right to live by working, . . . the organization of work, and the assurance of well-being by work," the abolition of taxes on goods of primary necessity and of the urban tariff (the *octroi*), free and complete education for all, and a special regard for women and children. Twice he repeated that there should be no vengeance and no attacks on property. The revolution is over, fighting should cease, "all Frenchmen are brothers." Not a single specifically communist demand appeared. Instead, "progressive equality" was the watchword. "Let us guard against demanding the immediate application of our communist doctrines."[12] Communists should be revolutionaries only in the sense that they support the revolution that has been made. At this point, Cabet did

[11] Gosse claimed (and Cabet denied) that he had manifested this desire; *ibid.*

[12] *Le Populaire,* Feb. 25, 1848.

not even caution the workers to be on guard against the *révolution escamotée* (stolen away).

The Icarian leader's moderation was seen as a blessing. The noncommunist press obviously breathed a deep sigh of relief,[13] and, although there were some rumors in the provinces that Cabet and 10,000 communists were ready to seize power, it was generally understood that the communists had rallied.[14] Daniel Stern, Lamartine, and Pierre Leroux all stressed later that Cabet's moderate tone and support of the provisional government had been crucial in keeping the working class from further violence.[15] What about the emigration? "The Revolution . . . opened a new horizon to his views," for "his followers flattered themselves that they would see their association realized on the soil of France."[16] Only on March 12 did Cabet finally comment on the emigration question, saying that the revolution had caused a change in plans, especially immediate ones, but that the "general design" remained. A month later, however, he admitted that many of those originally slated to emigrate were no longer interested.[17] During March and most of April Cabet probably wished he could scrap the project altogether. He hardly ever spoke of it (although he had to announce the arrival of the advance party in America), and the major reason for Gosse's attack on Cabet was that he ignored the advance party and the colonial project because of the revolution. He was also criticized for not calling a halt to the Texas expedition given his new orientation.[18]

Cabet thus took his place among the quarante-huitards, and an important place it was. He was generally recognized as the "chef des communistes";[19] he headed the largest club in Paris, tren-

---

[13] Cabet printed excerpts from various newspapers on their reactions to his manifesto in *Le Populaire,* March 4, 1848.

[14] *La Fraternité* had shown the same kind of moderation in its manifesto of Feb. 25, but this fact caused little reaction in the press.

[15] Stern, *Histoire,* I, 168; Alphonse de Lamartine, *History of the French Revolution of 1848* (London, 1870), 409; Leroux, *La Grève de Samarez,* II, 377–78.

[16] L. Garnier-Pagès, *Histoire de la Révolution de 1848* (Paris, 1861–1872), VI, 331; Lamartine, *History,* 357.

[17] *Le Populaire,* March 12 and April 9, 1848.

[18] Le Citoyen Jacques Bonhomme, *Cabet, Pacha d'Icarie* (Paris; [1848]).

[19] *La Voix des clubs* remarked in its first number that Cabet "gathered

chantly analyzed the course of the revolution, was the principal leader of the demonstration of March 17, and aided Blanqui in his hour of need; finally, and disastrously, he took the brunt of the rabid anticommunisst drive that preceded the elections to the national assembly. The greatest tribute to Cabet's role in 1848 came from Martin Nadaud, who, at the time he wrote it, had left Icarianism behind and been a Representative and one of the leading warriors against the reaction. Writing to Blanqui on July 31, 1850, he said:

> In February three men gave proof of a great energy of character: Blanqui, Raspail, and Cabet. Furthermore, I repeat, nothing was spared in order to wither them. One preferred the counsels of those who had always pledged themselves to the privileged and to the linxes of the stock exchange rather than to call upon these pioneers of humanity who had never deviated for a single moment, who would rest only in the tomb, these martyrs of modern times who inscribed upon their flags: Abolition of the exploitation of man by man.[20]

Cabet's work in the revolution[21] marked a return to his former political strategy. Rather than appearing as a sectarian pontiff, he merged the interests of his party with those of the entire socialist left and, by allowing the emigration project to sink into the background, regained the allegiance of the wide Icarian, but not neces-

---

around the flag of Fraternity and Solidarity an immense army of workers who were distinguished by the elevation of their sentiments, the level of their minds, and the certainty of their character." Garnier-Pagès attested that among the communists the Icarians were the only ones of any importance (*Histoire*, IV, 82–83). A foundryworker, upon hearing the chant "à bas les communistes" on the streets in early April, decided to look into Cabet's writings, as if this were the only place to go in order to see what all the noise was about (Cormon to Cabet, April 8, 1848, Papiers Cabet, I, BHVP). Proudhon spoke of the communists rallying to the provisional government but was referring only to Cabet's manifesto (*Représentant du peuple*, March 29, 1848). The *Républicain de l'arrondissement de Sédan* identified three brands of socialism in 1848: Fourierism, Saint-Simonism, and Cabet's communism. The most interesting view of all came from London; the *Quarterly Review*, in a long article on the *Voyage en Icarie* and its impact, perhaps revealed the attitude of the general public at the time when it commented casually on "Blanqui, who supports Cabet and Communism" (LXXXIII, [1848], 167).

[20] Bibliothèque Nationale, Manuscrits, MSS Blanqui, Nouv, Acq. Fran., 9581, p. 223.

[21] The main study of Cabet in 1848 is Pierre Angrand, *Etienne Cabet et la République de 1848*, 34–79.

sarily Cabetist, communist element. His greatest influence was felt during the first month of the revolution. His club, the Société fraternelle centrale, which met in the large Salle Valentino in the heart of Paris, brought together each week some 5,000 individuals[22] and was always accorded first billing in the reports of the *Voix des clubs.* As might be expected, these meetings were conducted in an orderly fashion, and Cabet emphasized his own addresses more than popular discussion. In the Société fraternelle and in *Le Populaire,* Cabet, while counseling prudence and reserve to the workers, denounced the slow shift to the right evident from almost the beginning of the revolution. By February 27 he was already warning the workers that they must continue to demand from the provisional government "all the consequences of a popular revolution," implying that he was not sure whether such could be expected from the group at the Hôtel de Ville. Thereafter, he and Proudhon served as the principal watchdogs over the actions of the government. Their earlier antipathy seemed to have dissolved; each quoted the other extensively on the lack of progress made by the new rulers of France. (Blanqui was more vociferous still, but he had opposed the government since its formation.) On February 29, Cabet openly recalled 1830 in criticizing the government's hesitancy on the questions of caution money and the stamp tax, but he especially attacked its establishment of the *garde mobile,* which he likened to a "praetorian guard." Then on March 4, viewing the choices made for departmental commissars, Cabet began "to fear that favoritism and the *esprit de coterie* has already provoked many bad choices in the personnel of the new functionaries. . . . If the provisional government does not attempt to compose an administrative personnel in a *social* manner, it will, instead of fortifying itself, prepare a counterrevolution of which it will be the first victim." The day before he had received a letter from A. Bertrand, a man of some education, who wanted to write for Cabet rather than "to occupy a post, however elevated, under the bourgeois regime that is being prepared."[23]

---

[22] Lamartine (*History,* 376) says 7,000 or 8,000, but the hall only held 5,000; 1,500 were turned away from the second meeting (*Voix des clubs,* March 13, 1848).

[23] Papiers Cabet, I, BHVP (the writer may possibly have been A.-V. Bertrand, painter, who fought on the side of the insurrectionaries in June; *Dict. biog.,* I, 212). The other citations are from *Le Populaire.*

In mid-March, Cabet published a full-scale assessment of the work of the provisional government entitled *Bien et mal, danger et salut après la Révolution de février* (Paris, 1848, signed March 12). The structure of the brochure revealed Cabet's opinion of the balance between "good" and "bad." The first thirty-five pages warn of a repetition of the legerdemain of 1830, while only three are devoted to the progressive moves of the government (including the proclamation of the Republic, freedom of the press, universal suffrage, showing a desire for social reforms, and a firm policy with regard to foreign powers). Eleven more pages speak of other errors, and another six suggest what should be done. The most pressing evil, according to Cabet, was the overwhelming influence of the group around *Le National* and in particular the mayor of Paris, Armand Marrast, who had a special entry into the high councils of the provisional government since Pagnerre, its secretary, was his puppet.[24] This situation meant bourgeois control over the destiny of the revolution. As an example of this clique's trickery, Cabet cited the fact that they had "annulled" Louis Blanc by sending him to preside over the Luxembourg Commission. Through *Le National,* Cabet also saw the stars of the Orleanists, Odilon Barrot and Thiers, on the rise. The grande bourgeoisie was already recouping its losses of February. Cabet also found Ledru-Rollin wanting, particularly with regard to equipping a truly popular National Guard. Cabet thought that the key to making the revolution develop in the interests of the people was the creation of a National Guard in which the workers would hold high rank and make up the bulk of the forces. As things were developing now, "There will not be a veritable national guard, but a bourgeois guard."[25]

While it was important that elections for the national assembly be postponed long enough to allow the consolidation of republican opinion, the National Guard was the crucial question. Specifically, Cabet proposed adjournment of the election of officers, a campaign to get all citizens into the Guard and armed, simple uniforms provided by the state, a small wage for service in the Guard, suppression of the garde mobile, and an assurance that the regular army troops would not be allowed (as *Le National* proposed) to return

[24] This opinion is supported by modern research. See R. Balland, "Pagnerre et ses amis," *Revue des révolutions contemporaines,* XLI (1950), 216.
[25] See *Bien et mal,* 47–58.

to Paris.[26] There was nothing in the least ridiculous about this heavy stress on the composition of the National Guard. The grand ideals of forty-eighters everywhere in Europe vanished into the air from which they came when the cannon and the sword of reaction came to confront them. Cabet was one of the few men among the idealists of 1848 who comprehended fully the need to arm the working man.[27] Yet—and this is part of his curious heritage—his eminent practicality on this question was offset by the fact that he had much to do with undermining the revolutionary resolve of the workers in the immediate aftermath of the February uprising. That more workers did not seek to join the National Guard may be attributed in part to the glow of brotherhood between classes that Cabet had helped to instill. The same problem that had caused Cabet to propose the Icarian emigration cropped up again: class antagonism was recognized, but class conflict could not be sanctioned.

Cabet's great moment in the revolution of 1848 came on March 17. The demonstration of that day had been first proposed by Cabet at the March 10 session of the Société fraternelle. Thereafter he met with Blanqui, the chiefs of the other major revolutionary clubs, and representatives from the Luxembourg Commission to decide on how to make the demonstration a reality. The two key issues were the adjournment of elections for the national assembly and the various questions connected with the National Guard. The latter were critical because elections for the Guard's officers were scheduled for March 20 and, especially, because the old National Guard had staged its reactionary demonstration the day before. Cabet, viewing the National Guard as the major problem, tended to moderate on the issue of the national elections. Blanqui, on the other hand, put national elections at the head of his demands, calling for at least a three-month postponement. Cabet's voice prevailed, and the bulk of the tens of thousands of militants were satisfied with his proposal to put off the national elections until May 31. When the demonstrators presented themselves at the Hôtel de Ville, Cabet led the deputation that presented their demands. Promises were made, and the vast troop broke up think-

---

[26] See *ibid.*, 41–42, 58–60.
[27] See also Société fraternelle centrale, *Deuxième Discours de M. Cabet* (*Séance du 13 mars*) (Paris, 1848).

ing that their hopes had been realized. But the provisional government was only willing to postpone the elections for the National Guard to April 5 and the national assembly elections to Easter Sunday, April 23. And this decision came only after Albert and Blanc had threatened to resign.[28]

March 17 marked the pinnacle of Cabet's popularity. He had been put before the national eye as never before. He had used his bonhommie magnificently in the confrontation of the deputation with the members of the provisional government and forced them to make forthright promises. In short, he was a true popular hero. But he was also a communist—a *communist,* a leveler, a believer in the *loi agraire,* a pillager, a defender of free love! This man had led 150,000 workers (were they all communists, too?) through the streets of Paris. And so, first as a whisper and then, as the elections of April 23 drew near, building to a deafening crescendo, was heard the horrible cry, "A bas les communistes! Mort à Cabet!" And as the cry grew louder, the République démocratique et sociale began to die.

Icarians in the Revolution

As Cabet moved into prominence (and then notoriety), several of his followers and many others who were ideologically in his debt participated in the affairs of the revolution. Only in Paris was there much chance for Icarians to engage in the actual fighting. Cabet claimed that although the Icarians did not involve themselves in the early phases of the struggle, after the "horrible fusillade on February 23 in front of Guizot's house had given the signal for Revolution, the Icarians everywhere became revolutionaries."[29] The author of *Pacha d'Icarie,* however, stated flatly that "Icarians

[28] The importance of Cabet on March is well known. Some historians criticize his moderation on the question of the national elections (see Jean Dautry, *1848 et la Deuxième République* [Paris, 1957], 124–25), but, as we have stressed, the National Guard issue was (quite justifiably) his main preoccupation. On the affair, see Angrand, *Cabet,* 44–47; Garnier-Pagès (who says that Cabet was the "soul" of March 17) *Histoire,* VI, 384–435; Stern, *Histoire,* II, 221–23; Louis Ménard, *Prologue d'une révolution* (Paris, 1849; reprinted by Cahiers de la Quinzaine, n.d.), 72ff; *Le Populaire,* March 19 and 23, 1848; and, especially, the careful assessment by A. Crémieux and G. Génique, "La Question électorale en mars 1848," *La Révolution de 1848,* III (1906–07), 206–12, 252 and 63.

[29] Cabet, *Chacun son devoir* (Paris, April 17, 1848), 2–3.

failed to fight and when they did the battle was essentially already won."[30] Cabet specifically mentioned the activities of only two of his adherents, Robillard (merchant baker) and Montagne (file-maker). Robillard, who was already a lieutenant in the National Guard, was raised to battalion commander in the heat of the fighting, while Montagne became a lieutenant. The records of these men were sufficient to merit their representing the Société fraternelle in the Club des clubs (along with Chameroy) and to lead them to consider running for the national assembly.[31]

More in line with Icarian principles was the work of moderation carried out by Icarians. At Mirecourt, Périgueux, and Nantes, Icarians were reputed to have pacified hotter heads among the workers, but we know specifics in only three cases. At Vienne on March 4 the Icarians published a declaration against pillaging.[32] Icarians at Rive-de-Gier succeeded in dissuading workers from attacking property when such designs were proposed; and M. and Mme Denise, Icarians, physically stood up to some marauders along the railway.[33] In Reims Cazé, a prominent Icarian, gave an impassioned speech calling for firmness but moderation on the part of the workers when the news of the revolution arrived from Paris; Butot, in his new function as municipal councilor, was instrumental in forestalling any further attacks on property after the arson committed by a band of workers at the large textile mill of Thomas Croutelle.[34]

In several cities Icarians (or at least people deeply influenced by Cabet's ideas) made other important contributions in the early events of the revolutionary year. At Mirecourt Julien Chambry and his friends, on hearing the news that the Republic had been declared in Paris, went immediately to the Hôtel de Ville "to place their demands," asking especially for arms to protect the revolu-

[30] Bonhomme, *Pacha d'Icarie,* 6.
[31] *Le Populaire,* Feb. 27 and March 7, 1848; A.N., C 941; Société fraternelle centrale, *Séance de 10 avril* (Paris, 1848), 9. A man called Maillard was instrumental in arousing the inhabitants of the Faubourg Saint-Denis to action on Feb. 24 (Victor Bouton, *La Patrie en danger* [Paris, 1850], 11), but since this name is quite a common one we have no way of knowing whether it was L.V. Maillard, the Icarian.
[32] Rude, "L'Arrondissement de Vienne," 309.
[33] *Le Populaire,* March 12, 1848.
[34] Gustave Laurent, "La Révolution de 1848," in his *Le Département de la Marne et la Révolution de 1848,* 48–50.

tion. They were turned down. They proclaimed the necessity for "a democratic and humanitarian republic" but were shocked by the indifference of the new authorities, who "are sold to the high bourgeoisie." Undaunted, they occupied themselves with preparing workers for their duties as voters.[35] Guay brought the Icarians of Niort together shortly after the establishment of the Republic was known and formed a club; he also went to other towns in the area to do the same. By mid-March, however, their meetings were already being disrupted by "misérables" in the pay of "bourgeois and aristocrats."[36] Icarian clubs were also formed in Toulouse, Marseille, Montpellier, Nîmes, Toulon, Reims, Vienne, and Lyons. At Toulouse, there was an opportunity for Icarians to be placed on the provisional council as well, for Saganzan and Balguerie were among the leaders of the workers who established themselves at the Hôtel de Ville; Antoine Cayré, writing on the revolution in Toulouse, says that the workers failed to press for the inclusion of these two men and therefore there was no socialist on the council headed by Joly.[37]

As one might expect, Icarians were in greater evidence in 1848 in Reims, Vienne, and Lyons than anywhere else outside Paris. The Rémois situation was the most important. On March 25, Butot and Cazé were invited to take part in the revolutionary municipal commission by its bourgeois directors because the latter "believed they could thereby arm the local authority with a more direct and more decisive influence on the working-class population."[38] This strategy was borne out by ensuing events. Cazé rallied the bulk of the working class to the provisional administration with his speech the following day. Butot went even further, cooperating nearly completely and even counseling the workers not to be too concerned if social measures were not taken immediately. The commission had indeed proposed a "special contribution" from the

[35] Chambry to Cabet, March 3, 1848, Papiers Cabet, V, BHVP.

[36] *Voix des clubs,* March 14, 1848; *Le Populaire,* March 16, 1848.

[37] "La Révolution de 1848 à Toulouse et dans la Haute-Garonne: Des Journées de février aux journées de juin," in Godechot, ed., *La Révolution de 1848 à Toulouse,* 144.

[38] A later statement by Courmeaux, leader of the social republican element of bourgeois opinion in Reims; quoted in Laurent, "La Révolution," 49–50.

"well-to-do citizens" of Reims to help the indigent, but such a measure was never implemented.[39] It became Butot's role to justify this sort of thing. When an Icarian named Génin, accused of participating in the attack of Croutelle's factory, sought Butot's moral support in the presence of other members of the municipal commission, Butot agreed with the others that Génin was a "hothead."[40] The main seat of Icarian power in Reims was the Comité électoral de la démocratie rémoise, which was formed on March 7.[41] But Butot established a separate club, the Club républican des socialistes pacifiques, the leadership of which consisted (besides Butot) of a lesser official, a physician, and a law student. If Butot had not sold out, he was certainly trying to make himself respectable. The Comité électoral soon fell into the hands of the non-Icarian demagogue, Gonzalle, who made every effort to emphasize Butot's estrangement from the working-class cause. The Comité put out a short-lived newspaper called *Le Républicain* that took socialist positions and aimed at promoting working-class candidates for the elections.[42] Nevertheless, despite his apparent role as a bourgeois stooge, Butot maintained enough popularity to gain 2,032 votes in the April 23 election in the Marne; even if this was not sufficient for election, it made him twenty-seventh on the list and third among the workers who stood as candidates.[43] The history of Butot is instructive on Cabet's general influence. The latter's emphasis on moderation and respectability obviously had a profound impact on Butot. In his profession of faith for the approaching election, Butot put heavy stress on his role as a pacifier, indicating that he saw nothing reproachable about his actions: "No liberty without order! And, hearing the call of the members of the provisional committee of Reims, I did not hesitate to accept the dangerous mission of joining these citizens to re-establish the order

[39] "Extrait du registre des délibérations du conseil municipal de la Ville de Reims, séance du premier mars 1848," ms. 1930, and M. Lacatte-Joltrois, "Abregé historique," IV, 63, ms. 1686, Cabinet des Manuscrits, Bibliothèque municipale de Reims.

[40] Génin to Cabet, n.d., Papiers Cabet, II, BHVP.

[41] Laurent, "La Révolution," 66.

[42] *Le Républicain,* 6 issues, March 3–April 4, 1848, Cabinet de Reims, V, 1213, Bibliothèque municipale de Reims.

[43] "Liste officielle des candidats ayant reçus plus de 2,000 voix," (Cabinet des Manuscrits, ms.) 1094, Bibliothèque municipale de Reims.

troubled by madmen, most of whom were brought to justice.[44] Thus, even though Cabet was taking a hard line in Paris on the National Guard, his chief representative at Reims was demonstrating the Icarian leader's influence in muting the revolutionary resolve of the working class. Still, the Icarian influence had been positive in Reims in one important respect. Gustave Laurent, who even tends to agree with the assessment of Gonzalle concerning the size of the Icarian group at Reims, is quite adamant in stressing that the *prise de conscience* of the Rémois working class must be attributed to Cabet's followers; that there was any worker movement at all in Reims in 1848 was due to "the humble group of Icarians."[45]

In Vienne the Icarian emphasis on order was evident. Many of Cabet's adherents were involved in club life, in either the Société républicaine, the Club populaire, or the frankly Icarian Comité électoral républicain des travailleurs de Vienne under the presidency of Cöeffé. Speaking before the Société républicaine on March 9, Ravat, the second most important Viennois Icarian, warned against the specter of '93, saying, "In the current situation we must give all our attention to keeping the most complete order." Three days later he reminded his listeners to remember the betrayal of 1830 but was confident that "the hour of our deliverance has sounded." Unlike Butot, however, he was not a complete pacifist, for he echoed Cabet in Paris in emphasizing that the worker "must continue to give a military character to his attitude" in face of bourgeois power. The leader of the Club populaire, Rouget, another Icarian, contended that the Icarians "have contributed the most in maintaining order during the grave circumstances that have just occurred."[46] But not all Icarians were satisfied with the pacific bearing of their group. Xavier Charre, for instance, broke with Ravat's Société républicaine to become president of the Blanquist Société démocratique during the second half of March. The latter's motto was "Union and Vigilance," and it linked itself directly to the Société républicaine centrale of Blanqui in Paris.[47]

---

[44] *Deux Mots aux citoyens electeurs,* printed letter in Lacatte-Joltrois, "Abregé," 70.

[45] Laurent, "La Révolution," 66.

[46] Reported in the *Voix des clubs,* March 16, 1848.

[47] On events in Vienne see Rude, "L'Arrondissement de Vienne," 267–71,

The legend reads: "[The Communists] are a set of brigands who claim that everyone has the right to live by working, that the earth is large enough to feed all its children, that wine brutalizes man, and a thousand other similar atrocities in the name of fraternity. Death to the Communists, Socialists, etc., etc." This is the best and most sympathetic of several surviving lithographs that relate to the anticommunist campaign of April 1848. Photograph: Estampes, Bibliothèque Nationale.

Faucon and Gluntz, leaders of the loyalist Icarians in Lyons, formed a Société fraternelle lyonnaise. This was reported in *Le Populaire* of May 4, but little mention of it is to be found elsewhere.[48] As is well known, working-class politics in Lyons during the revolution were dominated by Benoit, Greppo, and their friends; both these old antagonists of Cabet were elected on April 23 to the national assembly. Yet the importance of Icarianism at Lyons in 1848 should not be underestimated. In the first place, several of the nonloyal Icarians of days gone by played significant roles, especially in club life early in the revolutionary period. Razuret was president of the Club Jandard, "the most important club of the Croix-Rousse," vice-president of the Club de la rue Perrod, and a member of Lyons' version of the Luxembourg Commission. Rémond served as president and Garçon as treasurer of the Club de la rue Perrod, while Raffin was an important member of the Club du jardin.[49] Participating in the deliberations of the executive committee formed after the revolution we find Auguste Morlon and Barre, chef d'atelier (the latter, together with Garçon and Razuret split away from Cabet in 1845).[50] There are indications that a rapprochement took place in 1848 between the loyalists and these men. Frédéric Olinet, who later went to America and was true to Cabet in 1848, nevertheless participated in the affairs of the Club de la rue Perrod and served as its secretary.[51] Above all, the spirit of Icarian communism pervaded the revolutionary atmosphere in Lyons in 1848. Jean Gaumont has stated it well: "If the catastrophic revolutionary tendency represented by the Babouvists was perhaps dominant at the beginning of the revolution, it was counterbalanced, and more and more so with the evolution of events, by the more moderate tendencies of the Icarians, hostile to the armed struggles of the barricades, who preferred the ballot on

---

274, 286, 313–14, 317–35; the quotes from Ravat's speeches may be found on 319. Ravat was also editor of the *Echo des clubs* and was elected as an officer in the National Guard on April 16.

[48] On April 11 the *Tribune lyonnaise* published a declaration of thanks by this club to the Parisian "victors of the barricades."

[49] Gaumont, *Histoire générale,* I, 378 and 357.

[50] From a manuscript by the revolutionary leader and friend of Benoit, Félix Blanc, "Le Comité exécutif de Lyon," printed in *La Révolution de 1848,* IX (1912–13), 350.

[51] *Voyage d'un Autunois en Icarie,* 16–17.

one hand and organization and association on the other."[52] Although Gaumont was not aware of the conflicts that cause us to differentiate the Icarians from the Cabetists, there is little reason to doubt the kind of generalized influence he posits. And his reference to association is the lead-in to the area where Icarian influence in Lyons finally came to rest—in the cooperative movement, to which we shall return in the following chapter. There is another facet of the revolutionary spirit in Lyons which, in all probability, owes a great deal to the influence of Cabet.

The most general characteristic of the writings [of the radical candidates for the election of April 23] is their religious spirit. There are very few of them in which Christ, the Gospels, "the true spirit of Christianity," are not invoked, even though one notices in them defiance toward the Catholic clergy. [Moreover] religious memories and memories of '93 stand side by side everywhere. Typical of this strange association, we find a placard (unfortunately without a precise date), entitled *La Fête-Dieu républicaine,* illustrated by both revolutionary and religious vignettes which assimilate the festival of the Supreme Being with Corpus Christi day.[53]

Although the mystical and religious nature of many Lyonnais workers was a factor in the success of Icarianism among them, it seems quite probable, especially in light of the Christ-First Republic link, that their religiosity in 1848 was also an effect of Cabet's influence.

These examples of Icarian participation in revolutionary events underline three essential points. First, Icarians—the loyalists and the ideologically indebted alike—were prominent revolutionaries. While the hatchet may not have been buried, the sectarians reemerged to stand side by side politically with those who had split with Cabet. Second, Icarians seemed to take up the old left-wing solidarity strategy that Cabet himself rekindled in 1848, involving themselves not only in their own revolutionary clubs but also in

[52] *Histoire général,* I, 380.
[53] M. Lévy-Schneider, "Les Débuts de la Révolution de 1848 à Lyon." *Revue d'histoire moderne et contemporaine,* XV (1911), 177. There is also an engraving that shows Jesus as a Montagnard standing on a rock and pointing to a word floating by in the heavens: *Fraternité.* Georges Renard, "Cabet et les précurseurs de 1848," *La Révolution de 1848,* XXVIII (1931), 183.

groupings linking several ideological positions. Third, the stance of Icarians appeared to vacillate between (or to try to combine) a stress on order and cooperation and militant vigilance. This was typical of Cabet and shows that his own tactical dilemma filtered down to the rank and file.

The Anticommunist Drive

If Icarians generally remained pacifists and defenders of order in the early days of the revolution, such was not their image in the public (or, rather, bourgeois) mind. For one of the most striking features of the entire revolution concerned them directly. This was the communist scare of late March and April. As it ran its course, Blanqui would be fatally slandered, Cabet destroyed, and the elections pushed in a reactionary direction. Again it is unnecessary to delve into the question deeply; the importance of the anticommunist campaign in the development of the revolution has been treated by others.[54] Let it simply be said that although the problem of the forty-five centimes,[55] the excellent electoral organization of *Le National* and the moderate republicans, and several other factors all contributed to the conservative outcome of the elections of April 23, the cries of "à bas les communistes" did their work as well in assuring the virtual absence of socialists and radical democrats in the national assembly. Charles Fauvety, writing to the *Représentant du peuple* on April 8, realized what was happening: "The epithet 'Communist' is lavished upon all democrats by the more or less conservative republicans. Under the weight of this word they attempt to crush all those whose ideal goes beyond a simple change in government."[56] One of the most trenchant contemporary analyses of the situation and its results was made by T. W. Thornton, Cabet's Owenite friend, in the columns of *The Reasoner*. After noting the loose employment of the term communist with regard to the grain rioters in 1847, he went on to say:

Ever since the revolution of February, pushed so much farther than the bourgeois had any notion of going, they have sought an opportunity

[54] See, for instance, Dautry, *La Révolution,* 126ff, and, especially, Angrand, *Cabet,* 50ff.
[55] See Rémi Gossez, "La Résistance à l'impôt: Les Quarante-cinq Centimes," *Études; Bibliothèque de la Révolution de 1848,* XV (1953), 89–131.
[56] Quoted in Angrand, *Cabet,* 52.

of undoing some of the work and of returning toward the ancient system. The last demonstration by that party, that of April 16, succeeded by means of the cry "Down with the Communists" etc., which rallied some 200,000 of the National Guard, many of whom probably apprehended some great danger from the communists. It seems to be forgotten that the 100,000 workmen who are branded as incendiaries and plunderers, are the men who overthrew despotism, and holding Paris and all its wealth entirely at their mercy, caused persons and property to be respected. A very ungrateful return for their noble conduct.

All these demonstrations have excluded the Socialists from the National Assembly, and amongst the rest M. Cabet, though notoriously an advocate of peace and persuasion to a degree that made him a great many enemies. Against him, as the leader, vigorous attacks have been directed, and everyone being suspected of being favorable to Communism is exposed to threats and violence, especially in the provinces. The effect will be to drive numbers of them from their country, to escape such blind fury.[57]

This describes the situation in a nutshell. Cabet, really persecuted now, defeated at the polls, and seeing the cause of not only communism but also democracy evaporate, once again began to take up the emigration idea seriously.

Perhaps the fundamental problem for Cabet and his party was that he became identified, in the minds of his persecutors, with the advocates of force. His strong stand on the National Guard was probably a factor in this identification, but the major reason (beyond sheer malicious misrepresentation) was his connection with the archrevolutionary of the nineteenth century, Auguste Blanqui. Although Cabet excommunicated his followers at Tours who had apparently become involved with Blanqui in 1846, he nevertheless held the latter in high esteem. Our source is again Martin Nadaud. He was in the Creuse campaigning for the April 1848 elections when word of the Taschereau document reached him; he immediately defended Blanqui before a public meeting because "I remembered that I had heard Citizen Cabet speak of [him] in a completely favorable manner."[58] The two had also collaborated on March 17, even though Cabet took a more moderate stand than did Blanqui. But the surest indication of their connection, especially in

[57] "Anti-Communist Demonstrations," *The Reasoner,* May 7, 1848.
[58] Nadaud to Blanqui, July 31, 1850, MSS. Blanqui, Bibliothèque Nationale.

the public mind, was the aid Cabet rendered Blanqui after the publication of the Taschereau document which implied that Blanqui
had been an informer in 1839. It was published in the *Revue
rétrospective* on April 1. Cabet showed his disbelief in the document immediately after its publication and on April 5 was chosen
to serve on a board of inquiry organized by the Club des clubs. He
then agreed to accompany Blanqui as a witness on a visit to Durrieu, editor of the moderate republican *Courrier français,* on April
14. At that point the anticommunist storm was already of significant proportions. The following day, fully knowing how impolitic it
was to do so, Cabet published what may have been the crucial fact
exonerating Blanqui but was also the one that made Cabet his leading defender in France. Cabet said, in *Le Représentant du peuple*
(*Le Populaire* did not appear on that day): "I declare that, Citizen
Blanqui having asked me to accompany him to Citizen Durrieu's,
I consented without hesitation, and that Citizen Durrieu recognized
that he had proposed to Citizen Blanqui that he meet with Citizen
Lamartine at the latter's place and with Citizen Ledru-Rollin at his
on the evening of March 31 and that these two interviews were
proposed by Citizens Lamartine and Ledru-Rollin."[59] This meant
that these two gentlemen knew about the document and intended
to use it to control Blanqui. It is not our place to argue this question, but one thing is clear: Cabet had just carried out the most
noble and selfless act of his life. His aid would link him to Blanqui
and in all likelihood explode whatever chances he had of with-
standing the growing anticommunist drive. He went ahead anyway,
and as one views the aftermath, this event was clearly the catalyst
that destroyed forever the hope of building Icaria in France.

The denouement was rapid. On April 16, Cabet was observed
riding a white horse beside Blanqui (in reality he was nowhere in
sight); that night his house, where his wife and daughter crouched
in terror, was besieged by screaming members of the National
Guard. The lives of Icarians were threatened on the streets. Louis
Ménard described the scene in the days that followed, the days just
before the elections: "The furor against the communists did not
stop on the evening of the sixteenth; for several days, Paris was
prey to a veritable terror. One no longer dared to speak of social-

---

[59] Quoted in M. Dommanget, *Blanqui colomnié: Une Drame politique en
1848* (Paris, 1948), 85.

ism, nor even of the organization of work, in the streets; a large number of citizens were mistreated and menaced with death for having defended even the principles of Louis Blanc before the National Guard."[60] As for the *chef des communistes*, his life was a veritable hell during those days. He could only return to his home on April 18, and still the streets rang with cries for his head. Then, two days before the election, he was removed from the two major electoral lists of the democratic and socialist left, those of the Club des clubs (where Ledru-Rollin's influence was paramount) and the Luxembourg Commission. Moreover, an official "Bulletin de la République," issued by Ledru-Rollin, warned against voting for the "communists," who are "enemies of the Republic." The outcome could not be doubted; neither Cabet nor any of the other renowned socialists (save Blanc and Albert) would sit in the national assembly.[61] And so, one week later, speaking before the Société

---

[60] *Prologue,* 80–81.

[61] On these events see *Le Populaire,* March 23–April 27, 1848; Angrand, *Cabet,* 50–57; Garnier-Pagès, *Histoire,* 443ff; Ménard, *Prologue,* 79ff. Rumors circulated that Cabet himself, or Cabet and Blanqui, or Cabet and Raspail, planned to take over the government, or kill Lamartine, or institute the Terror, etc. Several brochures attacking communism circulated: L.-J.-G. Chénier (a descendant of the poet), *Avis au peuple français sur ses véritables ennemis* (Paris, n.d.); Guénée and Tandou, *Un Voyage en Icarie, vaudville en un acte* (Paris, 1848); Lamartine, *Lettre au Citoyen Cabet: Protestation contre le communisme* (Paris, 1848); Gandon, shoemaker, *Réfutation du communisme* (Batagnoles, 1848). Examples of pure red-baiting are: Anon., *La Cabétise, ou Voyage en Ignarie* (Paris, [1848]); J. P. Schmidt, *Du Pain, du travail et la vérité* (Paris, 1848); and D. A., *Lamartine, président de la République* (Paris, [April 1848]). Among the pamphlets in which candidates for election disclaimed any connection with communism are: Victor Considérant, *Aux Habitants du département du Loiret* (Paris, April 8, 1848), where he reminds the world that the Fourierists defended property and had always opposed Cabet; and F. Grille, *Pamphlets électoraux: no. 4* (Angers, [March 1848]), wherein the author claims that he, as a "democrat, would rather have kings than communism." Most of the foregoing are to be found in the magnificient collection of 1848 materials at the BHVP (Fonds Liesville). Other works opposing Cabet and his communism appeared in 1848 and 1849; three deserve particular mention because their length and the detailed manner in which they criticize Cabet indicate the importance that communism had taken on in the public eye: Ernest Merson, *Du Communisme: Réfutation de l'utopie icarienne* (Paris and Nantes, Aug. 1848), is a 370-page polemic; P. Nicholas Deschamps, *Un Éclair avant la foudre, ou le communisme et ses causes* (Avignon, 1848–49), a two volume diatribe, maintains the conservative Catholic position against communism; J. A. Mattabon, *Etudes socialistes: Du Communisme: Les Icariens* (Paris, 1849), is a serious critique of Icarian doctrine by a bourgeois democrat.

fraternelle centrale, he said quite bluntly: "We shall therefore occupy ourselves only with our emigration and, in order the better to prepare it . . . we will no longer have political discussion, but only discuss arrangements for the emigration."[62] Then came the accusations after May 15; again Cabet played no role. Finally, in one last attempt, he ran in the elections of June 4. Again defeat. This was the election that brought Leroux, Hugo, and Proudhon into the chamber (as well as Thiers and Louis-Napoleon). Cabet finished sixteenth, grouped with Thoré and Raspail, while only eleven were elected. His attitude toward the emigration was now definitive; he would "henceforth devote himself entirely to *Propaganda* in favor of the Icarian doctrines and to the continuation of our *Emigration*."[63]

Thus (again) the Icarians, persecuted in one city, would move on to another. On Cabet's instructions, the advance party had gone ahead into the wilderness beyond the Mississippi, even though the revolution had broken out, and was supposedly laying the foundations of Icaria in Texas. In fact, however, at the very moment when Cabet was announcing that the movement would abandon France, the advance party was confronting the brutal fact that their new nation was a vast wasteland of dust and sagebrush; several would die before the summer was out, dissension would break out among them, and Gouhenant, the leader, would be accused (unjustly) of having been paid by the government of the July Monarchy to undermine the entire project.[64] Cabet knew these facts by midsummer but did not communicate them to his following, thinking that somehow things could be worked out. (One can imagine that the news of the difficulties in Texas, coming on top of the tragic events of the revolution, must have brought him to the verge of insanity—the American project simply *had* to succeed.) Icarian faithfuls, thinking that all was going smoothly in Texas, now set their sights on escape. As Julian Lecerf, a Parisian worker, put it: "All the hopes that the revolution of February had awakened in me have fallen one by one. I had dared to hope that through truly democratic institutions, we could one day arrive at the realization

[62] *Dixième discours du Citoyen Cabet,* 12.
[63] *Le Populaire,* June 8, 1848.
[64] See Prudhommeaux, *Cabet,* 232–35.

of Community in France." As it was, however, "only Icaria holds out any hope."[65]

While all Icarians would agree with the first part of Lecerf's statement, only a few of them actually focused their hopes upon the colony. In the summer and fall of 1848 the Icarian movement as such became a series of emigration offices, but the response to the new call of "Allons en Icarie" was a mere whisper. The movement had already been decimated by the persecution of April and May. The Icarians at Périgueux may be taken as an example. After the revolution broke out, "hundreds" of Icarians or Icarian sympathizers could be counted there, yet the communication sent by the Périgueux Icarians and printed on May 28 bore only sixteen signatures and explicitly stated that communism had been completely crushed by the reaction—"we can no longer stay here."[66] On May 2, Laty of Autun had written, "In the name of humanity, conserve yourself for the country and for the *small number of friends* who have remained faithful to you."[67] The new call for emigration found few takers. A list of those from Nantes willing to emigrate is poignant evidence of what had happened all over France; of the hundreds who had followed Cabet's banner during the forties, ten indicated in August 1848 that they would like to join the emigration.[68] Two departures took place in the later months of 1848, but they were quite small. Prudhommeaux clearly states that thereafter

it was necessary to renew constantly the appeals for funds and to entreat restive adherents unremittingly. Little by little, the truth appeared to all clearsighted minds: this Icarian movement, which in January 1848 seemed so consequential, was condemned to end as an *essai en miniature,* a sort of laboratory experiment not without interest to the historian but without a durable impact on social evolution.[69]

There can be no doubt that the Icarian communist movement in France died during the summer of 1848.

But the great persecution of April and May 1848 was not the

[65] Lecerf to Cabet, Aug. 22, 1848, Papiers Cabet, XIII, BHVP.
[66] *Le Populaire,* May 28, 1848.
[67] Laty to Cabet, May 2, 1848, Papiers Cabet, XIII, BHVP, (my italics).
[68] Pedron, the correspondent of *Le Populaire,* was not among them. Letter of Aug. 17, 1848, Papiers Cabet, IX, BHVP.
[69] Prudhommeaux, *Cabet,* 219.

real executioner. It was instead the pattern of thinking manifested
in the new decision to escape. All that this amounted to was a
revival of the same set of variables and questions that had been
involved in the original call. At the very heart of the matter was
Cabet's position with regard to the problem of class antagonism.
Although he had been a staunch defender of the rights and interests
of the workers in the early months of the revolution, we have seen
that he and his followers did everything they could to keep order
and would not abandon their passivity. Although Cabet, from a
very early date, excoriated the bourgeois for betraying the revolution made by the workers, he continued to preach the brotherhood
of all Frenchmen and hoped that the class antagonism that he
recognized could be overcome. In short, he refused to give up the
possibility of class collaboration. His alternative in 1848, as in
1846–1847, was to opt fully for working-class exclusivism and
working-class revolutionary action against the bourgeois, or, in
other words, really to join his forces with those of Blanqui. But he
went into hiding on April 16 and May 15 and carefully explained
(*Le Populaire,* April 16, 1848) that tactically he had nothing in
common with Blanqui. Given his outlook, escape could be the only
answer after these events. Most of his followers would not escape
with him. Instead they turned to other endeavors, particularly, as
we shall see, involvement in worker's cooperatives. But they could
also do something else; they could fight.

The June Days stand as the great watershed between collabora-
tionism and exclusivism. Whatever the real nature of the warfare
of June,[70] in the mind of the French working class the horrors of
those days and the recriminations that followed made the breach
between the bourgeoisie and the proletariat seem irreparable. Let
us first assess Cabet's view of the situation. Once again, he was not
in any way involved in the hostilities; in fact, he was probably in
the Midi trying to rally support for the emigration when the insurrection broke out on June 23.[71] But he understood the significance

[70] Rémi Gossez argues convincingly that Marx's bourgeois-proletarian
confrontation was an oversimplification; "Diversités des antagonismes sociaux vers de milieu du XIXe siècle," *Revue économique,* VII (1956), 439–
457.

[71] Cabet was arrested, however, on the basis of allegations to the contrary.
A report from the Prefect of Police to the Minister of the Interior, drawn

of the uprising. In an excellent brochure on the revolt Cabet fully acknowledged the reality of class antagonism and predicted that, without amnesty, "social war" would become endemic in France. But note his phraseology: "If you remain in the way of hatred and vengeance, there will be hatred and vengeance everywhere, being provoked and growing each day. . . . Will this not be a perpetual state of war?"[72] Somehow he still felt that class hatred could be buried by an act of will, and the general aim of the brochure was to plead for amnesty lest class war become the dominant social reality. Cabet could not disabuse himself of the notion that class antagonism could only lead to anarchy. Nevertheless, he had not misread the history of the revolution of 1848. The June Days were the result of the failure of the bourgeois-dominated government to develop a strong policy of social amelioration. "It is the Government, it is *Le National,* it is *La Réforme,* it is especially Ledru-Rollin and Lamartine, who have ruined everything."[73]

But did responsibility for the unhappy evolution of 1848 rest fully in the hands of two-faced bourgeois democrats? The glow of unity that characterized the month of March, the working-class generosity and noncombativeness, the wait-and-see attitude, drew a great deal from Icarian doctrines of legalism, pacifism, and civil courage. The strongest statement of this opinion was made by Pierre Leroux (although he felt that this influence was beneficent):

Who, in '48 did more good than Cabet?
To whom does one owe it?
To Etienne Cabet more than any other person.

---

from a note from the subprefect at Bar-sur-Seine, stated that a veterinarian named Martin testified that he rode with Cabet in a diligence headed for Paris on June 22. Cabet was alleged to have told him that he was "impatiently awaited" in Paris. Furthermore, one Mme Loisel claimed that she saw Cabet during the insurrection in the rue des Gravilliers (Quartier Feydeau) telling several workers gathered around him that "if they did not succeed today, they would succeed later." This report is located among the documents relating to the investigations of the insurrections of May 15 and June 23–26 in the Archives de la Ministère de la Guerre (dos 3753) (Vincennes). Similar sightings of Cabet had of course been reported on April 16 and May 15; the tribunal believed Cabet's assertion that he was in Marseilles during the insurrection and threw out the accusation.

[72] Cabet, *Insurrection du 23 juin avec ses causes, son caractère et ses suites, expliquée par la marche et les fautes de la Révolution du 24 février* (Paris, 1848), 17–18.
[73] *Ibid.,* 25.

It was us; and, at the beginning, it was principally Cabet, because he was in intimate rapport with the working classes. It was Cabet who, having made the consoling and pacifying idea of a fraternal society glow in the eyes of the Masses, made the singular idea of a revolution of the guillotine and the scaffold, the sword and the gun, odious to them.[74]

Leroux lauded Cabet for saving the revolution from turning to carnage, for instilling in the workers a sense of probity and respect for the ideal of the brotherhood of all men. But did the Icarian chief spare the revolution from the agony of June, when the workers, reaching the limits of this probity, fought an essentially defensive battle in disorganized desperation, a battle that they had little chance of winning? If we accept Leroux's assessment of the extent of Cabet's influence, what the balm of his rhetoric really did was to contribute to the probability that the revolution would indeed be conjured away by the bourgeoisie. When the revolution broke out, a large number of those under his influence were still dreaming of the never-never land across the seas, and most of those who involved themselves in the developing revolution, as we have seen, were working among their fellow laborers to keep them from striking out against their exploiters. Cabet the endormeur bade the people rest when the situation demanded a revolutionary readiness, a militant vigilance, on the part of the working class. Although the wealth of the bourgeoisie and the sheer weight of rural France might still have precluded any meaningful working-class gains, Cabet's inability to surmount his reservations about the use of force—despite developments in his own thinking that pointed in this direction—both before and at the inception of the revolution made its reactionary outcome all the more likely.

Georges Duveau has left us this hypothetical picture of the evolution of the Icarian mind in 1848:

Thus, in forty-eight, our cabinetmaker did not begrudge his confidence in the Provisional Government, for he was convinced that in a trice Lamartine, Marrast, Louis Blanc, and Marie were going to construct an Icaria. But when he saw his comrades nonchalantly pushing a few wheelbarrows on the Champs-de-Mars, his dream took a more disabused turn. He believed, not without reason, in hostile, mysterious

[74] *La Grève de Samarez*, II, 377–78.

machinations in the heart of the government; he said to himself that the *manière forte* would be without doubt preferable to the ingenuous abandon that he showed in February. He rereads Buonarroti, and thus June is brewing.[75]

June was too late, however. A willingness among the Icarians to use the *manière forte* was necessary before the revolution, and certainly from its inception, if concrete benefits for the workers were to result. Etienne Cabet, perhaps more than any other man, had been in a position to create the strength of conviction, based on a readiness to fight, to force a positive solution to the social question in France. Instead, he had chosen first to flee and then, when the revolution occurred, to remain firmly in the mold of pacifism.

Is there any justification for this seeming failure on Cabet's part? Perhaps. More recent history has taught us to be wary of the belief that there does not exist an intimate connection between means and end. Can the good and the perfect issue from violence and destruction? Must not the means place an indelible imprint on the end? Cabet never really put it quite this way, but one of his adherents, J. Moreau, a Parisian worker, was aware of the problem; his simple language traverses a century of disappointment with the fruits of revolutionary violence and bears the essence of the utopian message. His words appeared in *Le Populaire* of October 31, 1847: "The convinced communist is horrified by destruction, and it is a strange contradiction to want to establish the good with the help of the bad. . . . [It] is always dangerous to employ violence to make reason triumph, because a man beaten is not a man convinced. I have a horror of blood; I believe that man has as his mission to build and not to destroy." He, therefore, would emigrate with Cabet. But while this may have been an intelligent and moving justification of Cabet's decision, it still begged the question. When pacific propaganda reached a dead end, and when escape was blocked by the absence of viable avenues, men had no choice but to reread Buonarroti and to be satisfied if something less than the good and the perfect—or, as Moreau would have it, reason—resulted.

[75] Duveau, *1848*, 232.

Epilogue and Conclusion

By the time Cabet sailed for New York, en route to New Orleans, on December 3, 1848, the Icarian movement had, for all practical purposes, ceased to exist in France. Small islands of Icarian faithfuls remained, but they focused exclusively upon the progress of the colony. It even appears that most of those who originally came to Cabet because of the emigration plan had also given up the Icarian cause. Le Havre, for example, did not experience the growth of a significant Icarian element until 1847, but by late 1848 Debut, Cabet's agent there, had to write: "I am today very unhappy with regard to the subscriptions and renewals. Some people have gone off one knows not where, while others claim that they are not making a sou and the 2 francs per month subscriptions trouble them too much at the present time." Out of eight subscribers recently contacted, only one, M. Grasz, had agreed to renew.[1]

After Cabet left to join his stricken adherents, huddled in New Orleans following the disasters of the Texas expedition,[2] *Le Populaire,* although it carried many articles sent in by Cabet and news of the new start made by the Icarians at Nauvoo, Illinois, became much more eclectic in its doctrinal orientation under the editorship of Krolikowski and Wahry. Even when Cabet returned in 1850 (to defend himself in person against the multiple charges, made by disillusioned participants in the emigration, that had resulted in his conviction in absentia the previous year)[3] and took over the helm

[1] Debut to Cabet, Dec. 4, 1848, Papiers Cabet, XII, BHVP.
[2] See Prudhommeaux, *Cabet,* 220–38.
[3] See A.N., BB[18] 1473 dos 6817; Louis Bellet, *Confessions d'un commu-*

of his newspaper again, there was little of the old doctrinaire attitude. *Le Populaire* had become an organ of the "democratic and social Republic" rather than the mouthpiece of a sect. To emphasize his interest in allying himself with the entire socialist left, Cabet made an attempt in 1851 to create a paper under the direction of Louis Blanc, Pierre Leroux, and himself.[4] This endeavor failed, but Cabet nevertheless proceeded to try to erase the sectarian stigma associated with his name by suspending the operations of *Le Populaire* and creating a new organ, *Le Républicain populaire et social,* which ran from October 11 to November 29, 1851. The coup d'état of December 2 brought its publication to an end. Thus, as the Icarian following in France evaporated, Cabet—while still gérant of the Icarian colony—threw himself into a hopefully united struggle against the approaching dictatorship. To this end he published two letters to Louis-Napoleon in October and November 1851 entreating him to resign; "Instead of the maledictions of History, you could already hear the applause of posterity" by doing so.[5] The extent to which Cabet played a role in the agitation that followed the coup d'état is uncertain. He left France for England in the last week of December, but little is known about his activity before that time. The military investigation of the insurrections of December resulted in his indictment for having "taken part" in the Parisian demonstrations; he was, however, placed in the "second category" of the "less guilty" established by the investigators.[6] This indicated that his physical involvement in the events was unlikely.

The situation in the Icarian camp during the rest of the Second Republic can, therefore, be described as follows: The few individuals in France who remained loyal Icarians were totally preoccupied with the colony; the latter could now be described as nothing more

---

niste-icarien: *Simple récits* (Paris, 1849) (for an example of the charges presented); Cabet, *Notre Procès en escroquerie;* and Cabet, *Défense du citoyen Cabet accusé d'escroquerie devant la Cour d'Appel de Paris (11 déc. 1850)* (Paris, Jan. 1850).

[4] J. Prudhommeaux, "L'Opposition socialiste sous la présidence de Louis-Napoléon: Louis Blanc, Etienne Cabet, Pierre Leroux en 1851," *La Révolution de 1848,* VI (1909–10) 68–69.

[5] Cabet, *Curieuse Lettre du citoyen Cabet à Louis-Napoléon* (Paris, Oct. 21, 1851), and *Deuxieme Lettre à Louis-Napoléon* (Paris, Nov. 2, 1851).

[6] Archives de la Ministère de la Guerre, "Insurrection de décembre 1851," dos 661.

than an experiment; and Cabet himself, after setting up the colony at Nauvoo, had returned to France in 1850 and progressively de-emphasized his role as a sectarian leader, joining instead the broader battle against Louis-Napoleon. This orientation may have amounted to a tacit recognition that Icarianism was now to be found only in the colonial endeavor, that the possibilities of a movement in France were gone forever. Simultaneously, it also showed that Cabet's older political strategy still animated his thoughts.

During the following decade the Icarian sect lived on in France but, as in the later years of the Republic, its membership was small and its eyes were fixed on America. J.-P. Beluze, who, after the death of Favard in 1847, emerged as Cabet's chief assistant among the workers in his inner circle, headed Icarian recruitment and fund-raising efforts in France during the first half of the Second Empire. A report by the procureur-général of Paris in 1858 tells us about the state of the Icarian group in France by that time.

It is learned from the information transmitted by M. le Préfet de Police on the Icarian society that the said Beluze is the principal agent of this society. At the death of Sr Cabet, he was confirmed by the community in his functions as mandatary, and the commission was maintained. This commission is composed of Mme Cabet, her daughter, and the said Beluze, who is seconded in some circumstances by two other Icarians in Paris.

The said Beluze has published, each month, as did Sr Cabet, a bro-chure addressed to the Icarians containing either appeals for funds or news relative to the Saint-Louis community.[7]

The said Beluze collects subscriptions [of money] destined to keep the little colony established in America alive. To this end, he maintains a steady stream of correspondence either with those rare adherents who still have faith in the theories of Cabet or with the members of the colony who constantly ask for financial aid and appeal to the brothers of the mother country.[8]

[7] Late in 1855, Cabet was dethroned as director of the Nauvoo colony and led those followers who remained loyal to him to Saint Louis. He died there on November 8, 1856 (because of apoplexy allegedly brought on when he was served the wrong food for breakfast by an unwitting chambermaid), before he had been able to organize his group effectively. The Nauvoo colony, relieved of Cabet's tyranny, lived on until the 1880s.

[8] A.N., BB^{30} 421 dos 1619P. For similar reports see A.N., BB^{30} 413 dos 1242P, 416 dos 1329P, 416 dos 1342P, 416 dos 1346P, 418 dos 1452P, 420 dos 1563P.

Cabet's Heritage

If the tiny cadres of Icarians after 1848 had no significance in the history of the French working-class movement, can we therefore conclude that Cabet's efforts ended ultimately in total failure? Was Icarian communism thus without historical consequence beyond a few struggling experimental communities in the plains of the United States?

Answers to these questions may be pursued by asking two more. First, in what directions did the majority of those Icarians who dissolved their ties with the Icarian cause move in 1848 and after? Second, how did Cabet serve to shape the history of the times during which Icarian communism made its deepest impact?

After the dream of a French Icaria was smashed in April and May of 1848, those Icarians who refused to follow Cabet's resurrection of the emigration scheme were faced with two major alternatives. If they felt that political means remained the only way to effect the transformation they desired, they would indeed have had to "reread Buonarroti," to raise the cry of armed revolution. Otherwise, they would have had to abandon the political arena altogether and apply themselves to economic association—in the realms of trade-union activity and cooperation. To follow either line meant rejecting a central tenet of Cabet's doctrine, even though considerable justification for either could also be found in his writings. On one hand, no one could forget Cabet's plea of "point d'indifference politique": the ultimate triumph of Community was a political question. Yet on the other hand, the ideal of fraternity, brotherhood, and solidarity could be realized through economic association. So it was that Icarians branched out in both directions although the latter, with its essentially pacific means, seems to have captured most of them. But Icarians were not alone in this regard. The defeat of the June Days caused a broad move toward economic action. The conscious worker in France felt frustrated with political activity of any sort but clearly recognized that collaboration with the bourgeoisie was a delusion. It was natural, therefore, that economic association, undertaken exclusively by the workers themselves, should follow; this course was further stimulated by the heavy restrictions placed on political organization by the government in July.[9]

[9] See Rémi Gossez, "L'Organization ouvrière á Paris sous la Seconde Ré-

We know of several instances of Icarian involvement in trade-union or cooperative activity. In August and September of 1848 a great strike among the workers in the woolens industry at Vienne developed when the municipality drastically reduced the number of men employed by the communal workshops. The excess supply of labor stimulated downward pressure on wages in the private sector. Although the municipal authorities perhaps overemphasized communist responsibility for the strike that unfolded after August 28, there can be no doubt that the Icarian weaver, Gagnière, was one of the most important leaders in the movement.[10] Although solidarity among the workers broke down in late September, the strike was by no means a total failure, for the "January minimum," a very low wage scale, was not reimposed by the employers. It would appear, then, that Icarians were at the forefront of the syndicalist movement at Vienne.[11] Although information is lacking, it is not unlikely that similar developments took place elsewhere.

But it was in the area of cooperation that the Icarian heritage was most strongly felt. Jean Gaumont gives heavy emphasis to this fact.[12] Worker cooperatives were hardly new phenomena in 1848. Gaumont argues convincingly that many cooperative experiments had been launched in France well before the attempt by the English Roachdale Pioneers in 1837. The first producers' cooperative motivated by communist principles, the Compagnie des industries-unies, was born in Paris in November 1845 under the direction of "Raisant and other well-known communists." The Prefect of Police of the Seine was convinced that the principal ideology animating these workers was that of Pierre Leroux. The company quickly established provincial connections, especially with a group in Lyons under Guillermain and Sauvant, who were also

---

publique," *1848 et les Révolutions du XIXe siècle*, XLI (1949), 31–45, and Gossez, *Les Ouvriers de Paris*.

[10] Rude, "L'Arrondissement de Vienne," 398ff.

[11] It is also true, however, that in no other city in France was the sectarian Icarian movement so strong; both Cöeffé and Ravat, as well as a number of lesser figures, would emigrate to Nauvoo. Moreover, Crétinon, an Icarian printer from Vienne, has left us one of the major sources on the history of the American community. See Rude, ed., *Voyage en Icarie: Deux ouvriers viennois aux Etats-unis en 1855*, 93ff.

[12] *Histoire générale de la coopération*, I, and *Le Mouvement ouvrier d'association et de la coopération à Lyon* (Lyons, n.d.).

labelled communists.[13] Aside from knowing that Frédéric Garçon was a member in Lyons, we are ignorant of Icarian involvement in this enterprise; but in view of the friendship and doctrinal affinity between Leroux and Cabet it seems probable that other Icarians, especially at Lyons where slavish devotion to Cabet personally was not very strong, associated themselves.[14] Moreover, at about the same time, an Icarian of Grenoble named Gavard wrote Cabet about a project that he had conceived to form a nation-wide workers' cooperative of consumption and production, sure evidence that cooperative ideas were already stirring in the minds of Cabet's adherents before the revolution.[15] But the post-June 1848 cooperative movement was replete with Icarian participation. Pierre Wahry was instrumental in creating the Parisian organization known as Union essénienne, whose aim was the universal and fraternal association of all workers through cooperatives. Although the trial of Jeanne Deroin's Union des Associations ouvrières revealed no names of known (former) Icarians, Gaumont stresses the importance of Icarian ideals in that organization.[16] The Société de la Presse du Travail, although it hoped for the immediate establishment of "bazaars" (one sees the influence of Vidal here), went beyond cooperation as such in that it wished "to create, through the press, a veritable representation of workers in industry, the arts, and Science, or to say everything by the single word, work."[17] Auguste Desmoulins, its founder, made efforts to win Cabet's friendship and did so to the extent that the latter printed the program of the Presse du Travail in his *Almanach* for 1852.[18] The extent of Icarian participation in this project is uncertain, however. At Lyons, the involvement of former Icarians in the cooperative movement was quite heavy during the Second Republic. The Association fraternelle de l'industrie française was founded by former

---

[13] Reports of Oct. 31, 1846, and Jan. 28, 1847, A.N., BB[18] 1441 dos 2089A.

[14] Gaumont, without adducing any direct evidence, claims a strong Icarian influence in this organization from the beginning; *Histoire générale,* I, 224ff.

[15] Gavard (mécanicien) to Cabet, July 12, 1846, Papiers Cabet, XII, BHVP.

[16] Gaumont, *Histoire générale,* I, 264–65, and 276–77.

[17] Auguste Desmoulins to Cabet, Aug. 8, 1851, Papiers Cabet, IX, BHVP.

[18] *Almanach icarien pour 1852* (Paris, 1851), 171–74.

Icarians Barre, Razuret, Raffin, and Rémond in January 1849. The preamble to its constitution stated quite simply that "The February Revolution gave birth to hopes that have not been realized. The workers have thus had to seek a remedy to their ills by themselves; they have found it in association. . . . From it we await the moral transformation of man and the coming of fraternity. . . . The question is no longer political; it is industrial, it is social."[19] The same year, Razuret, along with Rémond and three others, founded a Société des travailleurs unis with the specific aim of eliminating "intermediaries and parasites" in the sale and exchange of tools used by the silk-weavers.[20] This society developed several subbranches, some of which included former Icarians; even André Poncet, a Cabetist loyalist at least until 1848, was involved in the direction of the Association des industries réunies. Furthermore, Chapius was one of the founders of a consumer's cooperative, which eventually had some 3,000 members, called the Société fraternelle des Castors.[21]

Perhaps the most important evidence of Icarian evolution toward cooperation is the history of J.-P. Beluze. In 1860 he broke with the Icarian cause in America, abandoning, in the words of Gaumont, "utopia for reality." He created and directed with considerable success until 1869 an organization called the Crédit du travail, the aim of which was to provide credit to workers desiring to set up consumers' and producers' cooperatives.[22] In 1863, Beluze published a brochure in which he laid out his justification for the plan. The most interesting aspect of this brochure is Beluze's attitude toward work. Cabet was not a worker and in fact seemed to view work as merely an unfortunate necessity. For Beluze, however, work constituted the principal basis for human fulfillment; "Work is the Source of independence and of liberty in man."[23] But only in the framework of fraternal cooperation can this liberty flourish. Beluze, along with the bulk of the Icarians who went into cooperation did not, however, break with Cabet in one

[19] Quoted in Gaumont, *Histoire générale*, I, 384.
[20] Razuret, *et al.*, *Société des travailleurs-unis: Utensiles de fabrique* (Lyons, 1850); Gaumont, *Le Mouvement ouvrier*, 29ff.
[21] Gaumont, *Le Mouvement ouvrier*, 34, 36–37.
[22] See Gaumont, *Histoire générale*, I, 460ff.
[23] Beluze, *Les Associations, conséquences du progrès: Crédit du travail* (Paris, 1863), 20.

essential respect; the ultimate aim was still the total transformation of society. Unlike the Roachdale Pioneers, they did not for an instant wish to compromise with a society based on laissez-faire. And their means would have to be slow and pacific; no great cataclysm could bring about the new world of social justice they sought. We confront here a spirit in the French working class going beyond the framework of cooperation, one that was to merge with the evolutionary socialism of Jaurès and others at the turn of the century. There can be little doubt that Cabet contributed significantly to this broader tradition.

Yet Cabet must also figure among the precursors of the revolutionary socialist tradition as well. Despite their leader's reluctance to view the class struggle as a positive historical force, some French Icarians drew revolutionary conclusions from Cabet's doctrine, particularly after his conflict with *La Réforme*. In 1848 Cabet himself became a revolutionary, even though he refused to take the stance of militant vigilance promoted by the Blanquists. Some Icarians, however, such as Charre of Vienne, joined the Blanquists before the elections. What evidence exists concerning the movement of Icarians toward revolutionary politics after the collapse of the Icarian movement in May? Although Duveau hypothesized that the *manière forte* grew in their hearts as the June Days approached, we are currently ignorant of Icarian participation in this bloody conflict. Cabet did not mention their involvement in either *Le Populaire* or the *Insurrection du 23 juin,* but this does not mean much. We do know that the Icarians of Mirecourt greeted the uprising with great enthusiasm and hoped for a new outburst after it was suppressed.[24] It is quite clear, too, that some former Icarians participated in revolutionary activity as the Republic marched toward reaction. Paul Guay of Niort was arrested after the coup d'état and condemned to transportation to Algeria. He was described as "one of the most active instigators" of the troubles at Niort on December 3, 1851.[25] At Reims, Etienne Gandon, shoe-

---

[24] *Rapport de la Commission d'enquête sur l'insurrection qui a éclaté dans la journée du juin 23 et sur les événements du 15 mai* (Paris, 1849), III, 171.

[25] *Dict. biog.,* II, 308. Razuret was also arrested at Lyons, but the authorities "found nothing that attached him to a plot against the safety of the state"; Archives municipales de Lyon, I² 54, Bibliothèque municipale de Lyon.

maker, Nicholas Fourcart, weaver, and Jean-Louis Guérin, carder, all former Icarians, were also deported to Algeria after the coup d'état.[26] By far the most interesting case involving an Icarian, however, was that of another Rémois, Génin, the man who wrote Cabet in 1848 of his innocence after his conviction for attacks on property at the beginning of the revolution. Out of work after his release from prison, he came to Paris and joined the garde mobile; he was in Reims, however, during the June Days. Shortly thereafter he was associated with Agothon Bressy, who became the most influential figure in the working-class movement in Reims from the latter part of 1848 until the coup d'état. Bressy combined socialist agitation with a truly remarkable effort to organize the Rémois workers into a grand cross-craft union. He founded a newspaper called *L'Association rémoise,* of which 204 issues appeared between January 7, 1849, and June 6, 1850. Although Bressy also drew from Buchez, Proudhon, and the Fourierists in forming his basic outlook, Gustave Laurent claims that he had relations with Marx and "studied and spread his doctrine."Génin's close relationship with this man indicates that the Icarian experience may well have been, for many French workingmen, like some of their German brethren, a fundamental step on the way to an outlook that would ultimately embrace Marxism.[27]

The broader question of the general role of Cabet and Icarian communism in the awakening of the consciousness of the French working class is thus posed. There can be little doubt that Cabet exercised a more profound influence on the workers of France than any other writer in the pre-1848 period. Perhaps Louis Blanc was better known in Paris, but beyond the capital Icarian communist doctrine surely outstripped all others in influence. In certain towns

[26] "Parquet de Reims: Les Proscriptions à Reims après le coup d'état: Requisitoire définitif," Dossier Courmeaux (unnumbered MSS), Bibliothèque municipale de Reims.

[27] We know that Génin was in Bressy's inner circle from the fact that he was arrested with Bressy at Mezières on suspicion of having attempted to incite insurrections in the Marne after the Parisian uprising of June 13, 1849. See *L'Association rémoise,* June 24, 1849, Cabinet de Reims, V, 1215, Bibliothèque municipale de Reims. The author of the entry on Bressy in the *Dict. biog.* (I, 298–301) is not convinced of his connections with Marx. Nevertheless, Bressy's program, stressing total organization and combination of economic and political action with working-class revolution as the long-range goal, certainly has Marxist overtones.

Cabet's communism was the first socialist ideology to make its way into the minds of the workers. That Cabet and the specific content of Icarianism itself were soon forgotten after the disasters of 1848 is evident. But no historian can ignore the fact that this man, ridiculous as many of his ideas might seem, and disagreeable as his personality may have been, formed the first large communist working-class "party" in European history and presented the communist idea for the first time to many willing listeners outside the confines of his direct following. But beyond the question of communism as such, Cabet did something else; he told the workers to emerge from their shell of apathy, to be conscious of their importance in society, and to recognize that through their collective action change could be wrought. And this change would be brought about through political involvement. In attacking secret societies, Cabet contributed significantly to the maturation of those militants already politically aware. His most eloquent appeal to the workingman in the name of political engagement had permanent meaning: "To remain indifferent to politics is to put one's condition in the hands of others, of the Parties; it is to deliver oneself to the torrent, to hazard; it is to accept dictatorship, the domination by Democracy as by Aristocracy; it is to make oneself a slave, a sheep, a brute; it is to be without a sense of one's personal interests, and guilty of ignoring the general interest when one could so easily serve it."[28]

Striking as this contribution may have been, however, Cabet personally vacillated between direct political engagement and a policy of utopia in which truth was more important than limited progress. In this complex figure we glimpse the frustrating contradictions that agitated the awakening of popular democracy in Europe. Short-range political action (the drive for universal suffrage, for social legislation of various kinds, for reforms within the system), had to be undertaken, but participation by workingmen with little experience or historical knowledge but a continuing sense of deference was likely to be limited and unenthusiastic unless they had a specific idea of the kind of society they might ultimately hope to create. *Voyage en Icarie, Le Vrai Christianisme,* and even the emigration proposal were of crucial significance, therefore, in providing this concrete vision of a new world. There would have been

[28] Cabet, *Ma Ligne droite,* 26.

no Icarian movement without the utopian plan. But neither would it have taken on the dimensions it did without the other Cabet, the propagandist and political activist. Cabet, however, found it personally impossible to harmonize his utopian dream, and his tactics for realizing it, with the political realities that he confronted on a day-to-day basis.

But working-class Icarians were not necessarily bound, as he was, to one *ligne droite*. They had no particular psychic investment either in the absolute truth of his "system" or in his means of reaching it. In analyzing what happened to Icarians in 1848 and after, it is clear that the heritage of Cabet in France was not in the realm of utopian experimentation but in concrete political and economic action carried out by self-interested workingmen. But would those workingmen have arrived at that point if the dream of Icaria had not previously captured their imagination? I think not. Thus, in a Mannheimian sense, utopia had provided a glimpse of a radically different form of social life; but for those who yearned for it, it could only be a distant symbol. The bulk of Icarians faced the realities of the here and now and struggled in the arena of contemporary society. More for them than for their leader, theory was brought into relative consonance with practice. This does not mean that Cabet was simply left behind by his followers. For he had, after all, provided the example. The entire life of this utopian, from the days of the Charbonnerie to the attempts to counteract the new Napoleonic dictatorship, revealed his practical side. Cabet the utopian was also Cabet the man of action. Because of this he broke the barrier that kept Fourierism and Saint-Simonism in the rarefied atmosphere of intellectual diletantism, at least so long as these doctrines remained unified wholes.

One comes away from a study of Icarianism with two fundamental impressions. The first is that great care must be exercised in drawing conclusions about the nature of a "mentality" or, more broadly, the spirit of an age, from a simple examination of thought. If Etienne Cabet's doctrinal works are read in isolation they not only reveal his utopian mentality but in fact make him appear as a utopian archetype. One is led to place him in the vanguard of the "political Messiahs," of the totalitarian democrats of the first half of the nineteenth century. Yet such categorization breaks down when the full scope of Cabet's life and his practical activity are brought into the picture. This is not to say that the latter is the "real" Cabet, because the utopian and totalitarian democrat were also there. But surely Amédée Dunois was right; the "Cabet who counts for history is the Cabet of the years before 1848, the founder and leader of one of the first proletarian groupings, of a veritable workers' party."

This leads to the second point. What occurred as Cabet's thought and action were digested by distraught laboring men in the forty-eight era? They extracted from the utopian Cabet only the vision of what society might be like, while generally rejecting both the antidemocratic and experimentalist strains of his developing thought. His counsel against conspiracies was almost universally accepted, and his attitudes regarding mass politics and mass revolution found widespread sympathy. His general outlook was thus ordered and pruned by a majority of his followers to suit their conception of reality. The Icarian experience, in short, should evoke a feeling of genuine confidence, even during a traumatic era of modernizing transition, in the political intelligence of the masses and in popular democracy, a democracy unmodified by any other adjective.

There can be no question that utopian socialism played an extraordinary role in the emergence of working-class movements and democracy in Western Europe. But until we move away from the simplistic notions on the subject bequeathed to us by "orthodox" Marxists and their equally doctrinaire conservative and liberal antagonists and get down to a concrete examination of the mechanisms by which its influence was spread and the ways in which it penetrated the minds of working people, this role will remain unknown.

Icarian communism must thus be understood as a specific phase in the reaction of the working masses to the upheaval produced by political and economic modernization. In France it was the first mass movement to accept the total overthrow of the emerging capitalist society. But worker-artisan experience was insufficient for the movement to rid itself of traditional encumbrances. Beyond that, there existed no concrete analysis that might have served to replace the sectarian framework. Many of Cabet's own followers saw that sect and emigration amounted to a disastrous cul-de-sac and mistrusted class collaboration and pacifism. Yet, on the whole, as the early months of the revolution of 1848 were to show, the average French urban worker was generous and tended toward mysticism. He was, in other words, in tune with the general outlook motivating most Icarians. To what extent working-class attitudes in 1848 were influenced by Cabet and to what extent Icarianism reflected the larger spectrum are questions that are impossible to answer. Icarian communism was a product of its milieu. French society was in that amorphous stage of transition in which new class lines could not yet be clearly perceived. The Icarian movement was rooted in this fluid situation. Its shape and its nature bore the stamp of the confused interaction of two different societies, one traditional, the other industrial. The struggles of the Second Republic and the rapid industrialization of the Second Empire significantly undermined the hold of tradition on the French worker, and the Icarian phase in the growth of working-class consciousness—the phase of artisan sectarian communism—came to an end.

‖ *Appendix 1.* Locales of Icarian Strength

City	Correspondent	Other leading figures	Subscribers to *Le Populaire*	Signatures on addresses	Stated estimates and other indices	Sue medal contributors 1846
Paris (Seine)		Herman Ewerbeck Louis Krolikowski Firman Favard, tailor Charles Chameroy, traveling salesman L. V. Maillard, merchant Robillard, *marchand boulanger* Martin Nadaud, mason J.-P. Beluze, cabinet-maker	527 (6/44) 1030 (11/45) (*banlieu* incl.) 952 (8/46) (plus 86 in the *banlieu*)	no general address made	over 5000 at Soc. frat. cen. meetings in 1848	4220
Lyons (Rhône)	Chapius, chef d'atelier, then Faucon, tailor	André Poncet, chef d'atelier Gluntz, tailor J.-J. Razuret, chef d'atelier Frédéric Garçon, chef d'atelier	256 (8/46)*	553 (7/43) ⋯ 1300 (1/48)	5000 1000 (3/44)	830

* The date of this and all the following numbers of subscribers is August 28, 1846.

Appendix I (*continued*)

City	Correspondent	Other leading figures	Subscribers to *Le Populaire*	Signatures on addresses	Stated estimates and other indexes	Sue medal contributors 1846
Reims (Marne)	Eugéne Butot, weaver	Mauvais, *employé* Cazé, entertainer Constant	54	99 (7/47) 443 (1/48)	400–500 (12/47)	214
Vienne (Isère)	Vincent Cöeffé, shoe-form maker	Ravat Gagnière, weaver	62	72 (9/45) ⋯ 87 (2/46) ⋯ 200 (9/47) ⋯ 180 (1/48)	400–500 "for 300" 150 in promenade	200
Nantes (Loire-Inf.)	Pedron, tailor	Feydeau Buisson, shoemaker	94	98 (1/45)	*Le Populaire* "the organ of the workers" (12–44) 500–600 (10/45)	212
Périgueux (Dordogne)	Pépin, mirror-maker		54	21 (11/45) ⋯ 23 (4/46) 47 (1/48)	for 100 "rapid progress" (5/46)	50
Thiviers (Dordogne)	Dupuy, nail-maker		6	7 (4/46) ⋯	for 30	33

City (Department)	Leader(s)					
Angoulême (Charente)	Finet, merchant		9	15 (10/46)....	for 200 (?)	—
Niort (Deux-Sèvres)	Paul Guay, shoemaker		24	124 (11/45) 20 (1/48)	for "all"	29
Luçon (Vendée)	Poupineau, woodworker	Madeline, weaver	—	—	24 arrested in 1847	—
Tours (Indre-et-Loire)	Desmoulins, physician		26	48 (1/45) 103 (10/47) 150 (1/48) (incl. Amboise)		80
Toulouse (Hte. Garonne)	Perpignan, shoemaker; Jules Chéydès, merchant	Sagansan, woodworker; Adolphe Gouhenant, artist; Chrétien	136	49 (11/45) 68 (2/46) 180 (1/48)	for 300 some stagnation (10/46) for 1000 (?)	—
Toulon (Var)	Frayssée, locksmith	Adolphe Elléna, printer & writer	54	24 (3/46)....	for 500	186
Marseilles (Bouches-du-Rhône)	Coignard, shoemaker's tools salesman	Bonnafous	27	10 (2/46) 115 (8/47) 71 (1/48)	for 43	240

Appendix I (*continued*)

City	Correspondent	Other leading figures	Subscribers to *Le Populaire*	Signatures on addresses	Stated estimates and other indexes	Sue medal contributors 1846
Givors (Rhône)	Faure, municipal councilor & knifemaker(?)	Louis Marchand	24	26 (9/42) 49 (1/48) 57 (1/48)	"much progress" (4/46) for "many others"	150
Rive-de-Gier (Loire)	Boussac		16	48 (8/47)		42
Saint-Etienne (Loire)			—	68 (1/48)	"have finally come out of our lethargy"	
Mirecourt (Vosges)	Julien Chambry, organmaker	Lair	14 (?)	21 (9/45) 53 (1/48)		30
Autun (Saône-et-Loire)	Z. Laty, former merchant		21	203 (3/46)	for 500 500–600 Almanachs placed (1846)	69
Rouen (Seine-Inf.)	Caudron, shoemaker's tools salesman	Brunel, shoemaker's tools salesman Paumier, physician of Marcomme	61	19 (5/46)	"more than 100" (12/45) for "many others"	203

The above seem to have been the principal centers of Icarian influence. Others of some importance include Rennes (Ille-et-Vilaine), Bordeaux (Gironde), Grenoble (Isère), Nancy (Meurthe), Mulhouse (Haut-Rhin), Massevaux (Haut-Rhin), Pithiviers (Loiret), Le Mans (Sarthe), Falaise (Calvados), Le Havre (Seine-Inférieure), Saint-Quentin (Aisne), (Seine-et-Oise), Choisy-le-Roi (Seine), Louvriers (Eure), and Albi (Tarn).

Appendix 2. Icarian Occupations*

Workers
  Traditional Craft Industries
    Tailors—89
    Shoemakers—65
    Bootmakers—17
    Cabinetmakers—28†
    Hatters—13
    Locksmiths—11
    Jewelers—10
    Lathe operators (wood and bronze)—9
    Blacksmiths—4
    Coppersmiths—4
    Wheelwrights—3
    Barrelmakers—3
    Saddlemakers—3
    Cardmakers—3
    Nailmakers—3
    Glovers—3
    Trunkmakers—2
    Basketmakers—2
    Mirrormakers—2
    Clockmakers—2
    Tinsmiths—2
    Carriage builders—2
    Carriage painter—1
    Glass painter—1
    Leather dyer—1
    Knifemaker—1
    Edge-tool maker—1
    Brushmaker—1
    Cooper—1
    Netmaker—1
    Gaitermaker—1
    Soapmaker—1
    Pianomaker—1
    Shoe-form maker—1
    Gilder—1
  Textiles—46
    Weavers—36
    Chefs d'atelier (Lyons)—7
    Carder—1
    Serger—1
    Folder—1
  Book Trades—7
    Printers &
      Lithographers—4
    Bookbinders—3
  Building Trades
    Stonecutters—14
    Woodworkers—12
    Masons—3
    Carpenters—3
    Painters—3
    Sculptors—2
    Camberer(Cambreur)(?)—2
    Roofer—1
    Plasterer—1
  Food and Service Industries
    Gardeners—3
    Diligence drivers—3

Pastry cooks—2
Bakers—3
Launderers—2
Cook—1
Dairyman—1
Butcher—1
Pork butcher—1
Waiters—2
Barber—1
Dry cleaner—1
Chimney sweep—1
Modern Industry
Machinists—13
Founders—5
Spinners—2
Filemaker—1
Sugar refinery worker—1
Gasworks worker—1
Masters
Bootmaker—1
Plasterer—1
Stonecutter—1
Shopkeepers and Clerks
Clerks (*employés*)—5
Wine Shopkeepers—3
Grocers—2
Merchant baker—1
Florist—1
Stationer—1
Fruit seller—1
Adjuster—1

Draftsman—1
Contre-maître—1
Bourgeois
Commercial
Salesmen (unspecified)—4
Linen salesman—1
Leather-goods salesman—1
Charcoal salesman—1
Restauranteur—1
File manufacturers—2
Casket manufacturer—1
Hat manufacturer—1
Trunk manufacturer—1
Distillery owner—1
Cap manufacturer—1
Entrepreneur—1
Tradesmen of some importance (*négociants*)—3
Professional
Lawyers—4
Students—4
Physicians—3
Writers—3
Teachers—2
Artists—2
Teacher in barber school—1
Civil engineer—1
Pharmacist—1
Librarian—1
Entertainer—1
Rentier—1
Peasants (*cultivateurs*)—2

* For the relevant sources, see p. 154.
† This includes 16 ébénistes and 12 (assumed) menuisiers.

Bibliographical Note

This study is largely based on archival manuscript sources and contemporary brochures and newspapers, above all those written or edited by Cabet himself. The majority of these references are not listed in this note but have been cited in the footnotes. Moreover, the reader will find a full bibliography in my doctoral dissertation, "Etienne Cabet and the Icarian Movement in France, 1839–1848" (University of Wisconsin, 1968), which is available through University Microfilms. Discussion here is limited to key source materials and those secondary studies that I found particularly useful or provocative.

Manuscript Sources

There are two extant collections of Cabet papers: the Archief Cabet: Collectie Brieven en Manuscripten, 6049 (folio), 4 boxes, at the Internationaal Instituut voor Sociale Geschiedenis (Amsterdam); and the Papiers Cabet, série 25, 16 dossiers, Bibliothèque historique de la Ville de Paris. The first comprises materials turned over to Jules Prudhommeaux by J. P. Beluze, Cabet's son-in-law and lieutenant in France after the founding of the Nauvoo colony. Besides a large amount of material relating to the American communities (Prudhommeaux's main interest), it contains a number of important Cabet manuscripts, draft letters, newspaper clippings, and memorabilia from the 1830s. The forties are poorly represented save for Cabet's important exchange of letters with the Société démocratique française à Londres. The second, used in this study for the first time, seems to be all that remains of Cabet's vast correspondence of the 1840s. The approximately 200 letters from Icarians found here have naturally been among my most important sources, especially on the internal evolution of the movement. They are as close as we are likely to get to the Icarian mentality and provide a remarkable collection for the study of working-class attitudes during the first half of the nineteenth century.

With the exception of several personal papers consulted at the Bibliothèque Nationale (Paris) and the Bibliothèques municipals of Reims and Lyons, the rest of the manuscript sources utilized are public documents. As is always the case in studies of popular protest and organization during this period, the Justice records (BB[18] and BB[30]) preserved in the Archives Nationales de France are of importance. Of the thirty-three dossiers cited, the most useful were: BB[18] 1409 dos 6043 ("Affaire des communistes de Toulouse," 1843, 125 pièces); 1415 dos 7135 ("Voyage de Cabet à Lyon," 1843, 25 pièces); 1423 dos 8701 ("Voyage de Cabet à Lyon," 1844); 1441 dos 1992 ("Mouvement communiste dans divers ressorts," 1848–1847, 103 pièces); and 1472 dos 6733 ("Sociétés secrètes, 1832–1848"). Dossiers from other Archives Nationales series (especially F[17] [Instruction publique] 6674 dos Association libre pour l'éducation du peuple) help in reconstructing Cabet's activities in the early 1830s and add much to Prudhommeaux's assessment of these years. Some helpful material was also located at the Archives de la Prefecture de police (Paris) and the Archives historiques de la Guerre (Vincennes).

I had originally assumed that a considerable amount of information might be gleaned from municipal and departmental archives in centers of Icarian strength. But trips to Reims, Châlons-sur-Marne, Lyons, and Nantes proved less useful than expected in uncovering information going beyond what is available in Paris. Moreover, in reading both Fernand Rude's study of Vienne and Maurice Agulhon's on Toulon I realized that I had found as much or more information on the Icarian party (if not on socioeconomic conditions) in those localities in *Le Populaire* than they had in local archives. This does not mean that further local study would not be fruitful (Marty's study of the Toulouse trial is indicative), but one is forced to wonder whether it might not yield diminishing returns.

For the socioeconomic context of Icarian communism I have relied largely on secondary studies and published contemporary works. In the case of Niort, however, archival work has yielded a variety of illuminating materials. Special thanks are due the chief archivist of Deux-Sèvres, Maurice Bjai, for his assistance. The "Enquête sur le travail agricole et industriel" of 1848 (A.N. C 943–969) is also useful in evaluating socioeconomic conditions in several areas.

Printed Sources

A bibliography of Cabet's works may be found in Jules Prudhommeaux, *Icarie et son fondateur, Etienne Cabet* (Paris, 1907). Several additional citations, in particular the valuable *Lettres aux électeurs* of

1831, are recorded in the bibliography of my dissertion. The footnotes in this book indicate the range of contemporary brochures, articles, and newspapers that relate to the Icarian movement and its political, social, and economic background. My aim here is merely to indicate the most valuable sources.

Cabet's theoretical positions are made explicit in two of his major brochures of the early 1840s: *Ma Ligne droite, ou le vrai chemin du peuple* (Paris, 1841); and *Douze Lettres d'un communiste à un réformiste sur la communauté* (Paris, 1841–42). *Toute La Verité au peuple* (Paris, 1842) and *Les Masques arrachés* (Paris, 1844) are perhaps the most important brochures analyzing (from Cabet's point of view) the internal conflicts of the movement. But without question the single most important source is *Le Populaire de 1841,* 1841–1851 (Bibliothèque Nationale, Lc² 1360. This collection is complete save for May and June 1843; the latter may be found at the Bibliothèque de l'Arsenal [Paris]). The evolution of Cabet's substantive and tactical thought, the vicissitudes of the movement, the indices of Icarian influence within various occupations and localities, the polemical exchanges with other groups of reformers, and information on an endless variety of other questions are all to be found in this newspaper. This underlines the tremendous significance that the study of the press still retains in historical research. Other newspapers, such as *L'Atelier, La Fraternité de 1845, La Démocratie pacifique, Le Travail* (Lyons), *La Tribune lyonnaise, Le Journal de Reims, Le Républican de Reims* (1848), *L'Emancipation de Toulouse,* and *La Voix des clubs,* also played a notable role in this study. The *Almanach icarien,* 1843–1852, provided important information, a reminder of the potential significance of the many almanacs published during these years for the history of the popular classes.

The 1830s and 1840s seem to have been the age par excellence of the polemical and informational brochure. Besides the seventy-three separate brochures by Cabet used here, I have drawn information from another fifty-eight attacks on and defenses of Cabet and Icarianism. The harvest was uneven, but again the notes show the significance of such works. Several memoirs of the era contain important information, particularly those of Joseph Benoit, "Confessions d'un prolétaire" (1871) ms 302, Bibliothèque municipale de Lyon, Sébastien Commissaire, *Mémoires et souvenirs* (Paris and Lyons, 1888), and Martin Nadaud, *Mémoires de Léonard, garçon maçon* (Bourganeuf, 1894). Among a variety of other contemporary sources, some dealing with or published by other socialist or communist schools, others elucidating aspects of political, social, and economic change during the thirties and forties, the following bear special mention: A. Audiganne, *Les*

Populations ouvrières et les industries de la France, 2 vols. (Paris, 1860); Louis Blanc, *Histoire de dix ans,* 13th ed., 5 vols. (Paris, 1883); E. Regnault, *Histoire de huit ans,* 6th ed., 3 vols. (Paris, 1884); Chambre de Commerce de Paris, *Statistique de l'industrie de Paris résultant de l'enquête faite par la Chambre de Commerce pour 1847 et 1848* (Paris, 1851); Anthime Corbon, *Le Secret du peuple de Paris* (Paris, 1863); Théodore Dézamy *et al., Le Prémier Banquet communiste* (Paris, 1840); Pierre Leroux, *La Grève de Samarez,* 2 vols. (Paris, 1863–64); J. J. Pillot, *Ni Chateaux, ni chaumières* (Paris, 1840); Charles de Rémusat, *Mémoires de ma vie,* ed. Charles Pouthas (Paris, 1959); Flora Tristan, *Union ouvrière* (Paris, 1843); and L. R. Villermé, *Tableau de l'état physique et morale des ouvriers employés dans manufactures de coton, de laine et de soie,* 2 vols. (Paris, 1840).

Secondary Works of Major Importance

Cabet, Communism, and Socialism

Angrand, Pierre. *Etienne Cabet et la République de 1848.* Paris, 1948.
——. "Notes critiques sur la formation des idés communistes en France," *La Pensée,* no. 19 (1948), 38–46; no. 20 (1948), 58–67.
Bonnaud, Felix. *Cabet et son oeuvre: Appel à tous les socialistes.* Paris, 1900.
Buffenoir. "Le Communisme à Lyon de 1834 à 1848," *Revue d'histoire de Lyon,* Sept.–Oct., 1909, 347–61.
Charléty, Sébastien. *Histoire de Saint-Simonisme (1825–1864).* Paris, 1965.
Cuvillier, Armand. "Action ouvrière et communisme en France vers 1840 et aujourd'hui," *La Grande Revue,* Dec. 1921, 25–35.
——. *Hommes et idéologies de 1840.* Paris, 1956.
——. *Un Journal d'ouvriers: L'Atelier, 1840–1850.* Paris, 1954.
Dautry, Jean. "Le Pessimisme économique de Babeuf et l'histoire des utopies," *Annales historiques de la Révolution française,* April–June 1961, 215–33.
Dommanget, Maurice. *Blanqui calomnié: Une Drame politique en 1848.* Paris, 1948.
——. *Les Idées politiques et sociales d'Auguste Blanqui.* Paris, 1957.
Eisenstein, Elizabeth. *The First Professional Revolutionary: Filippo Michele Buonarroti.* Cambridge, Mass., 1958.
Evans, D. O. *Le Socialisme romantique: Pierre Leroux et ses contemporains.* Paris, 1948.
Faucheux, L., and L. Morauzeau. "Les Débuts du communisme en Vendée: L'Affaire Madeline," *Etudes: Bibliothèque de la Révolution de 1848,* XV (1953), 77–88.

Fotion, Janice. "Cabet and Icarian Communism." Unpublished Ph.D. Thesis, State University of Iowa, 1966.

Galante, Garonne, A. *Filippo Buonarroti e i rivoluzionari dell' otto-cento, 1828–1837.* Turin, 1951.

Garaudy, Roger. *Les Sources françaises du socialisme scientifique.* Paris, 1948.

Hammen, Oscar J. "1848 et 'le Spectre du Communisme, " *Le Contrat social,* II (1958), 191–200.

Holinski, A. "Cabet et les Icariens," *La Revue socialiste,* XIV (1891), 539–50, XV (1892), 40–49, 201–5, 315–21, 449–56, XVI (1893), 296–307.

Johnson, Christopher H. "Communism and the Working Class before Marx: The Icarian Experience," *American Historical Review,* 76 (1971), 642–89.

———. "Etienne Cabet and the Problem of Class Antagonism," *International Review of Social History* XI (1966), 403–43.

Lehning, Arthur. "Buonarroti's Ideas on Communism and Dictator-ship," *International Review of Social History,* II (1957), 266–87.

Loubère, Leo. *Louis Blanc: His Life and His Contribution to the Rise of Jacobin Socialism.* Evanston, Ill., 1961.

Manuel, Frank. *The New World of Henri de Saint-Simon.* South Bend, Ind., 1963.

———. *The Prophets of Paris.* Cambridge, Mass., 1962.

Prudhommeaux, Jules. *Icarie et son fondateur Etienne Cabet.* Paris, 1907. 2d ed., Paris, 1927.

Puech, Jules. *La Vie et l'oeuvre de Flora Tristan.* Paris, 1925.

Ramm, Thilo. *Die grossen Sozialisten als Rechts- und Sozial philo-sophen.* Vol. I, Stuttgart, 1955.

Ranvier, A. "Une Féministe de 1848, Jeanne Deroin," *La Révolution de 1848,* IV (1907–08), 317–55; V (1908–09), 421–30, 480–98.

Rude, Fernand, ed. *Voyage en Icarie: Deux ouvriers viennois aux États-unis en 1855.* Paris, 1956.

Shaw, Albert. *Icaria, a Chapter in the History of Communism.* New York, 1884.

Soboul, A., ed. *Babeuf et les problèmes du babouvisme* (Colloque in-ternational de Stockholm). Paris, 1963.

Spitzer, A. B. *The Revolutionary Theories of Auguste Blanqui.* New York, 1957.

Volguine, V. "Jean-Jacques Pillot, communiste utopiste," *La Pensée,* no. 84 (1959), 29–53.

Weill, Georges. "D'Argenson et la question sociale," *International Review for Social History,* IV (1939), 161–70.

Economy, Society, Politics, and the Working Classes

Aguet, J.-P. *Contribution à l'histoire du mouvement ouvrier français: Les grèves sous la Monarchie de Juillet (1830–1847)*. Geneva, 1954.

Agulhon, Maurice. *Une Ville ouvrière au temps du socialisme utopique: Toulon, 1815–1851*. Paris, 1970.

Bezucha, Robert. "The 'Pre-industrial' Worker Movement: The *Canuts* of Lyon," in Bezucha, ed., *Modern European Social History* (Lexington, Mass., 1972), 93–123.

Boussinesq, Georges, and Gustave Laurent. *Histoire de Reims depuis ses origines à nos jours*. [Vol.] II, *Reims moderne*. Reims, 1933.

Briquet, Jean. "La Signification sociale du compagnonnage," *Revue d'histoire économique et sociale*, XXXIII (1955).

Cameron, Rondo. "Economic Growth and Stagnation in France, 1815–1914," *Journal of Modern History*, XXX (1958), 1–13.

———. *France and the Economic Development of Europe*. Princeton, 1963.

———, ed. *Essays in French Economic History*. Homewood, Ill., 1970.

Chéramy, R. "L'Année 1848 dans de département de la Marne." Diplôme d'Etudes supérieures (1946). Ms 1511, Bibliothèque municipale de Chalons-sur-Marne.

Chevalier, Louis. *Classes laborieuses et classes dangereuses*. Paris, 1959.

———. *La Formation de la population parisienne au XIX⁰ siècle*. Paris, 1950.

Creveuil, Georges. "La Condition ouvrière et la crise de 1847 à Nantes," *1848 et les révolutions du XIX⁰ siècle*, XXIV (1948), 39–61.

Daumard, Adeline. *La Bourgeoisie parisienne de 1815 à 1848*. Paris, 1963.

Dautry, Jean. *1848 et la Deuxième République*. 2d ed. Paris, 1957.

Dolléans, Edouard. *Histoire du mouvement ouvrier (1830–1870)*. Paris, 1957.

Dunham, Arthur L. *The Industrial Revolution in France, 1815–1848*. New York, 1955.

Duveau, Georges. *1848*. Paris, 1965.

Festy, Octave. "Dix Ans d'histoire corporative des ouvriers tailleurs d'habits (1830–1840)," *Revue d'histoire des doctrines économiques et sociales*, V (1912), 166–99.

———. "Le Mouvement ouvrier à Paris en 1840," *Revue de l'Ecole libre des Sciences politiques*, VI (1913), 266–97.

France. Office de Travail. *Les Associations professionnelles ouvrières*. 3 vols. Paris, 1901.

Gaumont, Jean. *Histoire générale de la coopération en France*. 2 vols. Paris, 1924.

Gille, Bertrand. *La Banque et le crédit en France de 1815 à 1848*. Paris, 1959.

Godechot, Jacques, ed. *La Révolution de 1848 à Toulouse et dans la Haute-Garonne*. Toulouse, 1948.

Gossez, Rémi. "Diversités des antagonismes sociaux vers le milieu du XIXᵉ siècle," *Revue économique*, VII (1956), 439–57.

——. *Les Ouvriers de Paris (1848)*. Paris, 1967.

Gourvitch, A. "Le Mouvement pour la réforme, 1838–1841," *La Révolution de 1848*, XII (1915–16), 93–131, 185–211, 265–88, 345–59, 397–417; XIII (1916–17), 37–44, 95–115, 173–92, 256–71; XIV (1917–18), 62–81.

Greffé, André. "La Ganterie niortaise: Etude geographique d'une survivance industrielle dans le Centre-Ouest." Diplôme d'Etudes supérieures (1949), Ms F n.a. 1220, Archives départementales de Deux-Sèvres.

Isambert, François. "L'Attitude religieuse des ouvriers français au milieu du XIXᵉ siècle," *Archives de sociologie des religions*, VI (1958), 7–35.

Labrousse, Ernest. *Le Mouvement ouvrier et les théories sociales en France de 1815 à 1848*. Paris, 1961.

——, ed. *Aspects de la crise et de la dépression d'économie française au milieu du XIXᵉ siècle, 1846–1851*. Vol XIX (1956) of la Bibliothèque de la Révolution de 1848.

Léon, Pierre. "L'Industrialisation en France en tant que facteur de croissance économique, du début du XVIIIᵉ siècle a nos jours," *Stockholm: First International Conference of Economic History: Contributions, Communications*. Paris, 1960.

Levasseur, Emile. *Histoire des classes ouvrières et de l'industrie en France*. 2 vols. Paris, 1903.

Lévy-Leboyer, Maurice. *Les Banques européennes et l'industrialisation internationale à la première moitié du XIXᵉ siècle*. Paris, 1964.

Lévy-Schneider, J. "Les Débuts de la Révolution de 1848 à Lyon: A Propos d'un ouvrage récent," *Revue d'histoire moderne et contemporaine*, XV (1911), 24–61, 177–98.

Lhomme, Jean. *La Grande Bourgeoisie au pouvoir (1830–1880)*. Paris, 1960.

Maitron, Jean, ed. *Dictionnaire biographique du mouvement ouvrier français: Première partie: 1789–1864, de la Révolution française à la fondation de la Première Internationale*. 3 vols. Paris, 1964–66.

Markovitch, T. J. *L'Industrie française de 1789 à 1964 (Cahiers de l'I.S.E.A.)*. Paris, 1965.

Moody, Joseph. "The Dechristianization of the French Working Class," *Review of Politics,* XV (1958), 46–49.

Pariset, E. *Histoire de la fabrique lyonnaise.* Lyons, 1901.

Rude, Fernand. "Le Mouvement ouvrier à Lyon," *Revue de psychologie des peuples* (1958), 223–46.

———, ed. *La Révolution de 1848 dans le département de l'Isère.* Grenoble, 1949.

Sée, Henri. *La Vie économique et sociale de France sous la Monarchie censitaire.* Paris, 1927.

Simiand, François. *Le Salaire, l'évolution sociale et la monnaie.* 3 vols. Paris, 1932.

Tudesq, A.-J. *Les Grands Notables en France (1840–1849).* 2 vols. Paris, 1964.

Weill, Georges. *Histoire du parti républicain en France (1814–1870).* 2d ed. Paris, 1928.

General Perspectives

Beauvoir, Simone de. "Idéalisme moral et réalisme politique," *Les Temps modernes,* 1, I (1945), 248–68.

Berneri, M. L. *Journey through Utopia.* London, 1950.

Buber, Martin. *Paths in Utopia,* trans. R. F. C. Hull. Boston, 1955.

Desroche, Henri. "Messianismes et utopies: Note sur les origines du socialisme occidental," *Archives de sociologie des religions,* VIII (1959), 31–46.

Duveau, Georges. *Sociologie de l'utopie et autres essais.* Paris, 1961.

Gurvitch, Georges. *La Vocation actuelle de la sociologie.* 2d ed. Paris, 1957.

Hobsbawm, Eric. *Primitive Rebels.* New York, 1959.

Leblond, M. A. *L'Idéal du XIX⁰ siècle.* Paris, 1909.

Mannheim, Karl. *Ideology and Utopia,* trans. Wirth and Shils. New York, n.d.

Manuel, Frank. "Toward a Psychological History of Utopias," *Daedelus,* XCIV (1965), 293–322.

Michelet, Jules. *Le Peuple.* Paris, 1843.

Roche, John, and Stephen Sachs. "The Bureaucrat and the Enthusiast: An Exploration of the Leadership of Social Movements," *Western Political Quarterly,* VIII (1955), 248–61.

Ruyer, Raymond. *L'Utopie et les utopistes.* Paris, 1950.

Smelser, Neil. *Theory of Collective Behavior.* London, 1962.

Soboul, Albert, ed. *Histoire sociale: Sources et méthodes.* Paris, 1967.

Stein, Lorenz von. *Geschichte der sozialen Bewegung in Frankreich.* 2 vols. Leipzig, 1850.
Thompson, E. P. *The Making of the English Working Class.* London, 1963.
Tuveson, Ernest Lee. *Millennium and Utopia.* New York, 1964.
Ulam, Adam. *The Unfinished Revolution.* New York, 1964.

Index